# ACKNOWLEDGMENTS

Though it's impossible to name every single person who helped in the creation of this book, we do want to name a special few.

Acknowledgments from Robin...

Ginette Degner, what would I do without you? You're a wealth of information who is always there when I need you. I couldn't do it without you!

A special thanks to my students, who graciously gave me the "use" of their Web sites as many of the examples in this book and who provide me with constant learning experiences.

And, thanks to my family, who are always so supporting, even when I'm locked in my office for days at a time.

Acknowledgments from Kerri-Leigh...

Thanks to all the family who encouraged and supported me through this project. I couldn't have survived, sanity intact, without you. Especially to Mamama for letting us use the cabin.

Thanks to Omid Pourzanjani for your patience, time, and hordes of information. To Debbie Smith, Scott Dahl, Lisa Ringler, and Karen Taylor for reminding me that I'm not insane (though perhaps a wee bit on the masochistic side)—my undying thanks.

Most of all, I appreciate the five people who kept me from breaking any number of laws when life seemed too insane: Theresa Brooks, for talking me through those Kodak moments. Deanna Padilla, for reminding me of my strength. Tamalyn Holland, for letting me run amok and not judging me when I did. To Robin—riiiiiight. And finally, my knight on an Internet-ready snowboard, who cleaned the kitchen and left me alone on the weekends—Jody, you're the best!

# ABOUT THE AUTHORS

**Robin Nobles** was the first search engine–positioning instructor on the Internet, having taught over 1000 students in her beginning and advanced online courses and in onsite workshops and seminars across the states. Her second book on the subject, titled *Maximize Web Site Traffic, Build Web Site Traffic Fast and Free by Optimizing Search Engine Placement*, was published in the fall of 2000.

**Kerri-Leigh Grady**, a born geek who joined the Computer Club in the fourth grade, is a software engineer, Web designer, and writer living in San Diego, California. She is the author of a PEARL nominated e-novel, several articles on fiction writing, and hordes of bad poetry. When she's not writing code, Web pages, fiction, or technical documentation, she researches computer security issues and drinks too much coffee.

# CONTENTS

## PART VI
# How Secure Is Your Web Site?

**PART VIII**
# Appendixes                                                   571

# INTRODUCTION

## Asking Yourself the Right Questions

If you're reading this book, more than likely your Web site is up and running and you're conducting business over the Internet, whether successfully or not. But since the initial design of your site, have you gone back to analyze various components of the site in order to get them operating at their full potential?

Have you stopped long enough to consider each individual Web page to make sure it's designed to attract visitors and relay information quickly and effortlessly? Have you considered how those individual pages are joined together to compose the entire Web site and whether visitors to the site can find what they're looking for without having to jump through too many hoops?

And what about the major search engines and directories? Was your site initially designed with search engine strategies in mind? More than likely, it wasn't. Because close to 85 percent of all traffic to most Web sites comes through the major engines and directories, analyzing your site in terms of those entities is crucial to the success of your online business.

Have you considered security issues? Remember that your customers will purchase goods and services from you only if your site gives them a feeling of security and trust. Even today, with literally millions of dollars of goods and services being sold over the Internet every month, many people are still concerned about giving out credit card information online.

As you can see, you need to consider numerous components when analyzing your Web site; we discuss these factors in detail in this book. Each of these components works together to create a successful online business. If you concentrate on one or two and let the others go, your site won't be operating at its full potential, and your bottom-line business figures will more than likely suffer.

## A Glimpse at Online Use

If, at any point, you question the power of the Internet, spending a few minutes looking at online use and e-commerce figures certainly will make a believer out of you. Estimating how many people are online can be compared to estimating how many grains of sand are in a gallon jar, however. Nua Internet Surveys (**http://www.nua.org/surveys**) takes a stab at it by estimating that there were 332.73 million users online worldwide as of June 2000.

In Figure I.1, you see the numbers broken down by geographical area, with the United States and Canada coming in first.

With all those users, how much are they actually buying online?

ActivMedia Search (**http://www.activmediaresearch.com/**) predicted Web commerce to double in the year 2000. It based its figures on the fact that by mid-2000, the number of substantial online businesses had expanded by a third to approximately 550,000, with those online businesses' revenues growing at an average rate of 130 percent over 1999's figures.

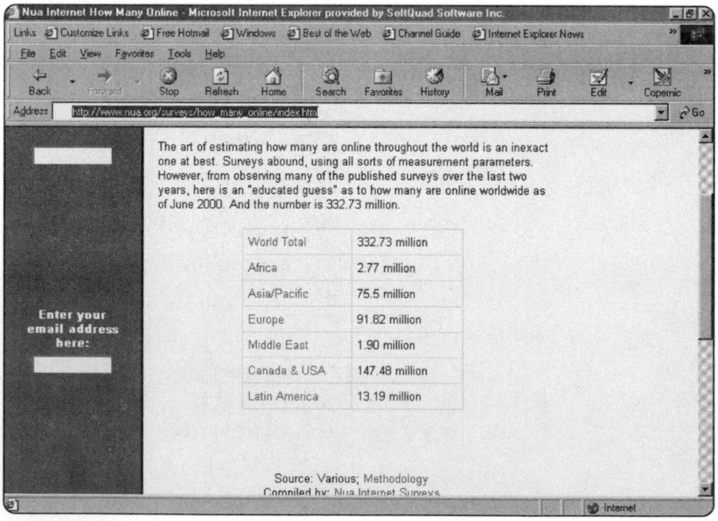

**FIGURE I.1**

Estimated online usage worldwide as of June 2000.

Using these figures as a guide, ActivMedia predicted that online commerce activity for the year 2000 would rise to $132 billion worldwide, which effectively doubled the $58 billion reported for the year 1999.

The days of having strictly informational sites are dwindling because nearly two-thirds of all new Web sites are selling goods and services online. In the past, Web sites were more concerned with the intricacies of actually setting up an online business. With the advent of software tools and technologies, however, e-commerce Web sites now are being slapped up in record numbers, with little thought as to their overall usefulness.

Now, more than ever, the importance of analyzing existing Web sites has come into play, as well as developing a means of reporting Web site activities and then using those reports to create a better and stronger online presence.

In Figure I.2, taken from Nua Internet Surveys, you can see that projected Internet-generated revenue will hit $1.234 billon by the year 2002.

With figures like that, it's obvious that the vast majority of revenue being generated is from business-to-business sales rather than from business-to-consumer sales.

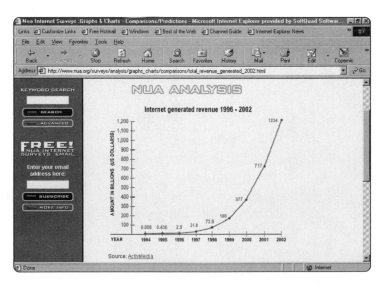

**FIGURE I.2**

Internet-generated revenue from 1994 to 2002.

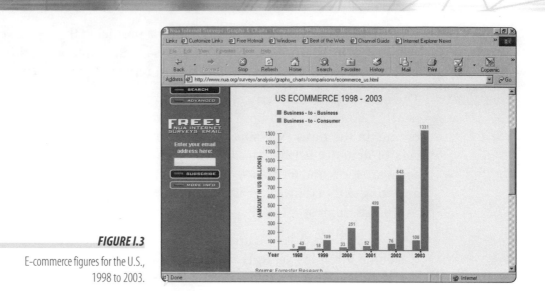

**FIGURE I.3**

E-commerce figures for the U.S.,
1998 to 2003.

According to Nua Internet Surveys, in the year 2000 in the U.S., business-to-consumer sales will reach $33 million, whereas business-to-business sales will top the chart at $251 million, as Figure I.3 shows.

## Components to a Successful Analysis of Your Web Site

Based on the statistics listed earlier, you can easily see the astronomical marketing power of the Internet. To tap into that power, you need to begin by analyzing your own site, which is the purpose of this book.

As we go over the various areas of an effective Web site analysis strategy, you may be tempted to believe that some of the areas are too elementary for your use. Before jumping to that conclusion, though, we challenge you to read the information and apply it to your own site.

Just because a company has spent hundreds of thousands of dollars having its Web site designed does not mean that the site will stand up under an analysis of the factors that make up an effective site. Evidence of that fact is placed in front of our noses every time we venture onto the Internet.

So take the time to consider the information presented here, and then apply it to your site. In return for your time and energy, you'll create a much more effective online business that will stand up under the closest scrutiny.

## How This Book Is Organized

The major sections of this book discuss the various components of a successful online business, as briefly mentioned here:

- **Web page and Web site analysis**

  According to the August 2000 issue of *Business 2.0*, the average duration of a page view is 50 seconds. So whether you like it or not, you have less than a minute to convince the average user to go further into your site, with the goal of converting the visit to a sale.

  This said, the importance of each individual Web page is obvious when it comes to the success of your overall site.

  You can't forget that each individual page is pulled together to create an entire Web site, though. So not only do you have to convince users that your online business can provide exactly what they are looking for, but you need to combine your pages in a way that makes it as simple as possible for your users to navigate through the mountain of information provided.

- **Capitalizing on return traffic**

  Are you providing the type of information that will bring visitors back time and time again? Is your Web site of such caliber that visitors will bookmark it? Do you offer incentives to get people to return, or is your content stagnant with little new to offer?

  Are you using the power of technology to capture the e-mail addresses of your visitors? Are you using an affiliate program to entice others to sell your products or services?

  Have you considered creating an online community for either your customers or your employees?

  Once you've gotten visitors to your site in the first place, your battle is only half over. Now you have to convince them to return.

- **Web engineering process**

  For years, architects and engineers have followed a process when creating their masterpieces. Software engineers only recently have begun to utilize the power of process and process improvement to work efficiently. Now the Web community has begun to follow suit, implementing process in Web design to improve the efficiency of design, maintenance of the site, and quality of the Web presence.

Using a Web engineering process, you can more easily and efficiently make changes to your site or, if you don't yet have a site, start your project with the knowledge that you'll reduce the number and severity of problems you encounter in building and maintaining your site.

- **Analyzing e-commerce solutions**

  When analyzing a Web site, you certainly want to take a good, long look at your e-commerce areas and make sure that they're working smoothly—taking a customer from first stepping foot inside your online store through closing the sale.

  Are you offering enough payment plans? Is your shopping cart laid out effectively? What other technologies are available that could benefit your site?

- **Creating engine-friendly Web sites**

  Certainly one of the current buzz terms is "search engine positioning," which reflects the fact that Web masters and designers are finally realizing the massive power of the major engines and directories.

  Because the vast majority of Web sites use techniques that are detrimental to search engine rankings, stepping back to analyze your pages in terms of the search engines can do nothing but strengthen your "findability" and traffic.

- **Analyzing security risks**

  In the year 2000, Nua Internet Surveys estimates that viruses and other destructive actions by computer hackers will cost businesses worldwide more than $1.6 trillion, losing 83.2 million hours of productivity because of computer downtime.

  Analyzing the security of your site covers areas such as operating systems, Web servers, data integrity and confidentiality, data protection and recovery, and the dangers of interactive Web sites.

- **Analyzing traffic**

  Most of the time, Web sites set up sophisticated logging systems that track every step users take throughout the Web site. But how often do people go back and analyze that data and actually use it to benefit their sites?

What parts of a log file are truly important? What can log files tell you, and how can you use that information to strengthen your site?

Simply logging the traffic does your site no good if you don't analyze that information and then use it to improve your site.

## This Industry Changes Rapidly

As you know, in any of the technology-related fields, changes are made on an almost daily basis. The way we're doing things today won't necessarily be the way we do things a year from now.

This fact hit home in the writing of this book. After all of the chapters had been written and final edits made, Disney announced its intentions to close down GO.com. They stated that they were trying to find a buyer for the GO search engine and directory. So, if the engine and related directory were sold, they would be moved to a new location. If they weren't sold, they would be shut down.

Since GO, formerly known as InfoSeek, has always been one of the major engines, this certainly created some havoc in the publishing of this book.

So, in the hopes that GO will be purchased and continue as a viable engine, the information on the search engine has remained in the book. However, you'll see several qualifying statements that will remind you of the possibility of the engine being shut down or moved.

The authors have set up a corresponding Web site for the book, which is located at **http://www.kerri-leigh.com/wsar**. To learn the final status of the GO search engine, be sure to visit our site.

## A Final Note

You've learned about the major components necessary for the effective analysis of your Web site. Now, you're ready to get into the meat of the book and begin analyzing your site.

Keep in mind that how you handle the information presented in this book is determined by the unique aspects of your site. If you're a healthcare facility, for example, you'll certainly approach certain areas of the book differently than someone who is selling antiques. The basic concepts and strategies are the same, however.

So before you begin, take a few minutes to consider your site. What are your goals now, and what are your projected goals for five years down the road? Ten? Who is your target audience? Is most of your traffic Internet savvy, or are your main customers new Internet users?

As you read through the book, always move forward with your goals and target audience in mind.

Above all, take the concepts and tips presented here and use them to create a dynamite online presence that is sure to enlist the trust and confidence of users, thus increasing the sales of your products or services.

Oh—and good luck!

# PART I

# WEB SITE DESIGN

# CHAPTER 1

# ANALYZING WEB PAGES FOR MAXIMUM EFFECTIVENESS

**In This Chapter**

Using Page Design Etiquette

Plotting and Layout

Including Contact Information

Copyright Issues

Going Interactive

Analyzing the Competition

Tools to Analyze and Develop Web Pages

Individual Web pages give your visitors their first impression of your Web site. The site as a whole relies on the design issues associated with each page. For this reason, the pages of your site are one of your first priorities when considering the needs of the audience you've targeted. Your site is the user interface for your products or services. You must take care to analyze the individual pages of your site for their effectiveness.

When analyzing Web page design, you should consider several essential issues. First, be aware of Web etiquette—what design elements are considered bad form or unprofessional? The Web is in constant flux, and new content breeds discontent if it is presented through annoying or inefficient elements of design. Also, studying your competition can help you determine what works and what's weak.

As a designer, you also should be very aware of the style of user interface the site offers and determine the best method of conveying information. In addition, you need to know what style elements of your user interface need special attention and what information you need to convey on every page.

If you already have a site or a detailed plan for a site, you can use this chapter to analyze the efficiency and usability of the pages you have. If you have not yet designed your site's interface, use this chapter to help determine the appropriate elements and layout for your type of site.

If anything we point out in this chapter seems obvious, we apologize. Keep in mind that much of what designers consider to be common sense often becomes common error to those who are unaware of or don't realize the importance of certain considerations. Even if you have designed Web pages for years, you might find a juicy tidbit you did not know about or had forgotten.

## Using Page Design Etiquette

No matter where your audience lives, works, or plays; no matter the intent of your Web site; several elements of Web page design apply to anyone, any company, in any situation. To encourage visitors to stay at your site and return to your site, you should go out of your way to make their visit exciting. However, the method you use to create excitement on your site also could create distractions or even annoyance. To avoid giving your visitors a negative impression, you must be aware of page design etiquette.

When analyzing each page for its adherence to etiquette, start by looking at your page from a visitor's point of view. Who is your target audience? What do they expect to receive from their visit? If your site attracts preadolescent children, for example, it should contain more color than text and more graphics or even animation than a site aimed at adults looking for the latest research in molecular biology. In general, however, the few rules in this section will cover a lot of common ground.

## Graphics

Images are fun. They're great. They help break up the monotony of long strings of text. But they also consume large amounts of bandwidth. If an image is too large, it can take forever to download, and you can lose customers who must wait interminable seconds while the image loads. Follow these guidelines for graphics:

- Keep your use of graphics to a minimum. Aside from the bandwidth issue, there are a few reasons to follow this rule. Graphics can be distracting if they are too numerous, too large, or animated. In terms of information, they are much larger than text, so they take longer to download. Visitors may begin looking at your site's information while images download, but if your graphics are relevant or even necessary to the discussion or data you present, the wait can be extremely annoying.

- Along the same lines, be aware of any animated graphics you include. Animation can be distracting, and because they are actually several images in one, they increase download time considerably.

- Double-check all images and other files you use on your pages. Images that have not been uploaded to the appropriate directory leave your site looking unprofessional.

## The Top Ten Mistakes of Web Design

According to Jakob Nielsen, author of *Designing Web Usability and Multimedia and Hypertext: The Internet and Beyond*, today's Web designers continue to make ten common yet crucial mistakes. Make sure you avoid these pitfalls:

1. Disabling the browser's Back button so users cannot return to previous pages in their history. Designers make this happen by opening new content in a separate window, using a refresh directive, or preventing page caching.

2. Opening new Web content in a separate browser window, causing the preceding mistake.

3. Using an unfamiliar user interface or not remaining consistent with Web standards. According to Nielsen, lack of consistency causes users to feel out of control because they don't expect the unfamiliar action. As an example, he points to the use of a radio button as an action button instead of a method of choosing an option.

4. No biographical information on the people behind the site. Nielsen's studies show that Web users like knowing who created or runs a site—it increases trust.

5. No archived content. Deleting old content leads to dead links and a less useful Web site. Nielsen estimates that archiving content might cause a 10 percent increase in cost to run the site, but the site's usefulness will increase by as much as 50 percent.

6. Relocating pages, which causes broken links from other sites to your pages.

7. Oblique headline text. Headlines often are used by search engines or tables of contents to link to a page, but if that headline information gives users no clue to the content, they will have to guess what you mean.

8. Spending resources to incorporate the latest fad rather than maintaining content and usability.

9. Slow download of pages, usually because of graphics, applets, and poor network design or hardware.

10. Content designed to look like an ad. Web users have learned to ignore banner ads, pop-up ads, and heavy animation, and they'll ignore your content if it looks like it could be any of these.

Readers responded with fervor to Nielsen's article, adding several of their own pet peeves to the list:

- Splash screens.

- Content structured so that a page cannot be bookmarked. Whether because of frames or scripting, this annoying format means users must return to the main page and search for the specific content again rather than using a link to go straight to that content.

- Links to non-HTML files without a warning to users about the content's new format—for example, PDF and other document formats.

- (For international users) Pages that aren't cached on servers closer to the user, causing exceptionally slow download times.

- Lack of contact information on every page.

- Lack of keyboard efficiency when using the Tab key while in a form, usually because of links between the input elements.
- Placing all the content in a complex table that takes a considerable amount of time to download. This is a problem because browsers may not display the table's content until the table tags have been downloaded.

To read more about Web usability, visit **http://www.useit.com**.

- To avoid large file sizes, you can test your images by converting them to GIF, JPEG, and PNG formats to see which is the best in terms of file size and appearance. Remember that a good rule of thumb regarding image format is that large or photo-quality images are best stored in JPEG format, while small images or images that use only a few different colors should be stored as GIF. Remember that GIF is an image type, whereas JPEG is actually a compression style for images, so a graphic in need of compression should be stored as JPEG.

## Sight and Sound

With all the capabilities of current Web technologies, it's tempting to add more bells and whistles than you really need. Keep these considerations in mind.

- If your page is cluttered with text, graphics, and color, your visitors will become distracted and will not gather the information you want them to glean. Color, varying fonts and text size, and multimedia goodies can enhance a page if used with plenty of balancing white space. The idea is *balance*.
- Font is another issue that should concern you. Use care when determining what font size and color to use. Varied font sizes can make a page more readable. But don't use fonts that are too small or too large. Too much text in a large font wastes valuable screen area, while text in fonts that are too small can make the page difficult to read, especially for users with low-resolution screens or vision problems.

- Too much noise on a page—audio noise, that is—also can become distracting. In fact, a good rule of thumb is to forget that the `<BGSOUND>` tag exists. Some music or background noise might not be offensive, but etiquette dictates that you give your visitors the choice of whether to listen.

- Most background music appears on personal and nonprofessional pages, and the format used—MIDI, for the most part—can become grating after listening to the song in loop for several minutes. Aside from music sites, how many times have you been to a professional e-commerce page "enhanced" with music or other background noise? Not many, and there's a good reason—it's not professional.

- If you insist on using sound, be sure to use a realistic sound byte or music sample. Many audio files used as background music tend to sound like synthesizer elevator music. Your visitors' coworkers in surrounding cubicles will think they're playing a video game instead of combing your pages for information. Also, if you choose to integrate sound on your pages, give your visitors the option to turn it on or off at will.

## Scroll Bars

Make sure that each page requires a minimum of scrolling. We discuss both types of scrolling: vertical and horizontal.

- If visitors find themselves scrolling through screen after screen of material (vertical scrolling), they will leave that page and possibly that site. If you must scroll through more than two screens to see the entire page, with very few exceptions, your page requires some adjustment. Generally, vertical scrolling says you have too much information on one page. Refer to Chapter 2, "Analyzing Your Site's Structure for Maximum Accessibility," for more information on data segregation, which can reduce this problem.

- Another type of scrolling that can be present is horizontal. Horizontal scrolling is a taboo, though some sites can get away with this tactic. Do not allow a page to "scroll right" unless you have a specific design reason for it. The most common cause of this phenomenon relates to the use of tables in a page. If your page designer creates a table with an absolute size parameter rather than a relative-size parameter, scrolling might occur. For example, you could make the following change to your HTML:

Switch this (absolute size parameter): `<TABLE WIDTH="650">`

To this (relative size parameter): `<TABLE WIDTH="75%">`

- Absolute size forces the table to be a certain number of pixels in width. The relative-size parameter, however, forces the table to adjust to the size of the specific browser display. By requiring the size to be a percentage as opposed to a specific number of pixels, you avoid the "scroll right" that can occur with an absolute-size parameter.

**TIP**  If it becomes necessary for aesthetic reasons to force an absolute table size, cater to the lowest common denominator. Be sure that the page is viewable on a small monitor without scrolling.

## Links

Be wary of how you use links—how often, where, and how you implement them. Use them copiously, since they are the basis of Web surfing, but use them intelligently. Links are a great way to extend the usability of your site, but if links are used incorrectly, your pages can become difficult to read and navigate.

### Controlling Links to the Outside World

When you link outside of your site, you might want those sites to open in a new window. In other words,

```
<A HREF="http://www.nolongermysite.com" TARGET="_blank">Leave My
Site</A>
```

Using the `TARGET` parameter allows visitors to remain on your page even as they visit another page. When they close that browser window your link created, they will find themselves back at your page, as if they never left.

Opening more browser windows on your visitors' monitors sometimes is considered bad form, however, because they have no choice in this extra drain on their computer resources. Consider how much you need users to stay on your site. Balance this need with the demand for good customer service.

### Incorporating Links into Text

When using links, think of the flow of your text. Your visitors are reading content on your site, and just as you want them to read without encountering typos or difficult fonts, you don't want to distract them with sudden requests to "Click here!" Consider which of the following examples is better:

- Our widgets are the best, according to critics 'round the world. **Click here**!
- Critics say our widgets are the best! **Here's why**.
- See why **critics say** our widgets are the best.

Obviously, the flow of the third example is better, and yet users can still tell what the link contains and how to get to it.

### Avoiding Dead Links—a.k.a., Linkrot

You should scan pages periodically to find any broken links. Broken links waste your visitors' time and leave them with the impression that your site is not well maintained or frequently maintained.

Along the same lines, keep in mind that when you reorganize your information that links to your pages from external sites will continue to point to your original page. Always leave a link or refresh from the original page to the new location. Don't do this only for your main pages, because most people will link to specific pages in your site. If you leave your potential visitors looking at a **404 File Not Found** page, you can count that visitor lost.

However, if you are able to set up a custom 404 File Not Found page (a page the Web server pulls up in case someone trying to reach one of your URLs is unable to do so), definitely take advantage of the opportunity. Using your custom page, you can redirect traffic to the main areas of your site, reducing the chance that your lost customer will give up and leave altogether.

## Diabolical Frames

When using frames, you must be very aware of etiquette. Frames are great for manipulating pages in ways tables can't, but they also can create a bit of angst in visitors to your page. If you use links to external sites, you should, for the sake of courtesy, use the TARGET parameter with the value top. This forces the link to open in your main frame—in effect, escaping your frames.

Many people consider frames evil because of the general lack of etiquette displayed by sites that employ this method. Some browsers don't support frames, so users sometimes receive blank pages because the Web designer didn't use the NOFRAMES tag. Framed pages also cannot be bookmarked—the bookmark will only reference the default pages for the frames. Finally, some browsers don't have the capability to print frame pages.

In some cases, when the page's designer hasn't considered smaller viewing areas (or monitors), a frame may adversely affect navigation or even the capability to view all the information. The key is to view any frame pages from every possible browser and system possible. Ask others to look at the pages and to give you feedback. You might be surprised at just how many have trouble viewing what you've created.

Also, frames can be detrimental to search engine ranking, which you'll learn about in Chapter 21, "Analyzing Technology That Can Be Detrimental to Search Engine Rankings."

## Colors

Finally, select the color scheme you use with care. Keep your audience in mind when you choose. Obviously, pastels most likely will not appeal to a battalion of Marines. On the other hand, they probably won't care too much to read white text on a black background, either. You also should remain aware of distractions when analyzing the color. Too much color, too much bright color, or not enough color can affect the way visitors view your page.

A sure way to lose your visitors to another site is through bad use of color scheme—is this too obvious an issue for us to point out? Absolutely not. Pages, colors especially, look different when viewed from different browsers and even different operating systems.

Also, make sure, whenever possible, to use a light background with dark (black, preferably) text. Why? When your users go to print out your page, they might find themselves getting exactly what you have on the page, minus the background. In other words, a big page of white, unreadable text.

## Plotting and Layout

When creating the layout of a Web page, you should keep in mind several points that usually have everything to do with the etiquette we just discussed. Some elements of good page layout deal more with aesthetics and ease of navigation than with etiquette, however. You might find yourself sacrificing some of the following guidelines. Remain aware of what you need to do to counteract the problems your visitors might encounter if you decide to use potentially dangerous design practices.

## User Interface

How do you interact with your Web site visitors? What format do you use to convey information, retrieve information, and keep visitors at your site? Some sites use site maps, graphics, and multimedia. Others use frames, tables, or text designs. No matter the format, these are all types of user interfaces (UIs)—how a site interacts with those who use it.

What are the types of UI to consider? There are more than we could possibly cover, with variations of variations. We will look at four UIs—image maps, frames, tables, and long pages of text—to help you determine what elements you might want to incorporate into your own design and what issues you should consider when making your design decisions.

### The Image Map

Some sites begin their users' journey with an image map, a large image with clickable areas that link to pages within the site. This image might include graphical representations of an area. A phone might link to contact information, for example. To advance through the site, users must click on one of the images within this main image. Other image maps use an image with text-like links to point out different areas of the site to the user. How effective is an image map as a page design method? It depends on the site and the target audience.

Image maps are tricky. The graphical interface might appeal to computer newbies, but most pictorial image maps (those using graphical representations of the site areas rather than textual representations) come with very little instruction, rendering them difficult to use unless users have encountered one before. To make your image map user-friendly, include text links under your image, as well as instructions on the use of an image map, or make sure your image map is composed of text images rather than pictorial ones.

Figure 1.1 shows a textual image map. It's very easy to see where to click in order to find widgets, gadgets, and technical support. On the other hand, a pictorial image map must have intuitive graphics that can tell users just as well where to find things. A picture of a widget would tell them where to click to get to the section on widgets. An image of a customer taking a sledgehammer to a widget might work in pointing to technical support. No matter what you choose, you must consider the ease of use for your customers. Will they be able to find what they need using your image map?

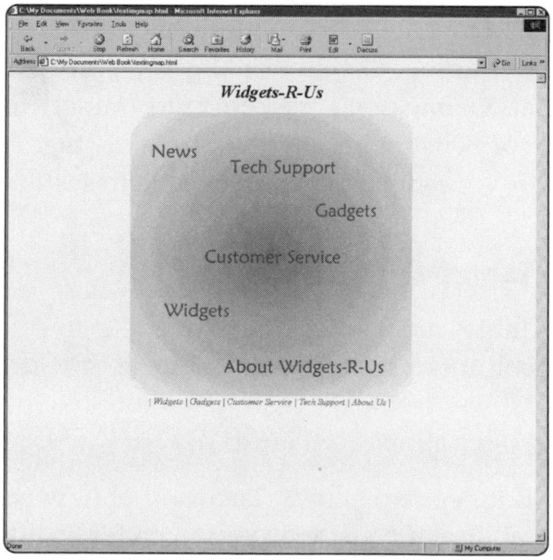

*FIGURE 1.1*

A textual image map interface.

Before choosing the image-map method of transportation about your site, consider the consequences. An image map is static and cannot change as your users move about your site. Using image maps may also require that you use a good deal of space on your users' Web browsers, making the image map a less efficient use of monitor area. Text, on the other hand, requires very little space in comparison, but it isn't as eye-catching, nor does it provide the amount of eye candy that images provide. Balance the pros and cons when deciding the effectiveness of this particular UI.

### Frames

Frames, like image maps, are tricky creatures. They can provide a great method of site navigation, or they can be a pain in the NIC for the person trapped in frames or even for the would-be customer whose browser doesn't support frames. What's a Web designer to do?

If you choose to use a frames format for your page design, do so with care. When—if—you link outside of your site, use the `_top` or `_blank` `TARGET` parameter. This ensures that the new page is loaded outside of your frames. You may have reasons for keeping your customers inside your frames, but keep in mind that customer service dictates a customer-friendly site, and trapping your visitors in your frames is definitely considered an act of war.

Once again, keep in mind that not all customers use the latest version of Internet Explorer or Netscape on a Windows or Macintosh system, and some don't even support frames. To keep from isolating some of your customers, use the `<NOFRAMES>` tag. This HTML tag ensures that all of your customers will be able to see the content of your page.

### Tables

Tables are a great alternative to frames, allowing your pages to have columnar content without locking your customers into frames. With tables, Web pages can look more like printed content than plain text pages allow. See Figure 1.2.

But again, you must be aware of how each system will interpret your table tags. Netscape tends to prefer well-formed HTML, so if you forget

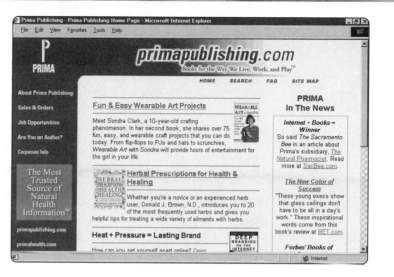

to close a tag, your page may lose content, or the format may change drastically. This tendency is greatly exaggerated where tables are concerned. What looks perfectly wonderful in Netscape may look like Picasso on hallucinogens in Internet Explorer, and vice versa.

Also, columns are great, but don't overdo them. Keep in mind that monitor sizes differ, and some are rather small. If you have more than two columns in your page design, you flirt with the possibility of causing horizontal scroll or too-narrow columns. If three columns or more are absolutely necessary to your intended page design, remember to test the page in every possible browser and system.

## A Single Page of Text

You've seen these sites. Everything is on one page. No external links. All links are within the page using anchors. These pages defy the rule of minimal scrolling. They defy the rules of data segregation. They defy the laws of physics.

Obviously, we feel one-page sites are a bad idea. Web surfers and customers do not tend to stay on a page if they have to scroll more than once or twice. So using one page and not making the most of data segregation becomes detrimental, regardless of whether you use graphics.

Look at Chapter 2. If you find yourself scrolling through screen after screen of just one page, you're in trouble. Pages (or worse, whole sites) that fall into this trap are in need of a great deal of redesign.

We don't intend to say that all instances of a long page of text or graphics are incomprehensibly diabolical. However, almost any page can and should be divided into several shorter pages.

### Analyzing Your User Interface

When analyzing the effectiveness of your UI, you must first determine your audience. Yes, we've discussed this before, and we will continue to discuss it *ad nauseam*. But don't underestimate the importance of knowing what your visitors need in order to get the most out of your site. Without an effective targeted UI, your site will leave its visitors feeling frustrated or bored.

Here are some of the questions you should ask yourself when analyzing the effectiveness of your UI:

- What is the primary purpose of my site? Should it be fun? Informative? Interactive? Real-time?

- What types of computer systems do visitors to my site use? Is there a chance they have older systems, small monitors, and slow Internet connections? Or do they use cutting-edge technology (and therefore expect my site to take full advantage of their systems' power)?

- How Web savvy are my visitors? If I use a site map, will my visitors be able to figure out how to use it? Do I include text links to areas within my site as well as the site map?

- Can visitors easily view all the information they need with my page's layout?

- Have I tested the page format with different browsers and systems? Does the format hold well enough for each system?

## Aesthetics

What determines aesthetics on a Web page? Obviously, we must again refer to the audience the page targets. Children will find other design choices more enticing than designs adults would choose. Here are a few key issues to consider:

- Does my page design have white space? Or is it cluttered with color, text, and images?

- Does my page design offer some type of eye candy, or is it bland?

- I want to avoid too much scrolling on my page, but do I compensate by crowding too much content into a small area? Or have I segregated my information instead?

- Does the design of my page entice visitors to look at the whole page, or is all the content concentrated in one area?

- Have I made use of links? Do the link colors distract from the color scheme I've chosen? Do the underlined links make an area look cluttered?

- Is my font readable? It should be large enough that everyone can see it but not so large that it forces the page to become longer than necessary. It also should use a font face that all browsers support and that everyone will be able to read (remember that the Web is an international playground).

## Plotting Your Page

If you have not yet created your site or are analyzing a possible redesign, you might start out your page design analysis by plotting your page. By plotting, you will be able to see what you plan to do with the page, and from this point, creating a prototype design will be a piece of cake (especially if you use some of the more powerful HTML editors to implement your design). In addition, plotting can help you see where the pitfalls might lie before you spend time creating the pages and filling them with content.

What do we mean by plotting? Look at Figure 1.3. As you can see, from here, you can gauge the size of the graphics you will include, the amount of text you will be able to include on the page, and so on. At this point, you could even include colors with text to make sure that your site is not "best viewed with UV sunglasses."

Begin by plotting the user interface you want to use. Then go through and make sure that it allows you to find everything you need quickly

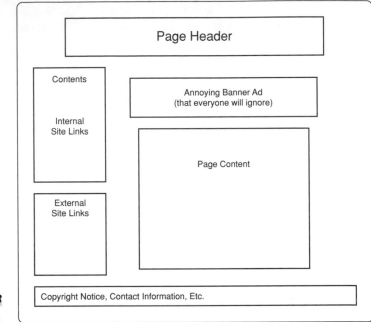

*FIGURE 1.3*

Plotting your page.

on that page. Check that you have remembered your contact information, navigation tools, and copyright statement. Once you have a layout you think will work, take it to your HTML editor. Consider the color scheme you need, the font sizes and colors, and so on. Look at general aesthetics, and make sure any content you use doesn't force much vertical scrolling and any horizontal scrolling.

In addition, watch for cluttering on the screen. Do you have too much content in any one area? Does the page's plot make your eyes move about the page to study all the content, or does it compel you to view only one section of little consequence?

## Including Contact Information

Have you ever visited a page that begged for feedback, but there was no way for you to give it? What about feedback forms that don't work and provide no other way to contact the Web master? It's frustrating, and it does nothing to entice visitors back to the site.

When creating each page, be sure to include either a link to a page with contact information or a method of contacting some representative of your company. If you're worried about spambots finding your e-mail addresses and abusing them, include only snail mail addresses or phone numbers. Use JavaScript or Perl to hide your e-mail address in forms.

Certainly, don't limit your contact information to an e-mail address or two. Give your customers the option of contacting you via phone, snail mail, or fax.

## Copyright Issues

Each page should have a copyright notice. At the very least, your first page should contain a notice that protects the rest of the pages within the site. Why?

First, some believe that a copyright notice lends more professionalism to your pages. Regardless of whether your content is valuable enough to warrant a copyright notice, if you include one, your content seems more valuable. If your content or the content you host could become a legal issue, however, make sure you post a copyright policy and include a prominent link on your page.

Second, some search directories prefer pages with copyright notices. We'll discuss this more in depth in Part V, "Creating Engine-Friendly Web Sites."

Even though your pages are protected by copyright as soon as they are created, a notice never hurts to remind surfers of the law before a copyright infringement occurs.

**TIP**  Remember that a copyright notice will not protect your content. Your code isn't safe unless you've used software or coding techniques to hide your HTML.

## Going Interactive

The best part about the Web as it grows and expands is its capacity to interact, to provide real-time feedback to its audience. Business sites should take advantage of this interactivity by using technology such as forms, scripts, ActiveX, Java, and so on. If your page offers the audience the opportunity to interact with others or with the site itself, you will find increased traffic to that page.

But again, there's beauty in balance. If you overdo the interaction, the site loses its appeal as it becomes cluttered or useless.

**TIP** A good rule of thumb is to use only one form—two at most—of interaction per page. This keeps the amount of activity on each page to a minimum so your user isn't distracted from the content.

Another potential pitfall with interactive pages is the download time. Scripts, applets, page preprocessing, and so on can add a significant amount of download time for your page. Your users won't want to wait around for the entire page to download because of an applet that may not even be necessary for the page's content.

What kinds of interaction can you use? We will discuss this topic more in Chapter 4, "Setting Up Polls, Contests, and Other Traffic-Generating Avenues," and Chapter 7, "Creating Effective Online Communities." For now, consider the following list of potential activities you can provide your site's audience:

- Polls allow your audience to interact with one another by voicing their opinion on some issue. Poll topics can be anything from silly to serious, depending on the audience.

- Chat areas give your visitors the opportunity to interact with each other about your product or your online community—in real time.

- Bulletin board areas provide two tools. First, multiple customers or visitors can interact with each other, discussing any issues related to your company, industry, and so on. Second, those discussions remain in the archive, searchable within your site or within search engines. A bulletin board can double as a guest book.

- If you make your site a portal (see Yahoo! for an example), you can offer such things as e-mail, free Web page hosting, auctions, maps, communities, and so on. Users often choose portal sites to become their start page or home page on their browser because these sites provide quick access to a variety of areas or tools.

- Contests give you the opportunity to see the feedback coming from visitors to your site, while offering an award that promotes your site.

## Analyzing the Competition

To analyze your own page design, you should start by looking at what your competition offers. This may not always be possible if your type of service is offered via secured areas to other businesses. You can find similar services offered online to the public on the Web, however. Check out these sites and find out what new methods or goodies they offer.

Here's what you should consider as you search other companies' sites:

- Look at their general page layout. Does the page draw your eye to the whole page, searching its content, or does it draw your eye to one particular area and away from other important elements?
- What kinds of interaction do they provide, if any?
- Are their graphics effective? If so, what kinds and how many do they use?
- Do they use anything that detracts from the page? Does something stand out to you as an effective use of page design?
- How quickly does the page download?
- Have they included contact information on each page? If so, what information have they provided, and in what format (for example, a mailto directive, a script, a form)?
- Can you easily find the information you need from the page within a few seconds?

## Tools to Analyze and Develop Web Pages

The following software tools can help you design your Web pages. Remember that tools only help you to create your page design and content, though. You must double-check your HTML code for dangerous design elements, such as absolute table width.

**FIND IT ONLINE**

- Microsoft FrontPage—**http://www.microsoft.com/frontpage**
- BBEdit—**http://www.bbedit.com/products/bbedit.html**
- Macromedia DreamWeaver—**http://www.macromedia.com/software/dreamweaver**

- Allaire HomeSite—**http://www.allaire.com/homesite**
- Arachnophilia—**http://www.arachnoid.com/arachnophilia**

The following browsers can help you analyze your pages as you test layout and aesthetics on each platform:

*FIND IT*
**ONLINE**

- Netscape Navigator—**http://www.netscape.com/download/ prodinfonfs_1.html**
- Microsoft Internet Explorer—**http://www.microsoft.com/ windows/ie**
- Lynx—**http://www.lynx.browser.org**
- Opera—**http://www.opera.com**
- HotJava—**http://java.sun.com/products/hotjava**
- Web TV Viewer—**http:// developer.webtv.net/design/tools/ viewer/**
- Konquerer—**http://www2.jorsm.com/~mosfet/screenshots.html**

## Conclusion

Many elements can determine the efficiency of the individual pages of your site, including layout, color, font, links, and graphics. Although not every page can or should follow the guidelines laid out in this chapter, you should be aware of the potential pitfalls associated with the use of certain elements in page design.

Always remember the importance of testing your pages on every possible browser and platform to ensure that no user will have a negative browsing experience on your site.

# CHAPTER 2

# ANALYZING YOUR SITE'S STRUCTURE FOR MAXIMUM ACCESSIBILITY

**In This Chapter**

Checking for Navigation Concerns

Translating Logical Structure into Site Sections

Using a Site Map

Assisting Users with Onsite Search Engines

The Database-Driven Web Site

Using Intranets, Extranets, and the Internet to Appeal to an Array of Customers

Establishing the Structure of Your Site

Finding the Right Technology

In addition to analyzing the individual pages of your site, as you did in Chapter 1, it's crucial to the success of your site to understand how those pages fit into an efficient overall Web site. This chapter examines everything from the relationships between the structure and organization of your site (both onscreen and behind the scenes) to the accessibility of the information for your users.

In Web design classes, you certainly learned effective ways of creating and developing a Web site. But how many times have you visited a site and not been able to find what you were looking for? Weren't these sites created and developed by professional Web designers? Sometimes in our quest to get our online businesses operating and functional in the shortest possible time, we overlook factors that can make a big difference in the overall effectiveness of our site.

Of course, to gain any perspective from the information in this chapter, you need to put yourself in the place of your users and ask yourself questions along these lines: Once potential customers get to my site, can they find what they're looking for, or do I lose traffic because my visitors are lost? Remember that you have 50 seconds to hook visitors before you lose them.

How easy is it to navigate your Web site, and what type of navigational tools are you using between your pages? How effective are those tools, and how can you make them even more effective? Are you using an onsite search engine? What about a site map?

If you're using a database to run your site, you'll have a different set of concerns, which we'll cover in this chapter. We'll also discuss various Web design issues that relate to the functionality of your site, explain how you can segregate the content of your site to improve its functionality, and outline the latest technology and tools to help you solve problems specific to your site.

## Checking for Navigation Concerns

When determining what navigation system would work best on your Web site, remember the most important point: *Keep it simple!*

Remember that new Internet users make up most of the traffic to any site. Though they may stop to "ooh and ahh" about your fancy icons and mouse rollovers, what they really want is to be able to move around your site in the easiest and quickest manner possible.

So don't try to impress your viewers with your fancy navigation system. Instead, create a system that is simple and functional. Think about what you appreciate most on a Web site. You want to find what you're looking for. So do your visitors.

One of the best ways to analyze the effectiveness of your navigation system is to plot it out on paper. By studying it on paper, you'll often see holes in your navigation system that you might not have noticed otherwise.

Two other keys are the flow of your site from page to page and the navigational tools you give your visitors. The capability to move from one place to another in your site should not test your visitors' patience but reward them with valuable information and a freedom that keeps them at your site rather than clicking away in frustration. This section gives you a number of things to consider and a list of guidelines to make sure the navigation system is both well structured and fully functional.

## Plotting Your Site

When plotting out your Web site on paper, consider what your most important Web pages are and how they're linked off the main page. Have you provided a link to all major sections of your Web site from the main page?

**TIP**  Make sure that all important pages of your Web site are within three mouse clicks from the main page. Why? Because the more loops and doorways you make your visitors crawl through to find what they're looking for, the better chance you have of losing them along the way.

So right now, take a few minutes to plot out your existing Web site.

What do we mean by *plotting out your existing Web site?* Start at the main, or home, page and write down all links leaving the main page that go to other pages of your site. You don't need to be concerned with links that lead customers to other sites, just those links within your site.

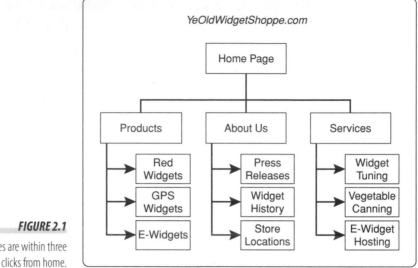

*FIGURE 2.1*

Plot a site to see if all pages are within three clicks from home.

Figure 2.1 shows how your Web site might be plotted out on paper. Note that any page can be drawn up within *two* mouse clicks of the home page.

In studying Figure 2.1, you'll notice that each page pertains to a particular topic. Ideally, this is the way your Web site should be set up, with data segregated according to the page. In Chapter 17, "The Importance of Search Engines to the Success of Your Online Business," you'll study the major search engines and learn why data segregation is so important.

What other pages are on your site? If they're important, how can you logically change the navigation to where they're within three mouse clicks? Make notes on your graph of areas that you need to change.

## Getting There and Back Again

When considering navigation, always keep in mind that you want your users to logically navigate through your site, especially in business-critical areas like your shopping cart section.

Always use a natural progression from page to page. In the text of your page, if you mention a related area on your site, by all means provide a link to that area. Then, to get your visitors back to where they were before, provide a way to return.

**TIP** One way to get your visitors back to a previous page is with a JavaScript snippet like this placed in your pages:

```
<H5><a href="javascript:history.back();" onmouseover="window.status=
'Return to Previous Page'; return true;"><font face=
"Arial,Helvetica,Geneva,Swiss,SunSans-Regular">
Return To The Previous Page</font></a></H5>
```

 **TIP** Simply add wording at the bottom of your page, such as "Return to the Previous Page," as used in this example, and your visitors can easily return to the page they just viewed.

Where does your shopping cart fit into the navigation of your site? Can visitors access the shopping cart from each of your product or service pages? We cover shopping carts in detail in Chapter 13, "How Effective Is Your Shopping Cart?", but for now, you need to consider how your visitors navigate through the shopping areas of your site.

## Testing the Navigation of Your Site

Next, look at your site's navigation elements to make sure it gets your users where they need to go. What areas are you linking to? Are there other areas of your site that may need to be included on the onsite navigation bar? Make notes of any areas that may need improvement.

 **NOTE** According to Jakob Nielsen, who is frequently sited as knowing more about what works on a Web site than anyone else, "lack of navigation support" is one of the top 10 mistakes in Web design. As stated at his useit.com Web site (**http://www.useit.com**), "Don't assume that users know as much about your site as you do. They always have difficulty finding information, so they need support in the form of a strong sense of structure and place."

 **FIND IT ONLINE** Now take a look at an example of a Web site that has an effective navigation system in place. Figure 2.2 shows the home page for Prima Publishing at **http://www.primapublishing.com**.

Note these important items on Prima's home page:

- Onsite search engine
- Site map
- FAQ
- About Prima Publishing

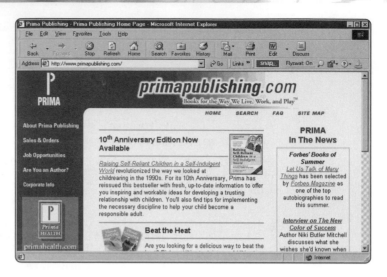

**FIGURE 2.2**

Prima Publishing Web Site.

- Sales & Orders
- Job Opportunities
- Are You an Author?
- Corporate Info
- News-related items about Prima
- What's new on the Web site

Whether you're interested in any of Prima's lines of books, working for Prima, writing for the publisher, or simply getting the latest information about the company, you'll find those links easily and quickly from the main page of the site. That should be your goal for your own site.

## Checking for Dead Ends

Another very important consideration concerns *dead ends* in your site. You should be sure that each page of your site, no matter how trivial or critical, has a link back to other important pages in the site. Key links include the home page and the main page of the section the user is browsing. Pages that result in a dead end give your visitors a reason to leave your site.

Suppose that Betty Browser wants to see what jobs are currently available at your company, so she surfs over to your Jobs area. In your Jobs area, you include nifty links to information about company locations, benefits, the office environment, and the jobs themselves. From each of the pages she can reach from this section, she should be able to return to the main Jobs page, the home page, and perhaps even the job listings.

**TIP**    When users search directories and search engines, they may come across an internal page of your site. If they like what they see on that page and need to find your home page, don't force them to type in your URL or even to guess where they need to go from this internal page. Give them an obvious link to get to the major points of your site.

## Checklist for Analyzing Navigation

When working on the navigation of your own site, ask yourself these questions:

- When visitors first arrive on my main page, can they easily determine how to get to the particular section of my site that interests them?

  Find a few people who have never been to your site and ask them to visit. Give them something to find, and see if they can find it easily and quickly. If they can't, you need to work on your navigation.

- Do I provide a prominent link to a site map? (Site maps are discussed later in this chapter.)

- Do I provide a navigation bar or buttons on each of my pages?

- Have I placed the navigation bar or buttons at the same place on each of my pages so my visitors will know where to find them? Don't make your visitors hunt for the navigation tools!

- Do I need to add any other items to my navigation bar?

- Is the wording on my navigation bar clear? In other words, make sure your wording tells your visitors exactly what's available in that area.

  For example, let's say that you sell software programs, but you also consult on software solutions. If your navigation bar only mentions "Software" or "Programs," will your customers know where they can find the information on your consultation services? Instead, use a label like "Products and

Services" to let your customers know exactly what they'll get if they click on that link.

- Do I provide navigation on the top and bottom of my pages? If your pages are long, this navigation capability is certainly something you need to consider, instead of making your visitors scroll back up (or down) to navigate your site.

- Here's something else to consider. When visitors first get to your page, what do they see on that page before they ever scroll down? Is there enough navigation on that portion of the page (before the *fold*, as it is termed) to get your visitors through your site? There should be!

- In the shopping area of your site, study your navigation closely. Can visitors easily add an item to their shopping cart and then continue shopping, so that they can click on a "Check out" button at any time when they're ready to pay? More information on e-commerce concerns is provided in Part IV, "Analyzing E-Commerce Solutions," but for now, think seriously about the navigation aspects.

**FIND IT ONLINE**

- Study the navigation systems of big e-commerce sites, such as Amazon at **http://www.amazon.com** or Barnes & Noble at **http://www.bn.com/**. When you add an item to your shopping cart, you will be given an opportunity to go directly to checkout, keep shopping, save your shopping cart items for later, etc. These options give visitors the flexibility they need to shop efficiently, wasting as little time as possible. That added convenience for them means more sales when they return later. In addition, even on those shopping cart pages, there are links to all major areas of the site. If they choose to continue shopping, they aren't dumped back at the home page, left to start again.

- Can every important page on my Web site be reached within three mouse clicks from the main page? Not only is this important in terms of navigation, but it's also important in terms of search engines, which we discuss in Part V, "Creating Engine-Friendly Web Sites."

- Does every page have a link to one of the important pages in my site to avoid losing visitors on a dead-end page?

## Translating Logical Structure into Site Sections

How many times have you gone to a Web site and been unable to find what you're looking for? You know it's there somewhere, but you certainly can't find it within a reasonable period of time.

Are visitors to *your* Web site able to find what they're looking for? *Are you sure?*

We've discussed navigation aspects for moving your visitors through your site in the most efficient manner. But you should certainly consider other ways to help visitors find what they're looking for once they reach your site. How you organize your site into sections (refer to Figure 2.1) plays an important role in the number of clicks a user must endure, and it also gives you a solid logical structure you can reflect on your home page and your physical structure.

### An "About Us" Section

One very important area for providing information is an "About Us" page. After all, you want to make sure you're giving your visitors a place where they can learn more about your company and its products and services. Before potential customers will consider purchasing your products and services, you must give them enough information about your company and its standards to prove to them that they can trust you and what you offer. If the "comfort" aspect is missing, you'll lose business.

In an "About Us" area, you can provide information such as …

- Press releases.
- Various departments in your company and their phone numbers, physical addresses, and e-mail addresses.
- A map to your main office.
- A listing of branch offices along with contact information.
- A listing of company officials and board members.
- The history of your company.
- Your goals.
- Plans for the future.

- Important alliances.
- Affiliate information.
- Advertiser information.
- Job information.
- Contact information for any Web site-specific issues.
- Stock or other information of interest to investors.

Make sure that a link to your "About Us" section is clearly visible on the main page of your site. Ideally, you'll also provide this link in your navigation system throughout the site.

*Find It*
**ONLINE** For a good example of an "About Us" section, visit eBay Auction at **http://pages.ebay.com/community/aboutebay/index.html**.

## Products and Services Section

Your Products and Services area is another crucial section of your Web site, and you need clear navigation to that section from every page of your site.

When potential customers land on your main page, if they're interested in your products and services, the first thing they're going to look for is a link to those products and services.

Make your link clear and prominent, and again, provide a link to your Products and Services area in your navigation system throughout the site.

What about dazzling potential customers with your new products or product lines? What about having a prominent link to sales that are going on in your company right now?

We cover the importance of data segregation in Chapter 18 as it relates to search engines, but you'll find that your Web site will operate more efficiently if you set up pages for each of your products and services instead of lumping them together in one lengthy page. Simply provide one major page that outlines your different products and services, and then link to individual pages for each of your products and services.

## Contact Information

One mistake many commercial Web sites make is that they don't provide contact information on all main pages of their site. You want to establish a sense of trust with your potential customers, and one way of doing that is to provide contact information. Let your visitors see that you have a physical address and a phone number, because it makes them feel more secure to do business with a company that has a presence in the "real world."

Some Web sites offer their full address, phone number, and e-mail address on the main page of the site. Then, on every other page, they simply provide a "Contact Us" link that goes to an e-mail address.

Remember that if visitors can't find what they're looking for on your site, they can always write and inquire, but only if you make it easy for them to do so. So provide that contact information, and by all means answer your e-mail!

Does your navigation bar contain a "Contact Us" link? Again, even if it only links to an e-mail address, at least you're giving your visitors an easy way to ask questions and to find what they're looking for.

Each visitor to your site is a potential customer. As opposed to brick-and-mortar businesses, a Web site doesn't have the advantage of a friendly person greeting each customer at the door. So if you don't provide an easy and quick way for your visitors to find what they're looking for, or a way for them to ask questions, you stand a good chance of losing their business.

## Customer Support

For your existing customers, you want to provide an easy way to find information about the goods and services they've purchased from your company. Again, a link to your Customer Support area should be prominent on every major page of your site.

After all, if you can't keep your existing customers happy, you'll have a difficult time convincing new customers that you can take care of their needs.

### Feedback Forms

Another important item to consider adding to every page is a link to a feedback form that allows customers to give specific feedback. This option gives your visitors and your customers the opportunity to contact you with problems, suggestions, questions, or praise they may have for your company, your products or services, or your site. The form should prompt users for plenty of information in order to get the specific feedback you need to improve your online presence. You might want to ask your visitors for information such as the following:

- Visitors' names and any contact information they feel comfortable giving (let them be anonymous, if they choose)
- What type of feedback they're giving—suggestions, questions, problems, dead-link notices, feedback that requests a response, etc.
- What area the feedback deals with—the site (what area specifically?), the company, a product, etc.
- Whether they would like a personal response
- Comments
- Any other specific information regarding the type of feedback (e.g., if they're notifying you of a dead link, which link is dead?)

Some surfers prefer to send e-mail, but feedback forms are another alternative to allowing your visitors to be as specific as they want to be, leaving you to continue to improve the Web site, product, or company.

Your Customer Support area should provide information such as …

- Contact information, including the e-mail addresses of various departments in your company, phone numbers, and physical addresses.
- Information on how to set up your products, if appropriate.
- FAQs for each of your products and services.
- An online users manual.
- Warranty information.
- A troubleshooting area.

**NOTE** Remember that a FAQ is a page of frequently asked questions and their answers. You can start up a FAQ by using the feedback forms from users or by using your test group to generate questions to include about your services, products, or site.

You also may want to include a forum that is monitored by your staff, so your customers can ask questions and enter into discussions about your products and services.

In addition, you may want to include an online form that your visitors can complete if their questions haven't been answered elsewhere.

Equally as important as providing the information is to make sure that navigation through your Customer Support area is simple and effective. Study your navigation system carefully and plot it out on paper. Look over the guidelines in the "Checking for Navigation Concerns" section, earlier in this chapter. Make sure that your current customers can get the help they need, and they'll do business with you again and recommend your company to others.

**FIND IT ONLINE**   For a good example of a support area, visit Qualcomm's Eudora Technical Support at **http://www.eudora.com/techsupport/**.

## Using a Site Map

Site maps can mean different things to different people. However, the type of *site map* we're referring to is simply a listing of all the Web pages on your site and often the page titles on the list are links to that page.

Many site maps are divided into various sections, such as Customer Support, Products and Services, Contact, About Us, and so forth. Under each of those sections is an alphabetical list of the Web pages that fall under that area. Site maps also can be divided into logical areas, as discussed later in this chapter. Or, if a company is small, an alphabetical listing of pages may be all that's needed.

Site maps aren't just for large Web sites. Any Web site can benefit from a site map. Not only is a site map beneficial for navigational purposes, but it's also crucial when working on building traffic from search engines, as we discuss in Part V.

Think of it this way. A site map is another means of navigating your Web site and helping your potential customers find what they want. You should provide as many means of navigating your site as you can, always with the idea that simplicity is your goal.

Let's go back to Prima's site and look at its site map at **http://www. primapublishing.com/map.asp**, which will give you some ideas of what you can include in your site map.

Prima's site map is divided into sections, as shown in Figure 2.3. Prima-Tech, which is Prima's technical line, is listed first, with information about each of the series books that Prima sells in that line.

But what if you don't know the name of the series? No problem. Prima also provides a category listing, so you can glance through its categories in areas such as Networking, Operating Systems, and the Internet.

Suppose that you know the actual name of the book, and it would be easier for you to simply look through a listing of all the Prima technical books to find the one you want. Farther down on the page, you'll find a link to an Index of Prima-Tech books. You'll also find links to "Help & Information," "Send Us Your Comments," "Book Proposal Guidelines," and a Prima-Tech FAQ.

Do you see how valuable a site map can be? It provides links to every bit of important information available on your site in an easy-to-find manner.

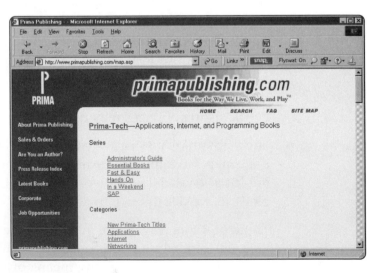

**FIGURE 2.3**

Prima Publishing's Site Map.

Another helpful feature of Prima's site map is the navigation bar to the left of the page. You'll find links to "About Prima Publishing," "Sales & Orders," "Are You an Author," "Press Release Index," "Latest Books," "Corporate," and "Job Opportunities."

No matter what visitors might be looking for on Prima's site, you can be sure they'll find it easily and quickly through the site map.

## Assisting Users with Onsite Search Engines

Onsite search engines are another means of helping your visitors find what they're looking for quickly and easily. Visitors can plug in what they're looking for, and the search engine will spit out the pages in order of *relevancy*, or the pages it considers to most closely match the search query.

Provide search capabilities on every page of your site, not just the main page. You don't want your visitors to have to go back to your main page to find your search engine.

**NOTE**

**FIND IT ONLINE**

To illustrate the importance of using an onsite search engine, consider Jakob Nielsen of useit.com's (**http://www.useit.com/alertbox/9707b.html**) research. He indicates that the majority of all users prefer searching to other methods of finding information on a Web site. His philosophy is that sites with more than 200 pages should offer search capabilities, including a search button on every page, global search through the entire site, and even Boolean queries on an advanced search page.

Nielsen's studies show that more than half of all users will use a search engine, whereas around one fifth will use links to navigate through a site. The rest may use either method. "The search dominant users will usually go straight for the search button when they enter a Web site: they are not interested in looking around the site; they are task focused and want to find specific information as fast as possible," says Nielsen. "In contrast, the link dominant users prefer to follow the links around a site: even when they want to find specific information, they will initially try to get to it by following promising links from the home page."

So where can you find an onsite search engine, and how difficult is it to set up?

SearchButton.com (**http://www.searchbutton.com**) provides onsite search engines to Web sites, and they provide customer support to guide you each step of the way.

One advantage to an onsite search engine through SearchButton is the log file information that is available. Through this information, you can track what people are searching for once they arrive at your site. We go into more detail about log files in an onsite search engine in Chapter 31, "Tracking with Log Files from Onsite Search Engines."

Onsite search engines are very simple to set up. With SearchButton, the engine spiders your site and indexes all of the information. Then you're provided with the code, and you simply plug that code into the HTML on your page.

Here's an example of the code:

```
<P>
<form method="GET" action="http://search.searchbutton.com/search">
</P>
<P>
<table border="0">
<TR>
<td colspan="2" valign="bottom"><font size="2"><strong>Search for:</
strong> </font></td>
</TR>
<TR>
<td valign="top"><input type="hidden" name="Site"
value="xxxxxxxxxx"><input type="text" name="query" size="30"
maxlength="64"></td>
<td valign="middle"><input type="image" src="http://
www.searchbutton.com/images/search-bug.gif" width="111" height="18"
border="0"></td>
</TR>
</TABLE>
</FORM>
</P>
```

It's a simple matter of signing up with SearchButton, having its engine's spider index your site, receiving a similar code, and cutting/pasting it onto your pages. Voilá! Your own site search engine!

# The Database-Driven Web Site

If you are not already using a database on your site, you should consider making a change. Databases have become standard fare nowadays, allowing you to serve up dynamic pages to your customer, depending on whom your visitor is or what the visitor is trying to find. Databases also give you the opportunity to track the activities taking place on your site—such as how many hits your new page got this week, who signed in to take part in a discussion in your chat area, and what the most popular download was this week.

The most common way to tie your database to your Web site is with ASP pages, which are easily created by using Visual Interdev, or with PHP pages. Several other methods are available, but these two formats provide a very efficient and effective means of tying your site to your database. *ASP,* or *Active Server Pages,* run on Microsoft's *Internet Information Server* (IIS) or by using modules on other Web servers such as Apache. *PHP,* or *Personal Home Page* (the name given this awe-inspiring language before it became the phenomenon it is today), is a hypertext preprocessor. In other words, when a page with an extension of .php3 or .php is requested by a surfer, the Web server "reads" through the page and fills in pertinent information before passing the page to the surfer. Types of information provided include database query results.

What is a *database query,* and what kind of results do we mean? When you query a relational database, you generally ask for information that fills specific attributes of a table, where a table is a collection of information. Suppose that you have a table called Widget, which contains a list of your widgets—the names, product code numbers, color, style, size, and wholesale price. If you run a query using *SQL,* or *Structured Query Language,* you might submit the following to the database:

```
SELECT widget_name, product_code, color, style, size, price FROM
Widget WHERE color="red"
```

This query returns all information included in the Widget table for red widgets.

Now let's see how that would look if you created a page using PHP that lists all red widgets in your catalog, which is stored in a MySQL database. The following code does not include the HTML that normally would surround the PHP, nor does it do any error checking.

```php
<?php
    $host = "localhost";
$usr = "widget";
    $passwd = "widgetsrock";
    $db = "Widget_Catalog";
    $query = "SELECT * FROM Widget WHERE color ='red'";
mysql_connect ($host, $usr, $passwd);
    mysql_select_db($db);
    $query_results = mysql_query($query);
    $num_results = mysql_num_rows($query_results);
    echo($num_results . " Widgets found.<br>");

    for ($i = 0; $i < $num_results; $i++) {
        $this_row = mysql_fetch_row ($query_results);
        for ($j = 0; $j < $mysql_num_fields($query_results); $j++){
            echo ($mysql_field_name($query_results, $j) . ": ");
            echo ($this_row[$j] . "<BR>");
        }
        echo ("<HR>");
    }
    mysql_close;
?>
```

If this database query returns only one row (in other words, there is only one red widget listed in the Widget table), the page might look like Figure 2.4.

Let's take this step by step.

First, you set the variables you'll need when calling on the MySQL database. So you need to set the hostname as `localhost`, the username as `widget`, the password to this database as `widgetsrock`, and the database name as `Widget_Catalog`. Our database query, `'SELECT * FROM Widget WHERE color="red"'` tells the database to return all fields (*) in the Widget table where the field name color is red.

Now you begin using PHP commands to connect to the database, query it with your `select` statement, and then run through the results. The

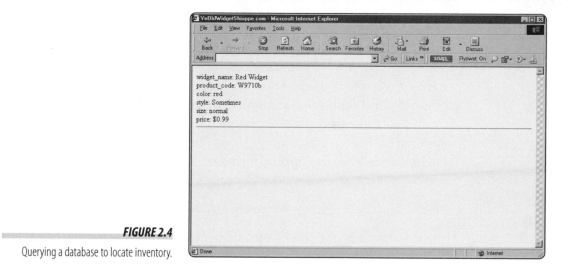

**FIGURE 2.4**

Querying a database to locate inventory.

command `mysql_num_rows` reveals the number of rows (number of re-sults) returned from the query. In this case, the `$num_results` variable is equal to 1. The command `mysql_fetch_row` gets each row of results so that each field can be printed.

When using a database to generate dynamic pages, remember not to sacrifice the usability of your site. The point of the database is to make your site less generic and more efficient, so remember to maintain navigability, aesthetics, and ease of use when you integrate the a data-base with your Web site.

**TIP**   Keep in mind that having your Web server parse every page before it goes to a browser adds a load to the server that it may not be able to handle. Make sure you have the proper hardware and software to deal with the added strain.

Some database-driven sites derive their entire page content from a template and the dynamic content from the database. Unfortunately, many users find themselves without the capability to return to the previous page on these sites because such a feature has been left out. Now is the time to give your users additional options. If they're search-ing your site with your database, they want to be able to return to any point in the search results at any time. Give them the option of which page of results to return to, or even the capability to return to the task they were completing when they began the search. When the site is navigable, it's also easy to use.

Along the same lines, be sure that your page isn't crowded with text, graphics, and multimedia. Maintain aesthetics so that users can easily find what they need from the page. Just because your site is dynamic and tied to a powerful database doesn't mean you need to throw in the kitchen sink. Take the opportunity to branch the page into several different pages, if necessary, to avoid sacrificing ease of use and aesthetics.

Here are just a few ideas for using your database to make a better site:

- If your database tracks hits, along with other metrics such as time of day, type of browser, country of origin, etc., you can better analyze your site's traffic.
- Have your customers fill out a form specifying their preferences, and tailor your site to those preferences.
- Automatically change the content of the page according to the date or time.
- Track purchases and take orders.
- Record a chat session so you can provide a transcript later.
- Automatically fill in information customers have already provided from other forms to save them the time and effort of retyping.
- Easily update information in several places throughout your site, instead of manually updating each HTML page.
- Through forms and your database, retrieve e-mail addresses and compile them to be used as a mailing list for your company's newsletter, sales promotion e-mail, an e-mail discussion list, and so forth.
- Tailor what's available on your Web site to each individual user.

If your company provides news on the Web, for example, each user could choose the type of news of interest, the location for weather forecasts, stock market quotes, etc. Each time the user visits your site, the database would pull the information created just for that particular user and display a page with the user's unique preferences.

This is an excellent way of providing an interactive Web site where your users will be able to retrieve personalized information.

## Using Intranets, Extranets, and the Internet to Appeal to an Array of Customers

Depending on the purpose your company serves, you may have more than one site to handle. The *Internet* allows you to give the general public access to the product, information, or services you provide. Your *intranet* gives your employees the capability to connect to one another in a secure area to get and share company, employee, or confidential product information. Your *extranet* will be similar to your intranet in that it is a private and secure network, except that the information it provides will be specific to the businesses with which you have networked.

So the Internet provides a site for the general public. Your intranet provides a site for only those within your company. And your extranet provides a site that connects you with companies with which you do business.

If you have all three nets at your company, you have an issue to consider with your employees, because you will have three separate sites. How will you make each site different enough that they are distinguishable from one another? You can achieve this difference by using varied color schemes, graphics, and even setups (see the following section, "Establishing the Structure of Your Site") while also maintaining a sameness that reminds your surfers where they are. But before you go to the effort, why is this an issue?

These sites and the pages within them must appeal to the customer. In each instance, you should consider the customer or employee to whom you are marketing. You want your Internet site to be attractive to the masses, but your intranet/extranet should appeal to its separate audience with its separate purpose. It should look and feel private and secure. Its content should be arranged according to the purpose it serves. And these attributes combined need to attract your users back to see new information as it is posted or to order a new product as it is revealed.

What can you do to make your sites different enough?

- Vary the colors you use. For example, you might want to use the blue of your company's logo for backgrounds, text, or image colors on your Internet site; but use a lighter version of that color for your intranet.
- Vary the page layout slightly, perhaps by putting navigation tabs at the top of your Internet site pages but using navigation buttons on the left side of your intranet site pages.
- Vary the images, perhaps by using the negative of your company logo or by using an entirely different theme.

What can you do to maintain continuity for those who move frequently from one site to another?

- Use logos and graphics with the same design.
- Use the same page layout.
- Use the same navigation tools with the same interface, including search engine, site map, etc.
- Use similar color schemes.

## Establishing the Structure of Your Site

When considering how your site is set up, you should be primarily concerned with two areas: the logical structure and the physical structure. By *logical structure*, we mean *how the site looks when you have it plotted on a page*. Where are the sections? How are they divided? What pages go into each section? How are the pages linked? On the other hand, the *physical structure* concerns *how the files that make up your site are structured in the Web server file system*.

Why are these areas important? Sure, you can easily set up a site that draws hundreds of thousands of hits per day. But—much as software engineers around the world refuse to admit it—Web development is almost the same as software development. For both types of development, an underlying structure must exist—something the users can work with. And in both, an understandable (if not pleasing) interface must be present for the users.

What are your options?

## The Logical Structure

When designing your site, consider all the navigation concerns discussed in this chapter. Your site can be divided logically into several areas, depending on the purpose of the site. If your main objective is to sell products, then your areas should be divided according to action.

Suppose that your company sells widgets in purple, red, and green; and those in green can be equipped with a Global Positioning System. Divide your pages according to each widget. The green GPS widgets should have a separate page from the green non-GPS widgets. But all these pages should be in the same section. Perhaps in another section, you want to allow customers to access technical support with a bulletin board system, a variety of articles, and contact information for your Tech Support division. Your Tech Support area is separate from the Products area, although you might include links from each area to the other.

On the other hand, say your Web site provides surfers with information on widgets currently on the market, including reviews of those widgets, customer feedback, and links to the widget companies' Web sites. In this case, you might decide the areas should be divided according to the company or the widget type. So each area would look pretty much identical to every other area, except the information would be different.

## The Physical Structure

The design of the physical structure depends on the needs of the Web designers and programmers who are developing and maintaining your site. If the site is large, the programmers may decide to divide the pages into a dozen or more directories. Let's use the widgets again as an example.

In the case of the widget products your company sells, the programmers may decide to divide all files in your site into images, *common gateway interface* (CGI) programs, products, career opportunities, company information and press releases, and tech support. Within these directories, they may further divide the pages. Programmers do this for several reasons. First, it's clean, simple, and effective. Second, if different programmers are developing different areas (in other words,

Charlie has the Tech Support section, Chris works on the Products section, and Sam deals with the Career Opportunities section), they may end up using the same or similar file names. When those files are uploaded, they will overwrite the files with the same names in the same directory. If those files go into different directories, though, the problem is eliminated.

**NOTE**   Good software engineering practice dictates that naming conventions for files are set up during your requirements phase. When deadlines loom and heads are about to roll, however, conventions sometimes disappear in the shuffle.

Take a look at the following physical layout (the actual file structure) at the top level of a Web site, as shown in Figure 2.5

Notice that very few files appear at the top level and that most of the contents at this point are directories containing more files. Each of these directories has been divided according to content. For example, the "newbooks" directory contains information regarding books that are currently available. The "reviews" directory contains information regarding reviews—both the articles themselves as well as information for reviewers to request review copies of future books—for the author. And "cgi" contains all CGI scripts used on this site.

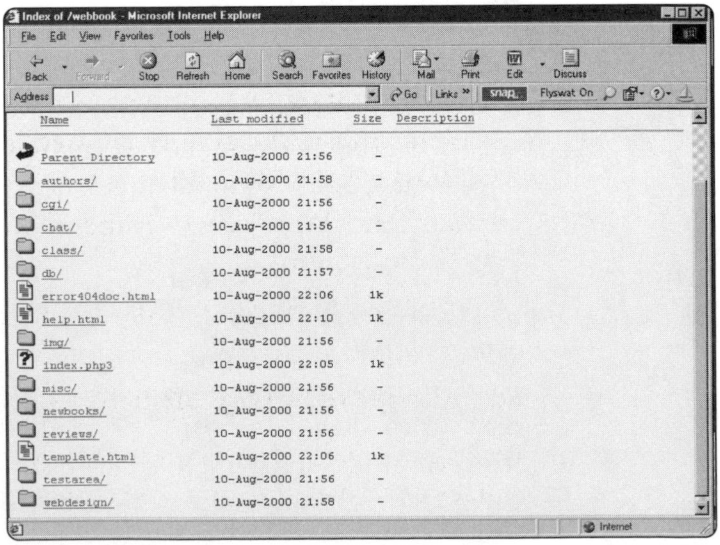

**FIGURE 2.5**

Organizing a site into directories.

By dividing the site into this physical layout, you avoid having the 100+ files contained on this site all on the top level. This method helps us bypass clutter and segregate our files into different areas for the sake of those implementing and maintaining the site.

 **TIP**    In each directory, make sure that one of the files is a default file—such as index.html or default.html. Users sometimes surf in from a search engine, and the page they find may not quite serve their needs. Savvy users may try to reach a "higher" level in your logical layout by asking for the default page in that directory of your physical layout. By giving them a default page, you have a better chance of keeping them at your site.

## Finding the Right Technology

A vast array of technology is available to you to create the perfect Web site that will keep customers coming back for more. Some software is free through different licenses (GPL, freeware, etc.), and those products are denoted by an asterisk (*) in the following subsections. The following lists have been separated according to function. We include a variety of choices for each section, but don't limit yourself—there are plenty of other alternatives out there.

### Web Servers

Web servers are the "engine" of your site, serving pages to Web surfers when they browse through your pages.

 *FIND IT* **ONLINE**

- Microsoft Internet Information Server—**http://www. microsoft.com/ntserver/web/exec/feature/ Datasheet.asp?RLD=71**
- Netscape's Web Server—**http://home.netscape.com/enterprise/ v3.6/index.html**
- Apache Web Server*—**http://www.apache.org**

### Scripting and Programming Languages

These languages allow users to interact with the Web page. The languages can do everything from creating pop-up menus for users to navigate the site to processing the input users submit via forms.

Programming languages are more powerful than scripting languages, but they are also more cumbersome.

*FIND IT*
**ONLINE**

- **Perl**—Perl is an acronym for *Practical Extraction* and *Report Language* and is one of the most popular scripting languages available because of its capability to parse and process text. It's used to create interactive forms and other CGI programs. In fact, it's the programming language of choice for writing Web applications. You can get more information at **http://www.perl.com**, **http://www.perl.org**, or **http://www.cpan.org**.

- **JavaScript**—JavaScript is used a great deal today to add immediate interactivity to a Web page, mostly in response to actions, such as rolling a mouse over a graphic. For more information, visit **http://www.javascript.com/**. For some interesting discussion and insight, see **http://javascriptweenie.com/**.

- **JScript**—JScript is the Microsoft Internet Explorer supported version of JavaScript, with information available at **http://msdn.microsoft.com/scripting/jscript/default.htm**.

- **VBScript**—Also known as *Visual Basic Script*, VBScript is a fast, portable interpreter for use in browsers and other applications that use Microsoft ActiveX Controls, Automation servers, and Java applets. See **http://msdn.microsoft.com/scripting/vbscript/default.htm**.

- **PHP**—An acronym for *Personal Home Page*, PHP is a scripting language that is embedded within HTML pages for server-side execution. You can get more information at **http://www.php.net/**.

- **Java**—Java is a programming language for writing client and server applications for the Web. For more information, visit **http://java.sun.com/** or **http://javaboutique.internet.com/**.

- **Visual Basic/ActiveX**—Visual Basic is a programming language from Microsoft that is graphically oriented and easy to learn. It can be used to create software ranging from database applications to commercial software packages (see **http://www.vbhow.to/**). ActiveX is a brand name from Microsoft (see **http://browserwatch.internet.com/activex.html**).

## Databases

Databases allow you to store and access information. Using a database with your Web site enables data tracking, automatic site updates, and customer recognition.

- MySQL*—**http://www.mysql.com**
- PostgreSQL*—**http://www.postgresql.org/**
- Oracle—**http://www.oracle.com/**
- Sybase—**http://www.sybase.com/**
- Microsoft SQL Server—**http://www.microsoft.com/Sql/**

## Search Engines

Onsite search engines allow your users to find pages on your site related to a specific keyword or phrase. We cover onsite search engines in Chapter 32.

- HtDig*—**http://www.htdig.org/**
- SearchButton*—**http://www.searchbutton.com**

## Site Logs

Logs help you track and analyze the traffic your Web site generates. We discuss log files in detail in Part VII, "Tracking Traffic to Benefit Your Site."

- Analog*—**http://www.statslab.cam.ac.uk/~sret1/analog/**
- Webalizer*—**http://www.mrunix.net/webalizer/**
- WebTrends—**http://www.webtrends.com**
- FlashStats—**http://maximized.com/products/flashstats/**

# Conclusion

Helping your visitors find what they're looking for when they arrive at your Web site will do much toward boosting online sales and developing customer loyalty. Make your navigation simple and user friendly, and provide different means of navigating your site.

For those visitors who prefer to click on links, make sure that your navigation bar or buttons feature links to every important area of your site. Use a site map to further outline your Web site's offerings.

For visitors who prefer the convenience of a search engine, use the power of an effective onsite search engine to help them find what they're looking for quickly and easily.

Tying a database to your Web site can drastically increase the functionality and interactivity of your site.

To maintain separation of data and ideas and to ensure data integrity, you should choose both a physical and a logical structure for your site and adhere to it.

# PART II

# CAPITALIZING ON RETURN TRAFFIC

# OFFERING FREE OR DISCOUNTED ITEMS OR INFORMATION

**In This Chapter**

Capitalizing on the Popularity of Freebies

Offering Discounts or Sale Items

Doling Out Good Advice

Maintaining Interest with Fresh Material

If you want your Web site to be bookmarked and visited over and over again, you have to give your customers a reason to come back.

This sounds so elementary, but it's often not easy to do. Sometimes it takes a little creativity, which is what this chapter is all about. All of the strategies in this chapter add up to one thing: providing relevant content to your site aimed at getting return traffic. For example, do you realize how many people spend hours and hours online searching for freebies? Have you stopped to consider how captivating the word "Sale!" can be? Have you considered writing articles related to your goods and services? Is there a way you could incorporate a reminder service into your Web site, so that your customers will automatically be reminded of sales, updates to the site, etc.?

In this chapter, we cover these ideas and more, and you'll learn how important it is to be able to retrieve the e-mail addresses of your visitors.

## Capitalizing on the Popularity of Freebies

Freebies on the Web is a business in and of itself. You can visit thousands of different sites that provide anything from free software to mouse pads to dog food.

When offering a freebie, keep in mind that you'll want to promote it on your Web pages, even with a simple graphic. Make it easily accessible, although not as prominent as your pay goods or services. You want your visitors to be able to find the freebies, but you want them to see what else you're offering as well.

But how can you use the popularity of freebies in your online business without spending a fortune? This section lists a number of ways you can add customer-friendly value to your site.

### Free Software or Services

When looking for ways to offer something free to customers, look first at the type of business you're running for products that either naturally coincide with your business or for products that serve a purpose that can also promote your company. Can you provide an online service for monitoring or analyzing your customers' systems, or something similar? Can you offer free trial versions of a software program? What about a free screensaver? If you're not in the software business, many of these can be altered to advertise your products or services.

### Services

What type of free services could you provide for your visitors? As an example, javElink will monitor URLs for changes at no cost. Once javElink gets you to visit the site to take advantage of its free service, it has the opportunity to sell you other goods and services. You can visit javElink, by the way, at **http://www.javelink.com/**.

The beauty of this concept is that javElink is able to market its free services in places that generally won't allow commercial advertising, because it's providing a free service to the Web community. Let's face it—the Web is meant to be free, right? So give users what they expect to find, then prove to them that you can be trusted and are worthy of their business.

Another important consideration is that when you provide a free service, you're able to ask the e-mail addresses of your visitors, which you can use later to send out newsletters, notices of discounts, special promotions, etc. Treat these e-mail addresses like gold, because they can be invaluable to you. Don't go overboard with the quantity of information you request, however, because you'll lose people who don't want to complete a lengthy form.

**TIP** Throughout this and subsequent chapters, we'll touch on the importance of permission e-mail marketing by reminding you to save the e-mail addresses of visitors to your site. We'll also discuss security issues as it pertains to harvesting e-mail addresses. However, for the purpose of this chapter, keep in mind that those e-mail addresses can be "gold" to your online business, giving you ready access to past customers, to customers who are interested in particular goods or services, or to visitors to your site who have requested more information.

If you want to learn how to harness the power of e-mail marketing, consider taking an e-mail marketing course written by expert marketer Stephen Mahaney of Planet Ocean (visit **http:/ /www.email-solutions.com/moreinfo**). The course is titled "A Business Course in Permission Email Marketing." Later in this chapter, we'll provide an excerpt from the course.

Through all of this, you're building credibility and name recognition, not to mention using free publicity to advertise your site.

Here are some other examples of URLs that offer free services and then use those services to market their pay goods and services. Do you have any ideas for services your company could offer?

*Find It*
**ONLINE**

- **Mouse Click Application (http://www.mouseclickapplication.com)** consists of a series of services for Web masters, including a search engine that optimizes tool, link popularity service, and a keyword density analyzer.

- **Netwhistle (http://www.netwhistle.com)** checks to see how often your server is down.

- **Dominator (http://www.e-gineer.com/e-gineer/domainator/index.phtml)** checks on the availability of domain names and trademarks.

- **Search Engine Simulator (http://www.delorie.com/web/ses.cgi)** lets you see what an engine sees when it visits your site.

- **Shields Up! (http://grc.com/)** lets you know how secure your system is from hacker attacks.

### Software Programs

Many companies will buy the rights to a software program and then give the program away on their Web site. In the program itself, they'll advertise their goods and services. And, on the Web, they'll advertise this free software program as well as their goods and services.

*Find It*
**ONLINE**

An inexpensive way of providing a software program to visitors is to get free *open source software* from a Web site like FreshMeat. With open source software, the source code is open, so you can add features to the program, make changes to it, customize it, and so forth. You then can provide free downloads of this software at your site, offer tech support, or set up a chat room or bulletin boards for users to discuss the program. Visit FreshMeat at **http://www.freshmeat.net**.

As other sites link to that software program on your site, you also have the opportunity to increase the link popularity to your site, which is very important in terms of search engine rankings. We discuss link popularity in Part V, "Creating Engine-Friendly Web Sites."

### Screen Savers

Another idea is to provide a free screen saver or wallpaper at your site, or better yet, a variety. Make it catchy and interesting and not strictly a sales pitch for your site. Then advertise your free download at the numerous shareware and freeware sites across the Net.

For as little as $75, you can have a screen saver created at 100ScreenSavers. com. Visit **http://www.100freescreensavers.com/customize.html**.

## Free Promotional Items

Although this area can be more expensive than others, it also can be an effective way to promote your business and to increase traffic to your site. Again, you can promote your freebies in lists and newsletters that generally won't accept commercial advertising. Then, once you get the traffic to your site, you can point them to your other goods and services.

Do you have product samples that you could provide to visitors? What about promotional items such as mouse pads, ink pens, or note pads? What about a free magazine subscription for three months? How about offering a free online game? Or a free online calendar?

Are you overstocked in any of your products? Are any of those products appropriate to be given away as freebies? If not, could they be given away in contests or sweepstakes (which we cover in Chapter 4, "Setting Up Polls, Contests, and Other Traffic-Generating Avenues")?

Keep in mind that you can limit the number of freebies given away on your site. For example, you could give freebies to the first 25 visitors a day, or change the time frame of when the freebies will be awarded.

Jelly Belly Online gives away 500 free samples every day to U.S. residents and 100 free samples to Canadian residents every day, but to make it fair, they change around the time when they offer the giveaways. Figure 3.1 shows a screen shot of the free samples page.

This site is in frames, and you can see the navigation bar running down the left of the page at **http://www.jellybelly.com**. They clearly mention their "Free Samples," but it appears toward the bottom of the listing.

**FIGURE 3.1**

Free samples at Jelly Belly Online.

Again, when your visitors complete the form to request the freebie, be sure to ask for their e-mail addresses and names. Harness the power of permission e-mail marketing by saving every e-mail address you can find for your visitors!

To get some ideas on freebies you can offer your visitors, visit About.com's Freebies site at **http://freebies.about.com/shopping/freebies/**.

## Discount Coupons

With discount coupons, you save the cost of shipping, because your visitors can simply print out the coupon themselves.

Even if you're a regional provider of goods or services, why not offer a discount toward your services to your Internet customers?

If a computer show, conference, or workshop in your particular industry is coming to your area, what about offering free or discounted tickets?

Visit Coupons.com at **http://www.coupons.com** or Save.com at **http://www.save.com** to learn how you can advertise your coupons through their networks and permission marketing companies.

*FIND IT*
**ONLINE** RegiSoft's offers an interesting twist to online coupons and vouchers. Its World Trade Server is a Java application designed to create value-added services in the form of e-coupons, e-vouchers, and e-tickets for mobile and e-commerce. The program then distributes these services throughout Internet and wireless protocols through consumers' Internet-enabled and cellular devices, which are redeemable at Web sites and brick-and-mortar locations. The World Trade Server is designed to cultivate customer relationships by providing profile-building and data-mining tools. Personalized e-coupons and e-vouchers arrive directly at consumers' cellular phones or PDAs (Personal Digital Assistants). Visit RegiSoft's site at **http://www.regisoft.com** to learn more.

## Partnering with Another Company

Instead of shouldering the entire cost of giving away promotional items, is there a company you could partner with? If you're in the travel business, for example, is there a company that might be willing to give away a free vacation? A discount on airfare? A reduced hotel rate?

Do any of your vendors have promotional items they would allow you to give away on your site? Is there a magazine related to your industry that might consider giving away free magazine subscriptions to your visitors?

Could you partner with a company and share expenses, thereby doubling your exposure? Both of you can market the promotional items in your newsletters, e-zines, Web sites, and more.

## Offering Discounts or Sale Items

Why not offer a discount on a particular good or service every week? In a very prominent place on the main page of your site, mention this discount, and update it with new information weekly. Keep it in the same location, so that your visitors will be able to look in the same spot every week to see what's being offered. Why not set up a weekly newsletter that announces your sales items to subscribers?

Another idea is to offer a page of items that are on sale, and again, provide a prominent link to it.

On Amazon.com's (**http://www.amazon.com**) toolbar at the top of each results' page, for example, you'll see a link to "Bargain Books." Some of the books are offered at huge discounts, whereas other books are simply priced under a certain dollar amount, which is particularly helpful when customers are ordering a gift and want to stay within their budget.

Figure 3.2 shows Amazon's Bargain Books page.

The bargains are even divided up into categories to make it easier on the visitors.

You can find another example at Sandals4Less.com (**http://www. sandals4less.com/**), where a link to "Birkenstock Sale Items" is prominently displayed, as Figure 3.3 shows.

As you can see, the site even offers a sizing chart, which is very helpful to its customers.

Using the Sandals4Less site as an example, the company could create a small graphic that would link back to its sales page. Then it could offer an additional discount, or possibly free shipping, to anyone who comes through that link. This is a large incentive for other sites to post those graphics, and it's an excellent way to build link popularity for the Sandals4Less site, especially if the sites are related to shoes.

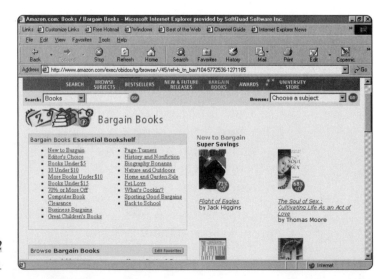

**FIGURE 3.2**

Amazon's Bargain Books page.

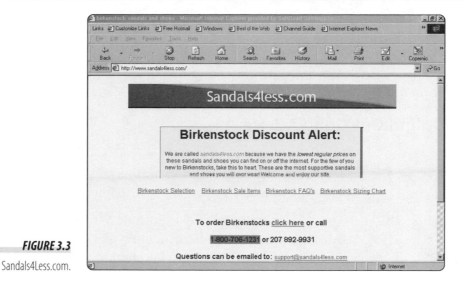

**FIGURE 3.3**

Sandals4Less.com.

**FIND IT ONLINE**

Coldwater Creek (**http://www.coldwatercreek.com**) offers a large graphic on its main page that links to its discounted items, as you can see in Figure 3.4.

"Save up to 60% off daily!" Yes, visitors will definitely click on that link, and they'll certainly bookmark the Coldwater Creek site, where they know they'll find discounts on a regular basis

**FIGURE 3.4**

Coldwater Creek.

So consider whether there is a way you can offer discount or sale items on your goods or services. Visitors are apt to bookmark your site and come back again and again if you give them a good reason to do so. Offering a discount is such a reason!

## Doling Out Good Advice

Is it possible for you to offer free articles of interest to your visitors? If you're a veterinarian, for example, can you offer articles on how to take care of a new puppy, or how to tell if you need to bring your dog to the vet?

By offering free information at your site, you're proving several things. First, you're showing your visitors that you are knowledgeable about the business and that you can be trusted. You're building credibility and name and brand recognition. Also, you're providing something that's free to your visitors—something that will make them want to return to see what you'll be offering in the future. Not only that, but you're filling your Web site with valuable content that will be appreciated by your visitors and the search engines alike.

### *Harness the Power of Permission E-Mail Marketing*

Here is an excerpt from "A Business Course in Permission Email Marketing" by Stephen Mahaney of Planet Ocean:

"Permission based email is the most cost effective marketing tool of all time — and the hottest business topic on the Internet today. To draw a parallel, think back a few years ago when companies were first discovering they HAD to get top listings on the search engines in order to succeed on the Internet. The process itself — and the tools involved to accomplish the task — developed into a passion and a science. The crucial piece of the search engine puzzle was "source code."

"Today, the same type of quiet frenzy is shaping up again within the arena of electronic direct marketing. Companies are scrambling to understand and appropriately unleash the power of one-to-one direct email to cut costs, provide support, maintain customer loyalty, and increase sales. This time the crucial piece to the puzzle is..."***permission!***

"Permission email operates on the premise that the recipient of your message has, in some way, established a relationship with you by indicating an interest in what you have to offer — and, in one way or another, given you permission to contact them."

For more information about the course, visit **http://www.email-solutions.com/moreinfo.**

**FIGURE 3.5**

Online Web Training.

 **TIP**  Master E-Book Generator lets your visitors create e-books with articles or other content that you provide. Visit **http://www.willmaster.com/master/ebook/index.shtml** to learn more.

**FIND IT ONLINE**  Figure 3.5 shows the main page of the Online Web Training site (**http://www.onlinewebtraining.com**).

Also, notice the link to "Recommendations." On this page, the site lists several resources it has found to be important in its industry. So visitors to the site can get an expert's opinion about software programs and services that might prove helpful to them.

By providing this free information, the site is building a reputation as being an expert in the industry, and it's certainly building name recognition. As people bookmark the site and tell others about it, the site's traffic is sure to increase.

 **FIND IT ONLINE**  In Figure 3.6, which shows the Web site of the National Writers Union (**http://www.nwu.org**), look at the toolbar on the left-hand side of the page. Notice the amount of valuable information available at this site, in addition to links to join the organization.

If you're a writer looking for a job, you'll hurry to click on the "Job Hotline" link. If you're in the process of signing a book contract, you'll certainly want to click on the "Contract Advice" link. The site offers

information about its many divisions as well as newsworthy items about the National Writers Union.

Although the purpose of the site is to promote the NWU and obtain new members, as well as to provide services to its current members, the site also provides valuable information to potential members.

## Free Shipping

Another slant on providing free information is to offer free shipping to your customers; or free shipping if orders consist of more than a certain amount; or free shipping on discounted items, during a special promotion, etc.

Find out what your competition is doing, then do it one better. Does your competition offer free shipping? Does your competition provide free information, freebies, or sales items? If not, you have the edge that you need over your competition.

Be the first in your industry to offer free shipping, and advertise that fact. Be the first to offer discounts or free information. Be the forerunner, and watch the traffic follow!

## Newsletters or E-zines

Why not send your customers and those on your e-mail list a monthly newsletter that lists articles by experts in your industry, new products and services, discounts, questions and answers, and so forth? Include a short "Tip of the Day" that your readers can look forward to, and post it on your Web site, along with past tips.

If you need content for your newsletter, why not ask your clients for articles related to their use of your products or services?

Be sure to have a prominent link where visitors can subscribe to your newsletter. And, when they sign up, prepare an e-mail that will be sent to new subscribers automatically. This e-mail can include information about your products, your company, or even a copy of your latest newsletter.

**FIND IT ONLINE** The e-mail marketing course by Planet Ocean that we mentioned earlier in this chapter is packaged with a software program for sending permission e-mails. Or visit the Bulk Email Software Superstore at **http://www.americaint.com/** for a variety of software programs.

**TIP** A popular way of retrieving e-mail addresses is to require your visitors to register in order to access another portion of your site, to use one of your services, to download a piece of software, and so forth. Require them to register, which brings them into your inner circle, and use those valuable e-mail addresses to announce new products or services, discounts, and so forth. Chapter 5, "Using Forms and Scripts to Capture E-mail Addresses," goes into more detail on this topic.

Be sure to archive your past newsletters and e-zines at your site. If your site has an onsite search engine, visitors can search through those archives for past articles. We cover onsite search engines in Chapter 31, " Tracking with Log Files from Onsite Search Engines."

You can advertise your newsletter, e-zine, or related lists through these lists:

**FIND IT ONLINE**
- Netsites—**http://www.egroups.com/group/netsites**
- New-List—**http://listserv.classroom.com/archives/new-list.html**
- Net-Announce—**http://www.erspros.com/cgi-bin/neta/na-webart.pl**

- BizLinks for Entrepreneurs—**http://youonline.net/free_sub.htm**
- CataList—**http://www.listserv.net/lists/listref.html**
- Email Mailing Lists—**http://www.cuenet.com/ml.html**
- InfoJump—**http://www.infojump.com**
- Huge Index of Mailing Lists—**http://www.geocities.com/ Eureka/6146/index.html**
- Low Bandwidth—**http://www.disobey.com/low/**
- The List of Lists—**http://catalog.com/vivian/ interest-group-search.html**
- ListQuest—**http://www.listquest.com/**
- Liszt—**http://www.liszt.com/**
- Directory of Publicly Accessible Mailing Lists—**http://paml.net/**
- Tile.Net—**http://tile.net/lists/addlist.html**

**FIND IT ONLINE**  Also, promote your newsletter on Usenet groups. To learn of related newsgroups, visit CyberFiber NewsGroups Directory and Search at **http://www.cyberfiber.com/index.html**.

**TIP**  If you need a source for maintaining a newsletter or e-zine list, visit one of these sites:

http://www.listbot.com/

**FIND IT ONLINE**  http://www.topica.com/

For tips on setting up a mailing list, visit:

http://www.useit.com/alertbox/20000820.html

For an article on how to set up your own newsletter or e-zine, read "Six Easy Steps to Launching Your Own E-zine" at:

http://www.academywebspecialists.com/information/ezines.html

## Expert Columns

What about offering columns by experts in your industry? When an expert in a particular industry writes an article or a regular column, visitors stand up and take notice, because they know they'll be able to learn some valuable information through that expert.

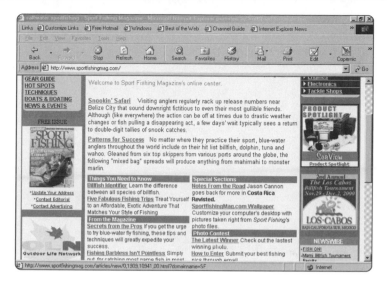

**FIGURE 3.7**

*Sport Fishing Magazine.*

Figure 3.7 shows Sport Fishing Magazine's Web site (**http://www.sportfishingmag.com/**); notice the various expert articles that are available.

You can read "Secrets from the Pros" or "Notes from the Road," both written by experts in the fishing industry. In fact, this site gives you a good taste of what's available in the print magazine, which is a big incentive to subscribe.

Besides offering articles by experts, what about interviewing experts? Many busy experts are more than willing to answer your questions, which is much easier for them than writing an article.

Or what about principal players in your company writing articles? Visitors take notice if the CEO or president of a company writes an article.

Another option is to provide speeches or interviews with experts on RealAudio or another audio service, and let your visitors actually listen to the speech online. Audio Web Pro produces streaming audio commercials for Web sites that allow visitors to listen without any plug-ins or server software. Visit **http://www.audiowebpro.com** to learn more.

In Figure 3.8, you see a Web site for a consulting company. How does the company prove that it's knowledgeable enough to consult with

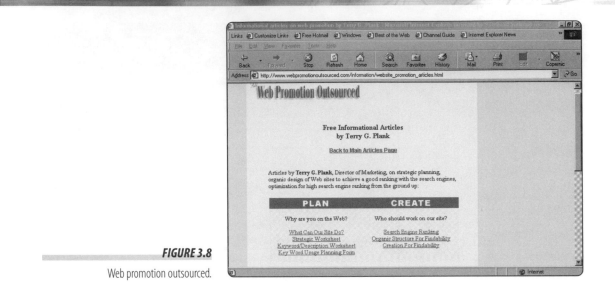

**FIGURE 3.8**

Web promotion outsourced.

you on your Web site? By providing an impressive number of articles by its primary consultant.

This is just the beginning of the listing of articles, but it gives you an idea of how much information this company provides at no charge to its potential customers.

Again, when using expert columns in your newsletters or online, be sure to archive past columns.

**TIP** If you're having problems finding an "expert" in your industry, visit Yahoo! and search for "experts" at **http://search.yahoo.com/search?p=experts**.

**FIND IT ONLINE** Or visit Experts.com at **http://www.experts.com/**.

## Questions and Answers

Many Web sites offer a place where visitors can send questions and have them answered online. Some companies even use these Q&As in their newsletters.

Let's say that you offer consulting services. Answer a few questions at no charge and post the answers on your site and in your newsletter.

Show your visitors that you know your stuff, and they'll be more willing to trust and hire you. Again, this is a good way to build credibility and name recognition, as well as to provide a reason for your visitors to return.

We've said it before and we'll say it again: Archive past Q&As and provide that valuable content to your site.

You can even visit related newsgroups and answer a few questions, then link back to your Web site, as a means of directing traffic through your site.

## Autoresponders

Autoresponders are another way of providing free information and reports to your Web viewers. Consider using autoresponders to answer questions that seem to be asked over and over again or to provide more information about your goods and services.

If you provide a free report via autoresponder, make the value of the report clear in an effort to boost requests for it. Again, save those e-mail addresses for future use.

Autoresponders can certainly save you a lot of time, because they're sent out automatically, and they also can save you from having to answer so many e-mails individually.

Some e-mail programs allow you to create your own autoresponders—such as Eudora Pro with its Auto-Reply function.

**TIP**

**FIND IT ONLINE**

MailLoop is a complete Internet e-mail, newsletter server, Web form processor, bulk e-mail, customer database, and autoresponder solution. All the software you need to automate your Internet venture is included and integrated into a single application. Not only that, but the software is simple to use. Visit MailLoop at **http://www.mailloop.com** for more information.

**FIND IT ONLINE**

Mailback.com and Autobots offer autoresponder services. Visit **http://www.databack.com/mailback.htm** and **http://autobots.net/** to learn more.

You can find more information on autoresponders in Chapter 5, "Using Forms and Scripts to Capture E-mail Addresses."

## E-books

E-books are popular these days for many reasons. They're so easy to use, and you have search capabilities that aren't available in print media. With the format of most e-books, you don't have to worry about someone cutting and pasting your work, so copyright issues aren't as much of a concern.

Many sites provide a download of a free e-book for their visitors, which is an excellent way of getting traffic. As visitors stop by to download the e-book, your other goods and services are placed in front of them. Not only that, but you build credibility and a reputation for being knowledgeable in your industry.

**FIND IT ONLINE** Be sure to advertise your e-book at places like eBooks Portal at **http:// ebooks. searchking.com/**, CNET's Download.com at **http://download. cnet.com/**, and the eBook Directory at **http://www.ebookdirectory.com/**.

**TIP** "The Ultimate Guide to Creating and Marketing eBooks," by Kristie Tamsevicius, is an excellent resource for those who are considering setting up an e-book for a giveaway or for profit. Visit **http://www.ultimateguidetoebooks.com** to learn more.

**FIND IT ONLINE**

**FIND IT ONLINE** You'll find numerous software programs that can help you create an e-book. EBook Edit Pro is one such program; you can find information on the software at **http://www.ebookedit.com/**.

## Free Course Related to Your Goods or Services

Would it be helpful to your visitors if you provided a free course or tutorial on how to get the most out of your products? Some goods or services obviously won't lend themselves to this concept, while others would.

If your company sells underground fences for dogs, for example, what about writing a course on how to set up the fence or how to effectively use the fence?

If you sell aromatherapy supplies online, what about writing a tutorial on using essential oils?

By offering free courses or tutorials related to your product line, you're providing a valuable service to your visitors, providing content that should help you with the search engines, and making your site more "bookmarkable" to get your visitors to return again and again to see what else you offer.

Plus, if you sell your goods or services through an affiliate network, you're providing more tools that your affiliates can use to market your products, which can add up to more money in your pocket. We discuss affiliate programs in more detail in Chapter 6, "Multiplying the Reach of Your Web Site through Affiliate Programs."

 **TIP**

**FIND IT ONLINE**

Ginette Degner, Director of Marketing with Harris Publishing, coupled one of the publisher's software programs with an online tutorial geared toward the Napster and MP3 audience. Through this tutorial, she shows how the company's software program can help Napster and MP3 fans learn how to download, convert, and burn MP3 files, and she targets the page to that audience. Visit **http://www.harrisdigitalpublishing.com/freeprograms/index.html** to learn more.

## Content Providers

If you don't have the personnel or time to provide content for your own site, or if you'd like to outsource that service to another company, you'll certainly find numerous content providers on the Net.

These content providers can provide you with branded content, courses, multimedia presentations, directories, and more.

A few examples of content providers follow. Visit their sites to learn more.

 **FIND IT ONLINE**

- Content Provider Network—**http://www.pocketcd.com/content.asp**
- Promo Loop—**http://www.promoloop.com**
- iSyndicate—**http://www.isyndicate.com/services/**
- Ezine News Wire—**http://www.ezinenewswire.com**
- Anaconda Products—**http://anacondapartners.com/ap_products.shtml**

Another option is to find content at other Web sites and then see if they'll let you use their content free or for a price. Many sites will allow you to use their content for free, as long as you keep their name on the content and link back to their site.

## Allow Your Content to be Used

If your site is full of beautifully written articles, news stories, courses, and content, other Web sites may be interested in using that content on their own sites.

Why would you want to share your content? One of your main goals is to build name recognition. The more your name is advertised and viewed, the more credibility and name recognition you'll have. Also, because those other sites will keep your name and URL on the pages, you'll be building link popularity, which we cover in Part V about working on search engines.

## Reminder Services

You may be familiar with Amazon.com's reminder service. You complete a profile, and the site sends you a reminder when your favorite author has a new book coming out, or when a book in your preferred topic area comes out.

Some shopping sites use services to remind their customers about upcoming holidays or personal occasions, and then they take that opportunity to let the customers know what's available that they might be interested in, including sales on their favorite items.

Travel sites often send out notices when flights to your designated locations are offered at lower prices.

By setting up a reminder service, you bring your customers into the security of your online business. You take the time to help them remember special events or to notify them of sales, and you offer tips to make their shopping experiences more convenient.

Could you set up a reminder service for your customers that will provide them with valuable information about your goods and services? In this manner, your company will be placed in front of the customers again and again.

In other words, think of ways of helping your customers and of making their experience interactive. By doing so, and by showing that you care, they'll come back again and again.

**TIP**

**FIND IT ONLINE**

Set up Whizdiary on your site, and visitors can schedule reminders directly from your Web site. You choose the content of those reminders and when they're sent. This is a good way of reminding visitors of upcoming events or sales. Visit **http://www.whizdiary.com/**.

Another reminder service that can be highly effective is Mind-It. Mind-It detects changes on your Web pages and notifies visitors by e-mail when there is a change in content, bringing them back to your site via a link. Mind-It is free—you just have to register to use the service.

As with all the techniques presented in this chapter, Mind-It's goal is to make your Web site "sticky" to get visitors to return again and again.

**FIND IT ONLINE**

Learn more at **http://www.netmind.com/html/wmmindit.html**.

## Maintaining Interest with Fresh Material

We've discussed various ways of getting your customers to bookmark your site and return again and again. But we haven't discussed one very important aspect of getting return traffic: keeping your Web site constantly updated with new material.

If you don't keep your Web site new and vibrant, you aren't giving your visitors any reason to return. They've already seen what you offer, so why come again?

If you constantly add new articles and columns by experts, however, or if you regularly offer discounts, you give your customers a good reason to return.

Consider putting a small "Last Updated on <date>" notice on the bottom of your pages, which lets your visitors know that the site has been updated recently.

**TIP** Ginette Degner with Service Brokers uses server side includes to update the dates on her site and offers this advice: "When offering bonuses with the purchase of your product, create a sense of urgency by adding an 'If you purchase by today's date' script on your page."

As you know, server side includes are a feature of CGI, in conjunction with your server, that allows you to dynamically insert a piece of information, such as the current date or time, on to any Web page.

*FIND IT*
**ONLINE** TextClock is a free Perl CGI script available from Matt's Script Archive at **http:// www.worldwidemart.com/scripts/textclock.shtml**.

You can find a C++ version at **http://www.worldwidemart.com/scripts/C++/ textclock.shtml**.

Or, visit ZDNet Developer's Script Library for a JavaScript version at **http://www.zdnet.com/ devhead/resources/scriptlibrary/javascript/time.html**.

Don't let your Web site become stagnant. Give it a new look and feel. Remember that this is the beauty of the Net—the capability to change things quite easily and with little expense. Capitalize on it by giving your visitors fresh and new content, and they'll reward you by visiting again and again.

## Conclusion

Give your visitors a reason to return to your site, and you'll begin building a group of loyal customers. Provide relevant and constantly updated content, and show your visitors that you're knowledgeable and can be trusted.

In the process, you'll build credibility and name recognition, which will only bring you more visitors.

# SETTING UP POLLS, CONTESTS, AND OTHER TRAFFIC-GENERATING AVENUES

**In This Chapter**

In Chapter 3, we discussed how you can offer free or discounted items and information to create a Web site that will be "sticky" and make your visitors return again and again.

Other ways of boosting traffic to your site, as well as getting that traffic to return, include polls, contests, and sweepstakes. Give them something interesting to do when they reach your site, and they'll want to return. Bore them to death, and you've lost customers.

Are you aware that you can set up a personal icon that can be used as a bookmark to your site?

What about offering a free fax service that lets your visitors fax any of your articles to another person? After all, every time your articles get into the hands of someone else, you gain a potential customer.

Offering awards is another way of building name recognition, and looking at your ad copy with fresh eyes can help make sure your text is as effective as any graphics or special features on your page.

Are you aiming your site at the international market? Are you considering topic-specific directories or vertical search engines as a means of boosting traffic to your site?

In this chapter, we'll cover these techniques as well as the importance of using interactive features on your site.

## Using Polls Effectively

You can use polls in a variety of ways, depending on the type of business you're in. You can create a listing of four or five items, for example, and then ask your visitors which they would like to see added to your site. Or have a poll and ask your visitors what they think of your site. Ask them what other goods or services they would like you to provide.

Have a poll on a news event, or take a poll on what features users would like to see on a pocket PC. The possibilities are endless, and they depend on the focus of your Web site.

You can even create a poll designed to start a debate, and then move the discussion to a message board or chat room. Get your visitors interested in the discussion, and they'll constantly come back for more.

We cover online communities in Chapter 7, "Creating Effective Online Communities."

 **TIP** At the Poll Control Center, you can create polls to use on your site. Visit **http://www.misterpoll.com/pollwiz.wga** to learn more.

 *Find It* **ONLINE** AnalogX, an excellent resource for free software programs, offers a program called CGIVote that lets you set up a voting or survey booth on your site. Visit **http://www.analogx.com/contents/download/network/cgivote.htm**.

You also can use polls to provide information of interest to your visitors. If you're in the insurance business, for example, and there's a controversial law that could greatly affect the insurance industry, your visitors probably would enjoy participating in a poll and seeing those results. Again, this is the kind of discussion that could then be taken to a message board for further debate.

 *Find It* **ONLINE** At the CGI Forum, you'll find scripts that you can use to create interactive polls on your site. Visit **http://www.cgiforum.com/directcgi/search.cgi?query=polls**.

## Offering Contests and Sweepstakes

Is your Web site conducive to offering contests or sweepstakes? Do you have any products that are overstocked in your inventory? Are they appropriate to be used as prizes in contests or sweepstakes?

Maybe you own a software development company, and an important computer show is coming to your area. What about offering a sweepstakes and giving away free tickets to the show to the winner?

Contests can be anything from a discount off your products to an expensive sweepstakes. You can offer a one-time contest, or you can run contests on a regular basis. Simply tailor the contests or sweepstakes to fit the focus of your site.

 **TIP** If you're having a rather large contest or sweepstakes, an important online press conference, a multimedia event, etc., be sure to advertise it at Yahoo!'s Net Events for added publicity. For *Find It* **ONLINE** more information, visit **http://www.broadcast.com/**.

## Using Personal Icons

In Internet Explorer 5.0 and higher, you can customize an icon for your business in the Favorites bookmarks section. Those customized icons also will appear beside the URL in the browser window.

So what's the big deal here?

Keep in mind that one of your main goals in working with your site is name and brand recognition. We've mentioned this before, and we'll mention it again.

You want to do everything you can to make sure your name and brand are recognized. Name and brand recognition are more difficult to accomplish online than in a brick-and-mortar business, because you don't have customers walking by your store, noticing the brands or recognizing your name. So you have to work a little harder at developing name and brand recognition on the Internet.

Using a personalized icon is another means of building name and trademark recognition.

Figure 4.1 shows a software program that will create customized icons for you.

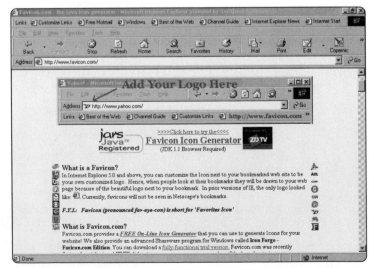

**FIGURE 4.1**

A Favicon customized icon can help build name recognition.

Note the large arrow with the words "Add Your Logo Here." This is one place where your customized icon would appear, as well as in the Favorites (bookmarks) section of Internet Explorer. This is simply another way of accomplishing brand name recognition. Regretfully, personal icons don't work with Netscape Navigator at this time.

*Find It* **ONLINE**   Visit Favicon at **http://www.favicon.com/** to learn more.

## Providing Fax or E-mail Services

You can use fax services in several ways. You can simply offer free fax services as a benefit to your viewers. Or you can offer a service that allows your visitors to send one of your articles by fax to someone.

### Offering Free Fax Services to Your Users

You'll find several free fax services on the Net, which can give you an idea of what you can set up on your own site. Visit these URLs to learn more:

*Find It* **ONLINE**

- Faxaway—**http://www.fax-away.com/free/**
- Free Fax—**http://www.freefax.com.pk/**
- TPC Fax—**http://www.tpc.int/sendfax.html**
- eFax.com—**http://www.efax.com/**

### Sending Articles by E-mail

Another idea is to provide a link to send an article by e-mail to someone, as Wired.com does. Figure 4.2 shows the form visitors complete to send an article by e-mail to a friend.

Notice that the form requires the visitor's e-mail address and name, the friend's e-mail address and name, and a box for adding a personalized message. Visitors also can choose to have the article sent back to themselves.

So for every article sent out from your site, you're retrieving two e-mail addresses to use in your e-mail marketing campaigns in the future. Not bad.

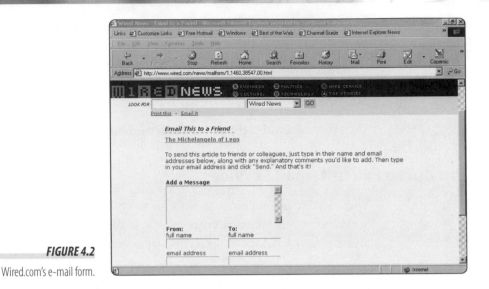

**FIGURE 4.2**

Wired.com's e-mail form.

## Offering Awards

Is your site conducive to offering awards in certain areas?

Suppose that you have a site that sells Web security solutions. You could offer awards to the best sites in that general area, broken down by categories. The best sites related to software programs would get an award in that category, the best sites in online solutions would get an award for that area, and so forth.

This is a way to increase traffic to your site as well as boost link popularity. After all, if you've given a site an award, that site will definitely link back to your site and refer traffic.

The award can be a small yet impressive graphic that can be linked back to your site. To make it easy on winners, be sure to include the HTML code along with your graphic, which will help ensure that the winners include a link back to your site.

## Producing Effective Ad Copy on Your Site

When considering how to capitalize on return traffic, don't forget the simple importance of producing effective ad copy on your site. Use terminology that conveys a sense of trustworthiness. Title your Web pages in this manner as well.

Use attention-grabbing words like these:

- Secrets
- Truth
- Free
- Improved
- Prosper
- Acclaim
- Win
- Vivid
- Monumental
- Security
- Breakthrough
- How-to

Be sure to watch your log files and track your sales to see where you're losing customers and where you're making the sale. If you're consistently losing customers on a particular page, go back over the ad copy on that page and beef it up. Do you have a "call for action" to get your customers to purchase the product or service? We talk about analyzing traffic and log files in Part VII, "Tracking Traffic to Benefit Your Site" so visit those chapters for more information.

When describing your products, prove to your customers the value of those products and how they can help your customers. Then go back over your products' varied features.

## Reaching a Global Market

According to A.J. Khan, president and CEO of Cyrsh Technologies Corporation, 49 percent of Internet users today do not speak English as their primary language.

Does your business cater to the international market? Have you considered the international market when creating your Web site and shopping areas?

If you haven't, and if global users visit your site, you need to make changes now to ensure that your international customers are awarded the same effective user experience as your English-speaking customers.

Cyrsh Technologies has taken one major step toward making the Net more global friendly with its error-tolerant and multilanguage search technology. PriceNet USA is a good example of the use of this search technology.

PriceNet users from all over the world, using different alphabets and languages, can type in what they're searching for as it sounds to them or in their own alphabet and language, and the technology resolves itself to the actual Web site. With Cyrsh Technologies' voice technology feature, even those who are blind can surf the Net.

To show you how Cyrsh technology works, we ran a search for "Unavercite of Jorja" (University of Georgia) at Cyrsh's site. Figure 4.3 shows the results of that search.

**FIND IT ONLINE**

You'll see how the site phonetically resolved itself by finding the University of Georgia's site. For more information, visit **http://www.cyrsh.com**.

If you're trying to gain a corner on the international market, consider translating your Web site, or individual pages on your site, into the

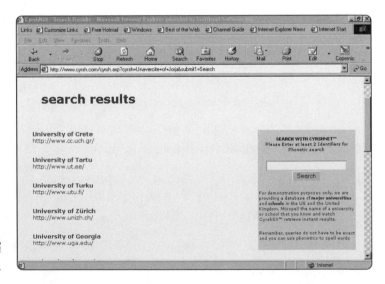

**FIGURE 4.3**

Searching for Unavercite of Jorja at Cyrsh.

languages you're trying to target. You can create interior or doorway pages in those languages, or you can purchase additional domains for your international viewers.

## Setting Up Related Directories and Vertical Search Engines

*Vortals,* which are vertical portals, are certainly gaining in popularity. You can visit a travel-related vertical directory or portal and search for sites aimed at the travel professional. Or visit a real estate directory or a government directory.

What exactly is a vertical search engine or vortal? Whereas a major search engine searches "horizontally" across numerous and unending categories, vertical search engines are topic-related search engines only, which is why they're called "verticals."

**FIND IT ONLINE**
You'll find several topnotch companies in the business of setting up vertical directories or engines. One such company is Quiver (**http://www.quiver.com**), which catalogs information provided by users into a directory and then uses data-mining technology to deliver relevant results.

Quiver is a vertical directory customized to a specific community, which is maintained automatically through a continuous analysis of bookmark and surfing data collected from a specific community of users.

Vertical search engines are increasing in popularity these days as well. Although directories have been around for a long time, vertical search engines focused on one industry only are fairly new. Vertical engines can be topic-specific or region-specific.

If you're looking for a way to boost related content and increase traffic, consider setting up a vertical engine on your own site. Vertical search engines lend themselves to practically any industry, and having a vertical engine on your site will certainly boost your link popularity.

Market the vertical engine heavily throughout related areas. People will begin to bookmark your site and visit again and again to use your vertical engine. Give them the capability of submitting sites to the engine as well.

**FIGURE 4.4**

GameBlitz, a vertical search engine for games.

**FIND IT ONLINE**

Web Wombat (**http://webwombat.com**) offers a global search engine, regional engines, or customized search engines. The company also builds corporate intranet search engines. Web Wombat created the vertical search engine for GameBlitz, shown in Figure 4.4.

**FIND IT ONLINE**

Notice the search window toward the top of the page. If you enter a keyword in that window, Web Wombat technology searches through hundreds of game-related sites for a match. You can find GameBlitz at **http://www.gameblitz.com**.

**FIND IT ONLINE**

Twirlix (**http://www.twirlix.com**) provides topic-specific search and directory solutions to vertical portals. Its technology integrates the advantages of search engines with those of Web directories. So its spider moves through the Web finding new sites, adding only relevant sites to that particular topic engine. Then Twirlix sorts those sites into category listings.

Figure 4.5 shows Twirlix's technology in action at AutoDesk Point A.

Lorin Horosz of Twirlix describes the search results:

> You should now have a page that illustrates the results that an end-user will find, complete with QualityRatings™ (based on 25 criteria that a human editor would use), QuickPreviews™ (a JPEG file preview of the homepage), as well as a site language indicator—all elements that help to streamline and enhance the navigation of information.

**FIGURE 4.5**

AutoDesk Point A's vertical search engine.

## Adding Interactive Features to Your Web Site

Interactive sites offer the advantage of being able to track your visitors to see which portions of your site appeal to them, as well as the capability to provide information of particular interest to each visitor. Another advantage of interactive features on a site is that they prevent the site from becoming stagnant by providing revolving content. If you follow up a visit with an e-mail or newsletter, you'll boost your chances at getting return traffic.

Using data mining, you can get to know your customers and create a site that's valuable to them. Cookies and data mining are covered in detail in Chapter 8 "Getting to Know Your Customer".

### Customizing Pages with Cookies

Going hand in hand with data mining is the capability to recognize your visitors when they return. A good example of a site that effectively recognizes visitors and gives an experience designed specifically for the individual user is Amazon.com.

In fact, Amazon is one of the first Net sites to use personalization software to customize pages for each customer. At Amazon, customers are greeted by name and then presented with recommendations based on each customer's preferences. These preferences are based on past actions being a good determining factor for future behavior. Amazon looks at factors such as purchasing history, book ratings, and behavioral data to predict future behavior. The site even sends targeted e-mail when new books go on the shelves that might be of interest to that particular visitor.

Once a visitor makes a purchase, his or her personal information is stored in files called cookies, making it easier for that visitor to make purchases in the future.

How successful is Amazon's personal approach? According to Amazon itself, sales rose from $15.7 million in 1996 to $147.8 million in 1997. Net sales for the second quarter of 2000 were $578 million. Plus, 78 percent of Amazon's sales in the second quarter of 2000 were from repeat customers. Not too shabby.

In Figure 4.6, you can see Amazon's personal approach: It mentions the name of the visitor and suggests books of particular interest to that visitor.

## Making It Easy to Bookmark Your Site

We've outlined ways of getting visitors to bookmark your site and return again and again. But how can you make it easy for them to actually bookmark your site?

**FIGURE 4.6**

Amazon's personal approach.

You know that pressing Ctrl+D while on a page will bookmark a site. But do your visitors know that?

**FIND IT ONLINE**

You can certainly list this tip on your Web site, or you can do one better by including a simple JavaScript that allows visitors to bookmark your site simply by clicking on a link. You can find the script itself, as well as an example, at **http://www.codebrain.com/javascript/bookmark/.**

## Using Recommend Scripts

Recommend scripts allow your visitors to recommend your site to other people. When a friend or business associate recommends a site, you're more apt to visit it, since you're going on a personal suggestion.

With recommend scripts, you'll create an effective e-mail that will automatically go out to those who are recommended to visit your site. This e-mail will seem as if it's coming from your visitor, rather than you, and will briefly outline your goods and services. You'll also automatically send an e-mail to the visitor who is recommending your site thanking him or her for the referral. This might be a good opportunity to mention your affiliate program, if you have one, because the visitor has already recommended your site to at least one person.

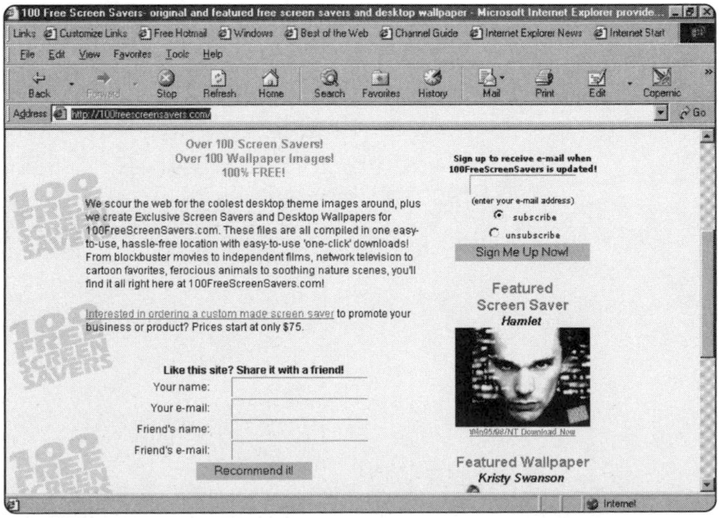

**FIGURE 4.7**

Recommend script at 100 Free Screen Savers.com.

Ginette Degner with ServiceBrokers.com uses a recommend script at 100 Free Screen Savers.com (**http://100freescreensavers.com/**), which you can see in Figure 4.7.

Master Recommend is a CGI program written with Perl 5 for your visitors to recommend your site to friends or business associates. "It is coded to minimize intentional and unintentional misuse, including spamming/blasting," it says at the site. Visit **http://www.willmaster.com/master/recommend/index.shtml**.

Or you can visit Recommend It at **http://www.recommend-it.com** for an easy way to set up a recommend script at your site.

### Offering an Online Scheduler

Do you operate a business where customers or clients constantly need to schedule appointments? Can you see how offering an online scheduling service could promote traffic to your site, since you're making it easy for your customers to make appointments for your services?

WebAppoint.com provides a real-time online scheduling service that allows your customers to schedule appointment times online with a simple click of the mouse. How much does it cost your business? Scheduling appointments is free, but WebAppoint provides additional services for a fee.

Visit **http://www.webappoint.com/** to learn more.

## Conclusion

Spend some time considering ways of boosting traffic to your site and getting return traffic. Whether you use polls, contests, icons, or recommend scripts, do whatever you can to make your site bookmarkable and to get your visitors to return again and again.

# USING FORMS AND SCRIPTS TO CAPTURE E-MAIL ADDRESSES

## In This Chapter

Setting Up Forms to Retrieve E-mail Addresses for Newsletters or Mailing Lists

Using Recommend Forms with Effective E-mail to Increase Your Site's Scope

Using Autoresponders

Languages to Benefit Your Site

E-mail is the bedrock of communication online. To maintain a dialogue with your customers, you must be able to e-mail them regularly with new information about your products, sales, or industry information. Knowing this, what are the best ways to capture those e-mail addresses?

We discuss spam in Chapter 10, "Incorporating Internet Ethics," but we want to make clear early on that unsolicited bulk e-mail is definitely *not* an acceptable tactic. You need to use more effective, less invasive methods of contacting and keeping in touch with your customers. We show you how to do just that in this chapter.

## Setting Up Forms to Retrieve E-mail Addresses for Newsletters or Mailing Lists

When customers enter your site, they are probably looking first for information. What better way to answer their questions than by setting up an e-mail list, periodic newsletter, or e-zine for their benefit? And by using these devices, you open the door to a sale. If your site is one-stop shopping for customers, they will be more likely to come to you. If you provide links in your newsletter or regular information about your products on your e-mail list, you can count your widget sold.

That's fine, but how do you approach customers with this idea? How do you capture those e-mail addresses, and how do you maintain those methods of contact?

### Selling the Idea

Your first task, before you even have the opportunity to capture those e-mail addresses, is to sell the idea of a newsletter to your customers. Usually you don't want to crowd your first page with information about your wonderful new e-mail list, but a nice headline-style announcement works fine as a link to the page with details. So before you jump in on your sales pitch, try grabbing your customers' interest so that they will want to know more about your newsletter. Figure 5.1 provides an example of this "grab" technique.

Next you need to pitch the idea. Make your customers want to be on your mailing list yesterday. Draw them in with details about what

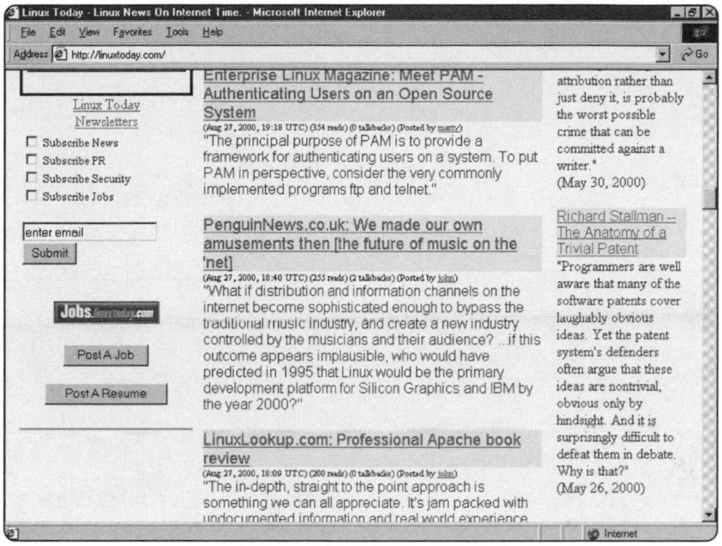

**FIGURE 5.1**

Linux Today allows users to sign up for a variety of newsletters by entering their e-mail address and choosing the mailings they want to receive.

your newsletter offers. What can you offer? Use this list to brainstorm for your content:

- **Industry news.** What new widget designs are due for release? What companies are on the leading edge of widget technology?

- **Trivia.** Who developed the first widget? When did Leonardo da Vinci first sketch one? Did you know that if you add baking soda to a widget, the resulting foam will clean up any carpet stain?

- **Giveaways.** Sponsor a drawing, and require an e-mail address to sign up for the drawing (as a way to contact the winner).

- **Helpful hints.** From one customer to another—how to get the most out of your widget.

- **Monthly/Weekly/Microsecondly specials.** What great deal can customers receive just by reading your newsletter?

- **Company news.** Are you looking for employees from those who know and love widgets the most—your customers? Has your company just been awarded an amazing patent? When is your company planning its Initial Public Offering?

- **Articles.** What have writers said about widgets? Any great poems out there dedicated to widgets?

- **Q&A.** Answer your customers' questions about widgets.

Incentive plays a huge role in getting customers to give you their personal information. By conducting a "drawing" and rewarding a prize to customers who sign up, you increase the likelihood of getting a few recipients you might not otherwise get. And after they receive your newsletter and realize its value, they'll be hooked for life. Alternatively, you could give away a gift with a purchase to those who sign up for the newsletter. You have numerous opportunities to reward your customers, so give that incentive.

**NOTE**    Another type of incentive rests with privacy issues, which are very important to today's Web surfers. At this point, it's a very good idea to place a link directly to your privacy policy. If you reassure your customers that their e-mail address goes no further than your database, you're more likely to get that address for your newsletter. We discuss privacy concerns and policies more in Chapter 10, "Incorporating Internet Ethics."

## Grabbing E-mail Addresses

You can use a few methods to capture e-mail addresses from visitors to your site. These methods generally fall into two categories: direct and indirect gathering.

Direct-gathering methods require that you give your visitors the option of signing up for exactly what they want from your site—e-mail notices, newsletters, etc. Indirect methods require that you capture e-mail addresses as a means of giving access to a specific service, site, etc. In other words, you might use an e-mail address as a login. This is considered an indirect method because you obtain an e-mail address that was intended for access to a specific area of your site. If you choose to use an indirect gathering method, remember to allow your customers to opt in or out of any e-mail you may want to send them. If you capture their e-mail address and begin sending them advertisements or other random e-mail, unless they specifically gave permission to you to send it, you are guilty of spam. Giving them a method of unsubscribing *after the fact* does not make your tactics any less underhanded.

---

### *Making E-mail Lists More Appealing*

Free and Web-based e-mail lists have increased in popularity in the last few years. According to eGroups, Inc. (**http://groups.yahoo.com/local/news.html**), 18 million members use more than 900,000 e-mail lists through its service. That's impressive! What's important about this claim, however, is that *18 million members already use eGroups to host their e-mail loops.* Why is this key?

When you ask your site's visitors to join an e-mail loop, announcement list, newsletter, e-zine, etc., they are much more likely to do so if they can administrate their account on that loop in one central location. Because of these Web-based mailing list services, your visitors can do just that.

However, if you use your own e-mail list through your server or your Web space provider, even if you allow members of the list to administrate their accounts on that list through the Web, their capability to access more than one e-mail list at a time diminishes.

Although you may find more benefits in hosting your own list, remember the functionality that the Web-based services allow and try to offer the same functionality to your mailing list members.

---

This section shows you a few uses for both direct and indirect gathering methods.

### Direct Gathering Method

You can capture an e-mail address simply by asking for it. When Valerie Visitor comes to your site, she sees an easy sign-up box on your page that automatically signs her up for your monthly newsletter. You can use a variety of methods to engineer this amazing feat. This is what a snippet of your HTML code would look like if you were calling on a Perl script to process the request:

```
Sign up for our monthly newsletter!<br>
<form method=post action="/cgi-bin/newsletter.pl">E-mail Address:
<input type=text name="email" size=20 maxlength=50><input type=submit
value="Sign Me Up"></form>
```

Then within your Perl script, you could store Valerie's e-mail address, send her a confirmation e-mail, and sign her up for your newsletter (if you don't use your own e-mail list method). Listing 5.1 shows what this piece of code would look like.

## Listing 5.1
## Using a Perl script to capture e-mail addresses and set up a newsletter through eGroups.

```perl
use CGI;
use DBI;
$query = new CGI;
$dbh = DBI->connect('DBI:mysql:customers', 'login', 'password');

# Get the e-mail address from the form submission…
$email = $query->param('email');

# Store that e-mail address in the newsletter table of the customers
database…
$insertion = "insert into newsletters (email) values ('" . $email .
"')";
$dbh->do($insertion);

# Use sendmail to send an e-mail to the e-list provider subscribing
this e-mail address…
open (MAIL, '| /usr/lib/sendmail -t -oi');
print MAIL <<EOM;
To: MistyValeEssentials-subscribe\@egroups.com
From: $email
EOM
close MAIL;

# Finally, send a message telling the subscriber to expect an e-mail
from you.
open (CMAIL, '| /usr/lib/sendmail -t -oi');
print CMAIL <<EOCM;
To: $email
From: newsletter\@mistyvale.com
Subject: Thanks from Misty Vale Essentials
Thanks for subscribing to the Misty Vale Essentials newsletter. We
hope you enjoy the articles, news, announcements, and tips we include
in every bi-monthly issue. If you ever have problems or concerns,
simply e-mail us at newsletters@mistyvale.com. To unsubscribe, send a
blank e-mail to MistyValeEssentials-unsubscribe@egroups.com.
```

```
Thanks, and enjoy!
MVE

EOCM
close CMAIL;
print $query->header, $query->start_html("Thanks!");
print "<h2>Thanks for Subscribing</h2>";
print "You will receive an e-mail from MVE and another from eGroups
about your subscription. If you have problems, questions, or sugges-
tions, feel free to <a
href=\"mailto:newsletter@mistyvale.com\">contact us</a>.";
print "Meanwhile, take a look at our <a href=\"newline.html\">new
line</a> of products.<br>";
print "We're offering a great discount when you purchase a <a
href=\"buyme.html\">gift set</a>.<br>";
print "<a href=\"http://www.mistyvale.com\">Return Home</a>";
print $query->end_html;
```

Obviously, this example is sparse and does not perform sufficient error and security checking. However, you can see that capturing that
e-mail address in this type of situation is easier than finding a Starbucks
in Southern California.

Remember to provide navigation back to previous areas, and don't
forget to take advantage of this nearly empty page to tout your products or services with announcements, advertisements, etc.

Another choice you have is to link directly to the e-mail list provider's
page for your newsletter, allowing users to sign up through that site.
By using this method, you ensure that subscribers realize the range of
services the provider offers, as well as how much control they have
over their own account with the provider. They know they remain in
control, and they'll appreciate that.

### Indirect Gathering Method

If you have chosen not to take advantage of such marketing techniques
as newsletters and e-mail lists, you can still grab e-mail addresses by
requiring them when your visitors log in to an area of your site. This
does not mean that you must charge your site's visitors to gain access

to a password-protected area. Instead, offer personalization by asking that users either log in or allow you to establish a cookie so that they won't need to log in each time they come to your site.

To keep your site user friendly, you might want to allow visitors to use your site simply as "Guest" rather than establishing an identity. In this way, your visitors avoid sacrificing privacy while still using all areas of your site.

But then, if you allow them access to everything on your site, how do you entice them to hand over their e-mail address?

Easy: Tell the truth, first off. Let them know that, if they give you their e-mail address, you will reward them with news about changes regarding your site, your services, or your products. Also, give them special offers available only to those who receive your e-mailings.

One other possibility exists. If users log in, all the work they did while at your site *is still accessible to them later.* Take Amazon.com, for example. Amazon provides recommendations based on your interests and the books you purchase. If Amazon were to allow guest accounts, those accounts would vanish when those users leave the site, and the next time they pop over to look for another recommendation, they must go through the process again to establish a temporary identity for which Amazon can recommend anything.

Not very convenient anymore, is it?

But by establishing their identity, visitors leave information with Amazon that it can use later to recommend books, music, movies, etc., as well as send visitors e-mails regarding specific products that might be of interest. Visitors can also supply their addresses for billing and shipping, so they won't have to enter the same data each time they purchase an item for someone. Amazon also offers a wish list that others can use to buy gifts for its visitors. That is convenience, and that is what entices customers to return to Amazon repeatedly to purchase products.

## Maintaining Interest

To maintain contact with your customers, you must keep their interest. How you do this depends a great deal on the goal of your site.

Why should they continue to receive your e-mail? Why should they come back to your site? Do you have something they need or want? Can you bring something to their Inbox every morning?

As we stated before, you can use several methods to entice customers, but only interactivity and frequency will maintain that interest.

One popular e-mailing that happens daily or weekly is news mailings. USA Today offers daily e-mail that includes short articles presenting the latest news. MSNBC.com offers its E-Mail Extra, which provides customized daily e-mail with the news each user wants to see.

Why does daily news in your Inbox act as an excellent example of maintaining interest? First, it's frequent. Every day, recipients can read the e-mail or delete it if they don't have time. They know they can turn off the service while they're on vacation and away from their computer, and as soon as they return, they'll be back to their daily news. The frequency reminds them of the news service, so on occasion, they check out the Web site to see whether something new is going on, or they go to the site to find more information about an article they read in their e-mail.

The interactivity is also a plus, especially with services such as MSNBC's E-Mail Extra. If Sally decides she no longer cares about celebrity news, she can simply go to the site and turn off that choice. Customized options can make all the difference. When Sally opens her e-mail, she knows she's going to get exactly what she asked to receive, so she knows the contents will be of interest.

Again, maintaining interest in your site makes all the difference. If your customers lose interest in the services you provide, they won't return, no matter how much glitz you add. Make the services interactive and frequent, and you'll snare your customers every time.

On the other hand, if you use an indirect method of capturing e-mail addresses, or you require visitors to opt out of receiving e-mail from you, be considerate. Show respect to these customers and potential customers by sending e-mail only to advertise sporadic or infrequent events, such as special sales, important Web site information, and so on, and only if they have not opted out of this service.

# Using Recommend Forms with Effective E-mail to Increase Your Site's Scope

Recommendations have become a staple of online purchasing, thanks to Amazon's efforts in this arena. Many shoppers look for recommendations from friends or family, celebrities in advertisements, and other shoppers when they hunt through brick-and-mortar stores, and the new medium of Internet shopping changes nothing in this respect. In fact, the Internet makes recommendations a necessity, because customers can't pick up objects, inspect them, and make sure they are exactly what they want to buy. Also, shoppers still want to know about the experiences others have had before they dive into a new purchase.

You can make your customers' lives easier by providing a forum for feedback and recommendations. Let's look at a few of Amazon's recommendation features to get a better idea of what you can do for your site.

## When First You Meet

Amazon provides personalized recommendations on its first page. If you have provided your e-mail address (in other words, if you've signed up to have an account at Amazon), Amazon greets you by name and gives you recommendations down the right side of the page.

These recommendations come from purchases you've made in the past and the ratings you've given those purchases.

In addition, you can go to a special page from the first page that allows you to view recommendations geared toward you. Figure 5.2 demonstrates that you can view recommendations for every type of product Amazon sells, from books and movies to music and z-shop items.

## Rate Your Purchases

As you can see in Figure 5.3, Amazon gives you the opportunity to rate on a scale of 1 to 5 the purchases you've made through its site. If you haven't used or read the purchase yet, you can keep the recommendation on hold by choosing the question mark. Or if the product was not intended for your use, and you don't want to include it in your recommendations, you can choose to have it excluded.

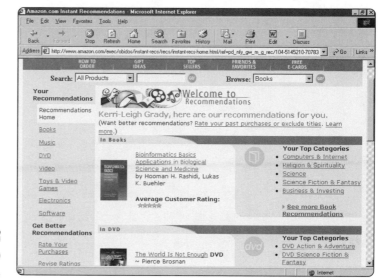

**FIGURE 5.2**

Amazon recommends products according to past purchases.

You can change your mind about the ratings you've given purchases at any time, allowing you to keep your recommendations up-to-date and applicable.

## Wish List

One of Amazon's greatest marketing tools is its wish list, where customers can tell *their friends and family* what they would appreciate as

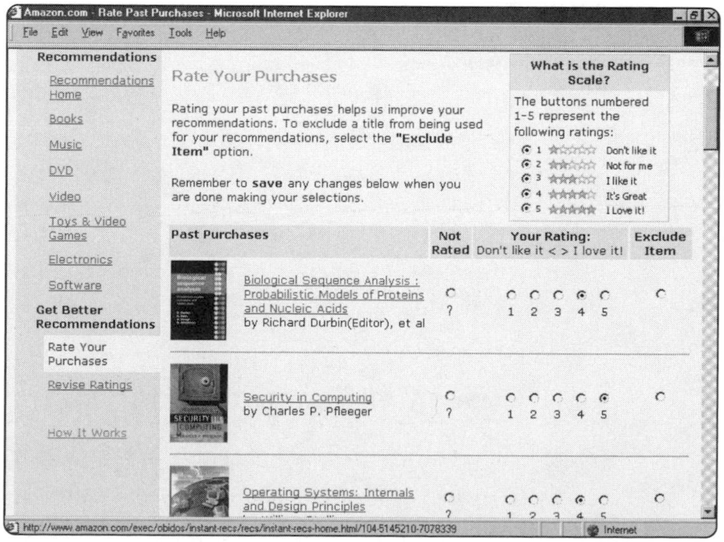

**FIGURE 5.3**

Amazon allows you to rate the purchases you've made through its site.

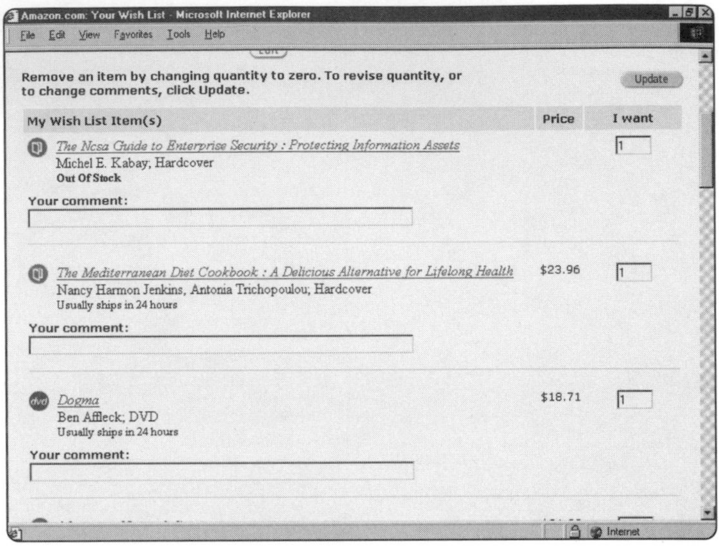

**FIGURE 5.4**

Amazon's wish list allows customers to spread the marketing wealth to their friends and family.

gifts. The wish list is perpetual and does not end just because the gift-giving season is over. You can continue your wish list throughout the year for your birthday or special occasions.

In Figure 5.4, you'll see that the wish list allows you to specify the number of items you want, and you can attach a comment to the item as well.

## New for You

Figure 5.5 shows Amazon's New for You section, which is actually not much different from its recommendation pages. The only difference is that the New for You pages consist entirely of new releases in the genres or subject matters in which you've expressed an interest.

In this area, you can avoid seeing old books and music that won't interest you, focusing instead on the newest releases or cutting-edge technology products.

## Customer Recommendations

Yet another brilliant marketing tactic that Amazon has used—and other online stores have borrowed—comes in many forms, but each form boils down to one thing: customer recommendations.

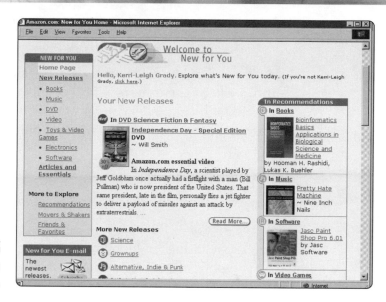

**FIGURE 5.5**

Amazon's New for You section recommends products that are new on the market.

Amazon offers four types of recommendations: Reviews, Other Purchases, Purchasing Circles, and Friends and Favorites.

### Reviews

Reviews are the most obvious method of recommendation at Amazon. First, each title that pops up in a search comes complete with a ranking (up to five stars) generated by reviewers.

Then when customers choose a particular title or piece of technology to view more closely, they receive reviews—short and long—that tell them exactly what others who have used, read, or listened to this product have thought.

Finally, reviews can be ranked themselves. If the review is deemed by other reviewers or customers at large to be completely useless, the ranking and the review may disappear from that product's review list.

### Other Purchases

Two sections of an Amazon product page fall within the Other Purchases description. The first section begins with a header that looks something like, "Customers who bought this product also bought…." A list of about five products follows this header, each one a similar book, video, or other product that anonymous customers purchased from Amazon at the same time they purchased the product in question.

At the end of a book product page is a similar header that says something like, "Customers who bought titles by Robin Nobles and Kerri-Leigh Grady also bought titles by these authors." Another list, this time of relevant author names, follows the header.

### Purchasing Circles

Amazon calls its Purchasing Circles service "specialized bestseller lists" because each circle defines its own bestsellers. What are the circles?

Each purchasing circle consists of a specific group with a single interest in common. For example, people in Honolulu, Hawaii, have a purchasing circle that recommends purchases to others with that geographical interest. Or people who work at Cisco Systems can see what others in their company are buying. Figure 5.6 shows the Association for Computing Machinery purchasing circle.

### Friends and Favorites

Like the purchasing circles, the Friends and Favorites section generates a list of recommended purchases from people you specify. In other

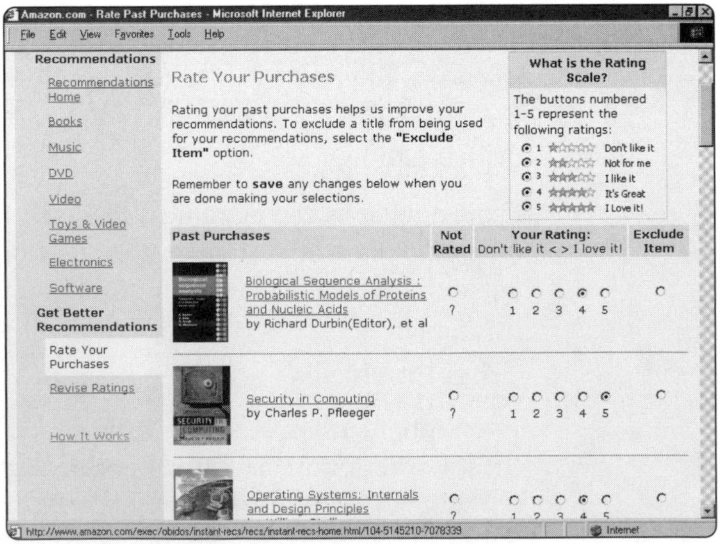

**FIGURE 5.6**

The purchasing circle for the Association for Computing Machinery

words, when Aunt Martha sets up her Friends and Favorites area, she can specify you as a favorite person, and she will be able to view any reviews or opinions you've posted on Amazon—with your permission, of course!

**FIND IT ONLINE**    To see the Friends and Favorites section, visit **http://www.amazon.com/ exec/obidos/subst/community/community-home.html**.

## Effective E-mail

Now that you're aware of the many marketing techniques available, what can you do with them? Easy: Use e-mail to get your message across, whether with recommendations, announcements, or special offers.

If you use e-mail to market your products or services, remember a few things:

- **Make it applicable.** Nobody wants to read recommendations for products that hold absolutely no interest.
- **Make it short.** Long e-mails are as bad as long Web pages. They'll be deleted if customers become bored or tired.
- **Don't spam.** Spam is evil. Make sure customers want the e-mail.
- **Remember the importance of frequency.** Have those e-mails released according to a strict schedule. Customers like knowing they'll have recommended Oprah reads within hours of Oprah's announcements. They like having a list of the latest fiction novels at the first of every month.
- **Remember the importance of interactivity.** If customers can customize their recommendations, they'll be more likely to read the e-mails you send, and they'll be more enticed by the products you recommend.

Don't forget the importance of e-mail. With it, you maintain contact with customers who might otherwise forget you exist.

## Using Autoresponders

Autoresponders, which are also called *mailbots* or *infobots,* allow anyone with an e-mail address to send a blank e-mail to a specified e-mail address. When the autoresponder receives the blank e-mail, it sends a prepared document to the originating e-mail address with information the sender requested.

How do autoresponders work?

When Mike sends an e-mail to autorespond@autorespondersrus.com, the mail server sends back a canned response written by someone at AutorespondersRUs.com. The e-mail tells Mike about its service—how to set up an autoresponder, how much the service costs, and how to contact the company for more information.

Mike decides he can get a better deal at OutofthisWorldMarketing.com, so he doesn't call AutorespondersRUs and doesn't waste anyone's time. That automatically generated e-mail did all the work for everyone.

Meanwhile, AutorespondersRUs now has Mike's e-mail address in its database.

As we discussed in the introduction to this chapter, unsolicited bulk e-mail is not acceptable. However, you can use autoresponder-generated e-mail addresses in other ways. Suppose that, after several weeks, Mike has not contacted your company, and you're curious about why. You can make personalized contact with Mike to find out how to better your services or even change his mind about his choice by offering a deal he can't possibly pass up. We discuss privacy issues, including spam, in Chapter 10, but think seriously about the consequences of misusing your visitors' e-mail addresses after they've made serious inquiries to your company.

## Languages to Benefit Your Site

The following list of scripting or programming languages can help you build more interactive sites that allow you to capture e-mail addresses. As we discussed throughout this chapter, maintaining contact with your customers is vital, so get to know your choices in interactive tools:

- **Perl.** Perl is the most commonly used language for *Common Gateway Interface* (CGI) scripts. CGI is used to capture and process data from forms.

- **JavaScript.** JavaScript is a client-side language, embedded in a Web page, that can provide client-side interactive functionality. JavaScript often is used to validate form information before the data goes to the server to be processed by a CGI script.

- **PHP.** The poor man's ASP, PHP allows you to run your pages entirely from a database such as MySQL. With PHP's database connectivity, you can also run site sessions to capture the activities and interests of your users.

- **Java.** Java allows you to create applets—miniature applications—to run directly in your Web page (client side). These applets are very powerful because they can interact with the server.

## Conclusion

Whenever possible, try to capture a willing customer's e-mail address in order to provide better service to that customer. Use e-mail not as a tool for spam, but as a method of establishing and maintaining contact with your customers. If your e-mail is targeted to your customers' needs and wishes, you'll have much happier customers.

# MULTIPLYING THE REACH OF YOUR WEB SITE THROUGH AFFILIATE PROGRAMS

**In This Chapter**

What Is an Affiliate Program?

Reaping the Benefits of Affiliate Programs

Setting Up an Affiliate Program

Managing an Effective Affiliate Program

Analyzing Your Affiliate Program Step-by-Step

Locating Affiliate Tools and Resources

Affiliate programs are one of the most overlooked elements of effective e-commerce and a veritable gold mine. This is especially true when your site needs to make money, but you can't rely on your products or services to guarantee your financial success.

In this chapter, we outline the importance of affiliate programs and show you how to set one up—whether it's yours or that of another company—and maintain it.

## What Is an Affiliate Program?

How many times have you been to a Web site that has banners or links to other companies? If you've seen these at least once (and we'll bet you've seen more like a million of those banners), chances are good you've witnessed an affiliate program in action. Banner ads and box ads are big in the world of affiliate programs, offering an easy method of running an effective program.

Affiliate programs are a means of offering a commission to an individual or company for referring a customer. A company with an affiliate program pays an affiliate, or associate, each time a new customer makes contact with the company's site. What "contact" means differs depending on the company, but there are basically three methods of making contact: ad impressions, click-through, and recommended purchases.

 **NOTE**   Keep in mind that a "commission" need not be monetary. You can offer anything from memberships to promotional materials in exchange for a link from a visitor's site.

### Ad Impressions

Making an ad impression is the action of loading an ad into a browser. A customer can make contact by viewing an ad on an affiliate's page (in other words, the ad receives an impression on the affiliate page). Let's say you have your own affiliate program for YeOldWidgetShoppe.com, and you've approved WidgetFiends.com to be an affiliate in your program. WidgetFiends places an ad on its Web page that links to your site. Each time someone brings up that WidgetFiends page with your ad, your affiliate program manager counts that impression on your ad, and you pay WidgetFiends a doubloon.

## Click-Through

Obviously, the ad impression method can mean very little in the grand scheme. Remember from Chapter 1, "Analyzing Web Pages for Maximum Effectiveness," that people begin to ignore banner ads or even to block them entirely with software. If a customer downloads your image and doesn't notice the ad, does that mean your doubloon was well spent? Perhaps, but depending on the reason you're using an affiliate program, you may want to beef up the stakes a bit. Offer a doubloon to WidgetFiends each time someone actually *clicks through* to your site from that ad on the WidgetFiends site.

Keep in mind that not all banner ads are considered affiliate programs. Some banners are simply paid advertising.

## Recommended Purchase

Another method of making contact with the customer occurs when the customer purchases a product or service from YeOldeWidgetShoppe.com after seeing your ad at WidgetFiends.com. After you confirm that the customer bought your widget or service for your widget because of WidgetFiends, you pay your affiliate a doubloon. An excellent example of this type of affiliate program is Amazon.com's Associates Program. To earn money from Amazon, you simply host a miniature bookstore on your site with a link to Amazon with your site's special code embedded in the linking HTML. Suppose that there are five really great books all about widgets, and Amazon sells them all. Place the book titles on your site with a link to Amazon, and each time someone purchases a book through your site, you get a few doubloons.

Meanwhile, you're busy washing your new car. Not bad for a day at the office.

## Reaping the Benefits of Affiliate Programs

 Affiliate programs have great potential for both added income for affiliates and new customers for merchants. According to the October 1999 Forrester Report, affiliate programs will be responsible for about 21 percent of online sales by 2003 (**http://www.refer-it.com/as99.htm**). Affiliate programs are almost the same as buying ad space and paying for the number of times the ad is viewed or leads to a sale. By offering

> ### Why is an affiliate program better than selling ad space?
>
> Riyaj Shaik, president and CEO of iSeed, Inc., says "Online merchants used to be resigned to shelling out huge advance payments to advertise on the pages of top Internet portals, gambling that their investments would generate profitable returns. But the proliferation of affiliate marketing programs has dramatically reduced online advertising risks, and pay-for-performance has become the name of the game." iSeed, Inc. offers Associate-It(**associate-it.com**), a portal site dedicated to affiliate programs.

an incentive to affiliates for "recommending" your services or products, you guarantee added exposure to the general Web populace.

Aside from increasing sales, affiliate programs can also add exposure to your site in other ways. Even if Web surfers "tune out" banner ads, they will begin to remember your company's name after ignoring your ads several times. In addition, popularity engines, which we discuss more in Part IV, "Analyzing E-Commerce Solutions," might count that link to your site, increasing your rankings in popularity-based engines such as Google.

The only drawback to affiliate programs, as we've discussed, is the proliferation of ads on the affiliate's site. If too many ads crowd a site, or if they detract in some way from the content of a Web page, the effect of the ad is nullified. The benefits far outweigh the possible disadvantages, however, because you can choose to track affiliate-related activity using alternative methods, and any small amount of name recognition increases the likelihood of traffic to your site and an eventual sale.

## Setting Up an Affiliate Program

You have two choices when you set up your affiliate program. You can choose a company to host your program, track the number of hits or sales generated from an affiliate, and provide reports concerning the affiliate metrics. Or you can choose to create your own tracking software. Either way, you have quite a few issues to consider, such as the following:

- **Cost effectiveness.** Remember when you build your program software that it will require maintenance as bugs, security issues, privacy issues, and other bugaboos are identified. In addition, the program itself will require regular maintenance—from how you use the program (per click, per purchase, etc.) to how you provide metrics and feedback to your affiliates.

- **Time.** How much time do you have to devote to your affiliate program? In truth, building, running, and maintaining your program is a full-time job. Do you have someone capable of taking on this position, or would you be better off using a broker service?

- **Method of use.** What is the most effective use of your promotion money? Should you pay per hit, per click, or per transaction? What is a fair rate to give your affiliates for their referrals?

- **Software.** Does the software you use accurately track different affiliates? Does it integrate with your accounting software? Does it track that links from affiliate pages appear according to any requirements you've set forth?

- **Server capacity.** Does your server have the tools and the capability to handle the additional processing your affiliate program will require? Remember, you will record and process information *each time someone "hits" your site—whether through retrieval of an image, click-through, or purchase.* You also must be able to create individualized pages—reports—for each affiliate to track the history its site has generated.

- **Security.** Do you have the means of providing security and privacy protection for your affiliates, or would a broker be better able to provide that for you?

## Using an Affiliate Broker or Ready-Made Software

Several programs available today can help you through various portions of your affiliate program—from creation to reporting to maintenance. At the end of this chapter, you can find a list of tools, including software and Web-based brokers, that you can use to create your affiliate program.

When you consider the options for each potential tool, keep these thoughts in mind:

- Is this cost-effective, or should you just create your own software or tools?

- Does this option offer real-time reporting?
- Does the program offer metrics to help you analyze the effectiveness of your program?
- Do you need to screen potential affiliates, or will your broker do this for you?
- Will you need to provide customer service, or will your broker handle this?
- Will the software or broker alert you to suspicious activity that could be fraudulent?
- If you choose to use affiliate-tracking software, will you need to upgrade your system to handle the additional capacity needs?
- How reliable is the software's or broker's tracking method?
- How effective and straightforward is the interface? Will affiliates find the sign-up process difficult or time-consuming? Will they be able to access reports regarding their accounts?
- How much security does the software/broker give both you and your affiliates?
- Does the software or broker offer the capability to pay different fee structures, or are you limited to one fee structure across the board? Some affiliate programs pay percentages in levels. If an affiliate sells 1 to 100 items, for example, it is paid a certain percent. If it sells 101 to 200 items, the percent goes up, and so forth.
- Does the software or broker ensure privacy for your affiliates? Has it posted a privacy policy? Do you agree with its privacy policy? Remember that many of your affiliates may be individuals with personal Web sites—and they may not want their information sold as if they were a business!

## Creating Your Own Tracking Software

The details involved in creating affiliate program software from scratch go way beyond the scope of this book, so in this section, we do not tell you everything you need to know to whip up your own personal affiliate software overnight. Instead, we discuss issues you need to consider as you develop the tools to track and maintain your affiliate program.

Because of the options available today to track affiliate program activity, we recommend that you create your own tracking software only if you have special needs that a broker cannot address. If you have unlimited time but limited money, for example, you might choose to develop your program from scratch in lieu of paying for a broker's services. Keep in mind, however, that software development requires more than a few hours of time with a compiler.

Also remember that this type of tracking software can create potential security and privacy issues. After all, you are tracking activity from *Web site visitors who may not want their activity scrutinized.* Make sure that development is the right choice for your circumstances given the time and risks involved. You may be better off giving the responsibility of development to someone else.

### What You'll Need

Depending on the type of program you want to put together and the amount of interaction this program will have with potential customers, your needs can vary a great deal. After you decide what type of tracking you want to use, you'll have a better idea of the scope of your needs. Here we look at a few necessities to create a basic tracking program.

Probably the most obvious tool you'll need is a database to track the information you gather. This database needs to be compatible with your other tools, and you must be able to access it from within Web scripts or programs.

Next, you'll need the code. This, of course, depends on the type of database you're using, as well as the scripts you use to create your Web site. Remember that even if you only need to count the number of times a particular server requests a banner ad from your site, you will be running this script or program on your server.

You also should consider whether you want to run everything in real time or you prefer to keep a log, which your tracking program processes later. Either of these methods has its own benefits, but you must decide which is better for your situation given the amount of traffic your site generates and whether you need real-time metrics from your program to be available.

What are the benefits of real-time processing? First, it's all real time. If you want to know right now how many click-throughs your site has received from a particular affiliate, you can view that information. Second, real-time processing is a plus to your affiliates, because they can see at any particular moment how well their advertising is doing or how much it's paying off.

On the other hand, logs reduce the amount of strain on your system. Either way, you keep the same amount of information stored in memory, but the system isn't required to process as much information to calculate metrics for any particular moment. In addition, if you provide individualized Web pages for your affiliates to see the log information, the pages can be static. Real-time metrics would require on-the-fly graphics and text.

You also may need software to create graphics, if you choose to use images to attract customers. Will you use graphical ads, such as banners, buttons, or squares? Do you need graphics to use in links to your site or to track the number of times a particular page receives a hit?

## Potential Issues

In addition to the tools you'll need, be sure to keep these issues in mind:

- **Interface.** Will your potential customers be aware of the affiliate program in use? Or will the affiliation be obvious, as in the case of Amazon.com's programs using separate and miniature bookstores?

- **Metrics and reporting.** How will you provide metrics to the affiliates associated with your program? Will you e-mail a weekly report to them, acknowledging their hits and giving the running total they have earned for the next payment? Or will you keep their report under password protection at your site?

- **Tracking.** What method will be most efficient and most reliable for tracking hits, counts, or sales from an affiliate's site?

- **Security and privacy.** Remember that your affiliates are customers, and some of those customers may give you private information that you should neither reveal nor subject to potential security violation.

### Getting the Word Out

After you set up your affiliate program, you'll probably realize that you need affiliates to make any of that work worth your while. How can you let the world know about your new affiliate program?

- **E-mail.** Use the e-mail addresses you've collected from your site's visitors—those who have elected to receive e-mail regarding the site, news and announcements, etc.

- **Advertising.** Use your own site to advertise by using graphics or text links to the area of your site that discusses your new affiliate program. Join a banner exchange program that allows you to advertise your affiliate program with banner ads. Pepper your site with references to your new affiliate program, and make sure those references target the right audience—people or companies with a Web site that would be interested in making money. We include a list of banner exchange programs at the end of this chapter.

- **Affiliate program directories and the search engines.** Get your program listed at directories that specialize in affiliate/associate programs. You can find a list of such directory sites at the end of this chapter. Similarly, make sure you optimize your main affiliate page for the search engines, then submit, submit, submit. Also remember that affiliate programs help boost your link popularity because related sites will link to your site through these affiliate sites. This translates to better rankings on popularity-based engines.

- **Two-tier program.** Using a two-tier affiliate program, your affiliates can earn money for referring new affiliates. How do you swing this without paying out money before you earn any? Let your direct affiliates earn a percentage of each sale generated by an affiliate *they referred*. This is known as a *two-tier program*— an effective way of advertising your affiliate program and gaining more affiliates.

## Managing an Effective Affiliate Program

As we mentioned before, maintaining an affiliate program can be a time-consuming task. To have an effective affiliate program, you should treat your affiliates as if they were customers—and they probably are! Give those customers their own affiliate manager to ensure that they will receive the attention they need to do their jobs properly.

You will need to remember the following issues as you manage your program:

- Your customer service for affiliates should be separate from, but no less important than, customer service for those who purchase your products or services. You should have at least one e-mail address set up specifically for affiliates that have technical questions or problems, need special attention, want to provide feedback and suggestions, etc. Also, prompt responses are important.

- Any upgrades you make to your service should be beta tested until everyone involved begins to experience feelings of psychosis. Remember that you're dealing with money, and if your affiliates are cheated because your upgrade messed with the system, you'll have very angry affiliates on your hands.

- Stay on top of security and privacy issues. When you use an affiliate program, you chance treading on someone's privacy rights. In addition, the use of cookies, CGI, etc. poses potential security risks that you may not be aware of until your system has been compromised.

- Watch for fraudulent behavior. What constitutes fraud in affiliate programs? If you pay per view on an affiliate's page, there may be a way for that affiliate to trick your system into believing that the ad on that page has been viewed more times than is actually the case. If you pay for click-throughs, make sure your program can detect unique users through session logs or other means.

- Offer your affiliates special discounts, services, or products that regular customers don't receive. The special treatment you give your affiliates not only motivates them to recommend your services or products through their sites, but the additional freebies, discounts, etc. can increase the demand for affiliate status. You'll increase your affiliate network and, in the process, improve your name recognition and sales.

- Analyze your setup regularly for effectiveness, security, privacy, and simplicity.

## Analyzing Your Affiliate Program Step-by-Step

In this section, you'll analyze your affiliate program based on both the program itself and the results you receive after your program has been publicly available and in use. Remember to check any log files or reports your software generates from the affiliate traffic.

### The Effectiveness of Your Ads

Use the metrics you gather to analyze your method of advertisement on a regular basis. Be aware of the following:

- What is the mean click-through–to–page view ratio for your affiliates?
- What is the click-to-order ratio?
- How many hits to your site are referred through an affiliate compared to the number that comes from different sources?
- Which ad or ad type (graphical or text) provides the highest number of click-throughs?
- Which affiliate generates the most sales? What content does that affiliate include on the affiliate site that complements your products (and probably helps to lead to those sales)?
- What is the total in sales generated from affiliates as compared to sales that come from other sources?
- Have you polled your site visitors to get feedback on various portions of your site, including the affiliate site that referred the visitor?

### The Interface

Your Web interface should follow the same general rules we discuss in Chapters 1 and 2. Remember that affiliates are customers as well as business partners—make their lives easy and entertaining even in this section of your site to ensure they return.

- Is the interface of your affiliate area self-explanatory?
- Is the interface uniform throughout your affiliate area?
- Is the interface of the actual program (how customers come to your site through affiliate sites) self-explanatory?
- Does the program interface require special knowledge or abilities that will make affiliation difficult or too specific for the general Web population?
- Does the program interface hinder navigation? Or can customers easily return to the affiliate site from your own?

## Ease-of-Use

You won't have many affiliates unless every aspect of your program is user-friendly and easy.

- Are underperforming ads easy to change on all affiliates' sites?
- Can affiliates view reports with a minimum number of mouse clicks and scrolling?
- Can you view reports and metrics with a minimum amount of mouse clicks and scrolling?
- Can you maintain the program, change options, and perform upkeep easily?

## Security and Privacy

Again, remember that your affiliates are customers, and those affiliates have security and privacy concerns for both themselves and those visitors on their sites. Consider the ramifications of security and privacy issues for affiliates and customers who find you through affiliate sites.

- Does your privacy policy address your affiliate program, or have you created a separate policy just for the affiliate program issues?
- In your security policy, have you addressed potential security issues related to your affiliate program?
- Can you safely upgrade your program without wreaking havoc?
- What sensitive affiliate information do you record that could easily be compromised?

- Do you have password protection set up for affiliates? Is your method for replacing forgotten passwords secure?
- Do you enable individual accounts for multiple employees of one affiliate to access that affiliate account? Do the individual accounts have unique logins for easy tracking of account access?
- Do you deactivate an account that shows signs of a security breach?
- Do you have off-site or physically protected backups of sensitive information for affiliates regarding sales, commissions, and metrics?

## Locating Affiliate Tools and Resources

The following tools and program directories can help you in your quest to make oodles of affiliate program money.

### Articles and Information

The following sites provide articles and other information regarding effective affiliate programs:

- AffiliateMatch—**http://www.affiliatematch.com/**
- eCommerceBase.com—**http://www.ecommercebase.com/ subcats.php3?id=23**
- OnlineBusiness.com—**http://onlinebusiness.com/ news_affiliate_marketing.html**
- ReveNews.com—**http://www.revenews.com/**

### Newsletters and E-zines

The following sites provide newsletters containing affiliate program information e-mailed to your Inbox:

- AffiliateMatch—**http://www.affiliatematch.com/**
- Webmaster-Programs—**http://webmaster-programs.com/Ezine/ Subscribe.htm**
- Affili Source—**http://www.affilisource.com/**

## Software

The following companies offer affiliate software that helps you set up and maintain your affiliate program:

- Be Free—**http://www.befree.com/**
- ClickTrade—**http://www.clicktrade.com/**
- LinkShare—**http://www.linkshare.com/**
- Pro-Track—**http://www.affiliatesoftware.net/**

The following companies will run your affiliate program for you:

- Commission Junction—**http://www.cj.com/**
- LinkShare—**http://www.linkshare.com/**
- PlugInGo—**http://www.plugingo.com/**

## Directories

The following directories are useful:

- Synergy Internet Marketing—**http://www.2-Tier.com/**
- **AffiliateMatch.com—http://www.AffiliateMatch.com/**
- iSeed—**http://www.Associate-It.com/**
- CashPile—**http://www.CashPile.com/**
- ClicksLink—**http://www.ClicksLink.com/**
- Internet.com—**http://www.refer-it.com/**
- Internet Productions—**http://www.WebAffiliatePrograms.com/**

## Seminars and Conferences

The following seminars and conferences can be a valuable resource:

- Affiliate Solutions Conference—**http://seminars.internet.com/**
- Internet Affiliate Marketing Summit (AffiliateForce)—**http://affiliateforce.com/**
- Web Marketing World—**http://www.thunderlizard.com/wmw.html**

### Program Links

The following program links are useful:

*Find It*
**ONLINE**

- FTPSearch—**http://www.affiliate-programs.org/**
- **Affiliate Tips—http://www.affiliatetips.com/**
- AssociatePrograms.com—**http://www.associateprograms.com/ search/newsletter.shtml**
- OnlineBusiness.com—**http://onlinebusiness.com/ news_affiliate_marketing.html**

### Banner Exchange Programs

These programs can help you generate traffic to your site by way of banner exchange. Keep in mind that many banner exchange programs require that your site be viewable by children. Don't apply if you don't qualify.

*Find It*
**ONLINE**

- BannerSwap—**http://www.bannerswap.com/**
- MyComputer.com—**http://www. bannerexchange.mycomputer.com/**
- Exchange-It!—**http://www.exchange-it.com/**
- Free Banners—**http://www.free-banners.com/**
- WebmasterExchange.com—**http://www.webmasterexchange.com/** (only for sites dedicated to Web design issues)

## Conclusion

Affiliate programs provide an easy way of attracting new customers to your site by allowing existing customers to help you market your company. Though the creation and maintenance of an affiliate program can be time-consuming, several tools and companies can help you construct a winning program. As you develop and maintain your program, keep in mind issues such as security, privacy, ease of use, navigation, and interfaces. Also, analyze your program metrics frequently to determine which ads work best and in what affiliate environment.

# CREATING EFFECTIVE ONLINE COMMUNITIES

**In This Chapter**

Your company sells computer chips, so why on earth would you need an online community? Or you manage a group of medical sites, so an online community couldn't possibly be an option.

In both instances, the thinking is wrong.

With few exceptions, an online community can be a valuable addition to any Web site. Online communities bring users into your fold and add a loyal following.

In this chapter, we discuss the benefits of online communities as well as describe important facets of effective communities. We cover how to manage your community and whether you want to let your community manage itself.

You'll learn how to boost the effectiveness of an online community and get a step-by-step guide in analyzing your own community.

## Reaping the Benefits of an Online Community

Whether you are creating on online community for the Internet, your intranet, or your extranet, the potential benefits of having a community are many.

In fact, online communities offer these benefits to visitors, employees, customers, and even the companies themselves:

- A sense of community and camaraderie. An online community is similar to having your company's own group or organization. "Members" can quickly feel a part of the community and can consider it their own.

- The heightened opportunity for return and referral traffic. Because it's "their" community, visitors more apt to return again and again and to recommend the community to their business associates and friends, particularly if they're able to learn valuable information from that community.

- Opportunity to establish special-interest groups that are an offshoot of your products or services. If you provide special interest groups that are an offshoot of your main focus, you give your members avenues for their individual focuses.

- Customer feedback on a regular basis. With an online neighborhood or community, your company has the unique opportunity to get invaluable feedback from customers and users of your products. If a product isn't working as it should, you can be sure you'll learn this information, and more, at your online bulletin boards or chat rooms. If your product has a kink in it, or if your services aren't up to par, you'll be in a better position to quickly make corrections or adjustments to get things back to where they need to be.

- Opportunity to add value where there was none before.

- Ability to post important announcements. Online communities give you the opportunity to post important on-the-spot announcements to employees, customers, or visitors—such as sales, contests, user tips, and more.

- Retrieval of e-mail addresses for marketing. In previous chapters, we discuss the power of permission e-mail marketing. With online communities, if you require your members to register, you'll be able to retrieve additional e-mail addresses that you can use in future targeted mailings and announcements about your company. See Chapter 5, "Using Forms and Scripts to Capture E-mail Addresses", for more information.

- Opinions about potentially new products and services. If you're considering developing a new product or implementing a new service, bring that idea to your community and get the members' reactions. Lack of enthusiasm can cause you to rethink your strategies, or heightened excitement might cause you to speed up the development. You can even use the online community to offer suggestions as to possible features for a new product.

- Enhance customer support. By recruiting experienced users of your products, you can offer expert advice and give perks to those who volunteer their time. The sharing of user experiences and problem solving can relieve some pressure from your customer support areas and encourage camaraderie.

- The building of valuable content on your Web site. With an online community, just think of the valuable content you're providing on your Web site, content that the Web community and search engines alike are bound to appreciate.

- The promotion of name recognition and credibility. An effective online community can build name recognition and credibility, and it can help your company become a leader in its industry.

- Avenues for free advertising for service-oriented sites. With online neighborhoods, you can advertise your company in free avenues, because you can focus on the free services and content you're providing to Web users.

  You can promote your community in lists and e-zines that generally don't take commercial listings, for example. You can post the community URL and information on newsgroups and have better luck at an increase in traffic than posting your company's URL alone. Companies that do business with you will more than likely be willing to promote your community on their sites. In other words, your potential for promoting your site in the cheapest way possible increases dramatically if you have an online community or are offering other free services to the Web community.

- A boost in link and click-through popularity with the search engines. Keep in mind that the increase in links pointing to your site due to your online community can greatly boost your rankings in the search engines. Most of the major engines place a high level of importance on sites with a high link popularity, as you'll learn in the search engine section of this book. Plus, with engines that consider click-through popularity when determining relevancy, having an online community where visitors stay on your site for lengths of time certainly can help your rankings on those engines.

- Ability to keep visitors at your site for longer periods of time. Not only do you want your visitors to remain on your site in terms of appealing to the search engines, but you also want to keep your visitors from leaving in order to present them with more opportunities to learn about your products or services. After all, the longer they stay and the more involved they become, the more apt they are to buy.

- A community that virtually runs itself once it's initially coordinated and set up. Once your community has been established and is up and running, you can even manage it so that it virtually runs itself, and the outlay of time to maintain the community is kept at a minimum.

- Does this sound too good to be true? Consider Usenet, where many of the newsgroups have been in existence for years without any formal oversight beyond the enthusiasm of their members. We cover how to manage your online community later in this chapter.

- Software programs make it easy to set up an online community. Certainly, you'll have the initial planning and creation of your online community to consider, but numerous software programs are available that will make it easier for you to set up areas of your community. We discuss those programs in "Assistance in Setting Up Your Community," later in this chapter.

## Selecting the Components of Your Community

What community areas are available, in addition to the obvious bulletin boards and chat rooms? Basically, you're limited only in terms of your imagination and pocketbook. This chapter gives you a listing of some of the features you may want to include in your online community.

In Figure 7.1, you'll see a screenshot of Talk City, a popular online community. Notice the number of community features offered at Talk City: games, chat events, neighborhoods, the event calendar, clubs, and more.

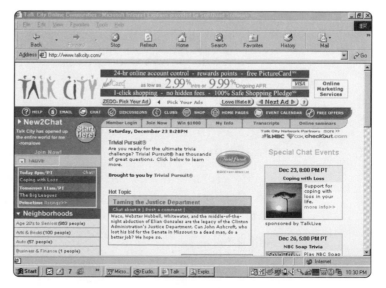

**FIGURE 7.1**

Talk City Online Communities.

## Bulletin Boards

An active bulletin board system is an important feature of any online community. When setting up your own bulletin board system, consider these points:

- Require members to register with their names and e-mail addresses, and issue passwords to use when posting messages.
- Post rules for using the forums, and require members to agree to the terms before being allowed to post for the first time.
- Post guidelines on how to use the forums.
- Divide the bulletin boards into categories and subcategories, making it easy for your members to post to the correct forum. Set up topics of interest to your members.
- In the beginning, monitor the use of the forums. Try to pick a member who seems to be leading that forum, and then ask him or her to moderate. Give your moderators passwords and special privileges.
- Let members suggest new bulletin board topics.
- If you have international members, consider setting up separate forums for different languages.
- Tell your moderators to try to keep the discussions on target. The key word in that sentence is "try," because members will use the forums in whatever manner is most useful to them.
- Ask your moderators to inform someone in your organization about topics that you need to know about, such as problems, requests for new products, etc.
- Archive all posts and make them searchable.

*FIND IT*
**ONLINE**

Figure 7.2 shows the guidelines for Excite's forums, which you also can find at **http://www.excite.com/communities/resources/standards/boards/**.

Excite's forums have been in existence for years, so they'll serve as an excellent guide in helping you create guidelines for your own bulletin board system.

*FIND IT*
**ONLINE**

Salon Table Talk is another online community; you can find it at **http://tabletalk.salon1999.com/webx**.

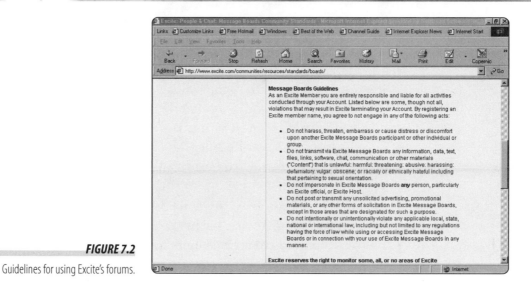

**FIGURE 7.2**

Guidelines for using Excite's forums.

## Talk, Talk, Talk

Online communities have a variety of choices when it comes to chatting among members. Certainly chat rooms are popular features of most online communities. But communities also can use chat software such as ICQ or AOL Instant Messaging (AIM), or even visit sites such as FreshMeat.net to find free programs they can modify specifically for their company or community. Communities also can participate in video conferencing using both audio and video capabilities, or they can provide live lectures or online courses.

### Chat Rooms

When Excite's communities first came into existence years ago, they found that offering a chat function was enough to get the community off the ground. In fact, many sites have used chat as a framework and have built content around it.

How can you encourage people to visit your chat rooms or forums? Set up specific times for discussing certain topics of interest to your members or potential members. Post those times in your calendar or special events area and on your Web site.

Many of the same guidelines for bulletin boards apply to setting up and monitoring chat rooms, but let's look at some additional suggestions:

- Decide what language censoring will be done, if any. Be sure to include that rule in the guidelines for the chat rooms, and made it widely known. Don't say that no pornographic words will be allowed in chat rooms if you're not able to monitor the situation closely. Instead, state the rules, and then protect yourself by stating that members are posting at their own volition, and the company accepts no responsibility for their conduct. Another option is to assign moderators to watch for foul or suggestive language, or even to use software bots to filter new messages.

- Require members to register with names and e-mail addresses, and require them to use a password to enter the chat rooms.

- Post chat rules and guidelines for how to use the chat rooms.

- Accept that people will use the chat rooms and bulletin boards in whatever way they choose.

- Assign moderators based on member strengths and interests. You may find that the best and most active moderators are those from within the ranks, instead of experts in the field or those you've pulled from outside of the community.

- Give away incentives to those who agree to monitor a forum or chat room. Make it worth their while to participate. For the benefit of your moderators, be sure to check with your accountant to see if any of those perks are taxable.

- Post a schedule of chat sessions, if you set up chat sessions on particular topics.

- Set up chat rooms on various topics of interest to your members and your company—for example, "New Product Development," "Ranting and Raving," "Product Improvements," "Strategies for Using the Product," "How to Use the Product," and "Technical Difficulties."

- Let members request that a new chat room be established.

- If you have international members, consider setting up separate chat rooms for different languages.

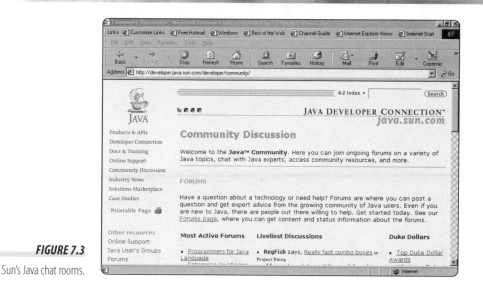

**FIGURE 7.3**

Sun's Java chat rooms.

- Make sure that your software allows you to save copies of the chat transcripts. Then archive the transcripts, making sure they're searchable.

- Make sure that your chat rooms and forums run on all platforms.

- Ask experts in the industry, company officials, or members to conduct chat sessions, and then advertise those chat sessions heavily.

Figure 7.3 shows Sun's Java forums and chat rooms divided into various categories based on member preferences.

Visit these chat rooms online at **http://developer.java.sun.com/ developer/community/**.

### Chat Software

Communities certainly can use chat software such as ICQ, AIM, or MSN Messenger as a means of chatting among members. Or they can purchase a license to rebrand an existing chat software program. Another option is to visit FreshMeat (**http://www.freshmeat.net**) to find free open-source software, and then to make changes to it or add features, making it their own.

Whatever software you use, make it easy for your members to download the software and use the features, and make sure to list "how to use" guidelines in your community chat area.

### Video Conferencing

With video conferencing, members can chat with other members across the globe using audio and video capabilities. Besides saving the expense of travel and time away from the office, video conferencing enhances communication and often speeds up the decision-making process.

Video conferencing can be PC-based or standalone. With room-based video conferencing systems, you can conduct meetings online and share applications and data, use presentation software, have access to network resources, and more.

Of course, many of the applications or benefits of using video conferencing depend on whether your community is being used through the Internet, your intranet, or an extranet.

**TIP** For more information, visit Intel's video conferencing page at **http://www.intel.com/ proshare/conferencing/**.

### Live Lecturing and Courses

 Going hand in hand with chat rooms is the capability of presenting a live lecture to your community. With EnterVision (**http://www. magicweb.com/technology.htm**), you can have TV-quality broadcasting over the Web by simply hooking up your source to a computer and then clicking on Play

 Mentor Technologies offers a vLab Classroom (**http://www.mentortech. com/vlab/class.shtml**), where students work independently on instructional modules and actually configure and control real network equipment. Optimizing the classroom experience, vLab Classroom uniquely combines training on a live network with the lecture and mentoring provided by the instructor.

## Venues for Special Interest Groups

Many successful online communities set up special interest groups that branch off from the main community, then create chat rooms and bulletin boards for those specific topics.

In fact, polls have shown that file sharing leads the pack of the most valued community feature, with special interest groups coming in a close second.

## Vertical Search Engines or Directories

In Chapter 4, "Setting Up Polls, Contests, and Other Traffic-Generating Avenues," we discuss vertical search engines and directories focused on one topic. A valuable addition to your online community would be a vertical search engine or a directory. Your members will be able to access the search engine and will be pointed to sites that are devoted strictly to your industry. They can submit their own URLs to the engine, and you can bet they'll link to the engine on their own site.

Onsite directories and vertical search engines hold much potential power in terms of popularity, content, return traffic, name recognition, credibility… and the list goes on and on.

If your site is geared toward the international community as well, consider using multilanguage search capabilities, as discussed in Chapter 4.

Quiver (**http://www.quiver.com**) provides vertical directories, which are great drawing cards for communities. Quiver's data-mining technology powers MyPrimeTime's directory, PrimeGuide, which in turn provides MyPrimeTime users with search results targeted just for them.

In Figure 7.4, you can see the PrimeGuide directory. You can view the directory online at **http://quiver.myprimetime.com**.

The directory listings are geared toward MyPrimeTime's major areas of focus: family, money, health, work, and play.

FindLaw (**http://www.findlaw.com**) is another vertical search engine and is composed totally of legal sites.

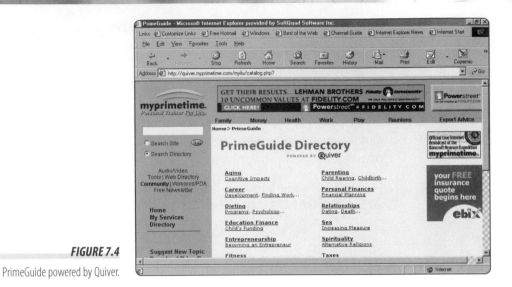

**FIGURE 7.4**

PrimeGuide powered by Quiver.

## Free E-mail

Think about it. If you give your members free e-mail addresses, every time they use that e-mail address, they're advertising *your* company.

Look at Yahoo! and its popular free e-mail program. Every time any of the members use that e-mail address, they're advertising Yahoo!.

Notice the number of features available in conjunction with Yahoo!'s e-mail in Figure 7.5.

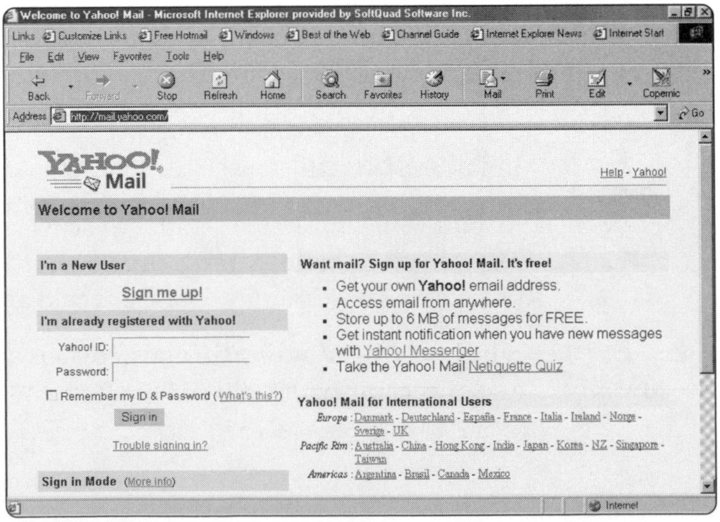

**FIGURE 7.5**

Yahoo!'s free e-mail service.

Members are given 6MB of space and the capability to access e-mail from anywhere.

## Mailing Lists

Some members may prefer to enter into discussions through e-mail, rather than an online bulletin board. So give those people what they want by setting up a mailing list.

Mailing lists can be moderated or unmoderated, depending on their use.

More information on setting up an e-mail list can be found in Chapter 3.

## Calendar of Events

You can use a calendar to post upcoming chat sessions, conferences in your industry, online workshops, projected dates for the availability of new products, and any number of things. Use this feature to re-mind your members of things they are likely to forget, and allow members to submit items to be placed on the calendar.

You can even set up a reminder service to automatically remind members by e-mail about calendar items that are important to them.

A slightly different twist to online calendars is *online calendaring*, which provides a way of interactively managing a group's calendar and con-solidating various calendars into one view.

For more information, visit Lycos Calendar by AnyDay at **http://anyday.lycos.com**.

## White Boards

A white board can be a valuable addition to an online community. It allows you to collaborate in real time using graphical information.

If you use Microsoft NetMeeting (**http://www.microsoft.com/windows/NetMeeting**), in addition to video and audio conferencing capabilities, chat, file transfer, program sharing, and desktop sharing, you'll also have white board capabilities.

**FIGURE 7.6**

Mimio's Whiteboard Demonstration.

Wanvas Online Whiteboard Editor is a shareware program, and MeetingTools by Databeam Corporation is an add-on whiteboard solution. Both are available through ZDNet's downloads section at **http://www.zdnet.com/downloads/**.

Mimio offers a WebEx service (**http://www.mimio.com/meetings/index.html**) where you can pay to have your meetings at their site. Mimio features a whiteboard, and you can participate in remote presentations, collaborative Web browsing, online text chat, opinion polling, and complete Windows application sharing.

In Figure 7.6, you'll see a screenshot showing a Mimio whiteboard in use.

## File Sharing

Believe it or not, file sharing is one of the most sought-after aspects of an online community.

Give your members the capability to share files with each other. Provide a place where they can upload and download files and provide search capabilities. If your members need software to use any of your community areas, be sure to provide that software as well.

As with all of your community areas, make sure that you post comprehensive guidelines and instructions for file sharing. Many of the programs listed in this chapter offer file-sharing capabilities, including Microsoft NetMeeting and Intel's video-conferencing tools.

## Articles and Q&As

Why not provide a place where members can write and post articles on particular topics? The information can be helpful to other members, plus new content will constantly be available, which will give members a good reason to bookmark the site and return.

Another useful and popular area of online communities is a Question & Answer section. Continually add new and relevant questions and answers based on problems solved in the community or through customer support, and your Q&A section will increase in value.

## Free Web Space

Another possible addition to your online community, depending on the nature of your business, is free Web space. Obviously, if your company is technology-related, most of your members will have their own Web space elsewhere. Having access to free Web space is always a plus, however. If your company is not technology-related, your members might appreciate having free Web space until they set up their own domains.

## Members' List

You might want to consider setting up a list of members and letting individual members enter their own information in a database. Then members who are looking for another member from a certain geographic area, or with a certain expertise, could search through the database for possible matches.

This members' list could be modified to include a job database, if desired, or any number of other features that could provide helpful and pertinent information to members.

As with all areas of your online community, make sure that you implement security features to protect the privacy of your members. See Part VI, "How Secure Is Your Web Site?" for more information on Web security.

## Group Buying

Some communities are built around the idea of its members banning together to purchase in bulk. Therefore, when appropriate, group buying can be a valuable feature of an online community.

## Invitation Services

Many communities offer invitation services to their members. Members are provided with design templates, address books, and even RSVP services to make planning functions much easier.

 *Find It* **ONLINE** Top invitation services include Envite.com, Yahoo Invites, Mambo.com, and TimeDance. Read CNET's review of these services at **http:// www.cnet.com/internet/0-1497812-7-1883617.html**.

# Getting Assistance in Setting Up Your Community

Obviously, your first step in setting up an online community is to decide which features to include. Instead of starting out with every feature known to man, start out slowly. Plan for the fact that setting up the community will probably be a larger undertaking than you had originally planned.

Keep this in mind, though. Make sure that your interface is simple and intuitive. Generally speaking, not all of your users will be computer geniuses, so develop your interface to be simple to use without massive instructions.

 **TIP** Subscribe to the Online Community Report (**http://onlinecommunityreport.com/**), a free, twice a month newsletter covering current events and innovations for online communications.

 *Find It* **ONLINE** For an article on setting up an online community, visit the Online Community Toolkit at **http:/ /www.fullcirc.com/community/communitymanual.htm**.

## Helpful Software Programs and Services

You'll find numerous software programs and services on the market designed to make setting up your online community much easier. Many of those programs are listed elsewhere in this chapter, but you'll find additional choices in this section.

---

### Tips from an Online Community Building Expert

Jim Cashel from Forum One (**http://www.forumone.com/capital/index.htm**) provides business strategies for online communities. What are the most-used community functions? Jim says that chat, message boards, and mailing lists top the chart. Other popular features include group calendaring, group buying, and invitation services.

When analyzing the effectiveness of a community, Jim states, "There are a number of relevant metrics for community success: traffic (page views), total users, growth, number of postings, revenue, and other desirable outcomes. The 'success' of an online community depends critically on the goals of the site. For example, some sites wish simply to save money on user support, so they start an online help community."

Jim believes that almost any online company would benefit from a community. "Any company or organization that engages with a community of users or stakeholders should think hard about online community technologies. Most would benefit from an appropriate adoption of technologies. That said, building and launching online communities is very difficult; it is paramount to consult with knowledgeable people and to plan."

---

When choosing software, you'll notice that some software programs are more appropriate for larger communities, whereas other software works best in smaller settings. So consider your needs carefully.

## Toolkits for Building Communities

When considering software for your online community, remember that many of the programs offer both chat and discussion capabilities, file sharing, and more, all in that one program. With other setups, you set up the components separately.

Some tools for setting up online communities follow:

***Find It*
ONLINE**

- LibWeb (**http://libweb.sourceforge.net/**) is a Perl library and toolkit for building online communities.
- Sharewire (**http://www.sharewire.com/**) offers free community building applications that will run on your server, such as site search, a directory, guestbook, calendar, surveys, and forums.
- Conferencing Software for the Web (**http://thinkofit.com/webconf/**) offers software for virtual teams, collaboration work groups, forums, and more.

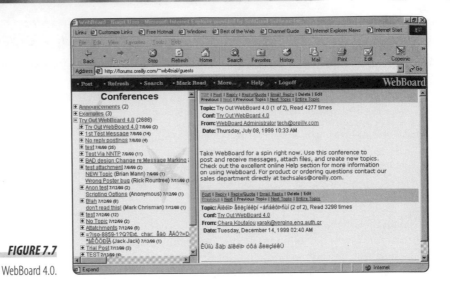

**FIGURE 7.7**

WebBoard 4.0.

- Web Crossing (**http://www.webcrossing.com/40/**), which is ideal for large or small communities, offers bulletin boards, newsgroups, mailing lists, email services, calendar services, and more.

- WebBoard (**http://webboard.oreilly.com/**) is an impressive high-end community software program that offers built-in support for two leading databases: WebBoard 4, Windows Edition for MSDE/SQL Server, and WebBoard 4, Windows Edition for Oracle 8/8i. The program supports up to 255 discussion boards and unlimited users, and its built-in Web server requires no configuration or special maintenance.

In Figure 7.7, you can see a sample of WebBoard 4.0, where bulletin board topics are listed on the left-hand side of the page, with actual posts listed on the right.

With WebBoard, you can post and receive messages, attach files, or insert graphics or links in the middle of the posts.

### Bulletin Boards and Forums

As you can see, the community toolkits offer bulletin boards and forums, or you can purchase them separately.

---

### *Seven Rules for Building a Community*

At the O'Reilly Software site, you'll find an article by Stephen R. Figgins titled "Seven Golden Rules for Building Community."

Those rules include the following:

- Plan it first.
- Grow in increments.
- Use it.
- Celebrate it.
- Record its history.
- Host it professionally.
- Keep the trust.

Read the article in its entirety at **http://software.oreilly.com/news.cfm?ID_News=189**.

---

- Boards2Go (**http://www.boards2go.com/**) provides free, hosted bulletin boards for Webmasters.

- Matt's Script Archive offers WWWBoard, a free Perl script-based message board, at **http://www.worldwidemart.com/scripts/wwwboard.shtml**.

- Allaire Forums, now Open Source software, is a Web conferencing software (**http://www.forumspot.org/**) that lets site developers using Cold Fusion set up and maintain online discussions.

## Chat Programs

Chat is certainly a popular feature for any online community. Look into these programs and determine whether they suit your special needs:

- If you want a chat program that operates on a large scale, works on most platforms, and offers a variety of features, consider iChat's Rooms. Users like the rooms because, with the Java client, there's no plug-in or additional software to download and install. Visit **http://www.ichat.com/community/rooms** for more information.

- For chat capabilities on a smaller scale, look into eShare's Expressions at **http://www.eshare.com/products/internet/expressions/index.html**. Expressions is easy to set up and run, and users can take part in online tours with other users, chat, or access bulletin boards.

### Conferencing Tools

Conferencing tools with video and audio features are certainly becoming popular with online users.

- Intel (**http://www.intel.com/proshare/conferencing/**) offers video-conferencing software.

- Evoke Communications (**http://excite.webconference.work.com/excite/index.shtml**) offers a suite of meeting services that allows up to 2,500 people to collaborate online. Evoke Collaboration is available for free for five users who want to test the service before buying. With this service, large-scale events or Web tours can be conducted with ease.

  Evoke's services also include Web conferencing, so that meetings can be conducted online. Participants can share charts and graphs, and the meetings can be recorded. Sales presentations, training sessions, and impromptu meetings can be set up in a flash.

- Lotus Development Corporation offers a suite of collaboration products called Sametime, which includes instant messaging, live document and application sharing, and virtual meetings. Visit **http://www.lotus.com/home.nsf/welcome/sametime** to learn more. Information on its e-learning solution, LearnSpace, is available at the same page.

### Vertical Search Engines and Directories

As mentioned in previous chapters, vertical search engines and directories offer many advantages to a Web site. Some companies that offer vertical search engines follow:

- SearchButton.com's Community Search (**http://www.searchbutton.com/solutions/features/CustomServices.html**) is a vertical directory with search capabilities that allow members to search through a ring of related sites.

- Quiver, at **http://www.quiver.com**, is a vertical directory customized to a specific community, which is automatically maintained through a continuous analysis of bookmark and surfing data collected from a specific community of users.

- Web Wombat, **http://webwombat.com**, offers a global search engine, regional engines, or customized search engines. The company also builds corporate intranet search engines.

- SearchLogic (**http://www.1port.com/**) features deep vertical Web search resources, including hundreds of thousands of topical links integrated with current news and database resources.

- Twirlix, **http://www.twirlix.com**, integrates the advantages of search engines with those of Web directories. Its spider moves through the Web finding new sites, adding only relevant sites to that particular topic engine. Then Twirlix sorts those sites into category listings.

**TIP** The CGI Scripts Forum (**http://www.cgiforum.com/**) has more than 20,000 scripts and resources. You can even learn how to write and install CGI, where to download Perl, how to test **FIND IT** CGI scripts for errors, and more.
**ONLINE**

## Remotely Hosted CGI

If your Web provider doesn't allow you to run your own cgi-bin, or if you don't know CGI programming, you can consider using some of the free remotely hosted CGI services available across the Internet.

**FIND IT** The Freebiescenter Directory (**http://www.freebiescenter.com/ ONLINE** **webmaster/cgi.html**) offers a listing of free forums, chatrooms, auctions, guest books, feedback forms, polls, surveys, and more.

## Managing Your Online Community

How involved in the day-to-day activities of your online community do you want to be? Does your company have the personnel—or the money to provide a staff—to manage the entire community, or will you need to rely on volunteers? If you have a members or e-mail listing, you'll also need tools for managing these. This section lists several considerations and tips for managing your community.

**TIP**    ListMaster Pro is a free program available from AnalogX that will allow you to easily manage an e-mail list. Visit **http://www.analogx.com/contents/download/network/lmpro.htm** to learn more.

## Recruiting Volunteers

Many successful online communities rely on volunteers to do the day-to-day monitoring of community activities. As members get more and more involved, they naturally step into leadership roles and moderate chats or forums, create calendars, work in the file-sharing area, and so forth.

How can you recruit members to assist? In the beginning, you'll need to monitor areas for members who seem to have an interest and expertise in those areas. Often, members will naturally assume a leadership position.

When considering how and where to recruit volunteers, keep in mind that some members are only looking for information. They have no problems to solve, and they probably won't participate much. Other members are problem solvers who can offer help based on experience. Still others are team builders you can recruit to assume leadership roles and help promote and build the community. Others simply enjoy participating in discussions.

In your bulletin boards and chat rooms, provide customers with experienced members—members who are often more than willing to answer questions and provide assistance to new customers and users. If you manage your community in such a way as to promote a level of hierarchy, your experienced members can greatly assist your customer service area and keep complaints and problems to a minimum.

What can you provide to those volunteers in return?

There may be password-protected areas of your site for paid subscribers only, and you may decide to give your volunteers access to that information in exchange for monitoring various areas in the community.

Another option is to give moderators discounts on goods or services, free tickets to trade shows or software programs, or similar perks. Make it worth their while to participate.

Certainly, paying the moderators is an option, but we're trying to suggest some non-paying means of compensating your moderators for their dedication and work. Be sure to check with your accountant, however, to see what perks might be taxable.

## Develop Goals and a Measuring System

In the beginning, develop clear goals for your online community. Establish weekly or monthly goals for getting new members, and review the figures regularly. In this manner, you'll be proving to the Accounting department the value of your community.

Check your log files regularly to see how much traffic your community areas get. This is an excellent measuring tool in determining the success of your community.

 **TIP** Why not take those annoying computer hackers and turn their expertise around to benefit your company? Get the hackers more involved in your site. Bring them into your fold and on to your side!

## If It Doesn't Succeed, Try Something Else!

Just because an original guideline or plan isn't working doesn't mean that you need to scrap the whole idea of an online community. Instead, rethink the strategies for that one area, see how it integrates into the total concept, and try something else.

Review your community functions on a regular basis to see how things are working and to see what changes might need to be made.

Visit successful online communities and see what they're doing. Contact them and ask for advice. Most of the time, Web masters are more than happy to tell you about their success stories.

## Develop Serious Usage Guidelines and Stick to Them

From the very beginning, develop a set of guidelines designed to prevent problems from happening. When problems crop up, add a new guideline about that area. The more structure you can create and implement in the beginning, the fewer problems you'll have down the road.

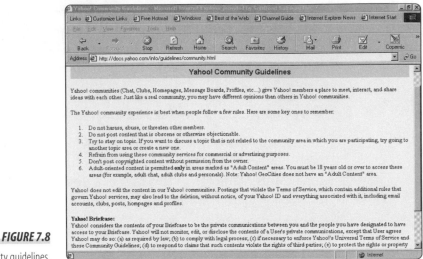

**FIGURE 7.8**

Yahoo! community guidelines.

Needless to say, all the guidelines in the world won't help if you don't make them readily available to your members. Why not require your members to indicate that they've read the guidelines and accept them before giving them access to the community areas?

Figure 7.8 shows see some of the guidelines for participating in Yahoo! community areas.

**FIND IT ONLINE**

You can find these guidelines at **http://docs.yahoo.com/info/guidelines/community.html**.

## Develop Guidelines for Removing Members

Regretfully, you may encounter a member who is doing nothing but causing problems. Develop a set of guidelines for removing problem members before the trouble ever occurs. Post those guidelines and follow them religiously. Let your members know what unacceptable behavior is, whether it's flaming on bulletin boards, using excessive foul or suggestive language, sabotaging any of your community features, and so forth.

In Figure 7.9, you can see Yahoo!'s guidelines for terminating membership. You can find these online at **http://docs.yahoo.com/info/terms/**.

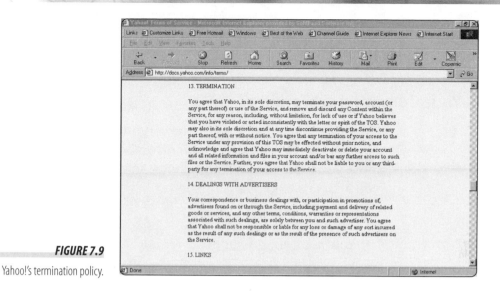

**FIGURE 7.9**

Yahoo!'s termination policy.

## Protect the Privacy of Your Members

Above all, you need to protect the privacy of your members and take security issues very seriously. Let your members know how you're protecting their privacy, and frequently monitor the system to make sure it has remained secure.

Figure 7.10 shows a portion of Yahoo!'s privacy policy.

For detailed information about Web site security, see Part VI.

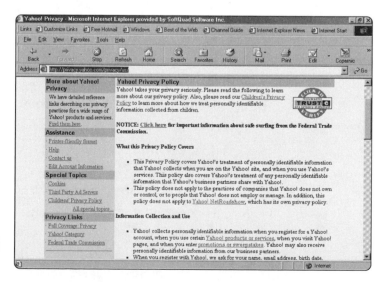

**FIGURE 7.10**

Yahoo!'s privacy policy.

**TIP**    For an excellent article on building electronic communities, visit **http://www.totalnetval.com/ 7-steps.htm**.

## Is Your Community Working?

How can you tell whether your community is successful? How can you tell whether it needs to be revamped? What can you do to promote your community and to boost interest? These lists should give you a means to gauge your success.

Your community is a success if:

- You're meeting your goals for adding new members.
- Your traffic is increasing in community areas.
- Your link popularity is increasing.
- The number of new interest groups or forums is greater than the number that is fading out.
- Twenty percent of your new members are coming from referrals from existing members.
- Members are participating in the various areas of your community.
- Attendance in your chat rooms or special chat sessions is increasing.
- Your customer support area is benefiting from the problem-solving capabilities of the online forums or chat rooms.

Your community needs a shot in the arm if:

- Your forum message threads are only five to six messages deep.
- You're not attracting your goal for new members.
- Your traffic is stagnant in your community areas.
- You're getting few referrals from existing members.
- Certain areas aren't getting used. Do you need to remove or revamp those areas?
- Your moderators aren't participating. Get new moderators!
- Members complain that your community features are difficult to use or confusing. Get someone from outside your community to test the features, and adapt the simplest user interface possible.
- Your special-interest chat sessions constantly have few attendees.

## Promoting Your Community

Once your community is up and running, or even pieces of it being functional, how can you get members?

***Find It* ONLINE** Announce your community features regularly on your Web site, newsletter, e-mail discussion list, etc. Set up specific chat sessions by experts in the industry or even your high-level executives. Advertise those events at Yahoo! Events (**http://www.broadcast.com/**).

Offer sales or discounts for new members who join. Announce your community in newsgroups, lists, and industry-specific Web sites. More information about how to promote your community, newsletter, and e-mail list are mentioned throughout this book.

**TIP** For an article offering online moderator guidelines and community building tips, visit **http:// www.well.com/confteam/hosting.html**.

Use the following tips to spread the word about your community:

- Visiting Liszt.com and searching for keywords related to your business. Join those lists and advertise your community. See Chapter 3 for a listing of other places to advertise your community.

**TIP** Where can you find lists and e-zines to post to? Go to Listz.com and search for keywords that are relevant to your community. Join those lists, and then promote your community in them. Visit
***Find It* ONLINE** **http://www.liszt.com** to find lists in your related area. Chapter 3, "Offering Free or Discounted Items or Information," also provides a listing of places where you can promote your community.

- Submitting your community's URL to the major search engines and directories as well as topic-specific engines and directories.
- Contacting related Web sites and informing them about your community.
- Using a recommend script, as mentioned in Chapter 4, which will allow your members to recommend the community to business associates and friends.
- Advertising your community in all of your print media. Offer discounts on goods or services to new members.
- Scheduling expert chat sessions and promoting them heavily.

- Informing your newsletter subscribers, e-mail list, customers, employees, and clients.
- Promoting your community on your own Web site and on each of your domains.
- Mentioning the community in all autoresponders and standard reply e-mail.
- Adding the URL to your community on your signature line.
- Visiting related newsgroups and inviting users to your community.

## Step-by-Step Analysis of Your Community

Answer these questions when analyzing your online community, and then consider what areas of your community might need improving:

- What online community features are you using? What features are you considering implementing in the future?
- Are you listening to feedback from members and considering additional features of interest to those members?
- Are search and archive capabilities available throughout all areas of your community?
- Do each of your areas have moderators dedicated to making sure that your community succeeds?
- Is your online community secure, and have you taken steps to make sure your members' privacy can't be compromised?
- Are you retrieving valuable e-mail addresses to be used in future advertising efforts?
- Are you using recommend scripts to make it easy for members to recommend the community to acquaintances?
- Are you using your community to make important announcements about product sales and proposed new products or services?
- How effective are your moderators in handling some of the technical or customer support problems?
- Do you make sure that new content is added to your community on a regular basis, such as new articles, questions and answers, and so forth?

- Have you considered adding a vertical search engine or a topic-specific directory?
- Have you posted a calendar, and do you keep it updated with upcoming events?
- Have you created comprehensive usage guidelines for your members as well as guidelines that call for the removal of a member?
- Review the section in this chapter called "Is Your Community Working?" How does your community measure up?
- Let people from outside your community test the interface. What was their reaction?
- Have you promoted your community on your site, in newsgroups, on lists, in your newsletter, in search engines and directories, and in print media?

## Conclusion

Online communities offer many advantages to a company's online presence. They can help boost your name recognition and credibility, keep visitors at your site, build link and click-through popularity, and create a sense of community and camaraderie with members.

With careful planning and implementation, your online community can almost operate itself, yet it can be an enormous traffic generator for most Web sites.

# GETTING TO KNOW YOUR CUSTOMER

**In This Chapter**

Data Mining—What Is It?

How to Mine Data

Translating Raw Data into Patterns

Respecting Privacy Issues

Gathering Your Data-Mining Tools

When considering the amount of data available to the general public nowadays, it helps to know that there are methods for extracting the data you need. Data mining is a necessary means of finding information about your customers in order to better serve them. However, data mining can also raise difficult privacy issues that you should consider before choosing to find everything you can about your customers and their habits. This chapter discusses the valuable resources available from the data generated by your site's visitors, the techniques you can use to gather and interpret such facts, and the inherent privacy issues involved.

## Data Mining—What Is It?

*Data mining* refers to software that scans data to find patterns related to customers. Data mining actually involves more than software, however. It's a new mindset developed from the world of e-commerce.

Consider the data in the world. Think of all information as a big database. In database systems, engineers attempt to normalize the database and its information so that the system is as efficient and sleek as possible, with no redundancies and no data errors, and with clearly defined relationships. If you were to order all information in this manner, you would be able to see the relationships clearly and identify your customers with no problems whatsoever.

In addition, the current definition of data mining implies unsolicited e-mail. If you know that your customers are out in the world somewhere, waiting to be identified, then you must be able to contact them somehow. The most common method of contact is by e-mail. You should be careful to avoid spamming, however. You can avoid resorting to spam in two ways.

First, identify your customers and their patterns in order to learn better ways to market your Web site. You know that your customers surf certain areas of the Web, so advertise there. You know your customers look for certain information, so tailor your site to be in the direct line of fire when they go to look for that information. In this way, you won't need to resort to e-mail, since your Web site does the advertising instead.

Second, redefine data mining so that you, as a business, are the active group, in opposition to the current passive idea of watching for patterns to emerge. Instead, hunt down patterns *within your current customer base.* After you identify those patterns, mold your sites to better fit the needs of the customers and to fit the expectations of those who have not yet found your site.

With the new face of data mining emerging, you will rely on word of mouth, proper advertising of your site, and relationship commerce (which we discuss in Chapter 15, "Implementing Relationship Commerce") to draw in new customers. You should do everything in your power to expand your capabilities in order to keep your current customers completely satisfied.

In this chapter, you will look at mining data from your current customer base in detail, and you will learn about software tools that allow for external data mining.

## How to Mine Data

The data-mining industry is huge. It incorporates data from every available source to find patterns not only in business, but also in technology, weather forecasting, pharmaceuticals, etc. Using pattern analysis, you can discover new combinations and trends that help to reshape and improve our lives.

In e-business, data mining is exceedingly useful to help discover the needs of your current customers and to expand your services and products to appeal to potential customers. In this section, we discuss the methods and means of acquiring and mining data from your visitors.

### Identifying Reach

What is *reach?* When you analyze the number of unique visitors to your site and what tasks they are using your site to complete, you identify the reach of your site.

Why is reach important? If you analyze your server logs, you may find that your site has had 10,000 *hits* in the last three weeks. Hits are not isolated to one single page, however. In fact, a hit is only the number of *files* accessed from your site. So if a single page on your site has four images of widgets in all their splendor, your server will calculate five hits—one for the page and four for the images on that page. From there, how do you determine whether 1,000 people accessed 10 files on your site or 5,000 people accessed two files each? By determining the number of unique visitors, you go a long way in learning how many people are actually using your site and how many pages they are viewing. You can find this information in your session logs (see Chapter 30).

When you can identify your actual hits and the number of pages on your site that people like to access, you can add to and modify your site to improve their experiences. When your site caters to the needs of your visitors, the number of unique visitors is likely to increase, and the number of pages your visitors hit will increase.

## Using Polls and Forums

Polls have two purposes in e-commerce. First, they establish consumer opinions on certain topics, helping you to isolate your market better and to provide more fodder in your data mining. Second, polls provide a bit of interactive fun for your site's users. Figure 8.1 shows an example of a Web poll.

Although you may have targeted your audience well, are you certain you haven't picked up stragglers who wouldn't normally frequent your

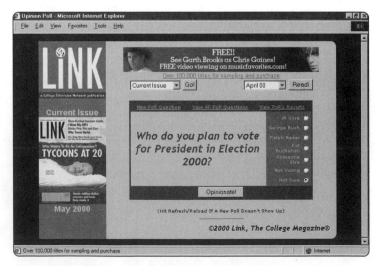

**FIGURE 8.1**

A Web poll at Link.com allows users to voice their opinions, find out others' opinions, and give the site designers a good idea of who frequents their pages.

site except for an odd tidbit that drew them there? Perhaps if you're more aware of who those stragglers are, and what content they found on your site, you can build onto your site to interest people like them. If you tailor your site to respond to these needs, you increase your site's reach by appealing to a broader group than you may have intended.

Meanwhile, there's nothing like a good controversy to bring people running. If your polls ask for opinions, controversy is bound to follow. By giving your audience the opportunity to voice its opinions (and then back up those opinions in a forum on your site), you achieve two goals in extending your site's reach. First, you draw people into revealing information about their beliefs (anonymously, unless you specify otherwise in your privacy policy) to help you build your site to fit their needs. Second, you entice a few of those in your audience to head over to the forum to discuss their opinions—and the controversy—they have expressed on your site.

Forums extend the reach that polls institute. Ideally, the forums will have discussion threads for your site's visitors to find topics of interest easily and to dive into discussion and debate with little effort. These forums will also remain on your site, providing you with hours of fun and a great deal of data to mine.

 **TIP**   Don't forget what a gold mine of data your communities contain. If you scan information in chat areas or threaded discussions, you can find a great deal of data you can use to improve the content and even layout of your site for its visitors.

## Creating Cookies

Although we discuss the ethical issues associated with using cookies in Chapter 10, "Incorporating Internet Ethics," we should point out here that cookies are a valuable way of tracking the clickstreams of your users. Because cookies are hotly debated for their lack of security and privacy, if you choose to use cookies, do so with care, and document as much as you can in your privacy policy about how cookies are used and what you'll do with the information you gather from them.

 **NOTE**   Remember that *clickstream* refers to the bread crumbs visitors leave behind as they surf the Web, and that these crumbs are bits of data in the form of site logs, session logs, history, etc.

Cookies are text files that a Web page sends to users' systems for storage and retrieval. Each time Sally Surfer hits up YeOldeWidgetShoppe.com, the site's code checks to see whether she has a cookie set. This cookie allows the site not only to greet her by name, but it gives the site company an opportunity to watch what Sally is up to.

Using cookies makes watching a clickstream easy. Browsers often will not store more than 20 cookies from any one site, however, and they will max out their limit on all cookies at 300. Aside from browser limitations, storing an excessive number of cookies is considered bad form. Use a cookie to establish that a session has begun, and only have it store as much information as your site's code needs to maintain that session.

On each page, for example, you can grab the cookie you've established for your site. Say the cookie stores the time of the last page change, plus some unique ID of that user. Compare the current time to the time on the cookie, store this information in the database, and then replace the cookie's time with the current time. This allows you to determine the length of the visitor's stay on each page of your site.

In addition, if you don't set an expiration date on the cookie, it will destruct when the browser closes. Again, Web etiquette demands that you use persistent cookies only to make the users' return to your site more convenient (for example, to eliminate the need to log in each time they return to your site). If you use a cookie to track each visit so that you can identify each time a user visits, you're being an Evil Web Master. Require a login if you choose to track individuals rather than visits. Don't clog up visitors' hard drives with dozens of cookies.

 **NOTE** Remember that a persistent cookie is one that does not expire at the end of the user's session or at some other definite time in the very near future. Persistent cookies may remain on a hard drive throughout several sessions.

## What Does a Cookie Look Like?

If you explore your temporary Internet files, you're likely to find a list of files that look like e-mail addresses, ending with @*somewhere*. If you are able to, you might see the file type, which will begin with the word *Cookie*. By opening these cookie files in any text editor, you can see the contents and just what the site might be tracking. You might not be able to tell what the text means, however, because cookie formats are specified in the code that created them.

Listing 8.1 shows an example of a cookie as it appears in a text editor:

### Listing 8.1
### Viewing a cookie file in a text editor.

```
ID
8852338
www.kerri-leigh.com/
0
2754789664
29367241
3156645832
29367041
*
```

### Creating a Cookie

Cookies are easy to bake. Using a pinch of CGI or other script (such as JavaScript), plus a splash of HTML, you'll have your own site-baked cookie to hand out to anyone whose browser settings allow them to accept it. The following two listings show simple examples of cookie creation using Perl and JavaScript.

Listing 8.2 shows a bit of Perl code to illustrate how to create a Perl cookie. Using the CGI Perl module, you easily can write code that generates a cookie containing the information you want stored there. To hold information the user inputs through a form, simply capture the form input and store it in the -value parameter. If you need to store more than one value, simply create a hash of those values and reference it when you create the cookie.

### Listing 8.2
### A Perl cookie.

```
#!/usr/bin/perl
use CGI;
$query = new CGI;
$cookieinfo{'name'} = $query->param('name');
```

```
$cookieinfo{'email'} = $query->param('email');
$perlcookie = $query->cookie (
    -name=>'My Groovy Cookie',
    -domain=>'yeoldwidgetshoppe.com',
    -expires=>'+2m',                #expire in two months! leave blank to
let It expire on browser close
    -value=>\%cookieinfo      #hold the name and e-mail
);
print $query->header(-cookie=>$perlcookie);
```

You also can use JavaScript to create your cookies, as Listing 8.3 shows.

### Listing 8.3
### A JavaScript cookie.

```
function jscookie (cookiename, cookievalue) {
  //cookie expires on close of browser
   document.cookie = "cookiename=cookievalue; domain=kerri-
leigh.com;" ;
 }
```

 **TIP**  Now, if you were looking for geeky but somewhat edible cookies, here's a great recipe:

> 2 cups crunchy peanut butter
>
> 2 cups sugar (woo hoo!)
>
> 2 eggs

Mix together. Try not to make a big mess. Preheat the oven to 350 degrees. Forget about the mess you've made. Eat batter raw if you don't mind flirting with salmonella. Otherwise, bake for about 10 minutes, unless your stove has a tendency to cook abnormally. Then just keep a good eye on your cookies. When they no longer look gooey, they're probably done.

## Tracking with Session Logs

Session logs are an interesting breed, defined by the methods you employ to track customers. Basically, a session is set either by hidden fields tracked by CGI code or by a cookie placed on the user's system. Code within the site keeps track of where users go, how long they stay on each page, what ads they may see while meandering through your site, and almost any other tidbit you can dream up.

The session then is defined as the time spent on your site—from the moment a user enters the site (and logs in or signs up) until the visitor leaves.

As the user views content, interacts with the site, etc., the code on your pages places information into the database, so that the information can be mined later.

We discuss session logs in depth in Chapter 30, "Using Referrer and Session".

## Viewing Server Logs

*Server logs* are files generated by your server each time some action is taken through your Web site. If someone requests your index.html page, for example, that request shows up in the server logs, along with the time of access, any errors encountered, and whatever other information you have configured your server to record.

 **NOTE** Don't get confused about server logs and session logs. Server logs are generated by your server according to the configuration your system administrator has used. Session logs are generated by scripts that track users on your site. We discuss these more in Chapter 30.

Obviously, these logs are full of gold and pearls. Using server logs, you can identify the most popular pages on your site, along with the browsers used by visitors to your pages, the IP addresses of your visitors, the errors encountered, etc.

Several popular software tools allow you to examine graphical data pilfered from your server logs. Figure 8.2 shows the results from one such tool.

 **TIP** In addition to the information you can find in your server logs, you should be aware that you can use reverse IP lookup to find the domain names of your users. This can be valuable for determining the geographical regions where your visitors live or even the connection types they use. If your reverse IP lookup returns a domain with a .de extension, for example, you know the user is in Germany. On the other hand, if the lookup returns @Home, you can safely assume the visitor uses a cable modem to get online.

 **FIND IT ONLINE** Visit eAmnesia (**http://eamnesia.com/hostinfo/ipinfo.jhtml**) to find a reverse IP lookup tool.

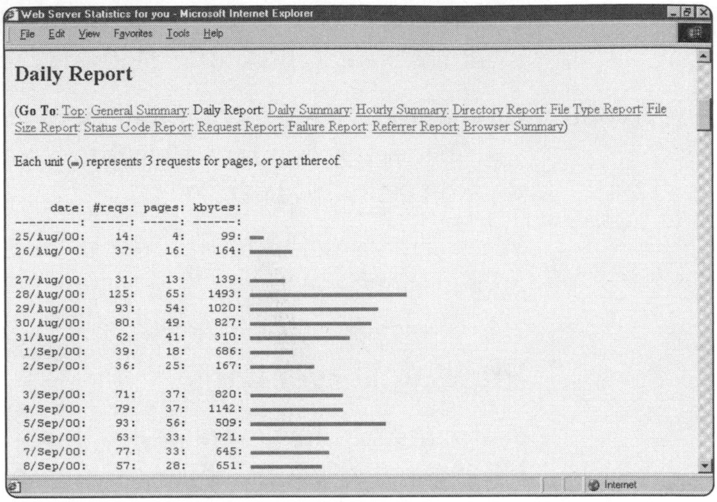

**FIGURE 8.2**

Page products by Analog, a Web server log analyzer

## Using Secondary Clickstream Services

You can hire a secondary source to analyze your server and session logs—in other words, to analyze and report on clickstream metrics. Some of the sites listed in "Gathering Your Data-Mining Tools," later in this chapter, provide tools that analyze clickstream data to add to server logs for data-mining purposes. By using a secondary service, you take the burden of maintaining the code and analyzing the resultant data off your server.

Often the secondary service simply requires a hidden image file placed on your site, and from the hit this generates on the service's server, it can find out who is using your site, when, and what browsers and capabilities your visitors have on their computers. No matter what method of data collection you decide to use, keep in mind the benefits of using a secondary service to help you in your data mining:

- The tools run on the secondary service's servers, reducing the drain of resources on your own system as clickstreams are recorded.

- Data mining takes a huge chunk of time and resources as software digs through clickstream information for patterns. Using a secondary service frees your own servers from the task of spending days plowing through the data.

- Most services format the resulting reports graphically, helping you to better understand the patterns that reveal themselves.

**CAUTION**  On the other hand, using a secondary source can create privacy issues. If you choose to use a secondary service, be sure to mention this in your privacy policy. You should already state that you collect clickstream data so that customers will know exactly what information you track and what you'll do with it. Customers will appreciate knowing that the information won't simply remain on your servers.

Some Web surfers will find the use of a secondary service distasteful, however, because more people are likely to see the results of what could be considered personal information. In addition, some people take offense that this information is transmitted away from your site. Always give your customers and visitors a choice about what information you track and how individualized that information is. See "Respecting Privacy Issues," later in this chapter, for other concerns about using secondary services.

## Translating Raw Data into Patterns

After you have mined data from all sources on your site, how do you determine patterns?

If your site is relatively small, or if your needs are small, you can run simple queries on your databases to determine averages, frequency, and patterns. What constitutes a pattern?

Consider the data in Table 8.1 as output from a query regarding the most recent widget sales at YeOldeWidgetShoppe.com. From this table, you can say with 83 percent confidence that women buy blue widgets. Patterns can be identified when rows have at least two matching columns. In this example, then, you match rows that contain a `Widget_color` of `blue` and a `Customer_gender` of `F`. You calculate the confidence level by dividing the number of resulting rows with blue widgets and female customers, and divide by the number of rows that contain a `Customer_gender` of `F`. There are five rows where women have bought blue widgets. Divide this by the six sales to women, and you can say with a confidence level of 83 percent that women prefer blue widgets.

What if your needs require huge amounts of data processing? Luckily for you, several companies offer software tools to help you analyze your data. In fact, some tools perform both data collection *and* analysis.

**Table 8.1. Finding Patterns in Mined Data**

| Widget_name | Widget_color | Customer_gender |
|---|---|---|
| Widgetizer | Blue | F |
| Widgetizer | Blue | F |
| Atta-Widget | Red | F |
| Atta-Widget | Blue | M |
| Widgetizer | Blue | F |
| Atta-Widget | Red | M |
| Atta-Widget | Blue | F |
| Widget Mobile | Red | M |
| Widget Mobile | Blue | F |

Because of the amount of data available to be processed and the nature of finding patterns, analysis could take hours, days, or even weeks. Be prepared to sink a great deal of time into finding patterns, but rejoice in the knowledge that, once you isolate those patterns, you will be able to create a better site for your customers.

You can find a list of software tools in "Gathering Your Data-Mining Tools," later in this chapter.

## Respecting Privacy Issues

Data mining may be an amazing technology that could potentially provide a variety of useful and pertinent information in almost any sector, but it is also rife with privacy-related dangers. Consider the context of data mining in this book: You are searching for patterns in the data you collect from *customer opinions, customer needs, and clickstreams (customer behaviors).*

Gathering information about your customers often places a heavy burden on your customers' privacy. Do you know if your customers mind that you collect information from their clickstreams? Do they care that you watch which ads they notice, what pages they spend the most time perusing? When you mine data, you take privacy loss one step further. As you search for patterns emerging in customer behavior, you will find generalizations about all of your customers, helping you to better target the needs of your customer base.

Fortunately for the customers whose data contributes to the pattern searching, data mining actually throws another layer of privacy protection onto the existing data. Why? Because the result of data mining is a series of generalizations about all of your customers. For example, most customers who buy widgets are male and in the 25- to 34-year-old age range. The most popular widgets among females are blue. Men between the ages of 18 and 24 are less likely to peruse technical support articles on widgets than how-to newsgroups for widgets. Though an individual's privacy was potentially compromised in gathering the statistics to form these generalizations, the resulting metrics are untraceable to any single person. Of course, this argument does not consider the persistence of the data that led to the generalizations.

Another concern involves the few cases of "hijacked" clickstream information that have become public in the last year, such as the case with ToysRUs.com, reported by Wired.com on August 8, 2000 ("E-Privacy's Foggy Bottom," Chris Oakes, **http://www.wired.com/news/business/0,1367,38041,00.html**). Site visitors were irate, believing that both ToysRUs.com and the secondary service—Coremetrics—had jeopardized privacy and personal security by transmitting clickstream data without the users' knowledge or explicit consent. Although the Coremetrics site declares that the company does nothing more than process the data sent to it by other sites, the issue created a storm of controversy about the relationship between the companies and the privacy issues that relationship created.

Although such outsourcing is common, the moral of the story remains: Communication is a top priority. If you use a secondary service, state this fact explicitly in your privacy policy, and give your customers the opportunity to opt out of participation.

The data-mining issue has both pluses and minuses, but if you treat the information you gather responsibly, you'll have more success in protecting your customers while still expanding your customer base as you learn how to appeal to a wider variety of widget buyers.

We discuss privacy in depth in Chapter 10.

## Gathering Your Data-Mining Tools

Data-mining tools include the metrics-generating tools that capture information from your server logs and database, the tracking software that follows a user's clickstream to record to your database, and the tools that analyze the data for patterns. You can find various data-mining tools at the following sites:

**FIND IT ONLINE**

- Accrue Software, Inc.—**http://www.accrue.com/**
- The Association for Computing Machinery Special Interest Group: Knowledge Discovery and Data Mining (SIGKDD)—**http://www.acm.org/sigs/sigkdd/**
- AZMY—**http://www.azmy.com/**
- Blue Data Miners, Inc.—**http://www.bluedatainc.com/**
- Coremetrics—**http://www.coremetrics.com/**
- Data Distilleries—**http://www.ddi.nl/**
- Data Miner Software Kit—**http://www.data-miner.com/**
- Data Miners—**http://www.data-miners.com/**
- Information Discover, Inc.—**http://www.datamining.com/**
- Intellix—**http://www.intellix.com/**
- KDnuggets—**http://www.kdnuggets.com/**
- MyComputer.com's SuperStats—**http://v2.superstats.com/**
- Web Side Story—**http://www.websidestory.com/**
- Webtrends—**http://www.webtrends.com/**

## Conclusion

Data mining, though deceptively simple, provides a powerful tool for determining your customers' general identity and the patterns behind their needs and activities on your site. Using everything from session logs and server logs to databases and CGI, you can easily record and analyze the data your customers' activities leave behind—their *clickstreams*. This analysis will help you create a better site that gives your customers exactly what they want and need.

A number of companies offer tools to help you collect and analyze the clickstreams on your site, and that number increases constantly as more Web professionals realize the power of data mining.

# THE WEB ENGINEERING PROCESS— TECHNOLOGY TO BUSINESS TO CUSTOMER

# ANALYZING YOUR ENGINEERING PROCESS

**In This Chapter**

Learning from the Software Engineering Institute

Applying Process Improvement to Web Development

Documenting Your Practices

Collecting Metrics

Keeping Your Site Under Source Code Control

Resources

Software engineering is a relatively new industry, and unfortunately, it shows its youth in its lack of process. Whereas other engineering industries have established processes that define their work, the programming field has not. Fortunately, the Software Engineering Institute has established criteria for defining and improving process in this industry. To ensure efficiency and quality in the design and maintenance of a Web site, we strongly recommend you consider these pages as important as the rest of the book—if not more so.

## Learning from the Software Engineering Institute

In 1984, the Department of Defense awarded a contract to Carnegie-Mellon University to develop the Software Engineering Institute. For the past 15 plus years, the SEI has developed software processes to improve the efficiency and reliability of systems that use software.

Why is this so important? Companies that design, develop, and/or maintain software without an instituted process tend to have a very haphazard method of working. Customers don't tend to like working with software that continually crashes, has inconsistencies, or contains an annoying or destructive bug. Yet, customers often do just that when the company that developed the software has no process that allows it to develop standards and to track bugs as they develop and test their software.

This may seem only mildly important until you consider the consequences of an impromptu design method. Consider these examples:

- Your group has been in development for two years on a project that should have taken six months. Unfortunately, because of a lack of process, the developers in your group have not been able to determine the full scope of requirements for which the testers are testing.
- The machine that administers radioactive treatment to cancer patients runs on software that has a few untracked bugs.
- Because of undocumented policies, several customers now are threatening to sue your company for not protecting their personal data from a cracker attack.

These instances may not apply to you, but they definitely give you the scope of what could possibly go wrong unless you spend a little extra time developing and sticking to a process.

## Applying Process Improvement to Web Development

What is process improvement? Obviously, you can assume that it means that a method of operation gradually improves. But what does this entail?

You also might see the idea of process improvement called the Capability Maturity Model. Again, it's easy to see what this might mean, but it may not be as obvious how to improve a process.

In the context of this book, what process(es) do you need to consider? In the field of software engineering, the process involves every aspect of software production, from determining requirements to software release. As for Web sites, you can assume the same process. A site should meet specific requirements in order to fulfil the needs of its customers. By the end of the Web process, you should have a product for those customers—in the form of a Web site.

In this section, we cover the process involved in Web development and how you can use the Capability Maturity Model to make your development process more efficient.

## Documenting Your Practices

To document your own Web development process, you should follow an adaptive process that allows you to move between stages as needed for efficient development. One such process is known as the *Spiral Model*. In this model, you begin by determining requirements for your site and then move through alternating stages of development and testing. When a developer finds a bug or suggests an improvement, the process moves back to developing requirements for the addition or solution.

Using the Spiral Model requires that you develop your site modularly. In other words, develop your site one piece at a time, beginning with the nugget of the site, and adding improvements as you continue. First, set up a group of requirements for an area of your site, develop that

## The Stages of Process Improvement

The SEI describes five levels of performance—called the Capability Maturity Model—for software engineering companies. Today most companies operate at Level 1, whereas very few operate at higher than Level 3, a more mature process level. What does each level signify?

- **Level 1: Initial**—The company uses no process whatsoever. All operations are done by the seat of the pants, and only by the heroic efforts of a chosen few does the company meet a deadline or customer specifications.

- **Level 2: Repeatable**—The Level 2 company has a process it has gleaned from experience, but it has not documented the process. In addition, the process it uses centers mostly on cost and scheduling issues, excluding the actual product.

- **Level 3: Defined**—A process is documented and standardized, and it's used among all areas of the company, not just on a single project.

- **Level 4: Managed**—In addition to a documented process, the company implements metrics collection—tabulating cost, time, success rates, and so on—and uses that information to accurately assess needs and schedules before a project even begins.

- **Level 5: Optimizing**—The company's documented process undergoes constant optimization. Improvements are made to the process according to the needs dictated by the gathered metrics.

area, test that area, reevaluate requirements according to testing performance, and then redevelop. This process continues in a "spiral" until the lifecycle of the Web site has ended (improvements and solutions are no longer required and development has ended—in other words, the site is due to go offline in 20 minutes, never to be seen again).

For a spiral process, shown in Figure 9.1, you should begin with a requirements document. Determine what your site must accomplish and what your project team will need in order to create the site. Next, develop a design document. In this document, you should make detailed decisions regarding your plan for the site and the implementation of your plan. After the site has been tested and before it goes online, create user documentation. This could mean as little as a privacy policy, a security policy, an "About us" area, and a FAQ to answer questions about the site. Or, it could mean an in-depth document that details step-by-step instructions on how to perform different tasks on your site.

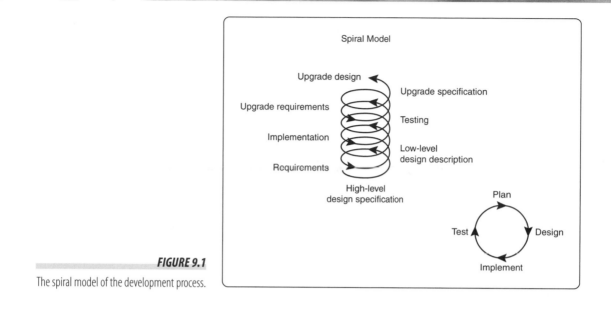

**FIGURE 9.1**

The spiral model of the development process.

In this section, we show you a detailed look at each of these documents and then provide you with some pointers on developing your own checklists.

## Requirements Documentation

Your requirements documentation should cover in detail every need that your site should fulfill. One method of breaking down your requirements is by first breaking down the elements of design you think the site should contain.

How do you determine what the site should contain? First, listen to the boss. What does your boss say the site needs to do? What does Marketing insist the site contain? Then listen to users. Poll them for opinions. If there's another site out there that does what your site will do, ask the users what could be improved. Ask what they'd prefer.

For example, you might list "online community" as a general requirement. What specific requirements does the community need to implement? Should the community be accessible to everyone, or will you require users to access the community through special software downloaded from your site? What will the community contain? Will it be limited to a bulletin board system, or will you include areas for users to have a real-time chat?

Perhaps you have aesthetic or navigation requirements specified by the general needs of your customers. Does the font need to be large for your vision-impaired audience, or do your pages use sound files to "read" content to the user? Are all pages within your company's domain required to follow a specific layout or color scheme?

From here, you should estimate a few metrics. What types of tools will you need to implement these general requirements? What technology must your team know or learn? How much money will these tools, classes, and so on require?

How much detail should you cover at this point? As much as possible. This segment of the process should be dedicated to preparing yourself for this project—to finding all the numbers and estimates you need to complete the project efficiently. When the documentation is complete, it can act as a starting point for additions and changes to the site to ensure consistency, so when your original design team has come and gone, the new team will have no trouble understanding the design and implementation requirements of the site.

## Design Documentation

There are two extremes when deciding the depth of detail you want to cover in your design document. You can choose to do a high-level design document, in which you cover a plan of attack in the development of your site, or you can choose a detail-oriented low-level design. A high-level design document lacks the detail of the implementation and only glosses over the plan your team will take with references to your requirements document. On the other hand, a low-level design document can be tediously long, with so much detail that your eyes glaze just looking at the title page. Your best bet is to choose a middle ground or to create both documents, beginning with the high-level design.

Start with your plan. Draft a list of requirements from your requirements document, or at least use your requirements as a starting point. Decide how you can implement the requirements, but do so in a high-level orientation. For example, assume that one requirement is "easy navigation," and your ultimate goal is a community about the wonderful world of widgets. Begin by listing the areas of the community and how you can set up links among those areas. Create a diagram to illustrate these areas and links.

Once you have an idea of the general plan, consider creating a secondary document that gives details about the design of the site. Even if you choose not to create another document, go through your high-level design and bring it down a few notches. In other words, include some detail about the plan implementation so that each developer knows exactly what colors, fonts, sizes, and layouts to use for each page element.

## User Documentation

User documentation is exactly what it sounds like—documentation meant to help your visitors use your site. In terms of the Web, user documentation refers to *Frequently Asked Questions* (FAQs), policies, and instructional areas.

 As any Web surfer probably knows, Web sites use a FAQ to provide visitors with a question-and-answer session with—you guessed it—frequently asked questions. What types of questions might you cover? Try posing questions regarding how to perform specific tasks at your site. Ask where to find important information. Ask how to contact your company. Ask any questions brought up during the testing phase of your site. In this section, we discuss what to include in each type of document. The list we use to analyze your documentation can be a starting point for your FAQ.

**TIP**  Consider including more than one FAQ on your site. Users have questions about a variety of issues, from navigating your Web site to product information, and the FAQ format is straightforward and rather popular.

What about policies? What types should you include? This depends on the purpose of your site, but the most popular nowadays include privacy, security, refunds, and delivery policies. A privacy policy should detail what types of personal information you gather from visitors to your site and how you intend to use it. You also might address the protection of information you've gathered—who else will see that information and how those third parties might use it.

**NOTE** The security policy you write should contain more information than you will publish to the public. You don't want every Joe Cracker knowing just how you will respond if he attempts to crack your site. On the other hand, you do want to reassure your customers that you guarantee you will do whatever you can to protect your site and their information. Your security policy also can serve as a warning to anyone interested that you will prosecute and that you will not ignore any malicious attacks against your site.

The refund and delivery policies are just two of a potential slew of documents related to your customer service. As we discussed in Chapter 1, "Analyzing Web Pages for Maximum Effectiveness," you also might consider a copyright policy to protect yourself or your customers from copyright infringement. Again, decide what is pertinent to your company's needs when drafting policies for users.

## Creating Your Process Checklists

The following lists will help you determine what you need to include in your documentation.

### Requirements Documentation

Your requirements document should give enough detail regarding your plan that you will be able to go directly from this document to the design document. You should address the following issues in your requirements document:

- Define terminology that may not be interpreted the same by everyone on the project. For example, define the term "community." What is involved in this community?
- Define parameters. For example, define bandwidth or optimal download times.
- Define how the customers are to use the site. What should they be able to do at your site?
- Define the depth of the logical structure of the site. For example, how many pages "deep" should customers have to travel to reach their destination in the site from the main page?

- How many areas does your site use? Will you vary the appearance of these areas to distinguish them? Consider any portal site, such as Yahoo!, for example. There are different areas for mail, auctions, and maps.

- What software will you need to create these sites? What software do you require to create or maintain graphics? Do you need a version control tool?

- What factors will affect your choice in layout and structure of the site and its pages?

## Design Documentation

The design document, no matter how specific you choose to be, should cover enough detail to allow you to begin implementation immediately. It should include the following items:

- What is the ultimate goal of the Web site (recap the conclusion of the requirements documentation)?

- What areas of the Web site should be defined? For example, will you have a Community Service area? A Products area? A Research area? Technical support? Define the contents of these areas.

- What aesthetic or design elements will you use to tie together the areas of your site?

- What color scheme will you use?

- What policy do you have for graphics? Text? Aesthetics of the page?

- What layout will you use?

- How will you divide the information? In other words, what logical structure will you use for the site?

- What physical structure will you use for the files of your site?

- What technology will you use?

- How will you interlink your pages?

- How will users access the areas of your site? Will they need special instructions or software?

- How will your design facilitate maintenance?

## User Documentation

Because there are so many different types of user documentation for you to include, we will cover all possible inclusions as generically as possible. Unless otherwise stated, you can assume that the list item would apply to any of the document types.

- How do users access the site?
- Do users need any special tools, software, hardware, etc. to access your site?
- Where can users find information about (*fill in the blank*)?
- Go through different tasks your users will want to perform, and list how to do them.
- How can users contact the company for tech support? Customer service? Sales? Suggestions?

# Collecting Metrics

As you test and implement your site, you should be collecting metrics to determine the usefulness of what you have done and to accurately determine the time, money, and success of future evolutions of your site's design. Even if your site is already developed, implemented, and drawing in visitors by the thousands, it isn't too late to implement metrics collections.

Where should you begin?

Start by determining which metrics will be useful to future testing or implementation. Do you care how many unique visitors come to your site? How many use a particular page? How often?

In addition to studying the results of your efforts on each page or on the site in general, you should gauge the amount of resources you spend on each phase of the development process. How much time did it take to create the prototype pages? How much money did it cost to implement the testing? How many bugs were discovered during and after the testing phase?

As you make improvements to your site, you'll move through the requirements phase, development, and more testing. Log the amount of time the improvement spends in each phase. Determine the number of resources required to move through the improvement. Determine whether the improvement changed the efficiency, aesthetics, navigability, and so on of your site.

These numbers will help you accurately estimate the resources you will need during future design implementations.

Your Web server logs contain a great deal of useful information, including the *Internet Protocol* (*IP*) address of visitors, errors that occurred during visits, types of files requested, and so on. If you need more specific information, though, other methods of collection are available. You might query visitors yourself by requiring a log-in. By using sessions and creating session logs, you can determine the amount of time spent on the site, the time spent on which pages, and what users found most useful. We discuss session logs in more detail in Chapter 4, "Setting up Polls, Contests, and Other Traffic-Generating Avenues," and Chapter 8, "Getting to Know Your Customer."

By logging metrics, you will be able to measure the amount of money, time, people-hours, and other resources future design implementations will require, and that future analysis will help you determine the importance of such implementations. By keeping and using metrics in your site analysis, you will improve your Web process.

## Keeping Your Site Under Source Code Control

Aside from documentation, source code control is the most necessary element of process improvement. Although it may seem peripheral to the idea of process, source control is essential to any project or group to ensure a mature process. Why? Let's explore what this concept is before we discuss its importance.

### What Is Source Code Control?

To start, we'll consider the topic of source code control in the context of Web design. If you have more than one designer working on your site, you may have divided the team to work on different sections of the site.

Say your company sells widgets. You might have one programmer designing the pages advertising your widgets and all the news about the company's latest certification successes. Two programmers are designing the database interface, where your customers, who build gizmos that provide the interface between your widgets and the end user, can order widgets and keep up with the orders. What happens when the two programmers working on the database undo each other's code each time they revise a file?

Uh-oh.

And what happens when all three programmers put the finished product together, only to realize that nothing integrates?

Double whammy.

Source code control prevents these nightmares from occurring. Using source control, you can not only keep two developers from undoing each other's code, but you can also save the most recent working version of the code in a safe place while you make changes. If those changes don't work at all, you can recall the saved version. You can even recall eight versions ago, if necessary.

So how does this affect process improvement?

Source code control tools can help you improve your process in several ways. First, these tools can help you gather metrics. The tools record the number of times a file is edited before it becomes part of a "release" (the final draft, if you will). From the information recorded with each version of the files, you can determine the average amount of time required and the amount of time required to repeat this type of task in the future.

Next, source code control tools help you to keep documentation. Each time you record a new version of a file, the tools request that you describe the changes you made to the file. This encourages documentation, and it can help you determine the process you use in terms of the amount of testing and debugging you will need to perform.

Finally, these tools allow you to keep safe copies of your files, meaning that your development will become more efficient. How so? It's easy to be efficient when you know you can fall back on your most recent version of a file while trying to improve it. And using source code control means you are using configuration management. *Configuration management* is a means of separating the code or version control from the code development. This separation aids in process improvement by forcing a process to enter where one may not have existed before. Because configuration management oversees the integration of the code (or in this case, the Web site), the documentation of the process, the integration or scheduling of debugging from testing results, and the final packaging of the finished product, it drives a process to occur. How? Configuration management sets up stages of development, and once those stages are clearly defined and documented, you have a working process.

**NOTE** You might hear source code control referred to as "revision control," "version control," "configuration control," "configuration management," or a slew of other similar names.

Now that you know what source code control is and why you should implement it, you should decide on *how* to implement it. What source control program you use depends on the operating system you use for Web development. Let's look at a few options.

## Source Code Control Tools

Several tools are available to help you protect your pages and code as you develop them:

*Find It* **ONLINE**

- **Rational ClearCase**—ClearCase for e-Business is available for Windows and UNIX platforms and supports Apache, Netscape, and Microsoft IIS Web servers. **http://www.rational.com/ products/clearcase/idex.jsp**

- **RCS**—The Revision Control System is available for UNIX by way of the GNU Project, although free versions also are available for Windows platforms. **http://www.gnu.org/software/ rcs/rcs.es.html**

- **CVS**—Concurrent Versions Systems, available on UNIX and Windows platforms. **http://www.cvshome.org**

- **MKS Web Integrity**—**http://www.mks.com/products/wi/**

- **Microsoft Visual SourceSafe**—If you are developing your site with any Microsoft Visual tools, SourceSafe is an option for your source code control. **http://msdn.microsoft.com/ssafe/**

- **Continuus/WebSynergy**—WebSynergy also integrates the Web design process with version control. **http://www.continuus.com**

## Resources

The following resources will help you in your quest for process improvement:

- The Software Engineering Institute at **http://www.sei.cmu.edu**
- Webcrisis.com: "Inability to Maintain" at **http://www.mks.com/press/coverage/wi/crisis.htm.** This excellent article delves into the pitfalls waiting for developers who don't use a configuration management process for their Web development.

## Conclusion

To maintain control of your Web development, you should create and use a process as defined by the Software Engineering Institute. Process implementation can save your development team time and money as you work to design and improve your site. Lack of process often leads to moments (or weekends) of chaos and heart palpitations.

Documentation and configuration management are at the core of the Web process as defined in this chapter. Both should be considered vital to the success of a development team and its process.

# INCORPORATING INTERNET ETHICS

**In This Chapter**

Protecting the Privacy of Facts and Actions

Avoiding Questionable E-Business Tactics

Writing and Displaying Your Privacy Policy

Tips for Preserving Privacy

Consulting Online Resources

Because of the reach of the Web and the capability for information to spread easily worldwide, Internet ethics plays a huge role in any e-commerce endeavor. From false press releases and fake virus alerts to compromised personal data and spam, the Internet provides a forum for a variety of unethical activities.

As a member of the e-commerce community, you have certain responsibilities to customers and potential customers to maintain their online security. Probably the most important issues to consider are privacy, securing personal or sensitive data from prying eyes, and tracking visitors at your site. Only slightly less of an issue is the opt-in versus opt-out controversy.

To ensure the trust of your customers, you should do everything in your power to ascertain that a breach of their privacy is highly unlikely. In this chapter, we discuss areas of vulnerability, ways to protect users, and how to write a privacy policy to assure your customers of their privacy rights within your site. We also provide a list of online resources where you can stay current with ethics issues.

## Protecting the Privacy of Facts and Actions

Privacy is a hot issue today, especially because of the amount of fraud perpetuated from lost privacy. From identity theft to stolen credit card numbers, Internet fraud is increasingly being discussed. The time, energy, and money that victims lose annually make privacy an all-important issue.

The U.S. Federal Trade Commission, in its May 25, 2000, report to the U.S. Senate's Committee on Commerce, Science, and Transportation, stated that of America's 90 million users, 69 percent used the Web to purchase goods or services in the third quarter of 1999. The FTC further stated that as much as 92 percent of these users are concerned about how online companies will use their personal information.

These figures are not at all surprising when we watch or read the news, only to hear of yet another privacy issue. Breaches of privacy happen too often, and many of these breaches receive heavy publicity, especially when they have been perpetuated through or by companies that have ensured privacy to the e-commerce crowd. This section shows you some of these examples and ways to avoid repeating these mistakes.

## Safeguarding Personal Data

In August 2000, TRUSTe, an organization that approves e-commerce sites' privacy policies and standards, received criticism when a security consulting company found cookies on the TRUSTe site that tracked the site's traffic. The privacy policy for TRUSTe listed no such notice for tracking in its privacy policy.

Privacy breaches also have been found on health-related sites. In fact, in August 2000, Kaiser Permanente accidentally sent sensitive personal data to incorrect e-mail addresses, compromising the privacy of its customers. Although the damage was relatively small, several messages did contain personal information related not only to patients' health issues, but also contact information and account numbers.

Kaiser Permanente On-Line is not the only health-related site to fall victim to such accidents or breaches. In February of the same year, the California HealthCare Foundation surveyed 19 sites to determine how well privacy is protected. Only three sites passed muster, with the other 16 violating their own privacy policies with sensitive patient information.

Obviously, these health site cases are extreme in that the private information these online companies made public was particularly sensitive. Unfortunately, these cases are not rare enough, and they do not comprise the entire spectrum of privacy issues. Most Web users, when they consider online privacy issues, may not stop to consider the more common—and more insidious—methods of information collection that could seriously compromise privacy.

Regardless of the amount and sensitivity of private data you store online, the security you use to protect that data should be as tight as possible.

Consider the amount of data you store about your customers. You may have full names, phone numbers, mailing addresses, e-mail addresses, and even credit card numbers. What else have you collected? Perhaps you have a purchase history in your database for every customer. Maybe wish lists, recommendations, employee numbers, family names, and other private information peppers your database.

Now imagine that someone cracked your system and downloaded 100,000 credit card numbers. Imagine that cracker threatened to post those credit card numbers unless you paid a dollar for each number. Then consider what your customers would do if they found out.

*When* they found out. In January 1999, one cracker attempted to extort money after stealing hundreds of thousands of credit card numbers from a large Web music store. Although this incident is rather extreme, it could easily happen again if Web stores don't make security a high priority.

Many Web users refuse to give out personal information—especially credit card numbers—because they don't trust online companies to keep this information secure. Their privacy and financial safety depend on their secrecy, and they'll sacrifice convenience in order to maintain that safety.

In the April 1999 issue of *Communications of the ACM,* Hoffman et al. report that most Web users who have never purchased anything online cite privacy and data security issues as the major reasons for not making an online purchase. In addition, the more skilled Web users become, the more likely they are to place greater emphasis on these particular reasons.

Why are Web shoppers so concerned about privacy and security issues? Perhaps the attention security and privacy breaches receive in the media helps to educate the Web public about the dangers of the Web. These concerns will never go away unless the online community makes more of an effort to secure private and sensitive information from prying eyes.

We discuss security issues in more depth in Chapter 27, "Minimizing Risks to Data Integrity and Confidentiality."

## Employing Ethics in Tracking Visitor Actions

What would you do if a perfect stranger hired a private detective to follow you every time you left your house? This detective would take pictures of you as you leave your home, watch as you drive down the street to pick up your kids from school, and sneak behind you at the grocery to record everything you show even the slightest interest in buying. You might be a wee bit disconcerted. You might even be angry at the sudden loss of privacy.

Many people feel this way about browsing the Web. They don't care to have someone watch their every move, recording tidbits of interest from their clickstream for later consumption by some amorphous group of nefarious marketing professionals. You don't have to be a Luddite to share this opinion. Privacy has become a luxury on the Web as we lose private information to the public, piece by piece.

Privacy online for many has more to do with information that someone could glean from tracking our travels through the Web, spying on e-mail, watching purchases we make, or even gathering information from forms that we input at Web sites. You may scoff at the likelihood of any outrageous instances occurring, but you have only to read the newspaper to learn that these practices have been perpetuated and are still in use by government, crackers, and e-business.

**NOTE**   The thought of tracking techniques acting as snooping detectives may sound like the plot of a particularly heinous B movie full of conspiracies and paranoia. However, these privacy concerns are so real that privacy advocates, companies that specialize in making Web surfers anonymous, and so-called "infomediaries," which provide your private information on your behalf according to some rating the infomediary has given a site's privacy policy, are becoming commonplace in the Web world.

As a Web professional, you may not understand what the fuss is all about. You see the necessity of tracking individuals through your site to provide a better, more personalized experience for them. You cringe at the thought of static pages that can't greet return customers by name. You'd rather sit through a year of 1985 music videos than consider having no list of recommended reading at Amazon. You understand that you've given up certain private information in order to have convenience and personalized attention that you can't even get at your neighborhood grocery store anymore.

Not everyone would agree with you, however. Some people will go to amazing lengths to remain anonymous online. For them, the entire Web experience allows them to remain unknown and unknowable. They want the capability to research Rogaine without worrying that their Inbox or mailbox will be inundated with hair-replacement ads. They need to know that nobody will ever find out about the three hours they spent reading all the latest news at the soap opera sites.

Even if your company's site has no interest in spying on its visitors, you should be aware of privacy issues. Why? First, Web surfers have become more privacy savvy, and if your site violates their privacy (even if you don't use the information they think you may have gathered), you'll lose respect and a potential customer. Second, you may outsource some task to a secondary company that has access to this confidential information. (We discuss this topic in more detail in Chapter 8, "Getting to Know Your Customer.") You will take the blame if that secondary company misuses the information, and you will receive backlash if the access becomes public knowledge. Finally, you may choose to use the information you've gathered from your site's visitors, and at this point, it becomes a definite privacy issue.

As a Web professional, you owe it to your privacy-seeking customers to honor their wishes. At the very least, you should keep their identities, or any identity marker, separate from their activities. If you need to track moves for the sake of session events (such as ads geared toward their interests during that session), do not record the information for later use. Keep the information temporary, and destroy it when the users leave your site or close their browsers. Ideally, you would offer anonymous browsing of your site to those who want to keep their movements confidential, while those who want the personalization and efficiency can log in to the system and approve the recording of their movements.

Whatever the needs of your site and the majority of your customers, always keep in mind the ethics of tracking your site's visitors. Some may consider the act as invasive as having a private detective peep into their shopping carts as they maneuver the local grocery store.

## Avoiding Questionable E-business Tactics

As in the brick-and-mortar business world, you have many choices when it comes to the tools you use to build your business. Technology can do some pretty amazing things, many of which are completely invisible to your Web site's visitors. But just because the technology is available doesn't mean you should use it to further your e-business cause. This section lists some of the gray areas when a questionable technique might bring you immediate satisfaction as a business owner, but could cause you to lose long-term customer recognition or result in you being ostracized from certain online powers.

## Clarifying Opt-in versus Opt-out Confusion

What are opt-in and opt-out? Simply put, they give visitors a choice between two options—inclusion or exclusion—regarding some service you provide. Let's look at an example. In Figure 10.1, you can see a series of check boxes that allow visitors to choose whether they want to receive the stated information.

Consider the section of the form that reads, "Would you like to receive our free newsletters??? You know you do." Generally the following list of newsletters would be considered *opt-in*, because you're choosing to be included in the mailing list for those newsletters. However, the author of the form has been courteous enough to fill out the form for us. Because we now have to uncheck the checked responses we don't want, we're actually opting *out*.

In the next section, the form reads, "What do you NOT want to receive?" Adjacent to this question is another list composed of "Nothing," "I'm confused," and "Lifetime supply of free widgets." If none of these were checked, the list would be entirely *opt-out*, because leaving the

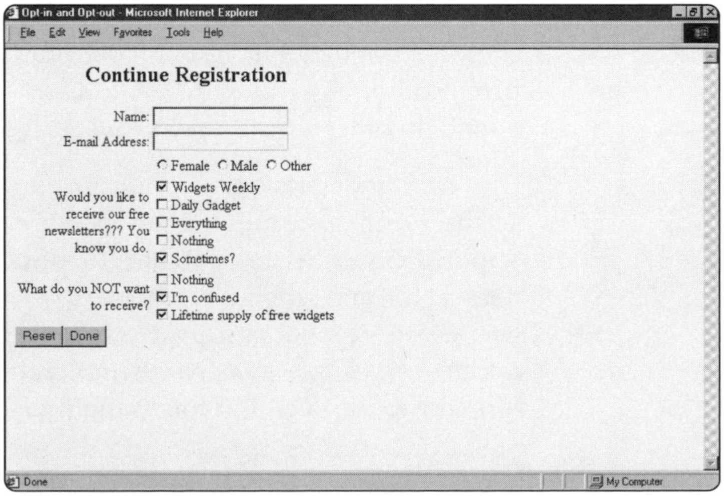

**FIGURE 10.1**

A bewildering example of opt-in and opt-out.

box unchecked means you'll get everything they offer. However, the author checked two boxes for us, so now we're opting in on those two responses ("I'm confused" and "Lifetime supply of free widgets"). In other words, we'd have to physically uncheck those responses in order to receive something in return.

**TIP**    Confused yet? Here's a simple explanation of opt-in vs opt-out:

If the visitor must physically choose not to take part in whatever your site offers, he must opt out.

If the visitor must make an effort to choose to take part in your offerings, he must opt in.

So by leaving this form alone and submitting it as-is, you would receive *Widgets Weekly,* the *Sometimes?* newsletter, and the *Nothing* newsletter. We've inadvertently opted *in* to all of these. However, we can change the responses as we see fit in order to opt in or out of other newsletters. You can see that this gets to be a more than a bit confusing. And confusion is a good tactic if you're trying to trick someone into receiving your free newsletters. This is where the controversy arises.

At the center of the opt-in versus opt-out controversy is the amount of control you choose to place in the hands of your site's visitors. To give customers full control of their destinies where your newsletters are concerned, you would have to give them the freedom to opt in to anything you offer. Some see a forced opt out as taking control away from the visitors to your site. If they misunderstand the wording of your choices, or if they just have an off moment when they don't even notice the choices at all, they'll find themselves receiving "unsolicited" e-mail. In other words, they've just lost some control over their Inbox.

Don't misunderstand us—by no means should you automatically subscribe your customers to newsletters when they were given no opportunity either to opt-in or to opt-out. Some choice is better than none at all, and when they choose to give their e-mail address to your site, visitors probably expect to find themselves opting out of several opportunities. Always give them that opportunity—allow your visitors to choose, even if it forces them to act in order to be left alone.

## Cornering Web Bugs

A very controversial method of Web visitor tracking is known as the *Web bug*. Essentially, a Web bug is a bug in the form of a GIF file that sends information about a user's visit to the page hosting the Web bug. Most often, these GIF files are clear GIFs—transparent and invisible except in the HTML source.

**NOTE**   We discuss the use of clear GIFs as a part of search engine positioning in Chapter 18, but don't be confused. Those clear GIFs do not transfer unwanted and private information—they are only for the benefit of the search engine spider.

Web bugs may or may not be legal, but most of the time, it is safe to say they are implemented unethically. When visitors hit a Web page, they cannot see a clear GIF Web bug. It is completely transparent. They have no idea that it has just transferred information about their visit. In addition, most Web sites fail to include information in their privacy policies regarding their Web bugs.

How do Web bugs work? Consider this piece of HTML source:

```
<IMG HEIGHT=1 WIDTH=1 BORDER=0 SRC="http://www.some-ad-company.com/
[ic:ccc]WebBugs/
bugme.pl?where=mycompany&page=buggy.html&time=10:01:53">
```

Here you can see that the supposed clear GIF is actually a Perl script that returns a 1x1 pixel GIF image. In the meantime, this call to the Web bug image has just transferred the company name, the particular page accessed, and the time of access. This Perl script also can access any other information your browser carries about the Web in its environmental variables.

Web bugs add to their own controversy by being able to communicate with any cookies the advertising company has been able to set on the user's browser. Remember that Perl can easily query the browser for specific cookies.

What do you need to know in order to protect your visitors' privacy?

First, if you choose to use Web bugs, do so ethically. Document their existence extensively in your privacy policy. Don't allow a third party to find out about your sneaky Web bugs and publish their existence throughout the online community; this only tarnishes your site's reputation and could affect traffic.

Second, give your visitors a choice about whether they want to be tracked, and as you dynamically generate your pages, leave out the Web bugs for those customers who want to surf your site anonymously. Your visitors will appreciate having a choice, and for those who don't care what you know about their visit, or who can appreciate the importance of certain tracking methods, you'll know that you have retrieved their information ethically.

Finally, don't use clear GIFs as Web bugs. Use a larger, more obvious image that tells your visitors that the bug is there. If the image is garish, however, and a clear GIF would work better, use a text warning to let your visitors know that the transparent Web bug exists.

By keeping your visitors' privacy and interests at the fore, you're sure to maintain their trust.

## Handling Cookies with Care

Simultaneously one of the most revered and reviled technologies to be incorporated into the Hypertext Transfer Protocol, cookies have a varied and pronounced reputation. In Chapter 8, we discuss how to create and view cookies and why you might use them.

For example, because HTTP does not account for creating *state* within a session, cookies can be used to force a session and to update state as users move about a Web site. *State* simply refers to the status of the entity concerned. If a user has entered a login and password, for example, that person moves from one state (before being logged in) to a new state (now logged in to the system).

Cookies also can be used to store information such as preferences, login IDs, and specific information a Web site may need in order to track users' movements or to provide more efficient service to users.

Since becoming known among the general Web public, cookies have been maligned as the harbingers of a world without privacy. In spite of the dangers they do pose to privacy, they can be very useful in making Web users' experiences more enjoyable.

Some of the uses for cookies that might require tighter security or more careful handling follow:

- Logging sessions so Web sites remember what the user has already done and doesn't need to repeat
- Remembering login information
- Remembering user preferences
- Tracking visitors through a site
- Managing affiliate program hits
- Storing shopping cart contents
- Tracking multiple visits

Obviously, cookies have great potential for both good and evil. Unfortunately, they can be misused and abused by sites that have no business even accessing the cookies. For example, if widgets-r-us.com places a few cookies on Surfin' Sara's computer as she navigates through their site, what's to stop YeOldeWidgetShoppe.com from poking through those cookies to find out what Sara's been up to lately?

If you choose to use cookies on your site, keep in mind a few rules of thumb:

- Don't overpopulate your customers' systems with rampant cookies. A little dab'll do ya.
- Don't go down in the history books for having The World's Biggest Cookie. Even chocolate chip cookies can be too big.
- Offer your site's visitors the option of going cookie-less. Don't restrict their movement about your site just because their browsers are set to accept no cookies.
- Unless the information is extremely paltry (for example, a login ID for your site and absolutely nothing more), don't keep cookies persistent. Set them to expire when the browsers close.
- When in doubt, use your own server to store information rather than relying completely on the user's system to maintain the information. If your site shoulders the burden of holding and maintaining the information, your customers will appreciate you more.

## Confounding the Evils of Spam

Many people complain when they receive junk mail—flyers, ads, circulars—in their mailboxes. Even more become hostile when telemarketers call at all hours to entice people to try some service or product. So it's no surprise that many also find *spam,* or unsolicited e-mail, distasteful.

This issue becomes even more hotly debated when we consider the waste of resources.

When Grady's Grocery sends out weekly ads highlighting specials on their delicious sandwich meats, they use their own time and money to create the ads. They pay for the postal rates, so these ads are delivered straight to your mailbox. Sure, it wastes two seconds of your time to leaf through your mail and, if you're not interested in the delish deli meats, another two seconds to toss the ad. Big loss.

The argument against spam centers on the lost resources the mailer imposes on the recipient. How is this? When the mailer composes her e-mail to the unfortunate 2,000 people on the mailing list she paid only $49.99 to receive, she uses her own time and resources. But this bulk mail takes a (slight) toll on the servers used to route the messages to their new homes, and it uses the recipients' memory and processing resources.

The wasted resources are admittedly slight for the recipients, but opponents of spam argue that those small amounts add up over time, and these bulk e-mails often cause undue burden to ISPs who must host the spam. In addition, spam e-mails become more sophisticated every day, using images and Java applets to spice up the pages. Again, this could become a hefty burden for ISPs, and it poses a potential security risk to anyone who opens the e-mail. The content of spam messages has also become a central point of contention, because many spammers use language or content that some find offensive.

Spammers have a reputation for faking e-mail headers or using unauthorized servers to relay their messages. They also may create temporary—free—e-mail addresses to use for spamming purposes, after which they shut down the account. The cost to them is minimal, and they receive recognition.

There are several arguments in favor of spam, including the right to free speech and an argument that the lost resources aren't as bad as the ISPs make them out to be. Besides, the ISPs are paid by customers (the recipients of the spam) to house any e-mail they receive, right? Many ISPs are cracking down on spammers, and more recipients of spam are contacting ISPs to seek action.

In lieu of sacrificing your reputation and your business, set up a mailing list so that interested parties or loyal customers may get the information you would otherwise send to them. If you send e-mail that your site visitors requested, always, always, always include an easy method for them to unsubscribe from your list, and assure them that you would not and do not send unsolicited e-mail.

If possible, allow your e-mail recipients to return to the site where they originally signed up for the e-mail notices from your company so that they may unsubscribe with the knowledge that they did, indeed, subscribe in the first place, and that they may renew the subscription whenever they choose. If you only give them the option of unsubscribing via e-mail (one of many tactics some unscrupulous spammers use to verify that your address was indeed valid and is ready to receive even more spam), you may further isolate your customers.

You may have the opportunity to purchase an opt-in mailing list, which means all the recipients listed have agreed to receive e-mail from whatever source. Make sure that the list isn't "dirty." In other words, be certain that everyone on the list did actually opt in at some point. Buy lists such as these from reputable sources so that you don't end up spamming some of the addresses that the source threw in just to increase the length of that list.

**CAUTION** If you earn a reputation as a spammer, you will find yourself blacklisted on some sites, and you may lose respect from potential customers. Spam is always a bad idea, even if your intentions are legitimate. Remember, if the recipient has not explicitly agreed to receive your e-mail, you are spamming that recipient, whether or not intentionally.

## Writing and Displaying Your Privacy Policy

As news reports of privacy breaches abound, privacy policies and their prominent display on every e-commerce site become necessary.

Web surfers have become savvy, and they actually pay attention to privacy policies. In August 2000, when Amazon e-mailed a notice to its members regarding a change in its privacy policy, the action made the news. The Web was abuzz, but the least visible question among the shouting was, "What's a privacy policy?"

What does a good privacy policy outline? Basically, everything. However, because you don't want your customers to fall asleep while wading through your policy (you want them to get back to purchasing your widgets), keep it as short as possible without sacrificing the content that your customers rely on to make informed decisions about the information they give you.

According to the September 1998 issue of *Communications of the ACM*, the Federal Trade Commission reported that most sites do not disclose a privacy policy for the sake of those who visit those sites, even when they collect personal information from visitors. Has this number improved?

*FIND IT*
**ONLINE**

Thankfully, yes! The FTC's "Privacy Online: Fair Information Practices In the Electronic Marketplace" (**http://www.ftc.gov/os/2000/05/ testimonyprivacy.htm**) announced that almost all online business sites now make a privacy policy available to the public, although only about 20 percent of these sites address the four core areas of privacy online (fair information practices).

The FTC's May 2000 report outlined current standards surrounding privacy policies. In a survey of commercial Web sites, the FTC found that 97 percent of sites collected some form of personal information, while only 88 percent disclosed information regarding their privacy policy.

The FTC report also defined fair information practices for privacy policies, broken into four units: notice, choice, access, and security. How does the FTC define each of these standards?

- **Notice.** This segment of your privacy policy is the most obvious. This standard defines what information you collect, how you collect it, and where that information can end up. How do you use the data you collect? Will a secondary source have access to the data? Will you sell the data?

- **Choice.** How do you give your customers a choice concerning how you use their private information once the commercial transaction has ended? Do you give them the option of opting in or out of having their information sold? Do you allow them to choose who can access their information? Do you give them a choice about how *you* use their information beyond the transaction?

- **Access.** How can customers access the information you have collected about them? This is important for two reasons. First, it gives customers an opportunity to find out just how much information they've leaked to you. Second, it allows customers to delete information they do not want used, and it gives them an opportunity to update or correct information.

- **Security.** Although you should have a separate security policy that details your responsibilities for site and data security, you should take an opportunity to refer customers and site visitors to that policy from within your privacy policy. This guarantees that customers are aware of the lengths you will go to in order to protect their private information.

During its survey, the FTC found that only 20 percent of privacy policies addressed all four units, and only 41 percent of policies addressed a bare minimum with the "notice" and "choice" units.

**NOTE** In order to fall in line with the fair information practices, be sure to address all four units of standards. Not only will you protect your customers from potential privacy risks, you will protect yourself from potential lawsuits surrounding privacy breaches. Remember, however, that you must follow the standards you lay down in your privacy policy, and remind your customers that the policy is subject to change.

## Tips for Preserving Privacy

As you learned throughout this chapter, privacy is a hot issue that should be taken very seriously. It is important enough that avoiding breaches of privacy should be incorporated into both your business practices and your engineering practices. Just as businesses must consider the ethics and legalities of their business practices, and just as engineers must consider the safety issues and ethics of their engineering practices, Web professionals must maintain an awareness of Web-related practices such as privacy and security.

Now that you know the importance of privacy, how can you avoid breaching the privacy of your site's visitors and customers?

- Live, breathe, and die by your privacy policy. If you must engage in some activity that places your customers' privacy at risk, detail this activity in your policy. Keep your policy up to date.

- Don't store extraneous information in an Internet-accessible location. Even though your customers give up convenience, it's better to have them re-enter credit card numbers and other sensitive data each time they want to make a purchase, rather than chance that the information will be stolen by a cracker.

- Encrypt as much as you can.

- Password protect everything possible. Make it very difficult for a third party to obtain login and password information for an account that they should not be able to access.

- Use cookies and session logs only with willing participants.

- Allow visitors to use your site anonymously. If login is required, provide a "guest" login.

- Stay on top of security alerts, and upgrade your system often to maintain the highest possible level of security.

- Allow visitors and customers to view the information you have collected about them. Whether your customers gave you the information or you generated the data from session logs, give them the opportunity to change or delete any information they feel should not be in your database.

## Consulting Online Resources

To give Internet ethics issues the proper treatment as a professional, you should be able to experience those issues as a consumer. For this reason, we have included the following list of resources that relate both to you as Web consumer and as Web professional.

**FIND IT
ONLINE**

- Anonymizer.com (**http://www.anonymizer.com**) provides privacy services to Web surfers, including anonymous Web surfing and anonymous e-mail.

- The Better Business Bureau's On-Line division (**http:// bbbonline.com**) provides services to the Web community to ensure reliability and privacy standards.

- IDzap (**http://www.IDzap.com**) offers anonymous Web access and hosting.
- Use the Internet Fraud Complaint Center (**http://www.ifccfbi.gov**) to report instances of online fraud.
- JunkBusters Corp. (**http://www.junkbusters.com**) is dedicated to eliminating junk mail, spam, telemarketing phone calls, etc.
- Privada (**http://www.privada.com**) provides privacy management solutions.
- PrivacyChoices (**http://www.privacychoices.org/resource.htm**) provides a list of online privacy resources.
- Privacy.net (**http://www.privacy.net**) is an online resource for privacy issues. To see what other sites can see about you, look at **http://privacy.net/anonymizer/**.
- PrivaSeek (**http://privaseek.com**) offers Persona, an infomediary.
- Somebody's Proxy Server (**http://www.somebody.net**) provides privacy and access to the Net.
- TrustE (**http://www.truste.com**) provides privacy services to Web sites, analyzing their privacy policies and keeping them informed of issues that might affect them.
- Zero-Knowledge (**http://www.zeroknowledge.com**) provides privacy solutions to Web businesses.

## Conclusion

Internet ethics is as an integral part of the Web engineering process. Just as an engineer who designs roller coasters must factor in the safety of the riders, a Web professional must determine the ethical issues—namely, privacy—that relate to the project at hand and make decisions regarding those issues and their execution.

In this chapter, you learned the importance of privacy awareness, the securing of sensitive information, and privacy policies. In addition, you looked at ethical concerns regarding spam, tracking users at your Web site, and giving your visitors the power to opt in or opt out of receiving information based on their affiliation with your site.

# PROVING YOUR TRUSTWORTHINESS

**In This Chapter**

The Importance of Trust

Avoiding a Sense of Distrust

Gaining Trust Company Endorsements

Crackers find new ways to sabotage e-business daily. From hijacking sites to defacement, illegal access to stolen information, the dangers are numerous. Lack of trust keeps a large portion of the Internet population from giving out personal information or purchasing products and services online.

As part of the Web engineering process, proving your trustworthiness is the key to generating rapport with customers who visit your site. Using strong engineering practices to build, debug, and deliver your site; and offering privacy to your customers will establish your site as reliable and customer aware. By proving your trust, you round out the Web engineering process and solidify your Web presence.

Several ideas we present in this chapter are considered part of relationship marketing, which we discuss in detail in Chapter 15, "Implementing Relationship Commerce." Relationship marketing, or relationship commerce, is essential to building trust.

In this chapter, we discuss elements of trust, which site elements can create a sense of distrust, how privacy and security policies help add to trust, and how to register with trust companies to verify your presence to the Web world.

## The Importance of Trust

By 2003, says eMarketer 2000 (**http://www.emarketer.com**), an Internet statistics provider, worldwide e-commerce sales are estimated to reach $1.44 trillion. If consumers don't trust your company, they won't give you a piece of that huge e-commerce pie.

What is trust? We can define this term by examining four facets:

- Quality of the product or service
- Authenticity of information
- Identity of the person or business
- Integrity of the person or business

There are numerous ways to gain trust and to help site visitors verify the quality, authenticity, identity, and integrity of your site's foundations; we discuss these methods throughout this chapter. Aside from carving out a piece of the $1.44 trillion in sales by 2003, why should you be so concerned about generating trust from your customers?

Word of mouth is one of the most powerful marketing tools around, but if customers don't trust you, will they speak of you favorably to others? Will they mention you at all? Probably not, and in the end, you lose name recognition as well as reputation.

If elements of your site generate automatic distrust, will visitors ever return to give you a second chance? Maybe, although it's not likely. If your site made an especially bad impression regarding trust levels, chances are good that visitors will remember your site and will remember not to go back, no matter how snazzy the new radio ads are for your site.

Trust is the cornerstone of e-commerce and is imperative to achieve success in this industry. As such, it is just as important as configuration management and privacy issues to the Web engineering process. If you develop, test, and release your site with the engineering process, privacy, and trust in mind, your site will deliver successfully to your target audience, and traffic will flock your site.

## Avoiding a Sense of Distrust

Without even trying, you may be able to inadvertently create a sense of trust among visitors to your site, but by ignoring the issue, you also take a chance at creating distrust. In this section, we discuss the elements of your site that you can analyze for potentially creating distrust. These elements are all related to quality, authenticity, identity, and integrity.

### Displaying Contact Information

When customers have questions your site doesn't answer, they will try to contact you. We've stressed the importance of including contact information on each page, but when considering contact information in terms of generating trust, the level of importance increases.

Suppose that a new visitor happens upon your site when searching an engine for the latest in widget technology. She leafs through page after page until she finds that you plan to release a new wireless widget for small budgets within the month, but you don't mention where she'll be able to buy that new widget. She wants to contact you to ask this question… except she can't find even a phone number on your site.

Will she trust you then? Probably not.

Offer a link to contact information on each page, or at the very least, provide a link on every page of your site to e-mail a company representative.

**TIP**    Along with displaying e-mail, *answer your e-mail*. Don't leave the would-be customer waiting for a response. If she doesn't hear from you, she knows that, although it's more expensive, she can get a wireless widget from a more reputable company. And instead of waiting, she'll head over to that company's trustworthy site.

## Establishing Good Security

Security is one of the biggest trust issues impeding e-commerce today. By not guaranteeing that your system is as secure as you can make it, you discourage potential buyers from offering up sensitive information, such as credit card numbers, phone numbers, and addresses. Customers would rather lose time and convenience to spend money at a brick-and-mortar store than jeopardize their financial and physical well-being by offering up private information for the world to see.

You can immediately lose trust from customers if your site lacks basic security during ordering or whenever they must give up private information in order to proceed at your site. If they don't see the neat little icon in their browser that denotes a secured section of the Web, they may very well leave, never to return.

In addition, you may lose trust if a cracker manages to infiltrate your system and gain access to sensitive information. You must stay abreast of the latest in security issues, especially where your server and the software on your server are concerned. If you plug security holes before a cracker takes advantage of them, you reduce the risk to your customers' information, and you maintain trust.

## Avoiding Spam

Nothing screams unprofessionalism louder than spam. When people receive unsolicited e-mail, they often think first of get-rich-quick schemes and untrustworthy companies that must resort to spam to get any traffic to their sites. Don't fall into this category. Use only e-mail addresses you secure through your site, and be sure that all visitors to your site who gave you their e-mail addresses were able to opt in or opt out of inclusion in your mailing list.

Also remember to include instructions in each *solicited* e-mail you send to let the recipients know how to unsubscribe if they feel they were accidentally subscribed or they no longer want to receive your e-mail. By placing control into the hands of the customer, you add to your own reputation and gain trust.

## Providing Customer Service

A sure way to lose customer trust is to mishandle your customers and then not make amends. Customer service is important in every business, whether brick-and-mortar or e-business. Because of the anonymous nature of the Web, however, customer service for e-businesses is imperative. A sure way to alienate your customers is to throw customer service out the window.

If customers contact your company (and be sure they can contact your customer service department) with a problem or complaint, address the situation immediately, and do what you can to repair the rift this problem has created in the trust level.

**TIP**   If customers are unsure of the quality of your product, you might consider offering samples and guaranteeing refunds if they are ever unhappy with your quality or service.

Most important, stick to your posted policies. If you deviate, you will lose the trust of your customers, and sales will fall.

## Offering Anonymity/Identity

Never, ever be anonymous to your customers, but allow them to be anonymous to you. What do we mean?

Let customers know exactly who you are. Include pictures of employees, if appropriate, on your company information pages. Let the customers see that there are actual people—not scheming thieves—

behind the scenes of your site. Give them a physical address so they know your company isn't a fly-by-night operation. Show them that you are in the public eye and don't mind the spotlight because you have nothing to hide.

Allow your customers to shield their identity from you as much as possible, however. Sure, if you have to deliver a product to their door, you'll need a shipping address. You'll need a name and credit card information if they want to pay by credit card. But do you really need to know their household salary, the number and ages of their children, and what types of junk mail they like to receive? Absolutely not. The information is helpful to you from a marketing standpoint, but it won't make or break your company.

Don't require customers to give any information that isn't absolutely necessary. If the customer is anonymous, you, as a company, are less able to take advantage of them or to compromise their privacy, security, or peace of mind. By default, trust levels increase.

## Using a Professional Site Design

Your visitors expect you to spend the time and money to ensure that all elements of your pages, from content to design, give off an air of professionalism. If your site does not look professional, it may radiate negative signals to your site's visitors. If the site is designed well with a solid page layout, you give the impression that you spent millions and millions on Web design, and visitors then know that you have a stake in the success of the company. You aren't a fly-by-night business without a care in the world for customer service. Figure 11.1 provides an example of a professionally designed Web site.

Specifically, what elements of bad design can scare away customers before you ever get the opportunity to prove yourself? In addition to checking out the tips in this section, review Chapter 1, "Analyzing Web Pages for Maximum Effectiveness," and Chapter 2, "Analyzing Your Site's Structure for Maximum Accessibility," for more information on site design.

### Correcting Typos and Grammar

Typos happen. Grammar checks don't always work, and techno-geeks aren't exactly famous for their ability to spell or write. Nevertheless,

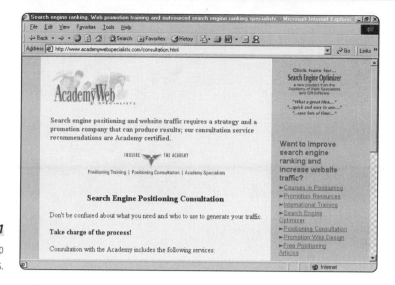

**FIGURE 11.1**

A professionally designed site can help generate trust from users.

you must show visitors that your site wasn't slapped together with a quickie page design program and the content thrown onto the page without a care for its presentation.

Be sure that employees who have knowledge or experience with technical writing or ad copy generate the content on your pages. Have several people proof the text for errors, unclear wording, or poor grammar. Prove to your visitors that your company is able to communicate to the general Web population with professionalism and style.

### Ensuring Ease of Navigation and Usability

If the pages of your site are useless or difficult to navigate, you will lose trust from visitors. Navigation problems and linkrot are signals that the site was not designed thoroughly and is not updated regularly. If the pages are useless, site visitors can easily infer that your company doesn't know what it's doing or wouldn't have enough quality in your services or products to do them any good.

 **TIP**   If you have the ability, remember to create a custom 404 error page so that users don't find themselves staring at a dead link from your site (see Figure 11.2). By giving them a page that links back to your home page, you increase the chance of keeping users on your site in spite of linkrot.

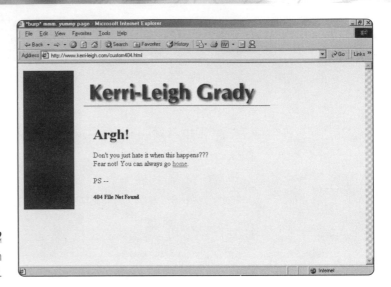

**FIGURE 11.2**

Use a custom 404 error page to avoid an
unprofessional appearance caused by linkrot.

Test your sites with designated testers who have varying levels of
experience and Web knowledge to find dead-end pages such as the
one shown in Figure 11.3. Gather enough information from them
regarding usability and navigation to ensure that your site screams
"We're professionals!"

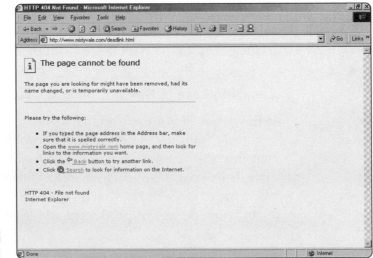

**FIGURE 11.3**

Don't let users encounter a dead link!

## Using Dated Pages

How trustworthy is a page if the information on it is a year old? How much can you trust a site that hasn't been updated since last spring? You can't. You don't know whether the company has fallen apart, is lazy, is a fly-by-night business, or just doesn't care. Regardless of the reasoning behind the lack of updates, you know one thing: That company isn't fit to take your money.

If you give this impression to your customers, you are bound to lose trust. Don't allow this to happen. If your site's content, by nature, doesn't change very often, at least use dynamic dates or be sure to touch up or change elements of the pages. Then include a bit of server side includes to show that your page was recently updated. Do this weekly. Even if your pages don't change in content, visitors to your site can see that you have at least accessed the files for your pages recently, so your company still exists and still actively takes orders.

This bit of HTML will display a last-updated message to your visitors if your server supports server side includes. Be sure to rename your page accordingly, usually with an .shtml extension.

```
<ADDRESS>This page last updated <!--#exec var="LAST_MODIFIED" -->.</
ADDRESS>
```

Also remember to check often for linkrot. This is the biggest signal to your visitors that you haven't updated your pages in a while.

## Providing Testimonials and Endorsements

As we mentioned before, word of mouth is powerful marketing. What better way to ensure word-of-mouth advertising than by offering testimonials to your site's visitors? If you provide good customer service, customers will write to thank you for the positive experience they had dealing with your site. By displaying these testimonials on your site, you let visitors know that others have enjoyed working with your company and that they are likely to have the same experience.

If you don't use testimonials on your site, however, you will not lower the level of trust, so don't despair if you are unable or unwilling to post customer comments on your pages.

**CAUTION**    Remember to ask permission from your customers before posting their comments on your site. If you offer a feedback page, be sure to use a disclaimer that lets the customer know the comments they submit become your company's property.

If you use auctions to generate sales and traffic to your site, be sure to request feedback from winning bidders. Keep your rating high, and when potential bidders check out your auction reputation, that reputation will bleed over into your company's general reputation. Visitors will trust your company if you have had positive feedback from auctions.

In addition, endorsements or certificates of approval from trust companies can help you increase trust levels. Such endorsements are becoming more common, so you may want to seriously consider pursuing such certificates. Before long, customers may assume the worst if your site lacks endorsement. (See "Gaining Trust Company Endorsements," later in this chapter, for more information.)

## Using Technology Wisely

When visitors encounter the latest technology on your site, they may well assume that you have large amounts of money and/or expertise, and trust levels creep up. Be careful that your bells and whistles don't make your visitors' experiences annoying, however. Watch for the following:

- Are the bells and whistles useful, or do they detract from usability of the page/site?
- Will the technology work on its own, or will visitors be required to take extra time to download and install a new plug-in?
- Does the technology impede navigation?
- Is the technology annoying?
- Do you give users the option (or do they even have the capability) to stop the technology or pause it?

Remember to consider the technology from the standpoint of your visitors, and be sure that you aren't using the bells and whistles strictly for the sake of looking cool.

## Forming Sound Partnerships

By teaming up with a company that has established trust online, you receive the honor of trust by association. Imagine that the largest widget company in the world announces that it has begun a partnership with a small widget accessory company. The companies have teamed up to give site visitors an easy way to order both widgets and widget accessories from one place. By partnering with the small, relatively unknown accessory company, the widget seller announces its trust in the accessory company's ability to deliver on its promises and guarantees to its customers.

Just call that insta-trust.

But just as you can gain innocence by association, so can you gain guilt by association. Be sure that *you* trust any partner you join. Review the company's policies and reputation before jumping into a partnership you may later regret.

**TIP**   Remember to monitor the sites of your affiliates to be sure they have followed any rules you set forth for them. You wouldn't want to find yourself associated with a disreputable site or one that would not appeal to (or that might even offend) your customer base.

## Displaying Privacy, Security, and Refund Policies

When customers consider whether to do business through your site, they may be very interested in the posted policies regarding privacy, security, and refunds. If you provide information to them, customers realize your company is open about its dealings and is willing to guarantee certain rights that customers retain.

Posting these policies actually places control back into the hands of the consumer. After all, if you state at your site that you offer a 30-day money-back guarantee for dissatisfied customers, they know you'll stick to it or risk a lawsuit. How does each policy type—privacy, security, and refund—protect the customer and add to trust?

Privacy policies let customers know which pieces of information they provide will be used by your company, and it allows them to discern whether they should provide certain information. If you are frank about who will have access to what sensitive information, and you allow them to modify, add to, or delete certain information, they remain in control, and trust increases.

Security policies let customers know the lengths you will go to in order to protect their information from crackers, as well as any guarantees you offer about the security of your site in general. For example, if your company stores information for the customer, and if some catastrophe, whether physical or cracker, results in the loss of that data, you might guarantee that off-site backups will restore information within a certain time period. Again, when customers know what you'll do to protect their interests, they'll trust your company more.

What if customers have a problem with the quality of the product or service they receive? Do you make guarantees to your customers, giving them control of the situation if they find the delivered goods unacceptable? Or are they stuck with the deficient product and out whatever money they spent receiving the goods? IF you let them know ahead of time what to expect from you by including a refund policy on your site, your trustworthiness will increase.

## Gaining Trust Company Endorsements

Three types of trust companies can help you on your way to proving your company's trustworthiness. They may provide endorsements, testimonials, or certificates for your company's site, depending on their purpose.

- **Customer trust.** These trust companies allow you to generate testimonials and ratings from customers.
- **Privacy trust.** Privacy trust companies actually help you protect your customers' privacy rights.
- **Identity authenticity.** These trust companies help you to verify to your customers that you are who you claim to be.

In this section, you will look at an example of each of these types of trust companies, and you'll learn how to sign up with them. You will examine the following companies:

- BizRate –(customer trust)
- TrustE –(privacy trust)
- VeriSign –(identity authentication)

## BizRate

When Netizens want to buy off the Web, they may not know who's reputable and who isn't. They might be diving into new territory, for example, buying electronics when they'd only bought books until now. How can they check out a site's reputation among other customers? They can skip over to newsgroups and wade through postings and flames, or they can visit a site such as BizRate.com, where customers are given the opportunity to provide feedback about their experiences with a particular company (see Figure 11.4).

**FIND IT ONLINE**

BizRate (**http://merchant.bizrate.com/oa/merchant_services/ index.xpml**) really serves a dual purpose. First, it acts as a convenient and central location for potential buyers to search Web-wide for a particular product. The customer then can research the companies offering the merchandise, their performance rating according to other customers, their policies, and their prices. In essence, this site acts as an online mall, except that it provides valuable information to customers about the reputation of the companies from which they may make purchases.

Second, BizRate gives companies an opportunity to find out more about the customers buying products from them, both after the sale is made and after the product has been delivered. BizRate also offers the capability to quiz customers about why they left a site without purchasing anything.

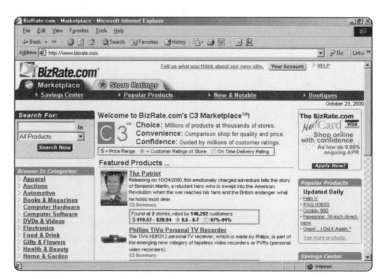

**FIGURE 11.4**

Rating a business at BizRate.com.

**FIND IT ONLINE**

What are the benefits to your company? First, you receive testimonials from people who have had good experiences. Second, if customers believe your operations have room for improvement, they have the opportunity to tell you so—anonymously. It's a win-win situation: You receive good feedback and ratings from satisfied customers, and you learn from suggestions provided by dissatisfied customers. A final benefit comes from the market research you can access from BizRate. Sign up for an account at **http://merchant.bizrate.com/oa/merchandising/apply.xpml**.

Customers have the opportunity to give feedback at BizRate after completing an order—a new window opens, allowing users to enter feedback on an HTML form. BizRate also follows up a few weeks after the transaction to ensure that the customer's opinion hasn't changed and to find out whether the contents of the order arrived on time.

## TRUSTe

As privacy policies gain in popularity, and as the general Web population becomes more aware of the importance of these policies, companies such as TrustE become necessary to the survival of e-commerce sites (see Figure 11.5).

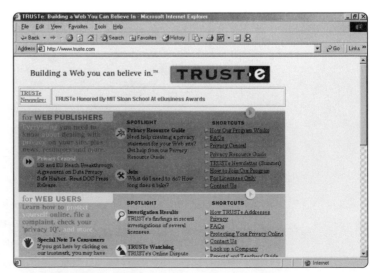

**FIGURE 11.5**

Getting an endorsement from TRUSTe.com helps reassure your customers.

TRUSTe (**http://www.truste.com/webpublishers/pub_join.html**) awards seals of approval, which they term "trustmarks," to sites that agree to what amounts to good customer service in the age of e-commerce. Many sites don't adhere to such standards, however, making organizations like TRUSTe extremely important in the fight to establish trust among customers.

TRUSTe, which requires an annual fee depending on your company's revenue, works with online companies to ensure that a privacy policy contains all the information customers need to know to make an informed decision regarding whether to reveal personal information on that site. This means that the privacy policy must detail who collects what information, how the information will be used, who will have access to the information, how users will be able to change/delete the information the company has, and what security protections are in place to guard against harm to the users. In other words, the privacy policy, which may be different for each situation, must be complete and truthful.

TRUSTe provides special attention and seals for sites targeting children.

In addition to helping companies create detailed and well-defined privacy policies, TRUSTe monitors the sites it licenses to ensure continued compliance to the policy. If customer complaints or an investigation reveals a breach of the stated policy, TRUSTe requires licensed sites to work with customers and TRUSTe to ensure a fair resolution of the problem.

## VeriSign

In 2000, an identity scheme made national news when PayPal, a company that allows individuals to pay each other online either with credit cards or directly through bank accounts, found its identity swiped. Someone had registered the domain **http://www.paypal.com** (using the number one, not the lowercase letter l), copied PayPal's site interface to its domain, and then sent out e-mails requesting PayPal users to log in through a link they provided. When the PayPal customers followed that link, the fake paypal.com site owner swiped the login information those customers provided, giving that person access to several PayPal accounts.

Because of problems such as this, identity authentication is growing in popularity. VeriSign provides this authentication, allowing a site to prove that it really is YeOldeWidgetShoppe.com rather than yeo1dewidgetteshoppe.com (that's the number one, not the letter l). When users visit your site, they can easily determine that they are safe by viewing your certificate, and you can let them know that you're authentic by posting VeriSign's seal on your site. Figure 11.6 shows VeriSign's home page.

VeriSign actually provides a range of services to help build trust among customers. First, it issues digital certificates to sites, individuals, and code developers to verify to customers that you are who you say you are. This is extremely important in light of the variety of schemes and scandals perpetrated online. The services don't stop there, however.

VeriSign also gives customers the capability to use SSL to help protect information in transit from their computer to yours. It insures your site in case of the misuse or abuse of your certificate by someone else. With VeriSign's product, you can accept and process payments securely. Finally, you receive added benefits such as a security analysis of your site.

Digital certificate authentication is very important in the e-commerce world, but other sites might also consider signing up for a certificate.

**FIGURE 11.6**

VeriSign.com offers authentication and other trust-building services.

Individuals, too, can protect their identities in e-mail by using a digital certificate.

**FIND IT ONLINE** To receive a digital certificate from VeriSign, visit **https://www.verisign.com/products/site/index.html** or call 650-429-5112.

## Conclusion

To round out your Web engineering process, you must consider and document all elements of proving your trustworthiness to your customers and site visitors. If your site does not generate trust, you will lose traffic and sales.

In spite of the precarious nature of trust in e-commerce, it is easy to generate enough trust to have the opportunity to prove yourself. And if your company follows through with solid customer service, you will maintain that trust level.

# ANALYZING E-COMMERCE SOLUTIONS

# ANALYZING THE E-COMMERCE PORTIONS OF YOUR SITE

**In This Chapter**

Defining a Well Laid-Out Design

Analyzing the E-commerce Portions of Your Site

How does this chapter differ from Chapters 1 and 2? At the beginning of this book, we discuss ways to make your site *in general* usable, navigable, and efficient. In this chapter, we cover how to analyze the e-commerce portions of your site *specifically* to determine the level of difficulty your users may have in using your site to purchase goods or services.

We start by defining parameters for an efficient e-commerce structure, and then define specific navigational and usability concerns that your site's visitors may come across. We end the chapter by analyzing your site's e-commerce sections according to points we make throughout the beginning of the chapter.

## Defining a Well Laid-Out Design

To secure and build traffic to your e-commerce site, you must provide consistency, ease of use, solid information, and a reason to trust your company's site to the customers. In this section, we define the elements that fulfill these requirements, giving your site the opportunity to create a usable, navigable, and efficient e-commerce area for your customers.

An e-commerce site that attracts and maintains traffic and sales has the following characteristics:

- User control of the browsing and buying processes
- Easy, obvious, consistent, organized, and fast navigation
- Consistent and straightforward page layouts that require minimal scrolling
- Customer service
- Tools to address security concerns

## Giving Control Back to the Users

When customers enter your site, they should immediately be given control of their browsing experience. When they come to buy from your site, they want to get in, buy what they came to buy, and move on to their next task.

If your site does not give control to your customers, allowing them to set the speed and activities they will achieve, they will leave your site.

You should consider the following points when giving this control to your customers:

- **Navigation, navigation, navigation.** If your customers cannot access any information they want within a few clicks of their current location, they will leave.

- **Don't force registration on your customers.** If they only want to browse, they can register their information later, when they're ready to buy. Forcing them to hand over personal information before they're ready to buy can turn some customers away from your site.

- **Offer a search engine on your site specifically for products.** Allow both fast and extended searches, and model these searches after popular search engines so that customers are more likely to recognize and more easily use the search facility. Give as many search options as you can generate to your customers, allowing them to search based on price or keywords in the description, or even by scanning a list from product types. Provide Boolean searches.

- **Give your customers as many options as you can, but don't allow the choices to make their navigation difficult.** Allow them to choose a low-bandwidth version of the site, for example, so that they only see images of products on individual product pages. Or give them the option of surfing your site without accumulating 40 cookies that track what they're doing and what they want to buy.

## Navigating E-commerce Areas

Navigation is important for every area of your site, but e-commerce areas often lack the ease of movement that customers find in other areas of sites. Unfortunately, it's easy to forget navigation as an essential component of e-commerce areas, because they employ more complicated elements, such as database access, Java applets, scripts, etc. Navigation falls by the wayside as usability takes hold as a seemingly more important element of the area. Don't let this happen to your e-commerce area. Navigation is even more important as users browse and search for products and services they want or need. If they get lost or can't find their way to the products, they will leave your site, never to return.

To avoid such a horrible fate, consider the following:

- The product listing for your site must be easy to browse.
- If you offer memberships (free or paid) to customers and want them to register, let them register at their own pace when they've determined they like what they see at your site. Include a link to your "sign up for a new account" page on every page they visit.
- Your site's search engine should not impede navigation. Give your users enough flexibility to search for products, and allow them to return easily to the search after they view product information.
- Keep product listings within three clicks of the home page.
- If new users must register during the ordering or purchasing process, allow them to continue afterward as if they had never been interrupted in their task. Automatically navigate back to the last task the users were performing before they began to register.
- Don't make your customers move through too many screens to get to the information they need.
- Cross-sell your products and advertise your services. On your Web Widget product listing page, include a link to lithium ion batteries to operate your Web Widget, along with links to free software downloads and a Web Widget chat area. Include an affiliate link to a company that creates handy leather covers that just happen to fit your Web Widget.
- Page titles should match the link text used to link to those titles. This helps to avoid navigation confusion, when users think the link has pointed to the wrong page.
- Search regularly for linkrot, especially after your site has been updated or upgraded.
- Make pages that list your products easy to scan. Use header tags for product types and regular- or reduced-size fonts for the

actual products below. If you use drop-down menus or page hierarchies to list products, keep the number of mouse clicks required to reach the product page to an absolute minimum.

- On every page, include a link that allows users to review the contents of their shopping cart.

- Every page should link back to the home page and allow customers to search *from that page* for new keywords.

- If your site offers members-only (paid) access to services, be sure that the services are interconnected and easy to access. Keep the number of clicks between pages to a minimum, and make sure that any information you offer is easy to locate and access.

## Using Effective Page Layout

E-commerce sites should provide a fast and easy way for consumers to access information, products, and services they need. One of the most important means of delivering these characteristics is in page design and layout. Much like the rest of your Web site, the e-commerce areas should follow a few simple rules to provide an effective source for all your customers' e-commerce needs.

- Scrolling is bad. If your pages must scroll, put all the important information above the *fold*—at the top of the page, before scrolling occurs. If you have too much information that absolutely must go on a single page, put links to the important information that sits below the fold at the top so that users can click to go directly to the text below without scrolling.

- Make sure product images are clear, yet small enough to keep the page from scrolling.

- Your "order" or "place in shopping cart" buttons should look like buttons or links. If they don't look like typical buttons or links, users may become confused about how to add to their shopping carts.

- Your "order" or "place in shopping cart" button should be at the top of the screen or next to the product name or image. If your page scrolls in order to include all information related to the product, place a *second* button at the bottom of the page.

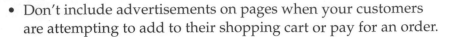

- Don't include advertisements on pages when your customers are attempting to add to their shopping cart or pay for an order.

- Keep your pages consistent in design. Make sure that every page looks exactly like the ones before it so that users don't have to hunt for information.

- Use headers and short paragraphs so that users can easily scan the pages. Web users tend to scan rather than read, so don't burden them with heavy passages of text—they'll leave the site.

- Be sure the price of an item and any pertinent shipping information (for example, a particular item is back-ordered and won't be in stock for four to six weeks) are very conspicuous. Don't leave your customers guessing.

**TIP**   Don't forget that the guidelines for e-commerce areas of your site are similar to those we discussed in Chapters 1 and 2. For example, use thumbnail images linked to larger images to reduce download time and to keep the page uncrowded.

## Providing Customer Service

Customer service is an integral element of e-commerce. Because consumers don't have the opportunity to interface directly with company employees, from customer service to sales personnel, they need the extra mile on customer service. If your site caters to their needs in this respect, you will gain trust from your customers, and those customers will return often to partake of the services and products you offer.

How can you pursue excellent customer service online?

Your company policies on everything from shipping and refunds to privacy and security should be well laid out with all the information any customer could ever want to read. The policies should be explicit about the customers' rights and any rights you reserve. Be lenient, however, especially in your shipping and refund policies. Because customers can't see or handle your products, they may not like what they find when they receive the product in the mail. If you refund your customers' money on return of the product, encourage them to return to your site to try something new. Incentives are great in this respect. The first time customers order a product they just don't like, offer a refund or an exchange, and in the exchange, include a free tawdry bauble, free shipping, or a discount with their next order.

Use a two-step ordering method. First, ask for contact information. Second, ask for payment information. This way, if users back out of the ordering process, you have their contact information. Send an e-mail to them, asking if they had problems with the ordering process, and give them technical support or customer support contact information.

As far as site and page design, consider the following ideas related to customer service:

- 24-hour response to customer service e-mail queries
- Real-time tracking of recent purchases
- Easily viewed purchase history
- Wish lists
- Alternative packaging, such as gift-wrapped products or plain shipping (For example, assume that the customer doesn't want his wife to know he just ordered a brand new widget for their anniversary.)
- Feedback forms
- Contact information or a link to a contact form on every page
- A variety of shipping methods (If World Wide Package Handlers regularly loses Wendy's packages, let her choose the United States Postal Service instead.)
- Free technical support tips and articles online
- The capability for customers to track the progress of their help requests

## Addressing Security Concerns

When customers order from your e-commerce areas, they will be very concerned about the level of security your site uses to protect their information. To ease their concerns, you need to take a few steps. As in all things, however, moderation is key. Consumers want to know their information is as safe as your site can possibly make it, but they don't want this knowledge to interfere with their experience at your site.

---

### A Quick Note on Following Through

No matter how wonderful your e-commerce areas are, no matter how many great reviews your site receives, no matter what you do to attract new visitors to your site, your efforts will be for naught unless you follow through with your customers.

What do we mean? Basically, give them the best customer service they can receive *offline*. When they order a product, ship that product within the time frame you specify on that product page or on the final ordering pages. Ship the product in quality material with enough padding to protect the contents. Include an invoice with the package that details what they've received, the price they paid, and contact information for customer service.

In addition, customer service representatives should be available at convenient times for every time zone you service. Provide a toll-free number, e-mail addresses, and even a real-time chat area just for customer service agents to communicate online with customers. Establish, publish, and stick to return policies for customers who are disappointed in the products they received.

By following through after the order has been completed, you reinforce the trust and good experience that your well-designed e-commerce site initiated.

---

## Let Customers Know They're Safe

Place a link to your security and privacy policies on each page of the order process. Place this link at the bottom of the page, even if your customers must scroll once to see it. Include *short* links within the ordering process at points where customers may feel nervous about providing information. For example, place a link from the link text "How We Secure This Information" next to the credit card information input fields. Link this text to a short pop-up window that briefly describes your secure ordering and any guarantees you place on that security.

**CAUTION** Be careful when using frames in secure areas. If a page within a frame is secure but the frame page is not, the lock or key icon the browsers use to signify a secured area will *not* appear.

## Manage Browser Security Notifications

When customers move into and out of secured areas, their browsers may be set to notify them of the change in security. Try to keep these notifications to a minimum, because they become annoying after several have popped up.

Keep customers in either the secured or unsecured areas for as long as possible to avoid forcing them to switch back and forth. Again, you can give control back to your customers at this point by allowing them to do all their shopping within a secured area. However, warn them that the extra processing required on both sides will slow down their shopping experience. In addition, be sure your server can handle the additional strain.

### Avoid Requiring Passwords Everywhere

Don't require your customers to provide their password more than once, unless you've asked them to verify a change in their account setup or information. If a customer wants to access his order history, for example, he must log in with his password. Five minutes later, he decides to order something new. He moves to the order process… only to be asked again for his password.

He provides this password, then decides to change his shipping address. At this point, he should expect to provide his password to ensure that he is who he says he is. In addition, he should expect to receive an e-mail at his default e-mail address confirming this change. When he moves back into the main site and wants to look one more time at his order history, however, he should NOT have to provide that password again. Users become annoyed when they must re-enter information they've already given, and passwords are no exception.

## Analyzing the E-commerce Portions of Your Site

The following checklists will help you determine whether your site and business use effective and helpful design elements within the e-commerce sections of your site.

### Main Pages

A *main page* refers to the start page for any area—be it your entire site or just the starting point for all Outdoor Widget products.

- Are all main pages consistent in design?
- Are there links to every area from each main page?

- Can customers quickly and easily find product information within three clicks of each main page?
- Can customers search from the main page?
- Can customers go to an extended search from the main page?
- Is contact information provided on each main page?
- Do the area main pages link back to the home page?
- Do you give your customers enough options to ensure a positive e-commerce experience at your site?

## Internal Pages

*Internal pages* refer to pages that fall "below" a main page in the site hierarchy. A product listing is considered an internal page, for example, whereas an online store's start page, which links to an internal product listing, is considered a main page.

- Are all internal pages consistent in layout and relative content?
- Are product lists easy to browse?
- Does each page show at least the number of items in the shopping cart, if not the contents of the cart?
- Must users re-enter passwords and other information, or is the login persistent?
- Do you use headers and short paragraphs for easy scanning?
- Do page titles match the text that linked to the page?
- Is contact information available on each page?
- Do your pages suffer from linkrot?
- Can customers search from each internal page?
- Do you give customers options for how to view your pages?
- Do you have a link to feedback information from each internal page?
- Does each page link back to the area main page and to the home page?
- Does each page include a link to review the contents of the shopping cart?
- Does each page give users an opportunity to log in or to open a new account?

## Product Pages

*Product pages* refer to pages that give specific information about your products. These do not include pages that list products.

- Are product pages consistent in layout and relative content?
- Are product descriptions clear, thorough, and concise?
- Is the product image available? Is it clear but small enough to fit well on the page? Does it increase the page's download time considerably?
- Is the product price clear?
- Is the turnaround time for shipping the product visible?
- Is the order button an obvious button? If it's a link, is it obvious to customers how to place the item in the shopping cart?
- If the page scrolls, do you have order buttons or links at convenient intervals on the page?
- If the page scrolls, do you have the most important information above the fold?
- If the page scrolls and there is important information below the fold, do you provide a link at the top of the page to get to the important information below the fold?
- Can users return easily to the browsing or searching that led them to the product page?
- Do you use headers and short paragraphs to facilitate fast scanning?
- Do page titles match the text that linked to the page?
- Can users search from each product page?
- Does each page link back to the area page and to the home page?
- Does the page offer cross-selling and related products or services for fast navigation?
- Is contact information available on each page?
- Does each page include a link to a feedback form?
- Have you checked each page for linkrot?
- Does each page provide a link to open a new account or to sign in to an existing account?
- Does each page allow users to review the contents of their shopping carts?

## Purchase Pages

*Purchase pages* are pages that users encounter while making a purchase.

- Are purchase pages consistent in layout?
- Have you eliminated advertisements or other distracting material from the purchase pages?
- If users aren't registered and your site requires registration, can they easily return to the purchase with no hiccups or glitches after registering?
- If users must log in, will the page automatically advance to the next purchase step after they provide login and password information?
- Does the purchase process end with access to a printable invoice?
- Do you send an invoice and order verification to users at their e-mail address?
- Do you provide customer support and tech support contact information throughout the purchase process?
- Do you use a two-step ordering process so that you can contact users if they back out without finishing an order?
- If you use frames within your purchase pages, do you load a new, secured frame page so that the secured icon (key or lock) on the browser window will appear?
- Can users navigate back to the previous task easily?
- Can users navigate to various areas or to the main page easily?
- Do you offer a variety of shipping methods?
- Can users ship to more than one address?
- Do you offer alternative packaging, such as for birthdays, or packaging that leaves off your company logo or name?
- Does each page offer contact information?
- Does each page have a link to feedback and technical support?

## Customer Support

*Customer support* refers to any pages or practices your company uses to aid in customer support.

- Have you given your customers enough options to make their experience at your site positive?
- Do you have clearly defined policies? Do you stick to those policies? Can customers easily find out about your policies?
- Do you have a fast response time to help or information queries?
- Do you offer online help request tracking?
- Do you follow up all customer service queries with e-mail?
- Do you follow through with the physical aspects of the purchase process?
- Do you accept and respond to user feedback?
- Do you allow customers to track purchases?
- Can customers view their purchase history?
- Do you provide customers with printable invoices?
- Do you offer technical support tips and articles free of charge?
- Do you offer real-time help or support from customer and/or technical support representatives online?

## Conclusion

Although navigation and usability are key issues when considering the layout and design of your site and your individual Web pages, they become even more important when considering the layout of your e-commerce pages. Customers will leave your site without buying—and they won't return—unless they can easily find and purchase the items they want or need.

By considering the individual pages of the e-commerce areas of your site, you can analyze your site's usability in terms of e-commerce readiness. Remember to consider the needs of your visitors and to design your site with their happy experience in mind. Be careful of pushy or annoying elements of design and content, and you'll increase your chances of success.

# TESTING THE EFFECTIVENESS OF YOUR SHOPPING CART

## In This Chapter

Shopping carts have become a necessity for any site that offers more than one item for sale. Because of the idea behind shopping carts (providing an easy way to "hold" items while continuing to shop), several issues come into play. The cart should not interfere with navigation or usability of a Web site, for example. Nor should it place private information at risk.

In this chapter, you will look at the issues surrounding shopping carts, as well as the issues presented by alternatives to shopping carts. Although we consider the product catalog and the payment process to be separate from the shopping cart, we consider usability and navigation issues when they relate to the shopping cart's ease of use.

## What Are Shopping Carts and Why Will They Change Your Life?

Any professional site that sells items to the online community uses a *shopping cart*. A shopping cart is nothing more than a software program that tracks what each user has placed in the shopping cart to buy, how much of each item, any preferences for that item (such as color or size), and what stage of the ordering process the customer is in. If the cart is part of the entire e-commerce solution, the software also takes the customer through the purchase, delivery, and tracking system. The shopping cart itself ends at the "purchase counter," when the user chooses a link to proceed to checkout and effectively dumps the contents of the cart onto the register counter.

The shopping cart's journey begins when Wendy Widget-Lover clicks on a button next to a picture of a beautiful orange-and-brown widget. The button says "Add to Cart." Later, Wendy also adds two gadgets and a mini-widget. She clicks on a button that says "Check Out" and finds herself looking at the contents of her cart. This is her opportunity to change quantities, delete items, or make any last-minute changes. She can also return to shopping from here, if she desires.

After Wendy approves the contents of her cart, she clicks on another button that says "Pay for Order." At this point, the shopping cart software hands off its contents to the software that will cover the purchase. Again, this may be the same software, but Wendy is in the final stage of her shopping (actual purchase), so the shopping cart goes away, just as it does in the grocery store.

## Cart Components

In effect, the shopping cart provides a means of holding on to information regarding who has what products, how many, what color, and whether the order has gone through a payment process yet. What are the actual components of a shopping cart? What will you need, starting from scratch, to have an effective shopping cart on your site?

- Web host
- Merchant account
- Secure server
- Procedures for fulfilling purchases
- Database
- Product catalog
- Interface and navigation plan

**NOTE**    As you plan your shopping cart, remember to consider scalability requirements. When your company's sales explode in six months, and your site traffic quadruples, you'll need to upgrade your system (or implement scaling procedures you've already created) to handle the added strain on your server.

### Web Host

Obviously, a Web host is necessary because you'll need a Web site. Whether you use your own servers, or you use another company's servers, you'll need a computer, somewhere, to provide Web space.

If you run a small business, and you neither want nor need the expense or hassle of dealing with your own Web space, you might consider using a storefront provided by another site. Amazon.com's zShops, for example, give e-tailers the opportunity to sell their wares through Amazon's interface (see Figure 13.1).

### Merchant Account

If you want to have a successful site with oodles of sales, you must accept credit card payments. Credit cards can increase your site's sales, but if you want to accept credit card payments, you must have a merchant account.

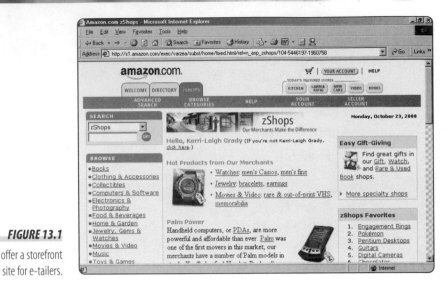

**FIGURE 13.1**

Amazon.com's zShops offer a storefront site for e-tailers.

When you have a merchant account, you become affiliated with a bank that will process credit card payments that you accept from your customers. A full discussion of merchant accounts is beyond the scope of this book, but you can find more information in Chapter 14 and at the following sites:

**FIND IT ONLINE**

http://wdvl.com/Internet/Commerce/MerchantAccounts/

http://ecommerce.internet.com/solutions/ec101/article/0,,6321_208591,00.html

### Secure Server

To process payments, you'll need a server that can handle secure transactions. In other words, it must be able to use *Secure Sockets Layer* (*SSL*), which provides a means of encryption. Customers want to know that their credit card numbers and other personal information are not available to prying eyes.

### Purchase Fulfillment

You'll need an order-fulfillment procedure: How do your employees process an order, taking it from the database, putting it together, and mailing it? What policies will you have regarding these orders?

Will you ship within 24 hours? Know the process of your order fulfillment so that orders are not lost, forgotten, or ignored.

## Database

To hold the order information, you'll need a few different interconnected databases. Inventory must be tied to orders, which must be tied to customers. If your operation is small enough, you may be able to use appropriate tables within the same database. Regardless of the structure of your database or databases, however, you need to be aware of how they are related and use the related information to improve your customers' shopping experiences by personalizing, making return visits easy, and speeding up the time it takes to check out.

## Product Catalog

You need a searchable product catalog containing product information, images, prices, etc. Your catalog, at the lowest level, will be nothing more than a collection of tables in a database. These tables will hold information such as size, quantity available, price, description, the image filename for this product, etc.

Don't forget the customer's relationship with your product catalog. You want your customers to be able to browse or search the catalog according to user-defined parameters. Suppose that Wendy wants to know about all the widgets you sell for less than $40. Your catalog should provide an easy-to-read, usable, and navigable interface to the database that actually holds the product information. Also remember that the catalog pages should load quickly. Wendy doesn't want to wait around for two minutes while a few image files and banner ads download to the page.

## Interface and Navigation Plan

When you design your shopping cart, you must keep in mind Web design issues that you normally consider for every other type of Web page. After all, the shopping cart you use reflects on your company's professionalism. If cart pages have green text on an orange background, users will run screaming from your site. If they have trouble figuring out how to check out, they'll leave, and they'll do so with a bad impression

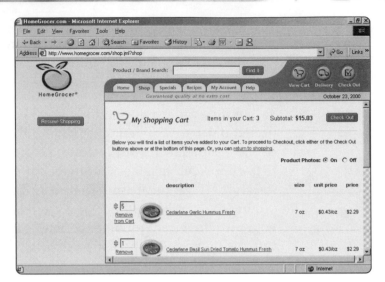

*FIGURE 13.2*

HomeGrocer also allows you to easily view the contents of your shopping cart at any point in the shopping process.

of your company. Figure 13.2 shows an interesting method of shopping cart use employed by HomeGrocer.com.

Shopping cart pages are no different from regular Web pages: Users still want to be able to see information without distracting animation or sounds. They want fast-loading pages that contain all the information they need, but without overloading them with too much information. They need to be able to get in, order what they want, and move to their next task. Just as you have with the rest of your site, you should plot your shopping cart's interface structure to be sure you have included the functionality your customers need and receive from the rest of your site.

Also keep in mind as you plan your shopping cart interface that navigation is even more of an issue here than anywhere else on your site. Why? Customers who add to their carts want to be able to return quickly to the last page they were on before going to the product information page.

Remember the example of Wendy searching for her inexpensive, $40-or-less widgets? She finds the New and Improved 99% Fat-Free Auto-Widget, visits the product information page, likes what she sees, and places the widget in her cart. After the new widget is in her cart, she wants to return to the search list she generated of inexpensive widgets.

What if it's not there? She has to hit the Back button on her browser—an etiquette faux pas. Your cart pages should give Wendy a link to return to the browsing or searching she was doing before she broke away to peruse the 99% Fat-Free Auto-Widget. This way, she returns quickly to her last task, without having to back out of the five or six pages she passed through to get to the final cart page.

## Getting Your Cart

If you don't already have a cart, you must decide on the route you'll take to get one for your site. A plethora of carts is available to you, depending on the needs you determine when you analyze your site's potential shopping cart. Here are some of your options:

- **Build your own.** Using CGI or Java, a database, and a little HTML, you can whip up your own custom-built cart containing all the functionality you need.

- **Turnkey solutions.** You can purchase an entire e-commerce package that includes shopping cart, product catalog, storefront, database, etc., avoiding the agony of programming, testing, debugging, etc. In addition, if you run into technical difficulties, another company's employees will find and fix the problem, saving your employees to complete their own tasks.

- **Merchant account carts.** Some merchant account providers include shopping carts with the merchant account they provide. You need only integrate the cart with your database, or upload your database to the merchant account site (if your account is off-site, such as with CCNow.com).

- **Standalone carts.** Some programmers build standalone carts that you can integrate with the rest of your system. In addition, some site design programs include shopping cart facilities that you can integrate with your site as you build it.

## When Shopping Carts Attack: Addressing Security Concerns

Like the clickstream issues we discuss in Chapter 8, "Getting to Know Your Customer," shopping carts threaten the security of private information from customers to your site. For this reason, shopping cart software must be as secure as you can possibly make it. In this section, you'll look at potential security issues and what you can do to avoid problems. You'll look at e-commerce security concerns in more depth in Part VI, "How Secure Is Your Web Site?"

## Where Are Shopping Carts Vulnerable?

What types of security breaches are possible with shopping carts? If you look at the shopping cart software alone, without considering the elements of security that come before the shopping cart is accessed and after the order leaves the cart to be processed by the server's payment processing software, there is very little left to consider.

Of course, as data is transferred in packets between the user and the server, those packets can be sniffed by a cracker. Using SSL for any sensitive information eliminates this concern, however.

How can shopping carts be compromised, then? In short, your site's visitors may tamper with the forms used to send an item to the shopping cart, which leads to huge discounts for these visitors. How is this possible? If you use the GET method for your forms, or if you use hidden input tags in your ordering forms, users can save these pages to their hard drive, alter the price listed in the URL or the hidden tag, and then submit the order to your site for processing. If you use real-time processing, there will be no opportunity to check the prices before the order is submitted. In addition, if you allow the product database to change values according to parameters submitted from your Web pages, you might compromise the security of your database price list.

## Taking Steps to Avoid Loss

You can take a few actions to avoid this potential breach.

Obviously, you might choose to use a shopping cart that queries the database separately for price information rather than relying on the price submitted via hidden input tags from users' browsers. This way, only the price listed in the database is used, and malicious users have no opportunity to change the price unless they gain access to the database.

If you offer discounts to certain users, be careful not to include the discount amount in any form fields. Use a discount key that your database tracks and that your software can reference in order to find the actual amount of the discount. For example, you might offer a 10 per-cent discount to any user who completes a customer survey to give you feedback on your site. After the user completes the survey, your software generates a random key, say UV9YHT003X, which then is recorded in a database table, along with the user's identity (to be sure the user doesn't try to get the same discount more than once), the expiration date, and the discount amount. You e-mail the user with a link to your site to receive the discount. For example, you might create a page with the following name:

> **http://www.YeOldeWidgetShoppe.com/widgets/
> discount.php3?dn=UV9YHT003X**

When users click on this link, the discount.php3 page brings up their discount information from the database. The users make an order, and the only parameter they ever see (or can alter) is the random key. The discount number cannot be changed unless users know the random key generated for a different discount amount. They would also have to know the real user's identity and that this real user has not yet taken advantage of the discount.

The point is to be sure to double check everything and to trust noth-ing users tell you if the potential exists for those users to be able to change that information.

## Analyzing Your Cart's Navigation and Usability

When you analyze your needs regarding shopping carts, and when you consider the needs your customers have, consider the following:

- Does the cart support secure ordering?
- Does the cart allow users to easily add, delete, and modify quantities as they view the contents of their carts?
- Can users navigate back to their previous task from the cart pages?
- Does the cart support international sales (can international customers pay with foreign currency)?
- Does the cart automatically calculate totals?
- Does the cart automatically calculate tax?
- Does the cart know, from the buyer's address, whether to calculate tax?

- Does the cart automatically calculate shipping costs?
- Does the cart allow you to choose different methods of shipping cost tabulation? For example, can you define shipping costs to be dependent on the amount of purchase, weight of the order, or items and quantities?
- Does the cart support the real-time processing of orders?
- Are orders persistent? In other words, can your customers leave your site without worrying that they will have to replace the items they placed in their carts? Are these orders recorded in your server, or do they use cookies? Consider the strain on your server if you keep all orders, and consider the customers you may lose if you use cookies only.
- If you use your server to keep incomplete orders, will the cart automatically dump the contents after a certain amount of time, or will you have to manually remove those orders?
- When customers move from one form to another within the cart or the ordering area, do the pages require them to re-enter information? Remember that customers may find this annoying and leave.
- Does the final cart page list all items, prices, any user-specified parameters (such as color or size), shipping and handling charges, tax, and an estimated date of arrival?
- Do you provide an estimated time of shipping and arrival on the cart pages?
- Do you include a total of items in the shopping cart on each page of the product catalog?

The following items are related to your shopping cart but involve either your product catalog or the ordering segment of the user shopping process. These factors are as important to consider as the shopping cart itself, because the shopping cart ties these items together, and in some cases, these segments are considered part of the shopping cart.

- Do you have recommendations on your catalog pages for related items or accessories to the product listed?
- Do the product pages specify whether an item is back-ordered?

- Do the product pages specify when the item will be shipped?
- Do the product pages include specific information regarding the item, its description, its price, and any information such as compatibility issues?
- After the order has been completed, do you provide a page for a clean printout—a receipt—of the final order?
- Do you confirm the order via Web or e-mail? Does the confirmation include the itemized list of products ordered, prices, extra costs, and contact information for customer or technical support?
- Does the ordering software allow users to choose multiple destinations for the products? In other words, if Wendy Widget-Lover orders six widgets, can she send one widget to each of her favorite aunts, who live in different cities?
- Do you provide a shipping tracking number with a link to the shipping company's site?
- Do you specify input fields on forms that customers will need to re-enter if they leave the page? If you ask for their Social Security number on one page, for example, you might (for security reasons) choose to have them re-enter the number if they make a mad dash to another site and then return to complete their order.

HomeGrocer.com, which opened its doors in 2000, delivers groceries to homes across America. At its site, users order from a wide variety of groceries—including produce—and schedule a delivery time and date. HomeGrocer's shopping cart is rather atypical, as is its site design, as you can see in Figure 13.3. Both work well for the type of usability requirements its customers bring to the site, however.

## Using Alternatives to Shopping Carts

If your site only sells one product, you don't want to deal with maintaining a shopping cart, or you don't want to sell anything directly from your site, you have a few alternatives—including auctions, e-mail orders, and printable forms.

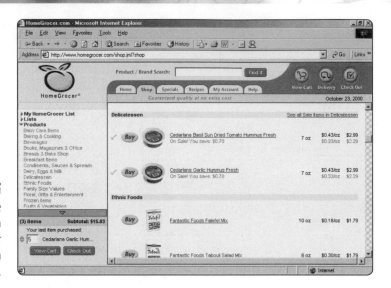

*FIGURE 13.3*

No matter where you are within the shopping area of HomeGrocer.com, you can always see how many items are in your shopping cart, and you can also easily gain access to those contents.

## Auctions

Auctions provide an easy way to sell your products without ever using a shopping cart off your site or even tied to your site. How does this happen?

When you place a widget on an auction site, you place the sale in the hands of that site. When bidders win the auction for your Super Deluxe Widget, they contact you to find out how to pay. You can choose to accept any form of payment (and if you have a merchant account, you can even accept credit cards) from customers. For more information about accepting different payment types, see Chapter 14, "Offering Various Payment Plans for Your Customers."

But what if you sell more than one item? Several e-tailers use auctions to sell more than one item at a time, and they encourage bidders to look at their full list of auctions to save on shipping if they win more than one bid. Keep in mind that some auction sites offer their own payment options for credit cards and even *electronic funds transfer* (EFT), allowing you to give up a small percentage of the winning bid price in order to give convenience back to the bidders.

Aside from the benefit of not needing a shopping cart, auctions can boost site traffic, which we discuss in Chapter 32, "Tracking Online

Sales to Determine the Effectiveness of Marketing Campaigns." The following sites host auctions. Be sure to read their policies thoroughly, because rules and costs differ among sites.

**FIND IT ONLINE**

- eBay—**http://www.eBay.com**
- Yahoo! Auctions—**http://auction.yahoo.com**
- UBid—**http://www.ubid.com**

## Purchase Forms

Using an HTML form, you can allow customers to e-mail you from your site with their ordering information. This type of ordering means you will not actually complete the order, however, so you will sacrifice real-time processing. Instead, users must send a payment using another means—usually postal service, phone, or fax.

You also can offer a form that users can print and then mail or fax to your company.

**CAUTION** Use purchase forms at your own risk. Your customers use the Web for convenience, and purchase forms actually make their lives more difficult because they must print their orders and mail the payments to you. Carefully consider this option before leaving your customers with purchase forms as their only payment option.

### Printing an Order Form

If you choose to have your customers print out an order form to mail to you, keep in mind a few issues of etiquette:

- Keep the order form short. In fact, query your customers with all the information you need, and then use a CGI program to format the information into a one-page form. This way, they won't worry that you can't tell what they ordered, and you won't ask them to waste a ream of paper with form elements that each occupy a separate line.

- Make sure that your form has dark text on a light background. Although systems differ, some printers will spit out the white text only, leaving users with a nearly blank sheet of paper… and no order.

- Keep your fonts simple and your point size large so that, if users choose to fax their orders to you, you will still be able to read the information provided.

### Phone/Fax Orders

It's always an excellent idea to offer phone and fax orders for those who are concerned about security issues with ordering online, but don't limit your ordering methods to just the phone, fax, or postal service, which can have a very negative effect on your site.

Sites that don't have credit card processing capabilities may not seem quite as professional: They look more like a home-grown e-store that someone slapped together (and didn't have the capital to invest in a professional site).

Also remember that the convenience of credit card ordering is gone. Instead, users must go to the extra effort of printing out and sending off an order form or calling your company.

Without credit card orders, you also lose out on the huge impulse shopping market. When your visitors have a credit card in hand, they can buy impulsively. If they must make an extra effort to purchase your items, however, they have time to rethink their decision to buy, and they may decide that they have better ways to spend their money.

For more information on the use of credit cards to collect payment and orders, see Chapter 14.

## Software and Solutions

The following lists can help you research your shopping cart needs. Whether you want to build or buy, you can find information from these sources to help you determine your best choices.

### Software

Use the following list to find software you'll need to satisfy your site's e-commerce needs.

- @Retail—**http://www.atretailinfo.com**
- Cart32—**http://www.cart32.com**

- CartIt—**http://www.cartit.com**
- Check It Out—**http://ssl.adgrafix.com**
- EasyCart—**http://www.easycart.com**
- Make-a-Store OrderPage—**http://www.make-a-store.com**
- Miva—**http://www.miva.com**
- SalesCart—**http://www.salescart.com**
- Shoptron—**http://www.shoptron.com**
- WebSiteTool—**http://www.websitetool.com**

### E-commerce Service Providers

Some companies specialize in providing services related to e-commerce. These companies can help your customers purchase goods from your site.

- Miva—**http://www.miva.com/products/**
- CCNow—**http://www.ccnow.com/overview.html**
- ClearCommerce—**http://www.clearcommerce.com**

ShopNow and Amazon's zShops are great alternatives to an e-commerce service provider.

- ShopNow—**http://stores.shopnow.com**
- Amazon zShops—**http://s1.amazon.com**

## Conclusion

Shopping carts are an integral part of e-commerce for sites that sell several items. Luckily, several companies and developers offer shopping carts, e-commerce solutions, and tools to create the carts your site needs.

When developing your own cart or investigating a cart or solution, keep these issues in mind: security, usability, and navigability.

# OFFERING VARIOUS PAYMENT PLANS FOR YOUR CUSTOMERS

**In This Chapter**

Taking Payments Online

Observing Security Issues

Analyzing Your Ability to Accept Payments

When you offer your customers the option of using a variety of payment methods, you increase the likelihood of a sale. As with any other aspect of your site, you need to consider the implications regarding ease of use, scope of appeal, and security.

Even if your site has a billing agreement with other companies for purchases, you might consider the contents of this chapter to guide you in expanding your services to individuals or small businesses. As you consider the various types of payment methods to use, keep in mind the following:

- Is it a fast method? Will customers have to wait for their products, or will the products be shipped as soon as a human can get to the order?

- Is it a costly method? Will you need a human to step in and process the payments manually?

- Is it an efficient method? The time required to make and process the order should be short, and the drain on your system should be minimal.

- Is the method widely used or supported? Is it likely that your customers will be able or willing to use the payment scheme you've provided?

Consider these issues as you analyze your site's payment processing capabilities to ensure the best outcome for your business and your customers.

## Taking Payments Online

 **FIND IT ONLINE**

According to Brian Cavoli of About.com (**http://adsonline.about.com**), business-to-business online sales in 1999 reached $43 billion. By 2003, that amount could reach $1.3 trillion. How does that much money change hands?

Online payments are the mainstay of e-commerce. Without the capability of an e-business to accept payments through its Web site, online sales would diminish. In this section, we discuss the myriad payment methods your site can use to draw sales.

## Credit Cards

Web buyers enjoy the convenience of relatively safe purchases they can make online by using credit cards. Why?

Credit cards are fast. Simply pull out the wallet, type in a few numbers, press a button, and voilá! For the additional cost of shipping and handling, and with only a few days' delay, your customers have brand new widgets arriving at their homes. Not bad.

 **NOTE**   Credit cards also help to expand your site's appeal to an international audience. With credit cards, they can purchase products for sale in foreign currency.

In addition to the ease of purchasing, the use of credit cards allows users to track monthly expenditures, and in some cases, the charges they make contribute to bonuses issued by their credit card companies. With these thoughts in mind, some consumers may choose credit cards because of the added benefits they receive.

Although credit cards are often the target of fraud, credit card companies are bound by law to hold their customers responsible for only $50 of any fraudulent billing. Some companies waive even this maximum, covering any amount billed illegally. Because of these protections, your customers are even more likely to use credit cards for their online purchases.

**CAUTION**   Unfortunately for you, fraud protections will not cover you. Some credit card companies charge the merchant for the fraudulent charges, so you should be sure, if you plan to take credit card payments, that you are aware of the potential for crime on your site.

What issues related to credit cards are important to you and your site?

- Which credit cards do you accept?
- If applicable, do sales compensate for merchant account fees and transaction fees?
- Do you perform any fraud checking on credit card orders you receive? Do you check that the billing address matches the credit card's billing address, for example? Do you use the services of a company that checks for suspicious credit card activity?

- Do you use your own merchant account, or do you accept payment through another company's account? If you use another company to accept credit cards on your behalf, how much fraud protection does it use, or how much protection can you put in place through your own means?

- Do you use encryption, Secure Socket Layer, or some other secure method of information transfer to ensure the integrity and privacy of the credit card information?

- How do you store credit card information (if at all)?

- How long do you store credit card information?

- Where do you store credit card information?

- Do you urge your customers not to charge with their ATM or bank account credit card unless those cards have fraud protection similar to that of credit cards? Remember that ATM cards deduct directly from a bank account. If a thief charges up that account, the victim is left with nothing unless the bank issues fraud protection.

- How quickly do you respond to the complaints of fraud victims?

After you analyze your policies related to credit card orders, it's a good idea to add that analysis to your security policy, plus a summary of your actions should credit card fraud occur through your site. We discuss security policies later in this chapter and in Chapter 26, "Analyzing Security Risks."

## Money Transfer Programs

Several companies have stepped forward to offer Internet transactions via money transfer. How do these types of services generally work?

First, the customer establishes an account with the money transfer company, signing up for a credit card or bank account to be charged or debited accordingly. Then, the customer purchases goods or services from your online business, which takes payment via the money transfer company. The money is transferred via debit from or credit charge to the customer's registered account, and that money is deposited into your business's account. The process is simple, and the charge to your company's account to receive the money is comparable to credit card charges from the bank that hosts your merchant account.

Many companies offer Internet transactions via money transfers, including the following:

- Achex, Inc.—**http://www.achex.com**
- Cybermoola—**http://www.cybermoola.com**
- PayMe.com—**http://www.payme.com**
- PayPal—**http://www.paypal.com**
- Yahoo! PayDirect—**http://paydirect.yahoo.com**

## Charging to Phone Bills and ISPs

A relatively new method of payment occurs via phone bill or *Internet service provider* (*ISP*) rather than credit card, checking account, and so on. With this method, customers use a dial-up modem to get online and can pay for goods through their local telephone bill. Some ISPs also support charges made directly to your customers' accounts when they shop online. How does it work?

Phone charges occur when customers choose to pay for products or services via the phone charge option. The modem disconnects from the Internet and dials a special number, which creates a charge on the phone bill.

ISP charges are possible because of software installed on your server (the merchant's) and on the ISP server. This method of payment means that users do not need to provide personal information, which secures some level of privacy.

The following companies enable customers to charge their purchases to phone bills or to their ISP account:

- eCharge Phone gives customers the option of charging goods to their phone bill. eCharge guarantees each phone order against fraud—a great incentive for both consumer and business. **http://www.echarge.com**
- iPIN allows customers to charge to their ISP, bank account, credit card, or wireless phone bill. **http://www.ipin.com**
- Trivnet's WISP allows customers to charge digital purchases to their ISP. **http://www.trivnet.com**

## Checks, Money Orders, and the Beauty of E-mail

Until recently, checks and money orders have always occurred via postal service. New methods of check payments are changing the way we do business online.

**FIND IT ONLINE**

Today, Joe Surfer can pay his bills online with bill-paying services such as CheckFree (**http://www.checkfree.com**) or Yahoo!'s Bill Pay (**http://billpay.yahoo.com**), which is guaranteed by CheckFree. You, as the recipient of such a payment service, can significantly speed up payment and simplify your customers' lives by accepting the electronic payment of bills. Many customers appreciate the capability to receive bills via e-mail. E-mail means they won't deal with extra paper they don't need, stamps, the post office, and file cabinet space. Customers can go directly from a link in the e-mail to a secure site where they pay the bill they just received.

PayByCheck.com (**http://www.paybycheck.com**) is another company that allows check payments, either electronic or paper. Like CheckFree, payments come directly from your customers' bank accounts and can be processed for Internet, phone, or fax orders.

## Phone and Fax Orders

Some customers refuse to transmit any payment or personal information via the Internet, in spite of any security measures you may use to ensure the integrity and privacy of the data. For these customers, it is imperative to offer an alternative payment method that doesn't involve the Internet.

Consider a few issues when setting up or analyzing this type of payment method:

- Do you offer toll-free numbers for phone and fax orders?
- How easy is the phone/fax process?
- Does your site offer an order form that customers can print out and use to fax their orders?
- Do you use product or item numbers to easily differentiate the products or services you sell? Remember that phone orders are verbal, so if your products sound similar or your customers could become confused, you should use another way to identify the exact items your customers are ordering.

- Do you accept checks for those too skittish to use credit cards even over the phone or fax lines, or to accommodate those who don't have credit cards at all?

- How long will you hold your products waiting for a check to clear if customers choose to pay by check?

- Do you use physical security methods to protect credit card numbers that could be visible to employees or possibly other customers?

## E-mail Orders

Aside from e-bills, as discussed earlier in the section "Checks, Money Orders, and the Beauty of E-mail," you might offer your customers the ability to order merchandise or services via e-mail. This option adds a few concerns. How will you process this order? Will it be automatic, using a text-processing script to parse through the page and produce the order? Will it require a human to enter the information elsewhere or process the order manually?

Your options are few. Either you have one person processing orders, entering order information into a database, and moving orders to the next person in the chain, or you require the customer to use a standard format in the e-mail that a program can parse. Again, this could be difficult depending on the circumstances. If you can't be sure that your customers are able—or willing—to follow the guidelines, this payment option is not viable unless you're willing to dedicate one person to processing the e-mail orders.

If you do allow this option, you need to analyze the following issues:

- Do you accept payment information (such as credit card numbers) in the e-mail? If so, do you accept encrypted e-mail? Do you require it?

- How do you format the e-mail for fast processing? How easy is it to replicate this format in e-mail? Will your typical customer have problems replicating the format?

- Do you place a link to a secure Web page in the e-mail so that customers may immediately pay for the goods they have ordered?

## Mail Orders

Some customers prefer to place orders via snail mail alone. Naturally, this is no different from classic catalog or mail orders. The only difference is that your catalog is stored online in a Web format. Here are some issues you need to consider, given this new format:

- Is your order form printer friendly? In other words, when your customers print out the form, will its format be readable and uncluttered?
- Do you state in your catalog the expected length of time for processing an order?
- Do you wait for checks to clear before sending products?
- Do you use any physical security to protect information you receive from your customers in physical form?
- Do you record any of your customers' information digitally? Do your customers know this?
- Is any digitally recorded customer information available to a network or to the Internet? Do your customers know this?

## Purchase Orders

The purchase order method of ordering and payment is perhaps most common among business-to-business transactions. Using purchase orders, your company can bill customers immediately after the orders have been placed. This order and payment method can be very efficient if used correctly.

When instituting or analyzing your ability to take an order via purchase order online, you should consider the following:

- Can you process these orders immediately? In other words, is your database able to check the validity of the purchase orders and immediately begin processing them?
- If you cannot validate a purchase order as the order is submitted, how much time does your system require to validate it? Does your system require that a human step in to validate? How much time and money will this require?

- Are your customers aware of how to make an order via purchase order? If there's a possibility that they have no clue, do you provide the information they need in a prominent location?

- How efficient is this method for your company's needs and for the needs of your customers? Would it be easier for everyone involved to accept company credit cards?

- Do you use any security methods or validations to ensure the safety of your customers' money and information?

## Observing Security Issues

In this section, we look at a few issues concerning the security of accepting payments via the Web. We explore this subject in more depth in Chapters 26 and 27.

Although several security issues could create a problem with payments on your site, the biggest security concern rests with stolen information. How will you protect your customers' information? Do you use encryption, SSL, or other security features to protect digital information?

Do you stop there, or do you also consider the physical security of information you have stored in your company's server (is the server locked away from prying eyes or physical damage)? Would the loss of the information be a *very bad thing*, or is the information easily replaced by the customer? For example, if your customer's last payment is stored on your server, do you have that payment information secured, not just from cracking attacks, but from power outages, corrupt files, or hardware problems? If you take payments through snail mail, is the paperwork generated by the transaction stored in a secure location, or is it vulnerable to prying eyes or even something as random as a tornado?

The possible problems with accepting payments are numerous. Your best hope when analyzing your security issues is to look at your system through the eyes of a thief or a tornado. Is the information secure? Will loss of the information be a *very bad thing* that results in lawsuits or general wailing and gnashing of teeth?

Pay special attention to this area of your site. Information is valuable, especially when it's tied to someone's bank account.

## Analyzing Your Ability to Accept Payments

When you offer payment methods through your site, you should tailor those methods to fit the needs of your customers—all of your customers. Because most business-to-business sales require predetermined payment methods such as purchase orders, we analyze the needs of business-to-customer sales in this section—but rest assured that these principles also apply to business-to-business sales.

The following list will help you determine the effectiveness of your methods of payment acceptance:

- Do you offer a variety of payment methods?
- For checks or money orders to be mailed, do you offer a convenient method of billing? Do you provide explicit instructions for mailing the payment?
- Do you have a separate shipping policy clearly stated for alternative types of payments?
- Do you accept a variety of credit cards, or do you only take a limited few?
- Do you accept e-payments? Do you have the capability to expand your system to accept from new banks or bill payment companies that begin to offer e-payment services?
- Do you offer credit balances? How many ways can your customers begin a credit balance?
- Do you offer payment through services that offer benefits to customers for using their services?
- How many indirect payment/order methods do you offer (e-mail, fax, postal mail)?
- How many methods of payment will you accept? Will the use of several methods require a large amount of your resources?
- Look to your lowest common denominator with your customers. Will the methods available appeal to all your customers, no matter what platform they use, their location, or their personal needs or desires?
- How fast is each payment process? Can the speed be improved by using automation rather than manual processing?

- How expensive is each payment process?
- How secure is each process? Have you enacted policies or plans to deal with potential security issues?
- How many people actually use the method you support or want to support? Is this method worth the time, effort, and money required to institute it?

## Conclusion

The possibilities are endless. You have several choices as far as payment methods are concerned, and it only takes an awareness of security issues coupled with the capability and need to offer several means of payment to have very happy customers.

Remember to consider the needs of individual customers when deciding on the types of payments you should or shouldn't accept. Keep in mind that some customers don't have the ability or desire to use credit cards, and also consider the security needs associated with different payment methods.

# IMPLEMENTING RELATIONSHIP COMMERCE

Relationship commerce, also called *relationship marketing* and *interactive marketing,* is not a new phenomenon, but because of the Web, the dimensions related to relationship commerce have exploded.

In this chapter, we define relationship commerce and its importance, and then we show you how to implement it using the Web.

## What Is Relationship Commerce and Why Is It Important?

Relationship commerce deals with creating a long-term relationship with customers. In other words, through marketing style, you forge a relationship with customers that you can maintain through continued interaction with those customers..

In the broad sense of the Internet, relationship commerce refers to a variety of methods and means, but all of these methods have the same core characteristics:

- They're interactive.
- They provide benefits and incentives.
- They provide and maintain customer satisfaction.
- They are entirely customer oriented.
- They build partnerships.

What do these characteristics mean for e-businesses? In terms of business-to-business e-commerce, relationship commerce means forging partnerships, which in turn build trust among customers and increase the targeted market of customers. Before, your widget accessory e-store appealed only to current widget owners. Now your partnership with a widget producer means your audience expands to those who are considering purchasing a widget with an accessory pack because they get the accessories at a discount.

In terms of business-to-customer e-commerce, relationship marketing means greater profit over an extended period of time. Customers know your company, they know you are customer oriented, they know you will interact with them, and they become loathe to try a competitor when they already have all they need with your company.

What are the benefits of relationship commerce?

- Relationships are long term, so customers stay with your company rather than moving to a competitor.
- Relationships build trust.
- Good rapport with customers leads to positive word-of-mouth marketing, bringing more customers.
- Business-to-business relationships mean partnerships, which open larger markets.

You can use the Web to build relationships with customers and to expand your customer base. This chapter shows you how.

## Building Relationship Commerce through Your Site

Chances are good that, just by virtue of being an e-business, you have implemented or are planning to implement relationship marketing on your site. If you have included interactivity, incentives, or relationship-building benefits in your site, you can rest assured that you are on your way to establishing and maintaining relationships.

In this section, you'll consider a few methods of building relationships with customers. To begin, consider how to establish relationships with customers that will keep them returning to your site and to your products.

### Using Personalization and Clubs

To personalize your site for each customer who wanders through the various areas, you'll need to know who they are and use their identity to appeal to their preferences. In Chapter 5, "Using Forms and Scripts to Capture E-mail Addresses," we discuss methods of capturing e-mail addresses and tailoring a site to the preferences of the visitors who use it. Use membership or similar enticements to track customers' interests, and then personalize your site accordingly.

By acknowledging your customers' dispositions and using information they provide to you, you can tailor your site to their every whim. What can you do to establish this personalization?

- Greet them by name when they arrive at your site.
- Use e-mail, autoresponders, and other direct marketing tools to follow up on orders or information requests.
- Use e-mail and site personalization to recommend products, services, or areas of the site similar to your visitors' interests.
- Use e-mail reminders of personal events provided by your customers (such as birthdays, anniversaries, etc.) or of events taking place on your site to appeal to your customers.

**TIP** Of-the-Month clubs are another excellent way of establishing a relationship with your customers. Every month, send a surprise product to customers who pay a monthly fee to join the club. For $12 per month, for example, Wendy Widget-Lover receives her Widget of the Month. In addition, you should give Wendy special discounts and seasonal gifts to show your appreciation for her loyalty to your company.

## Offering Benefits

By offering benefits to members or special customers, you can increase the level of relationship you build with customers. With these benefits, you offer a trade. You receive e-mail addresses, names, or other information that you can use to dynamically tailor your site for each customer, and in exchange, your customers receive regular bonuses that let them know they're appreciated.

What kinds of benefits could you offer?

- Discounts
- Gifts with purchase
- Free shipping or free shipping upgrades
- Free downloads, software, analysis tools
- Screen savers
- Free reports or other information
- Access to members-only areas of the site (see Chapter 7, "Creating Effective Online Communities," for ideas)
- Access to e-mail lists
- Free e-mail address

- Free Web space
- Long-distance calling cards
- Vacation certificates

 **TIP**   Use your affiliate program, which we discuss later in this chapter, to provide benefits like these to your customers.

## Portals

Portal sites serve an important purpose in the realm of relationship commerce. They provide one-stop shopping for almost all of a Web surfer's needs, and in that respect, they help the company behind the site to form a relationship with each user, no matter how many of the offerings users take advantage of. Examples of portal sites include Yahoo!, Lycos, and AltaVista. These sites offer services such as these:

- E-mail
- Search engines
- Search directory listings
- People finder
- Maps
- Phone listings
- News
- Chat
- Auctions
- Shopping
- Yellow Pages
- Personal calendars
- Personal address books

Your site doesn't necessarily have to be a portal site, but by taking a cue from those sites that do try to be the starting point for all Web activity, you increase the networking you do with visitors to your site and generate relationships that will endure. Imagine the loyalty your customers will have for your company when you provide them with free e-mail, address books, calendars, chats, and auctions.

If you choose to transform your site into a portal site, try to consider the following:

- Always maintain relationship commerce with customers. Remain customer oriented.
- Functionality in excess leads to reduced usability. Don't inundate customers with free services unless those services are well-organized and in no danger of eclipsing one another.
- Absolutely do not sacrifice customer service to make way for more free services.

## Newsletters

Newsletters allow your company to keep in touch with customers and to inform them of news and events surrounding your site. They keep your name fresh in the minds of your customers, and they expand your opportunity to create enduring relationships. Using newsletters, you can let your customers know about the latest news at your site and within your company, any upcoming sales or special offers, new benefits of membership, etc.

You also can include articles pertinent to your industry, which gives your customers the opportunity to learn something new or to try a new hands-on experience related to your industry. For example, articles could address how to build a model airplane using the 13-inch widget, located in the YeOldeWidgetShoppe shopping area. Or you could include a recipe that uses a standard widget. Use your imagination!

**TIP**  Send out your newsletter regularly to remind that your site is still active.

## Communities

Online communities can help establish not only a relationship with your customers but also among your customers. We discuss online communities in Chapter 7, so we won't go into detail here, but we do want to make the point that with community, you establish relationships.

These communities can help your customers in more ways than you might consider at first. They provide an outlet for conversations regarding common topics, for example. They allow customers to maintain contact with one another. They give customers an opportunity to share ideas, files, etc. They help customers with their business-to-business needs, from Web conferencing to instant messages. Meanwhile, your company benefits from inclusion in the relationships your customers build among each other.

## Maintaining the Relationship

Once you have established a relationship with your customers, you'll need to find ways to maintain the rapport. You have several options for implementing maintenance, but they all boil down to one issue: Customer Satisfaction.

Because relationship commerce relies on customer-oriented activities, customer satisfaction is key. If customers find themselves against a wall with your customer service, you will lose the relationship you built with them. To maintain customer service, consider the following:

- **Be accessible.** Give out as much contact information as your customers need to contact you. Also help them give you as much information as you need with appropriate prompts within contact forms. For example, ask them to define exactly the area of the site where they experienced a problem.

- **Be prompt.** Reply immediately to their correspondence with an autoresponder that tells them when their e-mail will receive attention and what they should do if, for some bizarre reason, they don't receive a reply within a certain time period. Then reply to them as soon as possible.

- **Be available.** Consider using a real-time customer service forum for customers to chat live with customer service representatives who are able to answer questions.

- **Empower your customer service representatives.** Give them the authority to do what they need to in order to resolve an issue or to placate an upset customer.

- **Follow up.** Use a customer service hierarchy that allows a supervisor to personally contact customers who have experienced problems. The supervisor then can ensure that the issues were resolved to the customers' satisfaction or make amends otherwise.

## Getting the Word Out

How do you let the general Web population know about your wonderful relationship marketing? Once your company has established relationship commerce as a vital element of your business, you will want to let everyone know that you can and will create and maintain a strong relationship.

When you announce your site, you want to stress the following:

- Your site is interactive.
- Customer satisfaction is your first priority.
- You will provide incentives to those who establish a relationship with you.
- You intend to forge a long-term relationship.

How do you announce your site, and how can you increase the reach of your site?

### Press Releases

Press releases are old hat in general, but be sure to remind your publicity personnel as they draft press releases to stress the elements of relationship marketing. The slant of these press releases, in fact, should center on the elements of your site that lend it to forging relationships with customers.

### Web-based Advertising

Advertising online, whether through banner ads or site reviews, should also center on the relationship aspects of your site. Draw customers to your pages with promises of community, customer-oriented service, quality, and interactivity. Let them know the incentives you're offering, and even consider starting out with an incentive to join. Advertise a random drawing of five widgets for those who sign up for your free online community, for example.

## Viral Marketing

Viral marketing isn't as unhealthy as it sounds. In fact, it refers to any word-of-mouth marketing that spreads like a virus. You can help out word-of-mouth advertising by encouraging it and simplifying the process. What are some examples?

- Give customers incentives for referring friends, family, acquaintances, etc. to your site.
- When customers encounter a neat new gizmo, make it easy for them to enter the e-mail addresses of friends to let them know about what they just found.

**NOTE** Remember to state your privacy policy clearly regarding the e-mail address you now have, and under NO circumstances sell the address or use it for spamming purposes.

- Offer customers the capability to fax an interesting article they found to family or friends—free, as we describe in Chapter 4, "Setting Up Polls, Contests, and Other Traffic-Generating Avenues."
- Let customers create a wish list of items from your site and e-mail that list to family and friends.
- Help customers send recommendations for products, services, articles, etc. via e-mail to friends and family.
- Give customers an opportunity to build a mini-community (for example, an online club or chat area) and invite friends and family to join.

## Affiliate Programs

Although we discuss affiliate programs in more detail in Chapter 6, "Multiplying the Reach of Your Web Site through Affiliate Programs," we want to remind you now that these programs provide an excellent opportunity to spread the word about your site, products, and services. In addition, they help to create a relationship between you and your affiliates.

Affiliate programs also give you the opportunity to offer benefits. You can reward affiliates not only with a percentage of each sale they refer, but also with discounts and other incentives. By creating a relationship with your affiliates, you reward those customers who agree to help you expand your customer base.

## Conclusion

Relationship commerce means centering your business on your customers by offering services with your products that engender long-term relationships. The best ways to move into relationship commerce are to become interactive with customers through your site and through e-mail, to create a community for customers so that they form relationships with each other as well as with you, and to make customer service a priority.

# GETTING THE TECHNOLOGY, SERVICES, AND SOFTWARE YOU NEED

**In This Chapter**

Analyzing Your Needs

Tools for Your Site

Services to Benefit Your Site

The Web is full of bells and whistles that can make your site zing with technology. New services become available daily—some free of charge—that add functionality to your site. Using certain software can help you boost traffic that returns daily to find out more about what you have to offer.

This chapter will help you determine what your site needs and what is available for your use. We also cover some of the tools you will find on the accompanying CD-ROM.

## Analyzing Your Needs

Before you research the tools, services, and technology available to you to boost the efficiency or effectiveness of your site, analyze the needs of your site. Consider the purpose of your site and what you offer to the public. Do you require any of the following?

- **HTML editor.** Even if your Web masters and content generators are HTML purists, using an HTML editor to create a layout (which the purists can tweak manually) saves time and energy.
- **Site design software.** Do you need help managing your site's layout?
- **E-mail list software.** Do you need software to set up and manage e-mail lists for newsletters, announcements, or interactive e-mail lists for customers?
- **Banner swapping.** Will you use banners on your site?
- **Affiliate tracking.** Will you run your own affiliate program?
- **Online community tools.** Do you need help setting up and maintaining bulletin boards, chat areas, polls, etc.?
- **Data-mining software.** Do you have data to mine? Do you need to mine it?
- **Traffic tracking.** Do you have analysis tools that will parse your server's access logs?
- **Site certificate.** Do you need to secure the trust of your customers?
- **Shopping cart.** Will customers want to order multiple items from your site?

- **Merchant account and merchant software.** Do you want customers to pay for items they ordered at your site?

- **Search engine submission software.** Do you need help submitting your site to the search engines and directories?

- **Search engine optimizing software.** Do you need help analyzing your site's search engine rankings?

- **Intrusion detection system.** Do you need to know when someone is creeping through your system?

- **Security analysis tools.** Do you need to find the security vulnerabilities in your site and server?

- **Server or information backup utilities.** Do you need to back up your data? (The correct answer would be yes.)

- **Database.** Do you need a database?

- **Perl.** Do you need a Perl interpreter for CGI scripts?

- **PHP.** Do you need a PHP processor?

- **ASP generator/editor.** Do you need software to help you build Active Server Pages?

- **Marketing analysis tools.** Do you need to track the effectiveness of your marketing campaigns?

## Tools for Your Site

We fully support Open Source Software, so we tend to concentrate on those tools and services provided as open source or freely distributed to the community. We list several sample tools in each section to give you an idea of what tools are available to you, however, regardless of their license types.

We discuss some of these tools in previous chapters. We list them here again for your convenience, as a quick reference.

### HTML Editors and Site Design Tools

HTML editors help you create Web pages quickly. Most editors use a word processor-style interface to help you create WYSIWYG pages. Some allow you to incorporate non-HTML languages or even database integration. Some of these tools allow you to develop site-wide design as you create individual pages by automatically creating links, site maps, site design templates, etc. The following list will give you a good idea of your choices.

- Microsoft FrontPage—**http://www.microsoft.com/frontpage**
- Macromedia DreamWeaver—**http://www.macromedia.com/software/dreamweaver**
- Allaire HomeSite—**http://www.allaire.com/homesite**
- Arachnophilia—**http://www.arachnoid.com/arachnophilia**
- Microsoft Interdev—**http://msdn.microsoft.com/vinterdev/default.asp**
- Tashcom ASPEdit—**http://www.tashcom.com/aspedit/**
- ColdFusion—**http://www.allaire.com/products/coldfusion**

## E-mail List Software

To keep your customers aware of what your company is doing or has planned, you might want to use an e-mail list to maintain contact. The following tools will enable you to create and maintain your own e-mail lists:

- MailLoop—**http://www.mailloop.com/** (included on CD-ROM)
- MailMaster—**http://www.gaudy.net/mailmaster/**
- Lyris—**http://sparklist.com/services/lyris/**
- LISTSERV—**http://www.lsoft.com/products/default.asp?item=listserv**

## Banner Advertising Software

To administer banner ads on your site, check out these tools:

- phpAds—**http://phpwizard.net/projects/phpAds/** (included on CD-ROM)
- bannerama—**http://www.bannerama.com/** (included on CD-ROM)

### Affiliate Program Management Software

To run your own affiliate program, you might consider one of these tools:

- Be Free—**http://www.befree.com/**
- ClickTrade—**http://www.clicktrade.com/**
- LinkShare—**http://www.linkshare.com/**
- Pro-Track—**http://www.affiliatesoftware.net/**

### Online Community Tools

To establish online communities, you should include polls, chat areas, portals, etc. These tools can help:

- php(Reactor)—**http://www.phpreactor.org/** (included on CD-ROM)
- sympoll—Creates easy-to-use polls. **http://www.ralusp.net/ html/escape/sympoll.php** (included on CD-ROM)
- JiveIt!—**http://www.hotdiary.com/**
- Web Crossing—**http://www.webcrossing.com/**

---

#### *php(Reactor)*

Angus Madden of php(Reactor) fame has used his software to create a portal site at **http:// www.ekilat.com/**. eKilat offers e-mail, greeting cards, discussion forums, and chat, among other services, to Indonesia and the rest of the world. What has Madden learned from his experience?

Offering a community where users can post their thoughts means return traffic—they'll come back to see how others have responded to their posts. In addition, because php(Reactor) uses advancing status to reward users who post frequently, users are more likely to return so that they may eventually moderate their own forum.

Madden also credits the use of greeting cards as the most effective means of Web site marketing. By including the option on each page of eKilat for users to send a randomly selected greeting card, he has seen an increase of 300 percent in cards sent. What's the big deal? "Although they may not seem appropriate for some sites, people love to send them, and each card is a personal endorsement for the originating site," says Madden.

## Data-Mining Software

The following software will help you mine data to help you fine-tune your site to your customers' needs.

- Accrue Software, Inc—**http://www.accrue.com/**
- AZMY—**http://www.azmy.com/**
- Blue Data Miners, Inc.—**http://www.bluedatainc.com/**
- Coremetrics—**http://www.coremetrics.com/**
- Data Distilleries—**http://www.ddi.nl/**
- Data Miner Software Kit—**http://www.data-miner.com/**
- Data Miners—**http://www.data-miners.com/**
- Information Discover, Inc.—**http://www.datamining.com/**
- Intellix—**http://www.intellix.com/**
- MyComputer.com's SuperStats—**http://v2.superstats.com/**
- Web Side Story—**http://www.websidestory.com/**

## Traffic Tracking Software

You can develop a strategy to maximize traffic by analyzing the traffic your site already has. The following software can help.

- Maximized Software FlashStats—**http://www.maximized.com/** (included on CD-ROM)
- WebTrends—**http://www.webtrends.com/** (included on CD-ROM)

## E-commerce Tools

E-commerce tools and solutions, such as those listed below, might include shopping carts, advertisement tracking, merchant tools, and catalog facilities, among others.

- Akopia Interchange—**http://www.akopia.com/** (included on CD-ROM)
- Merchant-Store—**http://www.merchant-store.com/**
- MyMarket—An e-commerce tool written as an example for a DevShed article. Read the article at **http://www.devshed.com/ Server_Side/PHP/Commerce1/**. (included on CD-ROM)

- @Retail—**http://www.atretail.com**
- Cart32—**http://www.cart32.com**
- CartIt—**http://www.cartit.com**
- Check It Out—**http://ssl.adgrafix.com**
- EasyCart—**http://www.easycart.com**
- Make-a-Store OrderPage—**http://www.make-a-store.com**
- Miva—**http://www.miva.com**
- SalesCart—**http://www.salescart.com**
- Shoptron—**http://www.shoptron.com**
- WebSiteTool—**http://www.websitetool.com**

### Search Engine Submission/Optimization/Promotion Software

To ensure that your site gets to and remains at the top of the search engines, you might consider the following software:

- Keyword Density Analyzer—**http://www.keyworddensity.com/** (included on CD-ROM)
- Search Engine Optimizer—**http://www.se-optimizer.com/** (included on CD-ROM)
- WebPosition Gold—**http://www.webposition.com/** (included on CD-ROM)
- Top Dog Software—**http://www.topdog2000.com/** (included on CD-ROM)
- Swiss Army App—**http://www.aesop.com/** (included on CD-ROM)

### Intrusion Detection Systems

The following tools will help you watch your server for possible intruders with ill intent:

- Network ICE—**http://www.networkice.com/html/ products.html**
- Cisco Intrusion Detection System—**http://www.cisco.com/warp/ public/cc/pd/sqsw/sqidsz/**

- RealSecure—**http://www.iss.net/securing_e-business/ security_products/intrusion_detection/index.php**
- Kane Security Monitor—**http://www.intrusion.com/Products/ monitor.shtml**

## Security Analysis Tools

Although you could download analysis tools from any hacker/cracker site, you might consider the following tools. Remember, however, that you need not spend a lot of money. The tools crackers use to compromise your site are mostly online and available for you to test against yourself. Just remember to be sure that, when testing your own site or server, you won't be harming someone else's. Isolate your server from others first.

- Big Brother—**http://www.bb4.com/** (included on CD-ROM)
- SATAN—**http://www.fish.com/~zen/satan/satan.html**
- SecurityFocus Pager—**http://www.securityfocus.com/pager/** (included on CD-ROM)

# Services to Benefit Your Site

The following services can help you create, maintain, and analyze your site.

## E-mail List Services

To keep your site's visitors informed of the activities at your site, consider the following tools and services.

- ListBot—**http://www.listbot.com/**
- E-Groups—**http://www.egroups.com/**
- SparkLIST—**http://sparklist.com/**

## Banner Advertising Services

If you decide to use a banner exchange to promote your site, the following list will help you find a service that is right for your needs.

- Banner Swap—**http://www.bannerswap.com/**
- Banner Exchange—**http://www.bannerexchange.mycomputer.com/**
- Exchange-It—**http://www.exchange-it.com/**
- Free Banners—**http://www.free-banners.com/**
- Link Exchange—**http://adnetwork.bcentral.com/**
- Traffic Exchange—**http://www.traffic-exchange.com/**
- Webmaster Exchange—**http://www.webmasterexchange.com/**

## Affiliate Program Management Services

The following services can create and maintain your affiliate program for you:

- Commission Junction—**http://www.cj.com/**
- LinkShare—**http://www.linkshare.com/**
- PlugInGo—**http://www.plugingo.com/**

## Online Community Services

If you want to use a community service rather than build your own tools, consider the following list.

- Delphi Forums—**http://www.delphi.com/**
- Yahoo! Clubs—**http://clubs.yahoo.com/**
- HotDiary's JiveIt!—**http://www.hotdiary.com/portalbuilder.html**

## E-commerce Services

The following e-commerce services will help you set up your own e-commerce enabled site.

- Miva—**http://www.miva.com/products/**
- CCNow—**http://www.ccnow.com/overview.html**
- ClearCommerce—**http://www.clearcommerce.com/**

## System Backup Services

The following companies will help you back up your system to avoid a loss of data.

- CBL Data Recovery—**http://www.cbltech.com/**
- Enhanced Software Technologies—**http://www.bru.com/**
- NetMass—**http://www.systemrestore.com/**

# Conclusion

The number of tools and services available to make your site better and more easily managed is astounding. In this chapter, we included a list of software and services we have referenced within this book or on the CD-ROM. Be sure to look at the licensing information carefully—we have included several General Public License tools.

# PART V

# CREATING ENGINE-FRIENDLY WEB SITES

# THE IMPORTANCE OF SEARCH ENGINES TO THE SUCCESS OF YOUR ONLINE BUSINESS

## In This Chapter

Because the majority of traffic to most Web sites comes through the major search engines and directories, having a good strong presence in the engines is crucial to the success and health of your Web site.

Simply slapping up your Web site, sticking in a few META tags, and submitting your site to the engines won't work. You need to understand search engine optimization strategies, and then apply them to your Web site and Web pages for maximum findability in the engines.

Are you aware that Yahoo!, the most important search tool, is not a search engine? Do you know and understand the importance of the Open Directory Project?

Which search engines and directories should you really concentrate on? How can you save time by submitting to engines and directories that are related to other search tools?

Which engines will bring you the most business? How popular are the engines and directories with online users?

We cover these areas and many more in this chapter. But this chapter is only the beginning of our discussion on using search engines and directories to draw visitors to your site. In the remainder of Part V, you'll get to know these tools in-depth and discover specific ways to get the most from them.

As we mentioned in the book's introduction, at the time of this writing, Disney had announced its plans to shut down GO.com. The search engine and its directory are both for sale, so whether the engine will be purchased and set up elsewhere or shut down totally, no one knows at this time.

Because of the importance of GO in the past and the uncertainty of what will eventually happen to the engine, we are leaving information on GO in this book. To find out what happened with the engine, please visit the authors' corresponding Web site at **http:// www.kerri-leigh.com/wsar** for more information.

## Why Are Search Engines and Directories Important to Your Online Business?

The vast majority of traffic to most Web sites comes through the major search engines and directories, and that's a statement agreed on by most search engine experts. In fact, NUA Analysis's Weekly Editorial dated February 19, 2001, states the importance of the search engines by noting that fifty-five percent of Internet shoppers made purchases at sites they found through the search engines, versus only nine percent who bought at sites found through banner ads. To read this article in its entirety, visit **http://www.nua.ie/surveys/analysis/weekly_editorial.html**.

So, for your site to be found in the search engines, can't you just submit your site using a handy submission service or a software program that will submit to more than 1,000 engines, and then start raking in the traffic and online sales?

It's not quite that easy. Simply submitting your site isn't what brings you the traffic. It's your ranking in the major search engines and directories that brings you traffic.

Let's say that your Web site pertains to English bulldogs. In Figure 17.1, you see a search performed at AltaVista, one of the major search engines, for "English bulldogs." The engine found 1,026 related Web sites for that *keyword phrase.* A keyword phrase is the topic of your Web page or Web site, and it is also how you believe most searchers will be looking for your site through the search engines. We cover how to choose keyword phrases in Chapter 17, "The Importance of Search Engines to the Success of Your Online Business."

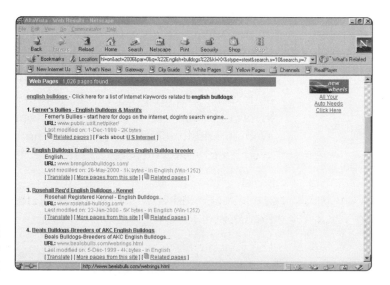

**FIGURE 17.1**

Search results at AltaVista for "English bulldogs."

**TIP**    Choosing the most effective keyword phrases for your Web pages is the single most important thing you can do for the success of your site. All search engine strategies begin with that keyword phrase.

In Figure 17.1, the top 10 Web pages for the keyword phrase "English bulldogs" appear on the first page of results. Each page of results has 10 Web pages on it.

If you were searching for "English bulldogs," how many pages of results would you go through to find a site of interest to you? Would you go through the first two pages of results, or the top 20 sites? The first three pages of results, or the top 30?

Few people will go any farther than the top 30 results, and many won't go past the top 10.

What does that mean to you as a Web site owner? If your site isn't found in the top 30 rankings, and preferably in the top 10, you'll lose traffic to your site and potential business.

Let's say that your own Web site is number 62 out of those 1,026 rankings. That's not bad, considering the numbers. But how many people will go through seven pages of results to find your site? Very few.

So you've learned that not only are the search engines and directories crucial to the success of your online business, you've also learned that *you must have top rankings in those engines in order to benefit from them.*

Even if you're using more traditional forms of advertising for your online business, being found in the top rankings of the search engines should be a priority.

Think of it this way. Have you ever flipped through the pages of a magazine, spotted an ad on television, or noticed a billboard advertising a particular online business, and then noted the business's URL or Web site address? Have you ever tried to find that business on the Web later? Were you able to remember that URL, which is often rather convoluted and difficult to remember?

If not, what did you do? If you're like most people, you went to your favorite search engine and tried to find the site. But if that site wasn't found in the top 10 to 30 rankings under the keyword phrase that you believed was relevant to the site, the Web site lost your business.

This is certainly something you don't want to happen to your own online business.

Therefore, one of the most effective—and least expensive—ways of promoting your Web site online yourself is through the major search engines and directories.

## Understanding the Differences between Search Engines and Directories

Search engines and directories differ in many ways, as we explain in this section. For example, the differences include where the listings come from, how sites are indexed, whether humans or spiders visit the page, and more.

### Search Engines

Search engines look at each page of a Web site separately from the other pages. Each page stands on its own, which means that you will want to submit each individual page of your Web site when possible if the page is important to the success of your business. With search engines, your site may have 25 pages listed, or 50, or whatever. In other words, you'll more than likely be able to get many more pages listed than just the main, or index, page of your site.

Also, each individual page needs to be *optimized* separately when working with search engines. To optimize means to create tags and text in accordance with a particular search engine's unique likes and dislikes, in an attempt to get your site placed higher in the rankings of that engine. So your tags, such as your title tag, META description tag, ALT tags, and so forth, will be designed for that one particular page, whereas another page will have different tags and a different focus.

Another important difference between search engines and directories is that search engines use *spiders* to index Web pages. Spiders are sophisticated software programs that crawl the Web, index the sites, and build an index of Web pages that we access when we search. Web site owners submit their URLs to the engine, and in response, the engine sends its spider to the pages to index them.

When search engines crawl and spider Web pages, they also follow links from those Web pages, so they often index those pages as well. Therefore, you can see the importance of providing links to all your important Web pages on your main page.

We discuss the following search engines later in this chapter, including links to find the engines.

- AltaVista
- Excite
- FAST/All the Web
- Google
- HotBot
- GO/InfoSeek*
- Lycos
- Northern Light

* GO may be shut down or purchased by a different company by the time this book is published, as mentioned in the introduction of this chapter.

## Directories

Directories, for the most part, consider the entire Web site as a whole. They generally don't look at individual pages. Therefore, Web sites usually are listed once in directories, and you can only submit one page of your site, generally the main page, although there are certainly exceptions to that rule.

**TIP**    You can sometimes get a couple of pages listed in the Open Directory Project and NBCi, instead of just the main page of your site. With Yahoo!, however, submit the main page of your site only. Don't take chances with the most important search service on the Web! For more information on how to submit to the ODP or to Yahoo!, see Chapter 25, "Strategies for Working with Directories."

Also, directories rely on submissions from Web site owners to build their index. Directories don't have spiders that go out and index pages. So if your site isn't submitted, it generally won't make it into a directory.

After you submit your site to a directory, a human editor usually visits your site and decides whether to place the site into the directory. So you'll need to make sure that your site will pass a "human editor" test, meaning that it needs to be a topnotch site that is obviously ready for business.

With directories, you don't need to be concerned with optimization strategies. META and other tags will do you no good with directories. Instead, your site is accepted into the index based on the submission form you complete and a visit from a human editor.

We discuss the following directories later in this chapter:

- Yahoo!
- Open Directory Project
- NBCi
- LookSmart

## Understanding the Relationships between Search Engines and Directories

Table 17.1 outlines the relationships between the major search engines and directories. If you can keep these relationships in mind, you'll save yourself valuable time when working with the engines, since submitting in one place can sometimes get your site listed in several others.

## Introduction of the Major Search Engines

In Chapter 24, "Engine-Specific Strategies," and Chapter 25, "Strategies for Working with Directories," we go into more detail about the major search engines and directories. In these chapters, we introduce the major players in the search engine industry and note some of their unique characteristics.

When working on your own Web site, keep in mind that you only need to be concerned with the major engines and directories—not the hundreds of smaller ones that will bring you very little traffic. Most of the traffic to a Web site comes from the major engines, so save yourself some time and energy by concentrating on them.

## 17.1 How Are the Engines Related?

| Search Engine/Directory | Provides Results to: | Uses Results from: |
| --- | --- | --- |
| AltaVista | LookSmart, Raging Search | Ask Jeeves, LookSmart, Real Names, GoTo |
| Ask Jeeves | AltaVista, Direct Hit | Direct Hit, AV, Excite, GoTo, WC |
| AOL Search | | ODP, Inktomi, GoTo |
| Direct Hit (owned by Ask Jeeves) | HotBot, Lycos, MSN Search, SimpleSearch, iWon, Ask Jeeves | ODP, Ask Jeeves |
| Excite | Magellan, WebCrawler | LookSmart, RealNames |
| Fast | Lycos | |
| HotBot (owned by Lycos) | | Inktomi, ODP, Direct Hit, GoTo |
| Inktomi | HotBot, NBCi, GoTo, Kanoodle, MSN Search, AOL Search, iWon | |
| GO/InfoSeek | Search.com, Web TV | RealNames |
| Google | Netscape Search, Topclick, Rocketlinks, Yahoo! | RealNames, ODP |
| GoTo | AOL Search, Netscape Search, AltaVista, Lycos, HotBot, NBCi | Inktomi |
| LookSmart | About.com, AltaVista, Excite, MSN Search, iWon | AltaVista, Direct Hit |
| Lycos | NetGuide Live | ODP, Fast, Direct Hit, GoTo |
| Magellan | | Excite |
| MSN Search | | Inktomi, Direct Hit, RealNames, LookSmart |
| NBCi | | Inktomi, GoTo |
| NetGuide Live | | Lycos |
| Netscape Search | | ODP, Google, GoTo |
| Northern Light | | Northern Light |
| Open Directory Project | Lycos, HotBot, Netscape, AOL Search, Google, Direct Hit | RealNames, AltaVista, GO/InfoSeek, MSN Search, Google, Excite, iWon |
| WebCrawler | | Excite |
| Yahoo! | | Google |

An exception to this rule is with industry-specific engines and directories. If you're in the metal tubing industry, for example, and there is a search engine or directory related to that industry, by all means, submit your site to it.

Submission URLs for the major search engines and directories are listed here, but you can also find them in Appendix B, "Recommended Web Sites".

**NOTE** Few technologies change as quickly as search engines. Search engines rank pages in their indexes based on their own individual *algorithms,* which are simply the characteristics of a Web page that the engine considers to be important at that particular point in time. Algorithms can change at any time, and they do. In this book, we give you general tips and strategies for working with each engine, but understand that things change rapidly in this industry. To keep up with the changes, study your competition regularly and subscribe to newsletters that publish changes in the industry. You can find information on industry newsletters in Chapter 18, "Basic Optimization Strategies," and in Appendix B of this book.

**NOTE**

***FIND IT*
ONLINE**

Unless otherwise stated, the data for the number of pages indexed comes from Search Engine Watch (**http://searchenginewatch.com/reports/**) as of June 6, 2000. Each search engine's ranking and number of unique visitors comes from Media Metrix as of March 2000. Concise listings of these stats are provided in the tables at the end of this chapter.

As you go through the rest of the search engines in this section, notice the number of engines that use RealNames or LookSmart results. Submit your site to LookSmart once, and you'll have a presence in several different engines as a result. We discuss the advantages of purchasing an Internet keyword through RealNames in Chapter 23, "Purchasing Keywords at the Pay Engines."

## AltaVista

***FIND IT*
ONLINE**

Founded in 1995, AltaVista (**http://www.altavista.com**) is one of the largest search engines and certainly one of the most popular. It's also one of the most difficult to work with.

In the past year, AltaVista has cracked down considerably on what it considers to be *spamming.* Spamming is any type of underhanded technique designed to manipulate search engine results. Although AltaVista continues to kick sites out due to shady practices, it has failed to explain exactly what it means by spamming, which makes working with the engine even more difficult.

We cover AltaVista's anti-spamming policies as well as other tips for this engine in Chapter 24.

Here's what you need to know about AltaVista:

- Web pages indexed: 350,000
- Fifth among top 20 search engines
- 11.953 million unique visitors

- If you ask a question, the results sometimes come back as "Ask AltaVista a Question," which means that the results are being pulled from the Ask Jeeves database.

- LookSmart provides directory results to AltaVista. Internet keyword information is provided by RealNames, and the actual search results come from AltaVista's index.

- iAtlas, a company now owned by AltaVista, provides Company Fact Sheets for many of the companies listed in the search results.

- The top three listings at GoTo are now being shown in AltaVista as "Sponsored Listings." For more information about purchasing keywords at pay engines such as GoTo, see Chapter 23.

In Chapter 24, you'll analyze some search results in AltaVista and learn what the engine likes to see in a Web page.

**TIP** Besides the strict spam guidelines that are firmly in place at AltaVista, another distinguishing factor associated with AltaVista is that it's a "theme" search engine. So, if you want top rankings in the all-important AltaVista, make sure that everything on your site points to one central theme or has one overall focus. Move other focuses to different domains. More information on AltaVista can be found in Chapter 24.

## Excite

**FIND IT ONLINE**

Excite (**http://www.excite.com**) is another highly popular search engine with a considerable amount of traffic passing through its portal doors. For many people, Excite serves as a one-stop site for retrieving news, chatting with friends, learning the latest sports scores, accessing message boards, and more.

Excite powers two other search engines: WebCrawler and Magellan. Submitting to Excite will also get your site in WebCrawler and Magellan, although their databases are much smaller than Excite's. Both of these smaller engines are now practically defunct, however; neither of them has indexed new pages in many months at the time of this writing.

Here's what you need to know about Excite:

- Web pages indexed: 250,000
- Fourth among top 20 search engines
- 17.471 million unique visitors
- LookSmart provides directory results to Excite's directory. So even if you're having a difficult time getting into Excite's index, if you're in LookSmart, you'll have a presence in the Excite engine.
- Excite is currently beta testing the use of Internet keywords, or RealNames, in its search results.

**TIP** Excite can take literally months to index a site. So, expect it to take a while for your pages to make it into this index.

Also, make sure your main page is indexed in Excite before submitting subpages. To be on the safe side, list links to all the important pages of your site on your main page.

## FAST/All the Web

**FIND IT ONLINE** A Norway-based company, Fast Search & Transfer, owns FAST (**http://www.alltheweb.com**), and its goal has always been to have the largest index of Web pages. At the time of this writing, it has fallen short of its goal, but the race for the largest index continues.

Another goal of FAST is to power other search engines similar to the way Inktomi operates. In fact, FAST's engine began to power one of the major search engines toward the middle of 2000: Lycos.

Here's what you need to know about FAST:

- Web pages indexed: 340,000
- Not listed in top 20 search engines in Media Metrix
- FAST powers the main search results at Lycos as well as Lycos's advanced search feature, its MP3 specialty engine, and its FTP search feature.

**TIP** Since FAST powers the main search results at Lycos, you'd expect the search results to be the same, yet they aren't, at least not at the time of this writing. What does this tell us? It signifies the importance of submitting to both engines, at least until the two indexes begin to match.

## Google

*Find It*
**ONLINE**

In many ways, Google (**http://www.google.com**) is a shining star among the major search engines. Like the most powerful search service on the Web, Yahoo!, Google was created at Stanford University, which certainly adds a lot to its credibility.

With more than one billion Web pages in its index, Google is the largest search engine in cyberspace, much to the dismay of search engines such as FAST and Northern Light, which have been struggling to get to the top of the chart.

To coincide with the rising importance of both site and link popularity, Google itself is a popularity engine. Google considers the *link popularity* of a site when determining its ranking, as opposed to Direct Hit, which considers *site popularity.*

Link popularity is the number of links pointing to a particular Web site, with the rationale that the more links that point to a certain Web site, the more important or popular that engine really is. Site popularity means click-through popularity, which means that Direct Hit counts the number of times a site is clicked on in the search engines, as well as the length of time visitors actually stay at the site, and this is what determines the popularity and ranking of the site.

Link popularity and size issues aside, Google continues to rise in importance for a number of reasons. First, it's a no-nonsense engine that provides one service to the Web community: searching. It's not a portal site like Excite, where you can almost get lost with all of the various bells and whistles available to visitors.

Instead, visitors go to Google for one reason only: to perform searches.

All of this aside, possibly the most important aspect of Google is its new alliance with Yahoo!

Here's what you need to know about Google:

- Web pages indexed: 560,000 fully indexed pages; 1.06 million, including partially indexed pages
- Eleventh among top 20 search sites
- 3.26 million unique visitors
- Google provides supplemental results to Yahoo!, which has certainly boosted Google's importance among the search engine community. What does this mean? It means that if you perform a search at Yahoo!, after you've gone through the results from Yahoo!'s own index, you'll be presented with results from Google.
- Google also provides search results to Netscape Search.
- The ODP provides directory results for the Google Directory.

Figure 17.2 shows search results at Yahoo! for the keyword phrase "giant panda."

Across the screen, notice the menu bar that indicates "Categories," "Web Sites," "Web Pages," "Related News," and "Net Events." In this

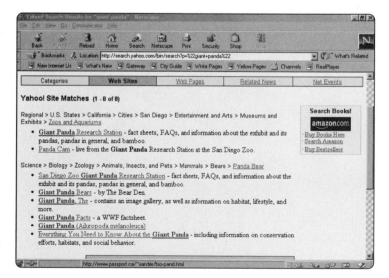

**FIGURE 17.2**

Search results at Yahoo! for "giant panda."

case, "Web Sites" is highlighted in blue. This indicates that these particular results are from the Yahoo! directory itself. If "Web Pages" on the menu bar is highlighted in blue, the results are from Google.

**TIP**   At the time of this writing, Google had begun to kick sites out of its index for no apparent reason. In their canned reply, they stated that they kick out sites for using unsavory practices such as cloaking or hidden text. However, most of the sites involved weren't using cloaking or hidden text. So, why are they kicked out?

Google isn't answering.

If this happens to your site, check your site carefully to make sure you aren't doing anything you shouldn't be doing. Look over our spam warnings in Chapter 24 and make changes as needed. Then, write to Google at googlebiz@google.com.

## HotBot

**FIND IT ONLINE**   HotBot (**http://www.hotbot.com**) is one of many search engines powered by Inktomi, though it certainly has the distinction of being the largest.

But what is Inktomi? Inktomi Corporation is a technology company, and one of its major components is the Inktomi search engine. Inktomi licenses its search engine out to other companies, such as HotBot and NBCi, that want their own search engine without having to build one from scratch.

So if you're in one of the Inktomi engines, does that mean you're in them all? Not necessarily. Each of the Inktomi-powered engines uses a different portion of the Inktomi index. Plus, each engine uses its own ranking algorithm, which means that if you rank high in one engine, you don't necessarily rank high in other engines.

Here's what you need to know about HotBot:

- Web pages indexed: 500,000
- Not listed among top 20 search engines in Media Metrix in March 2000
- 5.67 million unique visitors in December 1999 in Media Metrix
- Inktomi provides results to HotBot, MSN Search, AOL Search, NBCi, iWon, Kanoodle, Canada.com, Anzwers, and GoTo.

- At HotBot, the first results you'll see are the top 10 listings from Direct Hit (called "Web Results Top 10 Matches"); then, ODP results (called "Related Categories"); and finally, results from Inktomi.

- GoTo's top three listings are now shown in HotBot results under "Featured Listings." Also, GoTo's #4 listing appears in the number ten position under HotBot's "Web Results" section.

- Lycos actually owns HotBot, although Lycos doesn't provide results to HotBot and doesn't use results from Inktomi.

 **TIP**    What is your best chance for getting in an Inktomi-related engine, including HotBot? It's simple: pay to submit your site.

If you pay to have your site submitted, your site will be indexed within 48 hours and respidered every 48 hours for an entire year. Just think about it! You can make changes today, then wait a day or two and see how those changes affect your rankings!

*Find It* **ONLINE**    To submit your site, visit **http://www.positiontech.com/index2.htm**.

## GO/InfoSeek

*Find It* **ONLINE**    Around the first of February 2001, Disney announced its plans to shut down the GO.com site. What this means to the GO search engine and directory, no one knows. Please see the sidebar in this section for more information.

Because we don't know what's going to happen to GO, we're keeping information on the engine in this book. GO has been a major engine for years, and it could easily be sold and maintained by a different company. If that's the case, you'll want a background of the engine and how it has operated in the past.

Formerly called *InfoSeek*, the GO search engine (**http://www.go.com**) is still often referred to as InfoSeek among those in the industry. To coincide with its connection to Disney, GO plans to become more of an entertainment and leisure engine, but the site won't be limited to those topics. This bodes well for sites in categories such as business and health, which will still find themselves in GO's search results.

### Disney Is Shutting Down GO.com

When Disney took over the InfoSeek search engine two years ago, it was certainly one of the most popular and viable engines. However, Disney's plans converted it to a portal, full of perks such as free e-mail, chat rooms, bulletin boards, and more. These "best laid plans" seem to have signaled GO's downfall; it's now being shut down or sold.

What's going to happen to the search engine and directory now? GO's FAQ's, found at **http://www.go.com/faq.html#search**, state the following:

> During the transition period, the GO.com Search and Directory functions will continue to provide search results and listings of sites reviewed by our GO Guides. After the transition period, these Search and Directory services—including the GO Guides program—may be transferred to or available through a different site or may no longer be available.

Upon publication of this book, you can find out the status of the GO engine by visiting the authors' related Web site at **http://www.kerri-leigh.com/wsar**.

Like many of the major engines, GO/InfoSeek is both a directory and a search engine. Unlike many of the other engines, however, GO creates its own directory, called the GO Directory, instead of pulling results from other directories.

Here's what you need to know about GO/InfoSeek:

- Web pages indexed: 50,000
- Third among top 20 search sites
- 21.18 million unique visitors
- Search.com, owned by CNET, is a branded version of the GO search engine. Search.com taps into GO's database for general searching but uses its own index for subject searches.
- If you want a strong presence in GO, submit to the GO Directory, since those results appear first in the search results at GO.

**TIP** Before Disney's announcement to shut down GO.com, GO had instituted a "pay submission" service. Submitting through this service would ensure that your site would be reviewed for possible inclusion within 48 hours, and that it would be respidered once a week for a year.

However, this service was removed with the announcement of shutting down or selling the service. If the service is purchased by another company, you may again see a pay-for-inclusion program implemented. This certainly seems to be the "wave of the future" with the major search engines.

## Lycos

Lycos (**http://www.lycos.com**) has always gone for long periods of time without indexing any Web pages, which is extremely frustrating to those who are anxious to get into the index. However, with its alliance with FAST, which now powers the main search results at Lycos, that will hopefully change, although FAST certainly isn't "fast" when it comes to indexing Web pages. In fact, after submitting your pages, you can expect it to take between four to six weeks for your pages to appear in the FAST index.

Terra Networks SA, a Spanish company, now owns the Lycos search engine. And Lycos owns 15 percent of the FAST engine.

Here's what you need to know about Lycos:

- Web pages indexed: 50,000 (plus FAST's index)
- Second among top 20 search sites
- 28.01 million unique visitors

- When you perform a search at Lycos, you're first presented with a "Popular Searches" section, which pulls results from sites that have been reviewed by Lycos editors and results from Direct Hit.
- In the "Web Sites" section, you'll find results from the ODP, FAST, and Lycos's own crawler.
- GoTo provides its top three results to Lycos in a section called "Featured Listings."
- Lycos actually owns the HotBot engine, but HotBot gets its main results from Inktomi.

**TIP** Want a stronger presence in Lycos? Consider purchasing keywords from GoTo, which we'll cover in more detail in Chapter 23. Besides the top three GoTo listings appearing under "Featured Listings" in Lycos's results, at least two more GoTo listings appear among the top ten results in the "Web Sites" section.

## Northern Light

Northern Light (**http://www.northernlight.com**) is a popular search engine among researchers because of its large index, as well as its capability to cluster results by topic. Northern Light also provides a

Special Collections index, which is a research version of its service. Searching the Special Collections index is free, but documents cost a few dollars each.

Here's what you need to know about Northern Light:

- Web pages indexed: 265,000
- Seventeenth among top 20 search engines
- 1.32 million unique visitors
- Northern Light is one of the few engines that doesn't provide results to other engines/directories and doesn't pull results from other engines/directories.

**TIP**    Northern Light has taken a strong stand against automated reporting software such as WebPosition Gold by blocking access to its index by those programs. Will other engines follow suit? It's certainly possible. After all, if hundreds of thousands of users check their rankings by using programs like Gold, it's certainly taxing the engine's resources.

## Introduction of Important Directories

More and more engines are using results from other directories, which has certainly increased the importance of directories in recent months. Plus, the most important search site out there, Yahoo!, is a directory.

Remember that directories don't build their indexes by using spiders that crawl the Web indexing new sites. Instead, directories build their indexes by submissions, and they employ human editors who visit the sites and decide whether to accept them into their indexes.

With directories, the information provided on the submission form itself is used to determine the ranking and indexing of a site, although the human editors can and do change titles and descriptions on the submission forms quite often.

Let's examine some major directories and find out why they're so important. You can find additional information about directories in Chapter 25, "Strategies for Working with Directories."

**NOTE**

**FIND IT ONLINE** Unless otherwise stated, the data for the number of pages indexed comes from Search Engine Watch (**http://searchenginewatch.com/reports/**) as of June 6, 2000. Each search engine's ranking and number of unique visitors comes from Media Metrix, (**http://mediametrix.com/**) as of March 2000.

## Yahoo!

**FIND IT ONLINE** When comparing the size of Yahoo!'s (**http://www.yahoo.com**) index to that of big-boy search engine Google, with more than one billion partially indexed Web pages, you might wonder why the general consensus is that Yahoo! is the most important search service on the Web.

Also the oldest search service, Yahoo! is important for many reasons. First, human editors work hard at making sure that Yahoo! results are relevant, which sometimes seems like an impossibility with the engines. Searchers trust Yahoo! results, which is quite obvious when looking at the number of unique visitors that grace its site every month.

Because Yahoo! is by far the most popular search service among Web searchers, getting into the directory can make or break a Web site. In fact, many Web sites find that traffic to their sites attributed to Yahoo! alone is more than traffic attributed to the rest of the search engines and directories put together.

When submitting your Web site to Yahoo!, remember that a human editor will visit your site and look around. The editor will look to see if all of your images load, your links work, and your site is considered of the caliber to be accepted into the lofty Yahoo! index. After all, only about 30 percent of the sites submitted to Yahoo! actually make it into the index.

Keep in mind, too, that Yahoo! considers Web sites as a whole, instead of considering individual pages separately. Therefore, submit only the main page of your site to Yahoo! and not the individual pages.

Here's what you need to know about Yahoo!:

- Web sites indexed: Approximately one million
- First among top 20 search services
- 47.55 million unique visitors

- As mentioned earlier, Google provides supplemental results to Yahoo!. So when performing a search at Yahoo!, visitors will first see category listings from Yahoo!, Web sites from Yahoo!'s index, and finally Web pages from the Google engine.

**TIP**   If your company has more than one domain, can you submit each separate domain to Yahoo! in hopes of getting them all indexed? Yes, as long as each domain offers totally different and unique content and stands on its own.

However, here's a word of caution. Don't link your domains together until you get them each listed in Yahoo!.

## Open Directory Project (ODP)

*Find It* **ONLINE**   Believe it or not, the Open Directory Project **(http://dmoz.org)** has been compared in importance to Yahoo!, which says a lot for this human-compiled directory. The ODP is unique in that the majority of its editors are unpaid volunteers, however.

These volunteers create categories and subcategories, add or reject sites to or from the directory, switch sites to more relevant categories, change titles and descriptions, and perform other general editing tasks. How many editors work at the ODP? In July 2000, the figure was at more than 27,000 and climbing fast.

What makes the ODP so important is its alliance with many of the major search engines. The ODP provides directory results to important engines like Lycos, HotBot, AOL Search, and Netscape Search. So even if your site isn't actually listed in HotBot's index, for example, you'll still have a presence on the engine if your site is listed in the ODP.

When submitting to the ODP, submit the main page of your site. You may be able to submit one or two interior pages, or the main page to another category. We discuss the ODP in more detail in Chapter 25.

Here's what you need to know about the Open Directory Project:

- Web sites indexed: 1.92+ million, as provided by ODP's site on July 15, 2000 (**http://dmoz.org**)
- Not among the top 20 search engines, according to Media Metrix (but the power of the ODP lies in providing directory results to so many of the other major engines).

- The ODP provides results to Google, Dogpile, EuroSeek, SavvySearch, and more. For a listing of sites that use ODP results, visit

**http://directory.netscape.com/Computers/Internet/WWW/ Searching_the_Web/Directories/Open_Directory_Project/ Sites_Using_ODP_Data**

 **TIP**  If you have a site whose main focus is to list various affiliate programs, don't expect to get it listed in the ODP. If there's one thing that can get you banned quickly from the ODP, it's trying to get affiliate sites indexed.

## NBCi

CNET and NBC joined forces to create Snap, which was a popularity directory. But toward the middle of 2000, NBC Internet took over Snap, renaming the directory NBCi (**http://www.nbci.com**).

One unique feature of NBCi is that sites submitted to it generally appear in the index within a few hours. These new submissions go into what is called the LiveDirectory, however. Once traffic to the sites increases, the sites are placed in front of a human editor for review. If accepted, the sites move into the main directory of NBCi, called the Top Sites Directory. Only about 5 percent of the LiveDirectory sites ever make it into NBCi's Top Sites Directory.

When performing a search at NBCi, results from the Top Sites Directory appear first, followed by LiveDirectory results, and finally supplemental results from the Inktomi engine.

Facts about NBCi:

- Web sites indexed: 800,000 in January 2000
- Sixth among top 20 search services
- 10.96 million unique visitors
- Like many of the engines, NBCi pulls supplemental results from Inktomi. NBCi also partners with GlobalBrain, which ranks sites based on click-through popularity.

 **TIP**  NBCi is now offering a pay submission service where you can pay to have your site reviewed for possible inclusion in NBCi's main directory, the Top Sites Directory. For more information, visit **http://www.nbci.com/LMOID/resource/0,566,home-1078,00.html?fd.ft.su.s-Id.s-1078.**

### LookSmart

**FIND IT
ONLINE**

Like Yahoo! and NBCi, LookSmart (**http://www.looksmart.com**) is a directory, not a search engine. LookSmart claims to reach 74 percent of U.S. Web users through its current network of alliances. In fact, LookSmart powers the directories of MSN, Excite@Home, CNN, and Time Warner, as well as more than 380 ISPs.

Here's what you need to know about LookSmart:

- Web sites indexed: Unknown
- Not listed among top 20 search services, according to Media Metrix(LookSmart's importance lies in the fact that it provides directory results to search engines such as Excite and AltaVista.)
- LookSmart uses AltaVista's index to supplement its index of sites, yet it also provides AltaVista with a branded version of its own directory. In fact, LookSmart is now solely powering AltaVista's directory, instead of AltaVista's previous marriage of ODP and LookSmart results.
- LookSmart also provides directory results to both Excite and MSN Search, and it uses Direct Hit technology to present search results ranked by site or click-through popularity.
- LookSmart users also are presented with Internet keyword results by RealNames, which we discuss in Chapter 23, "Purchasing Keywords at the Pay Engines."

**TIP** You have to pay to submit to LookSmart, unless you have a non-profit Web site. Is it worth the cost? Yes, since LookSmart provides directory results to two of the major engines, AltaVista and Excite, to name just a few.

**FIND IT
ONLINE**

To learn more about submitting to LookSmart, visit **http://submit.looksmart.com**.

## Search Engine Statistics

Although we covered the popularity and number of pages indexed in the individual engine and directory sections in this chapter, it will be helpful to you to be able to view those statistics in one central location.

Also, we've included a table showing the top 10 search engines for referring traffic to a site. Let's begin with a table showing the most popular search engines.

## Popularity of the Engines

***Find It*** **ONLINE**

Table 17.2 shows the popularity of the major search engines and directories, as provided by Media Metrix, a leader in statistical information, available at **http://mediametrix.com/landing.jsp**. The figures provided here are for March 2000.

### Table 17.2. Top Search Engines in March 2000

| Ranking | Site | Unique Visitors (in millions) |
|---------|------|-------------------------------|
| 1 | Yahoo.com* | 47.550 |
| 2 | Lycos.com* | 28.011 |
| 3 | GO.com | 21.185 |
| 4 | Excite* | 17.471 |
| 5 | AltaVista Search Services* | 11.953 |
| 6 | Snap.com Search & Services* | 10.961 |
| 7 | AskJeeves.com | 8.793 |
| 8 | LookSmart.com | 8.763 |
| 9 | GoTo.com | 7.296 |
| 10 | iWon.com | 6.917 |
| 11 | Google.com | 3.262 |
| 12 | Dogpile.com | 3.091 |
| 13 | WebCrawler.com | 2.159 |
| 14 | MetaCrawler.com | 1.893 |
| 15 | GoHip.com | 1.713 |
| 16 | MyWay.com | 1.485 |
| 17 | NLSearch.com | 1.323 |
| 18 | Mamma.com | 1.279 |
| 19 | Links2Go.com | 0.865 |
| 20 | Yahooligans.com | 0.771 |

*Represents an aggregation of commonly owned/branded domain names.

*Unique Visitors:* The estimated number of total users who visited the Web site once in a given month. All Unique Visitors are unduplicated (counted only once).

Sample Size: More than 50,000 individuals throughout the U.S. participated in the Media Metrix sample.

## Number of Pages Indexed

*FIND IT* **ONLINE**

Table 17.3 shows the number of Web pages indexed as of June 6, 2000, as taken from the Search Engine Watch Web site. You'll find updated information, as well as additional statistical information pertaining to the search engine industry, at this impressive Web site: **http://searchenginewatch.com/reports/sizes.html**.

## Search Engine Referral Traffic

*FIND IT* **ONLINE**

Learning which search engines send the most traffic to Web pages certainly can help you decide which engines and directories you need to concentrate on. The information in Table 17.4 is provided by StatMarket as of April 3, 2000, and is taken from the Search Engine Watch Web site (**http://searchenginewatch.com/reports/statmarket.html**).

### Table 17.3. Web Pages Indexed

| Ranking | Search Engine | Millions of Pages |
|---------|---------------|-------------------|
| 1 | Google* | 1,060 |
| 2 | WebTop.com** | 500 |
| 2 | Inktomi | 500 |
| 3 | AltaVista | 350 |
| 4 | FAST | 340 |
| 5 | Northern Light | 265 |
| 6 | Excite | 250 |
| 7 | GO | 50 |

*Google has indexed 560 million Web pages. Because of the way it uses link data, however, it has partially indexed another 500 million pages. So the size of its index, including indexed and partially indexed pages, is more than one billion Web pages.

**Although WebTop has an extremely large index, it is not considered one of the important major search engines and isn't very popular with users. Therefore, information on this engine is not included in this book.

### Table 17.4. Top 10 Search Engines Generating Traffic

| Ranking | Search Engine | Percentage of Traffic Generated |
| --- | --- | --- |
| 1 | Yahoo! | 53.4 |
| 2 | AltaVista | 18.0 |
| 3 | Excite | 6.7 |
| 4 | GO | 5.7 |
| 5 | Lycos | 4.3 |
| 6 | Snap | 3.3 |
| 7 | GoTo | 3.2 |
| 8 | MSN | 2.3 |
| 9 | WebCrawler | 1.2 |
| 10 | Ask Jeeves | 0.7 |

## Conclusion

Considering the major search engines and directories is certainly one of the most important aspects of Web site analysis. Because of the amount of potential traffic that can come through the major engines, failure to create engine-friendly Web pages can signal disaster to any Web site.

If you can keep in mind the relationships between the engines and directories, and make it a point of keeping up with those relationships as time goes on, you'll save yourself some valuable time in promoting your site. We'll expand on the concepts presented here in subsequent chapters.

Again, visit the Web site designed by the authors of this book to learn the status of the GO search engine: **http://www.kerri-leigh.com/wsar**.

# BASIC OPTIMIZATION STRATEGIES

**In This Chapter**

Choosing Effective Keyword Phrases

Placing Your Keywords for Best Results

Creating Captivating Titles and Descriptions

Building Additional Doorways into Your Site

Content Is Crucial!

Keeping Up with Industry Changes

Finding More Information

How do you go about creating a Web page that's "engine friendly?" What steps can you take that will help your pages be found in the search engines' results? Then what can you do to get those pages at the top of the results?

First you need to understand that *search engine positioning* is a process. It's much more involved than slapping up a few META tags and going back to your cup of coffee. To be successful, you must do the following:

- Consider each page of your Web site carefully.
- Choose keywords that will bring you traffic, which will convert to sales.
- Place those keywords strategically on your pages.
- Create titles and descriptions that will captivate searchers.
- Build new pages that focus on certain areas of your business or individual products and services.
- Keep up with changes in the industry.

These simplified steps skim the search engine positioning surface. But if you can get this information fixed in your mind, you can learn the more focused skills that will skyrocket your pages in the rankings.

## Choosing Effective Keyword Phrases

The single most important thing you can do in terms of search engine strategies is to choose the best keyword phrases for each individual Web page.

**NOTE**  Remember that when working with search engines, each individual page is considered separately, so you'll optimize each page separately, choosing different keywords depending on the content of the page.

Suppose that your company sells school supplies. Instead of using the keyword phrase "school supplies" in your tags and body text on every page in your site, you'll want to fine-tune that phrase, depending on the content of each page. If you have a page that concentrates on backpacks, for example, your tags and text on that page should center on the keyword "backpacks." If you have a page that deals with math supplies, everything on that page should point to related keyword phrases.

Although this certainly sounds like an easy task, believe us, it isn't. Also believe us when we say that if you choose the wrong keywords, your traffic will suffer.

Your goal is to choose keywords that will bring you traffic that ultimately will convert to sales. Having hundreds of thousands of hits on your site won't do you any good if no one buys your goods or services. If you should find yourself in that situation, you need to do some serious work on your keywords.

When considering which keywords will give you the most focused traffic, keep these important considerations in mind.

## Choose Keyword Phrases Versus Single Keywords

Did you know that most people search for keyword phrases rather than single keywords? As the world becomes more Internet savvy, people are discovering ways of fine-tuning their searches. They're learning that a search for "computers" will produce millions of results, many of which aren't related to what they're really looking for. But a search for "computer tutorials" will produce much more focused results.

Not only that, but let's think about this in terms of competition. If you choose a keyword like "computers," which produces more than 10 million results in AltaVista, how easy do you think it would be to achieve a top 10 ranking for that keyword? In a nutshell, almost impossible.

But if you choose a keyword phrase like "computer tutorials," the competition drops down to 4,000 results. Now we're getting somewhere!

Also think about it in terms of who will be searching for your site. Let's say that the luck of the gods was with you when you created your Web page, and you managed to get a #5 ranking under the keyword "computers." But let's say that your site sells computer tutorials.

Therefore, the vast majority of the traffic you'll receive will be looking for something that your site won't offer, and the chances of converting that traffic to sales won't be good.

Research has shown that choosing general keywords won't create more sales. Your traffic may skyrocket, yes, but that traffic won't convert to money in your pocket. After all, the visitors came to your site looking for something that you don't offer. So they left.

## People Search Using Lowercase Letters

Research has also shown that the majority of users search in all lower-case letters, even when searching for a proper noun. Most searchers would type in "san francisco restaurants," for example, versus "San Francisco restaurants."

So capitalize on this by making sure that you use the lowercase version of your keyword phrase whenever possible. If your keyword phrase is a proper noun, you can use the lowercase version on your page in places your visitors won't see, such as ALT tags, style tags, keyword META tags, and more, which we discuss later in this chapter in "Placing Your Keywords for Best Results."

**TIP** Some engines are *case sensitive,* which means that searches for keywords in lowercase, capitalized, and uppercase variations will produce different results. Other engines are not case sensitive, and still others are partially case sensitive, which complicates matters further.

Therefore, be sure to search for all variations of your keyword phrase in the engine. If you get varying results, you'll know that the engine is case sensitive, and you'll need to make sure to use all variations of your keyword phrase in the tags and text on your page.

## Take a General Keyword and Pair It with a Specific Keyword

Rather than choosing a competitive and general keyword like "real estate," add a specific keyword to it—for example, "half moon bay real estate." By doing so, you've eliminated much of your competition, making it much easier for you to achieve a top ranking under the keyword phrase that is very focused on your company.

## Use Misspelled Keywords!

Is your keyword phrase commonly misspelled? If so, capitalize on those bad spellers by using misspelled versions of your keyword phrase in your tags that aren't visible to the users.

For example, is your business located in "Los Angeles"? Have you considered using misspelled versions of the city, such as Las Angeles, Las Angels, or Los Angels?

## Use the Longest Version of Your Keywords

If one of your keywords is "market," consider using longer versions of the keyword—for example, "marketing," "marketable," "unmarketable," etc. In this manner, if someone searches for any of those variations, they'll find your site.

Another good rule to follow is to use the plural version of your keyword phrase.

 **NOTE**   Some of the engines use *word stemming,* which means that they also will search for word stems of your keyword. So a search for "America" will also produce results for "American."

To see if an engine employs word stemming, search for versions of your keyword phrase at the engine.

## Check Your Competition

Besides checking to see how many people have searched for your keyword phrase, you also want to see how many other Web pages have been created and optimized for your keyword phrase.

So after you've spent some time arriving at a list of 25 to 50 keywords, place those keywords in order of importance to your site.

Before deciding which words to use on your pages, however, visit one of the engines and search for each keyword phrase. How many results do you get?

If you get a million results, that keyword phrase is too competitive. Can you fine-tune the phrase by adding a descriptive or regional word? If you choose a keyword phrase that's too competitive, you'll have an extremely difficult time getting a top ranking. Plus, the traffic won't be targeted, so it more than likely won't convert to sales.

If there are few results for the keyword phrase, however, you won't get enough traffic from that keyword phrase. Again, your goal is to increase targeted traffic, so be sure to pick a keyword phrase that will give you the best chance of meeting that goal.

Start with a keyword phrase that produces several thousand results. Get a top ranking, and then gradually go after the more competitive keywords and increase your traffic in that manner. The more popular your site is in terms of both link and click-through popularity, the higher your rankings will be. At that time, you'll stand a much better chance at achieving top rankings for the more competitive keyword phrases.

## Use a Step-by-Step Approach to Choosing Keywords

Because choosing the most effective keywords for your pages can literally make or break an online business, spend a lot of time picking out ones that will bring you traffic that will convert to sales.

---

### *Caution—Don't Use Trademarked Terms*

When choosing keywords, use trademarked terms with extreme caution. Lawsuits are springing up everywhere, and you don't want to find yourself in the middle of one.

The whole problem with using trademarked terms came to the surface when certain Web masters used trademarked terms to lure visitors to a site, even though the site didn't sell those particular products.

Let's say that you sell stereo equipment over the Internet. You sell Brand A, but you don't sell Brand B. But in order to boost traffic to your site, you add Brand B keywords to your page. In effect, you're taking targeted traffic away from Brand B, when you don't have a license to sell its products. If Brand B finds out, you're in trouble.

But how could Brand B possibly find out if you use Brand B keywords in some of your tags? Corporations hire people who do nothing more than search for the illegal use of their trademarked terms, and believe us, they'll find you.

In fact, one of our students found this out the hard way. She wanted to advertise her search engine positioning services, so she used the keyword "WebPromote" written in that manner. The WebPromote company found out, and their lawyer sent a rather nasty e-mail. The student contacted us, and we explained why this was a problem, then walked her through getting back on the safe side.

But what if you have a page that compares your product, Brand A, to your competition, Brand B? Can you then use Brand B's keywords in your tags and text on your page? Possibly, but keep in mind that this won't prevent someone from suing you for trademark infringement. Judge whether it's worth the potential problems before going this route.

Consider the following approach:

1. Write out a focused description of each individual Web page. One or two keyword phrases should be highlighted on every page.

2. Do you sell goods or services? Product names make excellent keywords. Be sure to read the "Caution—Don't Use Trademarked Terms" sidebar in this chapter.

3. Start with a main keyword, and then add descriptive or regional words.

4. Write down as many ways as you can to describe your business, products, or services.

5. Visit competing sites and see what keywords they're using.

6. Consult a thesaurus. For an online thesaurus, visit **http://www.thesaurus.com/**.

7. Visit GoTo's Search Term Suggestion Tool (**http://inventory.go2.com/inventory/Search_Suggestion.jhtml**) for keyword ideas. GoTo is in the process of eliminating access to the Search Term Suggestion Tool, and it will soon become available only to subscribers.

8. Visit WordTracker (**http://www.wordtracker.com**) and register for a free trial of its services.

Both GoTo and WordTracker will tell you how many people have been searching for your keyword phrase over the past 24 hours. Look closely at these numbers. You certainly want to choose terms that will bring you traffic. So, if only one person searched for your keyword phrase, you may want to rethink your keyword choice.

 **TIP** For an in-depth article on choosing the right keywords and where to place those keywords, visit **http://www.onlinewebtraining.com/information.html**.

## Placing Your Keywords for Best Results

We've outlined several ways to help you choose the most effective keywords. Now you need to know where to place those keywords on your pages.

**NOTE** The goal in placing your keywords is to put them on your pages in such a way as to increase the *relevancy* of those keywords.

"Relevancy" is how well a document provides the information a user is looking for, as measured by each search engine's algorithm. The higher the relevancy, the higher the ranking in the search engine results, as a general rule.

More information on relevancy can be found in the "Proving that Content is Relevant" section of this chapter.

Before we begin, keep in mind that each page is an entity in and of itself when it comes to the search engines. So focus each page on one or two keyword phrases only. Don't try to optimize a page for more than that, because you'll end up diluting your important keyword phrase. In all likelihood, you'll find yourself ranking high under other keyword phrases anyway, but focus on one or two only.

Also keep in mind that your Web page's ranking is determined by which keywords a search engine determines your Web page is relevant to and how often those keywords are searched for. The ranking criteria differ from search engine to search engine.

If you organize your keywords to be consistent with a search engine's ranking criteria, your ranking with that particular engine will go up. That's why it's so important to study what each engine considers relevant.

When considering where to place your keywords, keep these important facts in mind:

- The engines consider the beginning of the page and the beginning of the tags to hold more *prominence.* By this, we mean that keywords placed at the beginning of your body text and tags will get more of a boost in relevancy than keywords placed at the end of the text or tags. So place your important keywords toward the beginning of your body text and tags!

- If you want a page to rank high under a certain keyword phrase, you have to *use* that keyword phrase in your text and tags! That sounds rather obvious, but you wouldn't believe how many Web masters are totally baffled because their page isn't getting a top ranking, yet they're not proving to the engine that the page is relevant to that keyword phrase by using it!

- Don't start out by using your keyword phrase in every single area that we've outlined here. Remember that simplicity is the key, and "less" often wins out over "more" in this business. Instead, selectively use your keywords in a few places, then submit your page to the engines. See what happens. If you don't get the rankings you want, go back over your page and optimize it again, adding your keyword phrase in more places.

- Pages located in the root domain generally have an easier time getting ranked high, versus pages that are in directories and subdirectories off the root domain. This goes against basic Web design guidelines, but it's something you need to remember.

**TIP** *The search engines like simplicity!* For such complicated technology, the search engines prefer simple pages over complex ones that use a lot of impressive technology.

Therefore, the simpler your page is, the easier it will be for you to get it in the top rankings in the search engines, unless you've chosen such a competitive keyword phrase that your efforts are in vain.

## Using META and Other Tags for Keywords

Because each search engine has a different ranking algorithm, and because that algorithm changes quite frequently, using your keyword phrase in these tags won't work for every one of the search engines. This section will give you a good guide for where to place your keyword phrase, however.

The most important tag on your page is your title tag, so be sure to use your keyword phrase toward the beginning of that tag. Headline tags are also very important, as is using your keyword phrase in link text.

For engine-specific information, see Chapter 24, "Engine-Specific Strategies."

**TIP**

**FIND IT ONLINE**

Search Engine Optimizer (**http://www.se-optimizer.com/**) is an effective tool for checking your page for various elements and offering tips and strategies for improving your page's ranking in a particular engine.

Submit Director (**http://www.submitdirector.com**) is an ideal service for small businesses. It will not only analyze your pages in terms of "search engine friendliness," but it will also submit your sites to the major engines.

The following list will give you some ideas of where you can place keywords on your page. We've used "Jeep CJ7 decals" as an example.

- Title tag

  ```
  <TITLE>Jeep CJ7 Decals</TITLE>
  ```

- META description tag

  ```
  <META name="description" content="Jeep CJ7 decals in a variety of
  styles in prices you can afford">
  ```

- META keyword tag

  ```
  <META name="keywords" content="jeep cj7 decals, JEEP CJ7 DECALS,
  car decals, automotive stickers">
  ```

 **NOTE** In working with our students, we have found that top-ranking sites in AltaVista often don't use META **tags at all. Our students generally could get better rankings in that engine if they didn't use** META **tags.**

- Headline tags

  ```
  <H3 ALIGN="CENTER">Jeep CJ7 decals are durable and long lasting</
  H3>
  ```

- Link text

  ```
  <A HREF="http://yourwebsite.com/keyword-phrase.htm">Click here
  for pictures of Jeep CJ7 decals.</A>
  ```

- Body text

  ```
  <BODY>

  <P>If you haven't been able to find Jeep CJ7 decals to help make
  your jeep look as good as new, you've come to the right place!</
  P>

  <P>We even have hard-to-find decals like the Golden Eagle, . . .
  </P>

  </BODY>
  ```

- ALT tags

  ```
  <IMG SRC="images/box.gif" ALT="jeep cj7 decals" WIDTH="415"
  HEIGHT="100">
  ```

- ALT tags using single-pixel images

  ```
  <IMG SRC="clr.gif" BORDER="0" ALT="jeep cj7 decals">
  ```

- Comment tags

  ```
  "<--jeep c7j decals-->
  ```

- Sample URL

  **http://www.yourwebsite.com/jeep-cj7-decals.html**

- Names of images

  ```
  "jeep-cj7-decals.gif"
  ```

- Sample domain name

  **http://www.jeep-cj7-decals.com**

  Using hyphens between keywords in the name of a domain will make it easier for the engines to recognize it as a keyword phrase. You may not want to use hyphens for the main domain of your company, however, because it's more difficult for people to remember to use those hyphens.

- Directory names

  **http://www.yourwebsite.com/jeep-cj7-decals/eagle.html**

- Subdomain names

  **http://jeep-cj7-decals.yourwebsite.com**

- `<NOFRAMES>` tag, even if you aren't using frames

  If your page lacks content, and if you don't want to add more content to the visible area of the page, consider using a `<NOFRAMES>` tag. Create a mini-Web site inside that tag that uses your important keyword phrase.

  ```
  <NOFRAMES>

  <P>If you haven't been able to find Jeep CJ7 decals to help make
  your jeep look as good as new, you've come to the right place!</
  P>

  <P>We even have hard-to-find decals like the Golden Eagle, . . .
  </P>

  </NOFRAMES>•     Style tag

  <STYLE>jeep c7j decals</STYLE>
  ```

- Font tag

  ```
  <FONT COLOR="jeep cj7 decals"></FONT>
  ```

- `META` author tag

  ```
  <META name="author" content="jeep cj7 decals">
  ```

- Background images

  ```
  <BODY background="images/background2.gif" text="#222222"
  ALT="jeep cj7 decals" bgcolor="white" link="#0033ff"
  vlink="#555555" alink="red">
  ```

In Chapter 19, "Analyzing Your Source Code," we'll analyze the source code of a Web page so you can see many of these tags in action.

**TIP**  Do you need to optimize every single page of your site? If the page is important, yes, optimize it. Use your important keyword phrase in many of the tags mentioned here and prove to the engines how relevant the page is to your keyword phrase!

## Considering Your Page's Keyword Weight

When deciding where to place your important keyword phrase on your page, you'll also need to consider the page's *keyword weight*.

Keyword weight, or *keyword density,* refers to the number of keywords that appear on your page in relation to the total number of words on the page.

You want your keyword weight to be in line with the keyword weight of top-ranking sites under your keyword phrase. In other words, if your keyword weight is 3 percent, but top-ranking sites under your keyword phrase have a keyword weight of around 5 percent, you'll want to increase your keyword weight.

Keyword weight can refer to the visible text on the page, all of the text plus tags, or even the weight of individual tags.

To determine the keyword weight of the visible body text of your page, cut and paste the viewable text of your Web page into a word processor. Have the program count the total number of words. Then run a find-and-replace operation, putting your keyword phrase in both areas. The program will search for your keyword phrase and "replace" it with the same keyword phrase, and it will tell you the number of times it replaced the phrase.

Take the number of times you used your keyword phrase and divide it by the total number of words on your page to determine your page's keyword weight. For example, if you used your keyword phrase five times on the page, and there are 100 words on the page, your keyword weight is 5 percent.

Although each engine prefers a different keyword weight, and the best way to determine what an engine likes is to study your top-ranking competitors, a good general keyword weight for your viewable body text is 3 to 5 percent.

**TIP** In addition to calculating your keyword weight manually as we've done here, you can use a software program or Web site to determine your page's keyword density. Not only will these services determine your keyword weight, but they will compare your keyword weight to top-ranking sites under your keyword phrase.

**FIND IT ONLINE** Keyword Density Analyzer (**http://www.grsoftware.net/search_engines/software/ grkda/grkda.html**) is an excellent software program that will determine the keyword weight of your page as a whole as well as the individual tags on your page.

Keyword Count (**http://keywordcount.com/**) is a Web site that will determine your keyword weight.

## Creating Captivating Titles and Descriptions

Your title tag is the most important tag on your page. Why? Because almost all of the engines place a lot of relevancy on keywords used in the title tag, and because the engines use the contents of the title tag in the search results. Also, the contents of the title tag appear at the top of the browser window.

Description META tags are important, too, because they often are seen in the search results. Many of the major engines don't consider the content of META tags when determining relevancy, however.

Write your title and description as if you're writing ad copy for an advertising campaign. Use words that will appeal to viewers and make them anxious to visit your site to learn more. Sell the idea of visiting your Web site through effective title and description tags!

Think of it this way. When you perform a search at one of the search engines, do you always choose the #1 ranked site and visit it first?

Most people will glance over the titles and descriptions of the sites listed, and they'll visit a site that has an appealing title and description and seems to offer what they're looking for.

So if you have a #8 ranking, yet you have a captivating title and description, you may actually get more traffic than the #3 ranked site if it has failed in the title and description department.

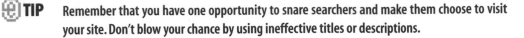

> **TIP** Remember that you have one opportunity to snare searchers and make them choose to visit your site. Don't blow your chance by using ineffective titles or descriptions.

What about using your company name in the title tag? Does your company have a significant amount of name recognition? In other words, how many people will be searching for your company's name?

More than likely, people will be searching for your company by using keywords that are related to the goods and services you provide, rather than your company name. So don't make the mistake of using your company name instead of an important keyword phrase in your title tag.

Of course, it's always a good idea to create a page that's optimized for your company name. But be sure to concentrate on important keywords on your main page.

Because the main or index page of a site is assigned more relevancy than interior pages, it's often easier to get an index page ranked higher than other pages. Capitalize on this by optimizing the index page for the most important keywords for your site.

## Tips for Writing Effective Titles and Descriptions

When creating titles and descriptions, keep these important suggestions in mind.

- Don't use dull or boring titles.
- Keep your titles and descriptions simple and easy to read.
- Use compelling words in the tags.
- Use questions in your title and description tags, and make your potential visitors think!

  If our students have a difficult time coming up with an effective title or description, we tell them to come up with an interesting question. Questions often can cause potential visitors to stop long enough to answer the question in their mind, and this pause can help them decide to visit your site.
- Use your keyword phrase toward the beginning of both tags.
- Don't use just a series of keywords in the tags. Instead, create captivating tags that will bring you business.

- Don't use ALL CAPS in the tags.
- Don't Capitalize The First Letter Of Every Word, because it's difficult to read and annoying.
- Don't overdo your use of keywords. Use your keyword phrase once in both tags.
- Make sure your title and description tags are interesting, make readers anxious to learn more, are easy to read and professional, include time and money if appropriate, and solve a problem quickly and efficiently.

## Analyzing a Sample of Titles and Descriptions

In Figure 18.1, you see a screen shot of a search at Excite for the keyword phrase "stock market." This screen shot will certainly point out the importance of creating effective titles and descriptions.

In Figure 18.1, are the titles and descriptions designed to pull traffic into the site? Are you impressed?

If you were searching for "stock market," which of these sites would you visit first? Which appeals to you and makes you want to visit the site?

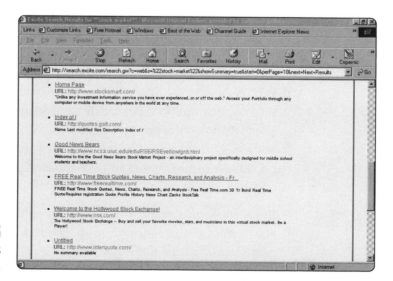

**FIGURE 18.1**

A search at Excite for "stock market" shows why titles and descriptions are important.

Notice how one of the sites uses "Home Page" as the title of the site. Another isn't using a title tag at all, so it's listed as "Untitled." That site also isn't using a description tag.

One of the sites is simply using a listing of items that are available at the site, and each individual word is capitalized, making it extremely difficult to read.

This is the second page of results, by the way. If these sites had used the keyword phrase "stock market" in the title tags, would their rankings have been higher?

## Building Additional Doorways into Your Site

As we mentioned previously, you can generally assume that you'll only be able to optimize a page of your site for only one or two keyword phrases. So what about the other 25 keyword phrases important to your business?

We also mentioned that each search engine has a unique set of likes and dislikes, and that the ranking algorithm of one engine is totally different from the algorithm of another engine. So pages that rank well for one engine may not do well with the others.

How can you be found under your additional keyword phrases and through the other engines?

Simple. You can create content-rich information pages, also known as *doorway pages*, and bring in traffic through those doors. Doorway pages are also called *gateway* or *splash pages*.

What are doorway pages? They're simply highly fine-tuned pages optimized for one keyword phrase and generally for only one engine. Everything on the page points to that one keyword phrase and that one engine. This is an excellent reason why you should segregate your data, because it's much easier to get a focused page ranked high in the search engines, rather than a page that tries to cover too many different areas.

Let's look at a screenshot of a sample doorway page, and then a screenshot of the main page of the site. Figure 18.2 shows a doorway page leading into the Wick Homes site.

**FIGURE 18.2**

A doorway page for the Wisconsin Home Builders, Wick Homes site.

The layout of the page and everything on the page points to one central theme: Wisconsin home builders.

Now, let's look at the main page for the site in Figure 18.3.

Notice that the layout of both pages is very similar. Visitors to the doorway page won't click on the main page and feel like they've entered a totally different site.

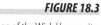

**FIGURE 18.3**

Main page of the Wick Homes site.

With doorways, you'll use the same strategies you've learned so far. You'll put a lot of thought into your keyword choice; you'll choose various places to put your keyword phrases; you'll make sure that the keyword phrase is used prominently on your page; you'll create captivating titles and descriptions; and so forth.

In the past, doorway pages were a "one-way street" into your site, meaning that traffic went from the doorway page into the main site, but not back through the main site to the doorway page.

When possible, consider linking from your main page to your doorway pages, because this can benefit your site in many ways. One-way street doorway pages sometimes are difficult to get top rankings on. After all, traffic isn't moving back and forth between those pages as it is in the main portion of your site. The only way someone will learn about one-way street doorway pages is through top search engine rankings. So those doorway pages will suffer from a popularity point of view.

So instead of using hidden links, as is a widely accepted practice these days, consider using visible links. The engines seem to be on the verge of cracking down on the use of hidden links. Therefore, save yourself some time and trouble by moving toward visible links with new pages that you create. Plus, with visible links, you have the opportunity to use link text that includes your keyword phrase, and most of the major engines place considerable relevance on link text. Remember that link text refers to the text that becomes a link—the words between the `<A HREF="...">` and `</A>` tags.

If you don't want to place a visible link to your doorways on your main page, at least add your links to a site map and link to the site map from your main page. Give the engines additional ways of finding your doorway pages. In Chapter 19, "Analyzing Your Source Code," we discuss this concept further.

## Adding Doorway Pages

When might you use doorway pages? Use doorway pages to create the following:

- Separate product pages
- Separate pages for each of your services

- A page that's optimized for your company name
- Regionally specific pages
- Pages optimized for specific engines
- Pages optimized for particular keyword phrases that you haven't been able to target elsewhere
- Newsworthy items about your company
- Any other pages with focused content

## Tips for Creating Effective Doorway Pages

When creating doorway or information pages, keep these valuable tips in mind:

- Use your important keyword phrase in your META tags and other tags.
- Fine-tune, fine-tune, fine-tune! The main thing to remember when creating doorway pages is to *focus*.
- Vary the content of your doorway pages. The engines don't like machine-generated doorway pages where keywords are simply swapped out.
- Create your doorway pages using the same general format as other pages on your site. You don't want your doorway pages to scream, "I'm a doorway page!"
- Use *content* in your doorway pages. Content can refer to related links, body text, FAQs, community-building devices, giveaways, etc.
- Don't create copies of your index page and use them as doorway pages. In the past, a common practice was to create five to ten copies of the main page of a site and name them index1.html, index2.html, index3.html, etc. Keep in mind that any engine that spots an index4.html knows that there are at least four other index pages floating around somewhere.

 **TIP**   For more information about doorway pages, visit Search Engine Watch at **http://searchenginewatch.internet.com/webmasters/bridge.html**.

 **FIND IT ONLINE**   Or, for an article about doorway pages, visit **http://www.onlinewebtraining.com/information/doorway_strategies.html**.

In Chapter 19, you'll study an example of a doorway page as we analyze the page's source code.

# Content Is Crucial!

The days of getting top rankings for a page that contains only the keyword phrase are over. Now, if you want top search engine rankings, you have to work for it.

When designing Web pages, keep in mind that you're trying to prove to the engine that your pages are relevant for a particular keyword phrase, which will cause that page to rank higher in the index.

The best way to prove the page's worth is to give the engine what it wants to see: related content.

## Proving that Content Is Relevant

In most cases, a Web site where all the pages are focused on a single topic will have an easier time getting top rankings for those related keywords than a site that offers just a page or two about a particular topic.

Why is that? Many of the search engines are moving toward being *theme* engines. This means that they look at Web sites as a whole, including the content of the pages and incoming and outgoing links. Think of it this way. When an engine crawls a site, it looks for links. If you're using link text with your keyword phrase, you're showing the engine that links off your main page are related in content to that main page. Or if the keyword phrase is in the URL of those links, the engine will notice that the pages are related in content.

By the same token, if you use related links to other Web sites, you're showing the engine that you're offering related content to your visitors.

As mentioned previously, *content* can refer to body text, related incoming and outgoing links, link text, tags, and other relevant areas of your page—such as polls, contests, bulletin boards, chat rooms, giveaways, etc. In other words, anything that can be related to the focus of your site can be considered the site's or page's content.

## How Can You Create a Content-Rich Page?

The best way to write content is to approach it from the point of view of writing an article about your important keyword phrase. Don't be afraid of length, because most of the engines like longer pages these days, even around 800 to 1,000 words.

Use mini-headings, generally beginning with a large headline tag and moving down the page using smaller headlines in a graduated manner. Begin the page with body text rather than a graphic. Engines can't see graphics, and only some of the engines consider the content of ALT tags when determining relevancy. So place body text before graphics whenever possible.

Keep your pages simple and highly focused. Don't use technologies that could be detrimental to search engine rankings. We cover problem technologies in Chapter 21, "Analyzing Technology That Can Be Detrimental to Search Engine Rankings."

Link your pages to other pages on your site and to related and important Web sites.

**TIP** A way to add content in a manageable amount without creating long pages is through a <NOFRAMES> **tag.**

You can add content through <NOFRAMES> tags even if your site doesn't use frames. Your Web visitors won't see the added content, but the engines will. Be sure to use your important keyword phrase in the <NOFRAMES> **tag.**

Keep in mind that visitors using Lynx or some older browsers will see the content inside the <NOFRAMES> **tag. Therefore, word the content in such a way that it will be non-disruptive to the rest of the page.**

When working on your pages, always take good notes. In this manner, if your rankings go down, you can backtrack and regain your good rankings. Also, you'll be able to see what's working and what isn't by reviewing your notes.

## Keeping Up with Industry Changes

The search engines change their ranking algorithms constantly and without notice. One day, your #1 site will fall to a #15, and you can suspect that the ranking algorithm for that engine has shifted and it's time to reoptimize the page.

But how on earth do you keep up with the industry changes?

Luckily, some excellent online and offline resources are available where you can learn more about search engine positioning and keep up with industry changes.

*Find It*
**ONLINE**

- Planet Ocean (**http://www.searchenginehelp.com/moreinfo**) offers a subscription service that features a monthly newsletter and access to its *Unfair Advantage Book.* Planet Ocean, a leader in the search engine industry, does a tremendous amount of research, backing up all of its articles with hard facts.

- Search Engine Watch (**http://www.searchenginewatch.com**) is one of the best sources for free information about search engines. You can register to receive its free monthly newsletter. Or for a fee, you can gain entrance to the subscribers-only area of the site, which includes a bi-monthly newsletter.

- The Vault (**http://www.1-internet-marketing.com/vault.htm**) provides "search engine secrets" that you won't find anywhere else, all documented by extensive research.

- Web Search at About.com (**http://websearch.about.com/ internet/websearch/**) offers a wide assortment of free articles and resources aimed at the search engine industry.

- *MarketPosition* (**http://www.webposition.com/newsletter.htm**) is a free newsletter published by First Place Software, maker of WebPosition Gold.

- Internet Day (**http://internetday.com/**) publishes a free newsletter that covers more than the search engines and is a good well-rounded source for online marketing information.

- Academy of Web Specialists (**http:// www.onlinewebtraining.com**) offers beginning and advanced online courses in search engine positioning strategies, so this is where to go if you want to work with an expert and get individualized help in boosting your site's rankings.

- *Maximize Web Site Traffic, Build Web Site Traffic Fast and Free by Optimizing Search Engine Placement* is a book written by one of the co-authors of this book, Robin Nobles. You can purchase this book through leading bookstores like Amazon or Barnes & Noble, or through **http://www.robinsnest.com**.

We've mentioned a few software programs in this chapter, but let's cover a few more, because there are some excellent software programs and services that can help you in optimizing your site. Keep in mind, however, that the programs will work much better for you if you understand search engine positioning strategies, because you then can use your knowledge and make the program operate more efficiently.

*Find It*
**ONLINE**

- Search Engine Optimizer (**http://www.se-optimizer.com**) allows you to run a URL through the program, and you'll be presented with a list of potential problem areas and ways that the problems can be solved. It's an easy-to-use program with a simple learning curve.

- WebPosition Gold (**http://www.webpositiongold.com**) is a popular software program that will provide ranking reports, analyze Web pages, submit your pages, and more. This program's ranking reports are worth the cost of the program, even aside from the other features.

- Keyword Density Analyzer (**http://www.grsoftware.net/ search_engines/software/grkda/grkda.html**) will analyze the keyword weight of your pages and compare it to other top-ranking pages.

- Top Dog (**http://www.topdog2000.com**) provides ranking reports for more than 200 search engines, including international ones, and it will also submit your pages to a couple of hundred search engines.

- PositionPro (**http://www.positionpro.com**) is a submission service that will submit your pages, then track your rankings. Its "analyze" function provides an amazing amount of information that will help you create pages that the engines are sure to like.

- WordTracker (**http://www.wordtracker.com**) will help you choose the most effective keywords for your pages by searching through the major search engines and letting you know what people are really searching for.

- Website Promoter **(http://www.cyberspacehq.com)** is a comprehensive yet easy-to-use program that will analyze, submit, and track your pages with the major search engines.

- Site Promoter **(http://www.sitepromoter.com)** will help you create pages that are designed to go to the top of the search engine's rankings and help you keep them there.

We've provided free trial versions of many of these software programs on the CD-ROM that comes with this book.

## Finding More Information

For more information about creating engine-friendly pages, visit these URLs:

*Find It*
**ONLINE**

- Search Engine Related Articles— **http://www.onlinewebtraining.com/information/ search_engine_articles.html**

- Search Engine Showdown— **http://www.searchengineshowdown.com/**

- Problems Using Trademarked Terms— **http://searchenginewatch.internet.com/sereport/9805- metatags.html**

- What People Search For— **http://searchenginewatch.internet.com/facts/searches.html**

- Back to Basics: META Tags—**http://www.webdeveloper.com/html/ html_metatags.html**

- How to Use HTML META Tags— **http://www.searchenginewatch.com/meta.htm**

- META Tag Lawsuits—**http://searchenginewatch.com/resources/ metasuits.html**

- What Can META Do for You—**http://www.hotwired.com/ webmonkey/html/96/51/index2a.html**

- Search Engine Tutorial for Web Designers— **http://www.northernwebs.com/set/index.html**

## Conclusion

Positioning your pages in the search engines requires considerable thought and planning. Remember to consider each page separately, and use tags on each page that are focused only on one or two keyword phrases.

Don't approach search engine positioning like a house on fire. Instead, try a few strategies, then wait to see how those strategies work before trying a few more.

Keep in mind that the engines like simplicity. Use good solid content on a simply designed page, focusing everything on the page toward one keyword phrase only, and your page stands an excellent chance at doing well in the rankings. Remember that your goal is to increase targeted traffic to your site—traffic that will convert to sales. If your traffic isn't converting to sales, you need to reconsider your keyword strategies as well as the overall design of your pages and site.

Finally, always take good notes when you're working on your pages. That way, if your rankings fall, you can backtrack and regain them.

# ANALYZING YOUR SOURCE CODE

**In This Chapter**

Examining HTML Areas that Can Affect Search
Engine Rankings

Do NOT Spam!

Revising Your Code to Improve Rankings

A Step-by-Step Analysis of Your Source Code

Using Analysis Tools and Services

In a nutshell, the source code is the guts of your Web site. It's also what the engines see when they visit your site, which is why it's so important.

When an engine's spider stops by your site to index pages, it doesn't see the beautifully created graphics, the impressive navigation bar, or the well-designed page in general. Instead, it sees the true skeleton of your site in all its glory.

What does this mean to you? It means that you need to step back from the visible design of your page and consider the page's skeleton because that's what the engines see. Problems with your HTML could conceivably present ranking problems. If the design strategies you're using push important keyword-containing text farther down on the page, your page could have ranking problems. If your HTML editor is running amok and adding irrelevant <META> tags, your site could experience ranking problems.

In this chapter, you'll take the basic knowledge you learned in Chapter 18, "Basic Optimization Strategies," and apply it further to your site as it pertains to your HTML. You'll also learn how to keep out of trouble with the search engines by not spamming, and you'll look at possible changes you can make that could help your search engine rankings.

## Examining HTML Areas that Can Affect Search Engine Rankings

The best way to learn how to analyze source code is to start with an example of a Web page and take it apart piece by piece. In this manner, you'll easily discover problems with the page, and you can see the skeleton of the page just like the engines see it. So let's look at an example of source code, and we'll tear it apart throughout this chapter.

### Looking at a Source Code Sample

The source code example in Listing 19.1 is optimized for the keyword phrase "search engines." There's a possibility that the page could rank high under additional keywords or keyword phrases as well. It's generally a good idea to optimize a page for just one keyword phrase only, though, especially if it's competitive.

Before we view the source code, let's see what the page would look like on the Web. In Figure 19.1, you'll see a screen shot of the page.

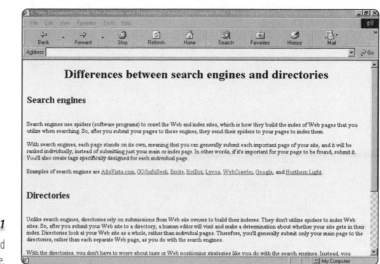

**FIGURE 19.1**

How the source code example would look online.

 **CAUTION**   Keep in mind that this example uses several spamming strategies that you won't want to use, which you'll discover as you move through the chapter. To make you aware of where spam occurs in this page's code, we've added HTML comment tags following each incident.

### Listing 19.1
### A Web page optimized for the keyword phrase "search engines."

```
<HTML>
<HEAD>
<META http-equiv="content-type" content="text/html;charset=iso-8859-
1">
<META name="generator" content="Adobe GoLive 4">
<META name="description" content="Learn the differences between
search engines and directories in distance learning courses.">
<META name="keywords" content="directories, search engines, distance
learning, directories, search engines, distance learning, directo-
ries, search engines, distance learning, directories, search engines,
distance learning, directories, search engines, distance learning,
directories, search engines, distance learning, directories, search
engines, distance learning, directories, search engines, distance
learning"> <-- See the Do NOT Spam section of this chapter--><META
http-equiv="refresh" content="1;URL=http://www.yourwebsite222.com"
target="_top"> <-- See the Do NOT Spam section of this chapter--
><META name="author" content="Joe Anonymous">
```

```
<META name="ROBOTS" content="NOINDEX">

<TITLE>Learn more about search engines and directories in distance
learning courses! </TITLE>

</HEAD>

<BODY>

<CENTER>

<H1>Differences between search engines and directories<BR>

<BR>

</H1>

</CENTER>

<INPUT type="hidden" name="HIDDEN" value="search engines"> <-- See
the Do NOT Spam section of this chapter--><H2>Search engines</H2>

<P><BR>

Search engines use spiders (software programs) to crawl the Web and
index sites, which is how they build the index of Web pages that you
utilize when searching. So, after you submit your pages to these
engines, they send their spiders to your pages to index them.<BR>

<BR>

With search engines, each page stands on its own, meaning that you
can generally submit each important page of your site, and it will be
ranked individually, instead of submitting just your main or index
page. In other words, if it's important for your page to be found,
submit it. You'll also create tags specifically designed for each
individual page.<BR>

<BR>

Examples of search engines follow:

<A HREF="http://www.altavista.com">AltaVista.com</A>,

<A HREF="http://infoseek.go.com">GO/InfoSeek</A>,

<A HREF="http://search.excite.com">Excite</A>,

<A HREF="http://hotbot.lycos.com">HotBot</A>,

<A HREF="http://www.lycos.com">Lycos</A>,

<A HREF="http://www.webcrawler.com">WebCrawler</A>,

<A HREF="http://www.google.com">Google</A>, and

<A HREF="http://www.northernlight.com">Northern Light</A>.<BR>

<BR>

<BR>

</P>

<H2>Directories</H2>

<P><BR>

</P>
```

```
<P>Unlike search engines, directories rely on submissions from Web
site owners to build their indexes. They don't utilize spiders to
index Web sites. So, after you submit your Web site to a directory, a
human editor will visit and make a determination about whether your
site gets in its index. Directories look at your Web site as a whole,
rather than individual pages. Therefore, you'll generally submit only
your main page to the directories, rather than each separate Web
page, as you do with the search engines.<BR>
<BR>
With the directories, you don't have to worry about tags or Web
positioning strategies like you do with the search engines. Instead,
you submit your site on their online submission form, and an editor
will visit.<BR>
<BR>
Examples are
<A HREF="http://search.yahoo.com">Yahoo!</A>, the
<A HREF="http://dmoz.org">Open Directory Project</A>, and
<A HREF="http://home.nbci.com">NBCi</A>.<BR>
<BR>
<BR>
</P>
<H3>What exactly is &quot;web positioning&quot; or &quot;web
optimization&quot;?</H3>
<P><BR>
</P>
<P>Web positioning, or Web optimization, is the art or science of
getting your Web site ranked, or positioned, in the search engines'
search results.<BR>
<BR>
The bottom line is this: If you want your Web site to be found, you
need to employ <A HREF="http://www.globalwebpositioning.com/">Web
positioning strategies</A> so that you can get the site into the top
rankings of the major search engines.<BR>
<BR>
And that's what distance learning <A HREF="http://
www.onlinewebtraining.com">search engine courses</A> are all
about.<BR>
<BR>
</P>
<H3>Very Important!!</H3>
<P><BR>
</P>
```

```
<P>The vast majority of the time, the top Web pages are very simple
pages without a lot of fancy tags and HTML.<BR>

<BR>

You'll find #1 sites that don't use an overabundance of tags. Most of
them don't use techniques such as frames, tables, or Java. They're
simple Web pages, and much of the time, they aren't very pretty.<BR>

<BR>

But, they're #1.<BR>

<BR>

So keep this in mind. The search engines like simplicity. A favorite
saying among writers/journalists is:<BR>

<BR>

<B>K.I.S.S. -- Keep It Simple, Stupid!</B><BR>

<BR>

</P>

<P>This certainly applies to <A HREF="http://
www.onlinewebtraining.com/site-map.html">search engine positioning</
A> as well.<BR>

<BR>

Also, &quot;more&quot; is definitely not better than &quot;less&quot;
in this business. The more times you use your keyword phrase does not
mean that your rankings will be higher than a Web page that uses the
keyword phrase a lot less. The more tags you use does not mean the
higher the rankings you'll get, either.<BR>

<BR>

So start out simple and build from there. Or if you're already using
a lot of &quot;extra&quot; tags, remove them and start over. You may
be very surprised at your rankings.<BR>

</P>

<P><BR>

</P>

<H4>Helpful links about search engines and distance learning
courses:</H4>

<P><BR>

<A HREF="http://www.onlinewebtraining.com"><IMG height="32"
width="32" src="images/circle.gif" border="0" alt="search engines"></
A> Take online search engine courses through distance learning at the
Academy of Web Specialists.<BR>

<BR>

<A HREF="http://www.searchenginehelp.com/acws/"><IMG height="32"
width="32" SRC="images/circle.gif" border="0" alt="search engines"></
A> Subscribe to an excellent newsletter about the search engines at
Planet Ocean.<BR>

<BR>
```

```
</P>
<NOFRAMES>
<P>You'll discover many differences between search engines and
directories. When working with directories, consider the human
element and create your pages accordingly. With search engines,
consider the spiders, and think carefully about what they actually
see on your pages.
</NOFRAMES>
<DIV align="left">
<P><Br>
<BR>
<BR>
<BR>
<BR>
<BR>
<BR>
</P>
</DIV>
<CENTER>
<!--See the Do NOT Spam section of this chapter-->
<P><FONT size="1">search engines, directories, distance learning,
search engines, directories, distance learning,</FONT></P>
<P><FONT size="1">search engines, directories, distance learning,
search engines, directories, distance learning,</FONT></P>
<P><FONT size="1">search engines, directories, distance learning,
search engines, directories, distance learning,</FONT></P>
</CENTER>
</BODY>
</HTML>
```

## Optimizing the <HEAD> Section of Your Page

As you learned in Chapter 18, the prominence of keywords on your page and in your tags is very important when considering relevancy. So the portion of your source code that is toward the top of the page is one of the most important areas of your page.

The first thing to consider when working in the <HEAD> section is that simplicity rules. Don't clutter up the section so that the engine has to dig through it to discover your important keyword phrases. Prominently display your keywords, and you'll stand a much better chance at getting top rankings.

In our source code example, we've highlighted the ‹HEAD› section in bold text.

## Creating an Effective <TITLE> Tag

In the ‹HEAD› section of our example, where is the ‹TITLE› tag? Remember that the ‹TITLE› tag is, by far, the most important tag on the page. Is it at the very top of the ‹HEAD› area where it should be?

No. It's buried beneath several ‹META› tags, as you can see in the following code:

```
<HEAD>
<META http-equiv="content-type" content="text/html;charset=iso-8859-
1">
<META name="generator" content="Adobe GoLive 4">
<META name="description" content="Learn the differences between
search engines and directories in distance learning courses.">
<META name="keywords" content="directories, search engines, distance
learning, directories, search engines, distance learning, directo-
ries, search engines, distance learning, directories, search engines,
distance learning, directories, search engines, distance learning,
directories, search engines, distance learning, directories, search
engines, distance learning, directories, search engines, distance
learning">
<META http-equiv="refresh" content="1;URL=http://
www.yourwebsite222.com" target="_top">
<META name="author" content="Joe Anonymous">
<META name="ROBOTS" content="NOINDEX">
<TITLE> Learn more about search engines and directories in distance
learning courses! </TITLE>
</HEAD>
```

Move that ‹TITLE› tag to the very top of your page, right under the <HEAD> tag. Then show the engine how prominent your keywords are by placing your important keywords toward the beginning of the tag.

## <META> Tags

Now let's talk about the ‹META› tags.

Because some of the engines consider the content of ‹META› tags when determining relevancy, the keyword-containing ‹META› tags need to be placed directly below the ‹TITLE› tag. So, in our source code example, we would need to move the <META> description and <META> keyword tags directly under the <TITLE> tag.

When analyzing your page, remember to keep the number of <META> tags down to a minimum. Believe it or not, the engines can easily get confused by what's important and what isn't. You can't take a chance when it comes to the success of your page, so remove all irrelevant <META> tags.

### Beware of Irrelevant <META> Tags!

Some HTML editors stick in irrelevant <META> tags or other tags in the <HEAD> section of your page. Most of the time, these tags are simply advertisements for the HTML editor, and they do your pages no good whatsoever.

In our <HEAD> example, notice the following tags:

```
<META http-equiv="content-type" content="text/html;charset=iso-8859-1">
<META name="generator" content="Adobe GoLive 4">
```

The HTML editor Adobe GoLive placed those tags in the page without our permission. Delete them! There's absolutely no reason to keep the tags on your page.

Other HTML editors, such as HotMetal Pro, will place a comment tag at the very top of the page directly under the <HTML> tag, like this:

```
<!DOCTYPE HTML PUBLIC "-//SoftQuad Software//DTD HoTMetaL PRO
5.0::19981217::extensions to HTML 4.0//EN" "hmpro5.dtd">
```

Delete it! Again, it does your page no good.

What about a <META> author tag? Does the tag contain our important keyword phrase? No. Will it help with your relevancy? No. Get rid of it!

But what about putting your important keyword phrase in your <META> author tag, rather than the name of the author? The Inktomi engines may consider the content of <META> author tags when determining relevancy, so you can certainly try that strategy with those engines. Currently, the other engines don't, but that's always subject to change.

In our example, we used a <META> robots <NOINDEX> tag. By using this tag, we're telling the engines *not* to index the page. Is that what we really want? Don't we want this page in the index? If we don't, we'll certainly want to keep in the tag, but keep in mind that not all the engines support the <META> robots tag, so you may have to use a robots.txt file instead.

**TIP**

**FIND IT ONLINE**

For information on how to create a robots.txt file, which you can use to keep spiders out of various pages on your site, visit a robots.txt tutorial at **http://country-art.com/class/robotstxt.htm**. The tutorial, which was created by an instructor of the Academy of Web Specialists, refers to an excellent software program, RoboGen, which will help you create robots.txt files.

### Beware of Redirect Tags!

In our example, we used a <META> refresh tag, as in the following:

```
<META http-equiv="refresh" content="1;URL=http://
www.yourwebsite222.com" target="_top">
```

As you know, redirect tags can serve a valuable purpose in Web design. Most of the major engines consider the <META> refresh tag to be spam, however, which we cover later in this chapter. So rather than use a <META> refresh tag, consider using a Java or server-side redirect instead.

If you feel like you have to use a <META> refresh tag, be sure to set it at 30 or above, rather than 1, as in this example. Yes, 30 is terribly slow, and your visitors can sprout new gray hair just waiting for the page to refresh. This is the safest strategy when using <META> refresh tags, however.

Also, if you use a refresh tag, be sure to keep the content of your page updated and relevant, so you're giving your visitors something interesting to read while they wait for the refresh.

### What <META> Tags Are Needed?

If an engine considers and uses the content of <META> description and/or keyword tags, keep those tags on your page, as a general rule. The rest can usually be deleted with no problems.

## Analyzing the Body of Your Page

In our source code example, what's the first thing in the <BODY> section of the page? A headline tag.

```
<BODY>
<CENTER>
<H1>Differences between search engines and directories<BR>
<BR>
</H1>
</CENTER>
```

Most of the major engines place a lot of relevancy on the contents of headline tags, so use them frequently. Many search engine optimizers start with a large headline tag at the top of the page and then gradually work their way down to smaller headline tags throughout the page. Try to use your important keyword phrase in each of the headline tags if at all possible.

 **TIP** Be sure to use headline tags instead of a larger font size because a larger font size won't help your relevancy nearly as much as a headline tag containing your keyword phrase. You can even consider putting the entire body text in a small headline tag, such as <H4>.

Also notice that our page begins with *text* rather than a graphic. When possible, try to begin your pages with text that the engines can read. Engines can't read graphics, so a graphic at the top of the page will push your important keyword-containing text down below the graphic. Some engines consider the content of <ALT> tags, but most of them don't, so don't think you can use that strategy to get away from starting the page with text.

Glance back over our source code example. Notice the number of times that our most important keyword phrase, "search engines," has been used. The phrase has been highlighted in bold text to make it easier for you to spot the keywords.

Notice that many of the paragraphs begin with "search engines," and that the keyword phrase is sprinkled throughout the body of the page. Toward the end of the page, the keyword phrase is used in link text and even in a <NOFRAMES> tag.

At the very bottom of the page, you'll see several keywords used in a tiny font size, which is considered spam. We've used this as a spam example, and we discuss it further in the "Do NOT Spam!" section of this chapter.

As we mention in Chapter 18, arriving at an appropriate keyword weight as compared to top-ranking sites for your keyword phrase is very important. So when creating and working on your own pages, check your keyword weight carefully. Don't go overboard with the use of keywords, but don't under-use them either. Instead, check out your competition and make your decision based on what's effective in top-ranking sites at that point in time.

Remember that if the page doesn't contain enough content, you can add additional content to your page through a <NOFRAMES> tag, as we've done here. Visitors won't be able to see the content of a <NOFRAMES> tag, but engines can.

## Linking to Relevant Sites or Pages

When creating your pages, consider linking to other related pages of your site or to other sites that offer related content. By doing so, you're proving to the engines that your pages are relevant for the particular keyword phrase. You can highlight certain words and hyperlink them to other pages, as in our source code example:

```
<P>The bottom line is this: if you want your Web site to be found,
you need to employ <A HREF="http://www.globalwebpositioning.com/">Web
positioning strategies</A> so that you can get the site into the top
rankings of the major search engines.<BR>

<BR>

And that's what distance learning <A HREF="http://
www.onlinewebtraining.com">search engine courses</A> are all
about.<BR></P>
```

Or you can link to other pages through a listing of links somewhere on the page, through your navigation system, through graphics, and even through hyperlinked punctuation. In our example, we added links to the major search engines and directories, which will prove to the engines that our page is relevant to our important keyword phrase.

Keep in mind that when an engine spiders your page, it is also looking for other links to spider. Give it links to other pages on your site, preferably in visible link form, which will help your interior pages get into the index. And because links to and from popular Web sites can help link popularity, be sure to add links to other related Web sites.

If you're afraid of losing traffic to other sites, hyperlink your punctuation and keep the color of the font the same so visitors won't realize that the punctuation is a hyperlink. Visitors certainly won't run their cursor over each and every comma or period to see whether it's hyperlinked to something else if the font color is the same as the non-hyperlinked text.

You can also use hyperlinked punctuation to link to other areas of your site to direct the engines to those pages. Using hyperlinked punctuation is preferable to using hidden links, which is still a popular strategy these days. Why is it preferable? Because if the engines get wise to using hidden links as a means of directing the spider to other pages, they may choose to ignore all hidden links or even consider hidden links to be spam. Hyperlinked punctuation will send up no red flags whatsoever, however. For more information on hidden links, see Chapter 20.

**TIP**   If you use hidden links, don't use the height and weight parameters for single-pixel, or transparent, images. If you use this strategy, the engine will have a more difficult time determining that transparent GIFs are being used.

## Keeping Your Pages Simple

One of the most difficult aspects of search engine positioning is the understanding that many Web design strategies are detrimental to search engine rankings.

Why? Because anything that pushes important keyword-containing text toward the bottom of the page can affect the page's rankings negatively. Or if a page contains little content, such as pages using Flash as the "splash" page of a site, you'll probably have ranking problems.

Problem areas include frames, tables, Java, JavaScript, Flash, image maps, and dynamic content.

In Chapter 21, "Analyzing Technology That Can Be Detrimental to Search Engine Rankings," we analyze technology that can hurt your rankings. But for the purpose of this chapter, just remember that anything that pushes your text toward the bottom of the page is potentially a problem.

Study your source code carefully. Remember that if *you* have to scroll past lengthy JavaScript, so do the engines.

# Do NOT Spam!

In our source code example, we use several spamming strategies as examples for you. In this section, we outline spamming strategies so you will know not to use them.

## Don't Stuff the <META> Tag

To begin with, notice the <META> keyword tag:

```
<META name="keywords" content="directories, search engines, distance
learning, directories, search engines, distance learning, directo-
ries, search engines, distance learning, directories, search engines,
distance learning, directories, search engines, distance learning,
directories, search engines, distance learning, directories, search
engines, distance learning, directories, search engines, distance
learning">
```

Notice how the keyword phrases are used over and over again. *Keyword stuffing* in your tags, as in this example, is considered spam, and it's something you want to totally stay away from.

How many times can you use your keyword phrase in your tags? Use your important keyword phrase one time in your <TITLE> tag; once, but no more than twice, in your <META> description tag; and in several variations and versions in your <META> keyword tag. For example, you should use your keyword phrase in all caps, all lowercase letters, and capitalized in your <META> keyword tag for those engines that are case sensitive. You can also use synonyms in the <META> keyword tag.

## Don't Refresh Too Often

Another spamming example we used is the <META> refresh tag. In the "<META> Tags" section of this chapter, we discuss the <META> refresh tag, which is considered spam by many of the major engines, including AltaVista, GO/InfoSeek, and Lycos. Don't use a <META> refresh with these engines. With the other engines, don't use a lightning-fast <META> refresh as in our example. Instead, be more conservative with the re-fresh speed, setting it at 10 or higher, preferably 30.

In our example, we also used the hidden value tag because in the past, it was a popular spot for placing keywords. The major engines con-sider placing keywords in this tag to be spam, however, so stay away from this method and only use the tag as it was originally created. Here's our example:

```
<input type="hidden" name="HIDDEN" value="search engines">
```

Yet another spamming example can be found at the very bottom of the page in our source code example:

```
<P><BR>
<BR>
<BR>
<BR>
<BR>
<BR>
<BR>
</P>
</DIV>
<CENTER>
<P><font size="1">search engines, directories, distance learning,
search engines, directories, distance learning,</font></p>
<P><font size="1">search engines, directories, distance learning,
search engines, directories, distance learning,</font></p>
<P><font size="1">search engines, directories, distance learning,
search engines, directories, distance learning,</font></p>
</CENTER>
```

In this example, we placed our keyword phrases in a very tiny font size at the very bottom of the page, and we used the keyword phrases over and over again. Most of the engines frown on this practice, and it can certainly get you into trouble if you try it.

## Watch for the Trouble Spots

What is considered spamming by the majority of engines? Review this list as you analyze your pages:

- Keyword stuffing, or repeating your keyword phrase over and over again in your tags or in the body of the page itself
- Repeating your keywords over and over again in a tiny font size, generally toward the bottom of the page
- Using invisible or hidden text—stuffing keywords in a font color that is the same as the color of the background of your page

- Using lightning-fast <META> refresh tags (some of the engines consider any use of the <META> refresh to be spam)
- Optimizing several pages for the same keyword phrase
- Creating identical pages with only the keywords swapped out
- Using keywords in your tags that don't pertain to your page's content
- Creating too many doorway pages
- Submitting too many pages at once
- Submitting the same page twice on the same day

In the AltaVista section of Chapter 24, "Engine-Specific Strategies," we cover more spamming techniques as they relate to the AltaVista search engine. Chapter 24 also contains engine-specific strategies.

**CAUTION**    At the Academy, we've taught students who have gotten into trouble with the engines by using spamming techniques, and they've come to us to learn why and how to get back in the engines' good graces.

This is what they've learned: It's not easy. When you're booted out of the engines for spamming, it's tough to get back in. For one thing, they get thousands of e-mails a day. You can write to them for weeks with no response.

And when you write to the engines, you often get a canned, automated response, which is no help to you whatsoever.

So take our advice. Don't spam. It's not worth it. Play it on the up-and-up with the engines, and you'll never regret it.

## Revising Your Code to Improve Rankings

Let's say that our example is your actual Web page. What could you do to improve your page's rankings?

It depends on which engine the page is optimized for, but let's say that you're targeting AltaVista for the keyword phrase "search engines." Here are some possible solutions:

- Move the <TITLE> tag to the top of the page and possibly move "search engines" more toward the beginning of the tag.

- Completely remove the <META> description and keyword tags, which is an effective strategy with the AltaVista search engine.
- Make sure that the text at the beginning of the page is appropriate as a description of the site because you're not using a <META> description tag.
- Get rid of the irrelevant <META> tags: http-equiv, generator, author, and robots.
- Get rid of the <META> refresh tag.
- Use more hyperlinked words or punctuation, and link to other areas of the site or to popular related sites.
- Use more ALT attributes with keywords in the tags.
- Use a style tag.
- Get rid of all spam, including the hidden value tag and the tiny text at the bottom of the page.
- Try to use the important keyword phrase in as many of the headline tags as possible.
- Use more link text.
- Check your keyword weight carefully.
- Add more content if the top-ranking sites for that keyword phrase contain more words than this page. Reduce the content if the competition uses less words.
- Consider increasing the content of the <NOFRAMES> tag if needed.
- Name the page after the keyword phrase (search-engines.html).
- Reduce the length of the <TITLE> tag to just the important keyword phrase.
- Because AltaVista is case sensitive, use your important keyword phrases in your <NOFRAMES> tag in all caps and in capitalized variations because you're not using a <META> keyword tag.
- Purchase a domain name with the keyword phrase in it (search-engines.com).
- Name image files after the keyword phrase (search-engines.gif).
- Put the keyword phrase in bold in the body text.
- Boost link popularity pointing to and from your site with related and popular Web sites.

## A Step-by-Step Analysis of Your Source Code

In Appendix C, "Checklists" you'll find a guide specifically for analyzing your Web page. For the purpose of analyzing your source code, however, answer these questions as they relate to your own Web page:

- Is the ⟨TITLE⟩ tag the first tag on your page?
- Is your keyword phrase used toward the beginning of the ⟨TITLE⟩ tag?
- Are you using one ⟨TITLE⟩ tag only? You can try using two ⟨TITLE⟩ tags with AltaVista and the Inktomi engines, but don't try it with GO/InfoSeek.
- Are you trying to optimize the page for one or two keyword phrases only?
- Did your HTML editor stick in any irrelevant ⟨META⟩ or comment tags?
- Are you stuffing your keywords over and over again in any of your tags?
- Are you using ⟨META⟩ description and keyword tags for those engines that consider the tags when determining relevancy, or for the engines that use the ⟨META⟩ description tag in the search results?
- Where does the body text of your page begin? Are you using technology that is pushing your keyword-containing text toward the bottom of the page, like JavaScript?
- Are you using a ⟨META⟩ refresh tag?
- Are you using a robots ⟨NOINDEX⟩ tag?
- Does your page begin with text rather than graphics?
- Does the first text on your page begin with your keyword phrase?
- Are you using headline tags with your keyword phrase?
- Are you using link text containing your keyword phrase?
- Are you using ALT and style tags for those engines that consider them?
- Are you using your keyword phrase toward the beginning of all tags?

- Is the page dynamically generated, possibly with a symbol in the URL? We cover dynamically generated pages in Chapter 21.

- Are you using a `<NOFRAMES>` tag to add additional content to the page, if needed?

- Are you linking to other relevant and important sites for your keyword phrase?

- Did you try using your keyword phrase in bold in the body text?

- Are you staying away from all spamming techniques?

- Is your page simple, without a lot of fancy technology?

- Is your keyword weight where it needs to be? Be sure to check your competition and adjust your keyword weight accordingly.

- Are you using your important keyword phrase toward the beginning of the body text, then sprinkled throughout the page, and ending with the phrase?

## Using Analysis Tools and Services

One of the best ways of analyzing your source code for HTML problems is with your HTML editor. Most editors have a means for you to check the page's syntax, and you should get in the habit of running all of your pages through that feature. It's so easy to leave off the ending of a tag, and you want to make sure your HTML is correct. If it's not, your rankings could be affected.

Be sure to review Chapter 18's "Keeping Up with Industry Changes" section for additional software tools and services.

Other tools and services follow:

**FIND IT ONLINE**

- Search Engine Simulator shows you what an engine sees when it visits your site (**http://www.delorie.com/web/ses.cgi**).

- LinkPopularity.com shows you the link popularity of your site (**http://www.linkpopularity.com**).

- Robots.txt syntax checker makes sure your robots.txt file is correct (**http://www.tardis.ed.ac.uk/~sxw/robots/check/**).

- Hi-Verify and Microsoft FrontPage verify Web site structure and design (**http://www.hisoftware.com/hiverify.htm**).

## Conclusion

When analyzing individual pages of your site, go to the guts or skeleton of each page and look at it through the eyes of a search engine. Make sure that your important keyword-containing text isn't being pushed to the bottom of the page.

Make sure that your HTML editor isn't sticking in irrelevant tags that could be hurting your rankings and that you're not using any strategies that could get you into trouble with the engines.

Spend time analyzing your source code, and your site will benefit in the rankings!

# ANALYZING YOUR WEB SITE DESIGN WITH THE ENGINES IN MIND

**In This Chapter**

Simplicity Counts!

Linking among Pages

Linking among Additional Domains

Using a Site Map or Hallway Page

Separating Data into Individual Pages

Capitalizing on Themes

Considering Directory Preferences

A Step-by-Step Analysis of Your Web Site for the Engines

A Step-by-Step Analysis of Your Web Site for the Directories

When analyzing Web design as it pertains to the search engines, you need to look at a totally different set of criteria than you examined in Chapters 1, "Analyzing Web Pages for Maximum Effectiveness," and 2, "Analyzing Your Site's Structure for Maximum Accessibility."

All of a sudden, you're no longer considering your users' experience, but the *engines'* experience. Certainly you can never lose sight of your users because they are obviously the mainstay of your online business.

If you're going to attract the search engines, though, you need to look at things a little differently, which we highlight in this chapter.

The engines like simple pages, and that's a fact.

Not only that, but you need to present your pages in such a way that the spiders will crawl them and give you maximum exposure. Or you need to use techniques such as site maps or hallway pages. Site maps provide links to all the pages on your site, whereas hallway pages strictly list the links to your doorway pages. Tied into the linking process is your link popularity, which we also cover in this chapter.

We comment in earlier chapters about the importance of segregating data, but it becomes even more important when considering the search engines. And going along with the concept of segregating data is the importance of themes, which is the latest search engine optimizing technique, and one you'll be hearing more and more about in the months to come.

## Simplicity Counts!

When performing searches at any of the major engines, have you ever noticed that the top-ranking pages are generally very simple pages with few bells and whistles? In fact, many top-ranking sites, except when link popularity is an issue, look as if they were created by a 10-year-old!

Why is that?

*Search engines like simplicity.* We've said it before, but its importance warrants saying it again.

Not only that, but the best time to optimize a page for the search engines is in the *design* stage, before the site is up and running. In this manner, you can keep search engine strategies in the back of your mind, and you'll know not to choose strategies that will put you at a disadvantage, especially if you're in a very competitive area.

Think of search engine positioning as a playing field. When you go out on the field, you'll automatically have several potential strikes against you in areas such as competition, the overall design of your page, the content of the page, the popularity of the site, and so forth. Your job is to give yourself as many edges over the competition as you can.

Doing away with frames, for example, will automatically even the playing field for you considerably. Staying away from Flash, dynamic pages, complex image maps, and Java will also help give you an advantage over the competition. In Chapter 21, "Analyzing Technology That Can Be Detrimental to Search Engine Rankings," we cover technologies that are detrimental to engine rankings.

When creating a Web site or redesigning a site, take the simple approach. Don't try to impress your users with complicated JavaScript that will push all your keyword-containing text to the bottom of the page. Don't create a splash page using Flash technology or a page that requires a plug-in in order to view it.

Instead, give the engines simple Web pages. Not only will the engines appreciate it, but so will your users.

Also, when possible, begin your pages with text. Remember that the search engines can't see your beautiful graphics. Some of the engines index the content of ALT attributes, but others don't, so you can't depend on them. Place your important keyword-containing text toward the top of the page and remind the engines of its importance.

Make your pages *content rich* rather than *graphics rich*. Give the engines something to spider and index!

Equally important as creating simple pages is having strong linking among those pages.

## Linking among Pages

**Fact:** Some of the major engines will only accept your index page through their submission process.

**Fact:** Even if the engines allow you to submit your interior or doorway pages separately, that doesn't guarantee that the pages will make it into the index.

**Fact:** Link popularity has an enormous impact on search engine rankings.

**Solution:** Link your pages together, and add links from the main page of your site to all important interior or doorway pages. Give the engines something to spider and index. And if you have additional domains for your company, link them together if their content is related. This can greatly benefit the link popularity of your site.

Although you'll certainly want to link your pages together from a navigational point of view, you're now considering linking from the eyes of the search engines. Therefore, on the main page of your site, add links to all important interior pages. Then when you submit the main page, the spider will find your other links and hopefully index those pages, too.

What about your doorway pages? If possible, provide a visible link to your doorway pages from the main page of your site.

But what if you don't want traffic going back to your doorway pages? You can certainly use hidden links, but use them with caution. Although using hidden links currently is a highly popular strategy, you may soon find yourself getting into trouble with the engines for using them. Hidden links are discussed further in Chapter 19.

Or, you may discover that the engines are simply ignoring hidden links and no longer indexing them. If you place too much importance on hidden links and aren't trying to link your pages together visibly, you may find that your Web pages aren't getting proper exposure if your hidden links aren't being picked up by the engines. Plus, using keywords in link text is generally very important with all the engines. You give up this benefit if you use hidden links.

As we mention in Chapter 19, "Analyzing Your Source Code," instead of using hidden links, try creating hyperlinks with punctuation and link to important doorway pages in that manner. Ideally, you should create a hyperlinked punctuation mark that's near your keyword phrase, if at all possible, to take advantage of the link text.

Another option is to provide a link to a site map or hallway page on the main page of your site, which the engines hopefully will see during a spider run. Include your interior and doorway page URLs on the site map or hallway page, and the engine will spot the links and index them. You'll learn more about site maps and hallway pages in the following section.

If you don't want an obvious link to a site map or hallway page, hyperlink an image in an area of the page where people wouldn't consider clicking, such as the logo at the very top of the page or a spacer GIF.

In other words, link your pages together as much and as often as you can. In this manner, you'll be presenting your links to the engines from several different pages, which will boost your chances at getting picked up in the indexes.

## Linking among Additional Domains

Because of the importance of link popularity, be sure to link your additional domains together. If the focus of your company is centered on one basic concept, you'll be boosting your site's link popularity by linking those domains together.

When purchasing additional domains, be sure to get domains with keywords in them. Consider this example:

**http://www.steel-pipes.com**

Should you put a hyphen or underscore between your keywords in a domain name? For the engines, it's a good idea because you're making sure that they recognize the words as a keyword phrase.

With the main domain of your company, though, you may still want to run those keywords together, like this:

**http://www.steelpipes.com**

It will be easier for your customers to remember the URL if you don't use hyphens. Plus, the non-hyphenated form is the default version on the browser, which is an important consideration as well.

By not using hyphens for the main domain of your company, you can send all customers through that doorway, and you can advertise that URL in all your printed materials. Then, you can promote the additional domains that contain hyphens when working with the search engines.

We've discussed the reasons why you would want to link your domains together, but is there a reason why you wouldn't want to do so?

The only time you'll want to stay away from linking your domains together is before you get each of the domains listed in Yahoo!.

Yahoo! won't list mirror sites or sites with very similar content. If you have several domains and are struggling to get Yahoo! to pick them up, you'll want to keep each of the domains separate from the indexed domain—at least until the site makes it into the index. Don't link the domains together, and use different contact information at InterNIC, even if you have to change the information prior to submitting your domains to Yahoo!. Try to make the appearance of your domains slightly different as well. Submit each of the domains to separate subcategories. Use Business Express, which gives you a better chance at getting the domains indexed. More information on Business Express can be found in Chapter 25.

Play it safe with Yahoo!, and you'll stand a much better chance at getting into the directory.

**TIP** To keep someone from purchasing the .net or .org versions of your domains, purchase them yourself, and use them for test domains, internal personnel information, and so on.

## Using a Site Map or Hallway Page

We cover site maps in detail in Chapter 2, "Analyzing Your Site's Structure for Maximum Accessibility," but that chapter centers around Web site design in general. When considering the search engines, a site map can hold the key to unlock the pages of your site for the engines, and it's crucial that you create one.

What do you need to include on your site map? Using the same format as the rest of your site, simply create a page that offers links to other important pages of your site. Don't try to optimize the page for the engines because you're not after a top ranking with your site map page.

Instead, you're after getting the page indexed and then letting the spider crawl the page and discover your other links during one of its runs.

Site maps generally contain links to all the important interior pages of your site. You may want to include a paragraph or two of text here and there on your pages, or descriptive sentences about each link.

Another effective strategy when working with doorway pages is to create a *hallway page,* which is simply a listing of your doorway pages with their URLs. Again, don't try to optimize the page for the engines. Simply put the page before the engines and let the spider find the links and index them.

In Figure 20.1, you'll see how site maps and hallway pages fit into the overall scheme of a Web site.

So, a hallway page contains links to doorway pages, whereas a site map generally contains links to interior pages only. Be sure to add a link from your main page to both your hallway page and site map.

You may even find that you'll want to create separate hallway pages for each of the major search engines to cover your engine-specific pages.

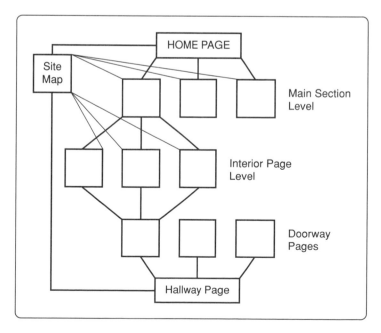

 **FIGURE 20.1**

Using a site map and hallway page on a site.

Use a robots.txt file, as described in Chapter 19, "Analyzing Your Source Code," and keep engines out of the pages you created for the other engines.

## Separating Data into Individual Pages

When creating your Web pages, keep the content of each page focused on one topic. Don't try to create a page that centers on several subjects because you'll have a much more difficult time getting that page ranked high in the engines.

By keeping each page devoted to one topic, all of your tags and content for that page can point to that one subject area, and you'll have a much easier time getting a top ranking for the page. This method is particularly crucial when working with competitive keywords.

The main page of your site can be a very general page that covers your company or site as a whole, optimized for a more general and broad keyword phrase because the index page will always get a boost in relevancy. Then from there, branch off into individual pages that each have a separate focus.

While it's important to fine-tune the content of each Web page, it's also good to remember the importance of themes.

## Capitalizing on Themes

Let's say that you have a Web site devoted to providing tips for repairing automobiles. In fact, everything on the entire site pertains to cars.

Someone else has a Web site that offers a wide assortment of information on numerous topics. The site offers pages on books, software programs, regional links, and automobile repair tips.

Your focused Web site will have a much easier time getting indexed and achieving a top ranking than the site without an overall focus or theme.

Many of the engines now are gravitating toward being *theme* engines, which means that they will consider the overall focus of the content of each Web site when determining relevancy. In other words, engines will look at the incoming and outgoing links to see whether those links are related to the site. The engines will see whether the site is linking to and from important and popular Web sites in a particular and related topic area, which will give the site a boost in relevancy.

Engines also will look at the site as a whole to see whether all the pages are focused on that one particular theme.

Why have the engines gone toward the theme concept? Michael Campbell, well-known Internet marketer and author of the popular *Vault* newsletter, explains that the search engines have tried everything to provide relevant results while cutting down on duplications and spamming. They reduced the importance of <META> and other HTML tags and then filtered out invisible text and the repetition of keywords. Didn't work. So they went to link and click-through popularity as a means of determining relevancy, but the problems remained.

Coupled with the spamming and duplicate Web page problems is the unruly size of the Web itself. How can the engines possibly store billions of pages and still provide relevant search results?

According to Campbell, here's where *term vector databases* came in as a building block for new technologies that can harness the power and size of the Internet while still maintaining relevant searches.

A term vector database has two main pieces of software built into it, as we alluded to earlier. One is *page classification*, where the engines decide the topic (or theme) of your page, and the other is *hypertext connectivity*, which looks at related sites linking to and from your site.

### Name Your Web Site Purpose in Two Words

"Can you do it?" asks Michael Campbell. "What is your Web site theme? Two words, three max. Try it. What is your site all about? Can you describe your Web site in two words? You'll need to answer these questions because themes are the new big winner in long-term search engine positioning."

Much of the information in this section comes from Michael Campbell's extensive research into themes. Visit the *Vault*, a pay subscription service, (**http://www.1-internet-marketing.com/vault/**) for the complete article.

Campbell explains themes from a computer scientist's point of view:

*Using a term vector database, they weigh page keyword density to calculate the page vector, which is compared and stored relative to the term vector. They then compute a Web page reputation by graphing interconnectivity and link relevancy, making sure the reputation of the page and the content on the page actually match. The closest matches get the highest search engine positioning.*

Yes, that's a mouthful, but it does explain the latest thinking in the search engine industry.

Your goal is to keep everything on your entire site aimed toward one particular topic. If your company has numerous focuses, such as selling computer peripherals, publishing books, and offering consulting services, you'll probably want to purchase additional and new domains for your company's other focused areas.

When considering theme search engines, keep these important strategies in mind:

- Center your entire Web site on one particular theme. Don't try to incorporate various topics into the same domain.
- Center each individual Web page on aspects of that theme. Don't deviate from that theme!
- Work hard toward building related link popularity by contacting related sites and asking them to link to your site, submitting your site to important directories, creating an affiliate program, and so forth.
- Add some related and popular outgoing links on your own site. If you're concerned about losing visitors who click off to another site, hyperlink your punctuation, which is one of Michael Campbell's tricks, or create a separate links list and link to that list from your main page.
- Don't use duplicate or nearly duplicate pages, and make sure that all your pages have unique content. Mirror sites won't work well with theme engines because of the engines' duplication and spam redundancy filters.
- Michael Campbell recommends taking your most popular two-word keyword phrase and giving it a 5 percent sum keyword

density and a 1.25 percent whole phrase density. He also recommends that one word have a higher individual density than the other. Make sure the whole phrase appears in the title and at least once in the body and as separate words spread throughout the document.

- Use <META> tags, and delete irrelevant <META> tags, as we discuss in Chapter 19. Use synonyms of your keyword phrase in your keyword <META> tag and in the body of your page.

- Keep your pages to a reasonable length. What is reasonable? Hard to say, but we recommend staying at less than 1,000 words per page, or even preferably less than 750 words.

- Use your keyword phrase in ALT attributes and link text.

- Make sure your resellers use their own look and content instead of copying yours.

## Considering Directory Preferences

We discussed how to analyze your site's design when considering the search engines, but what about the directories?

Directories are a totally different entity because a human editor visits your site. Therefore, you need to make sure that your site is ready for human inspection!

As editors of the *Open Directory Project* (*ODP*) ourselves, one thing that always presents problems for us is to have to download a plug-in to view a page. Most editors won't do it. It's easier to reject the submission.

Requiring your visitors to download a plug-in is a bad idea all the way around because no one wants to take the time to download and install a plug-in. They want the information that your site provides, and they want it fast!

Also, don't create such a technology-intense page that it causes an editor's or visitor's browser to crash. This could lead to instant rejection.

When considering the directories and your visitors in general, be sure to provide contact information on your pages. Yahoo! often won't index a page without contact information and a physical address.

We go into more detail on working with the directories in Chapter 25, "Strategies for Working with Directories," but here are a few things to keep in mind:

- Make sure all your graphics load, and make sure they load fast!
- Do all your links work? Don't take chances. Check your links yourself before submitting your site to the directories.
- Is your site ready for traffic? Is there enough content to attract visitors?
- Be sure to place a copyright notice on your home page.
- Provide a "last updated on <date>" statement, and make sure that you've updated your site recently before submitting your site.
- Don't submit mirror sites. Just as the search engines don't like mirror sites with the same content, neither do the directories. They want to provide unique content for their visitors.
- Many editors don't like to have to go through a splash page to get to the "real" site. Direct editors to the real meat of the site instead.
- Most of the directories don't want to list affiliate sites that are there for the sole purpose of selling products through affiliate programs.
- Make sure that your text is easy to read. Don't use a point size that is too small or too large. Don't use bright backgrounds with colored fonts because it's difficult to read and downright annoying!

## A Step-by-Step Analysis of Your Web Site for the Engines

In the following step-by-step analysis, we incorporate what you learned in previous chapters. Ask yourself these questions about your Web pages and site in general:

- Are your Web pages of a simple design that will allow the search engines to find your important keyword-containing text easily? Or are your pages technology intense, or do they push keyword-containing text toward the bottom of the page? Remember that anything that pushes your keywords toward the bottom of the page is detrimental to search engine rankings.

- Have you made sure to place links to all your interior and doorway pages throughout your site, via visible or hidden links, through a site map, or on a hallway page? Have you linked to your site map and hallway pages on the main page of your site?

- Is your data segregated so that each page is focused on one central topic or theme? Have you created additional pages, if necessary, and optimized them for additional topics that are important to your business or Web site?

- Is your Web site in general focused on one particular topic or theme? If not, have you considered purchasing additional domains for your other important topics?

- Did you spend a lot of time coming up with the best and most effective keyword phrases for your pages? Did you search for those phrases at the engines to see how many competing sites there are? Did you also use GoTo's Search Term Suggestion Tool or WordTracker to see how many people have searched for those keyword phrases lately? More information on GoTo's tool and WordTracker can be found in Chapter 18.

- Did you ask someone else's opinion about the keywords for your site? In our search engine positioning classes, we've found that brainstorming among students or with the instructor can be exceedingly valuable because it provides a different look at how someone might be searching for your site.

- Do the tags on your individual pages focus on the topic of those pages? Have you used different <TITLE>, <META>, and other tags on each page?

- If you're using frames, are you using a <NOFRAMES> tag complete with content-rich information about your site? If you're using an image map, have you provided HTML links to your other pages as well? If you're using tables, are you using your keywords in your tables? Does Java push your important text toward the bottom of the page? We cover these areas in more detail in Chapter 21, but be sure to view your source code, and make sure that your keyword-containing text is prominently displayed at the top of your page.

- Are you using irrelevant <META> tags that could confuse the engines?

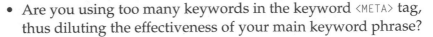

- Are you using too many keywords in the keyword <META> tag, thus diluting the effectiveness of your main keyword phrase?

- If your page doesn't have much content, have you added more content through a <NOFRAMES> tag?

- Are your keywords used toward the beginning of all tags and body text and then sprinkled throughout the body of your page, using the keywords toward the end of the page as well?

- Did you study Chapter 18, "Basic Optimization Strategies," carefully to see where else you could use your keyword phrase?

- Did you capitalize on the fact that most engines like both headline tags and link text by using each of them?

- Are your title and description tags captivating and a sales pitch to draw visitors to your site? Or are they dull and boring? Are you using your important keywords toward the beginning of both tags?

- If you have been unable to get top rankings under a particular keyword phrase or for certain engines, have you created engine-specific pages for those keyword phrases?

- Are your pages content rich, with both incoming and outgoing links to related and important sites? Longer pages do quite well in the engines these days, so remember that!

- If your pages haven't achieved top rankings, have you gone back over the various areas of your page to see where you can add keywords? Have you tried removing some keywords from your pages? In this business, sometimes less is more effective than more.

- Have you worked hard at building a good, solid link popularity for your site?

- Is your site simply a mirror of another site, or does it provide valuable and unique content?

- Have you checked your keyword weight against that of competing sites and adjusted yours accordingly? We cover the importance of studying your competition in Chapter 22.

In Appendix C, "Checklists" we provide a guide you can use to analyze your Web site in terms of the search engines. We also include the checklist on the accompanying CD-ROM, so be sure to print out a copy.

## A Step-by-Step Analysis of Your Web Site for the Directories

Use this step-by-step analysis to make certain that your Web site is ready for a human editor. This is particularly critical these days, with the importance of the directories increasing every day.

In Chapter 25, we offer more tips on working with the directories. For now, ask yourself these questions:

- Is your Web site ready for business and traffic? Is your e-commerce section functional?
- Do all your graphics load? Do your links work?
- Have you provided contact information and a physical address on your pages?
- Is there a copyright notice on your pages? Some directories, such as Yahoo!, like to see copyright notices.
- Does your site require a plug-in in order to view it properly?
- Are you using technology-intense pages that can cause a browser to crash? Have you cross-tested your pages with other browsers to be sure JavaScript runs without causing a pop-up error message?
- Will editors have to go through a splash page to get to the real meat of the site? Can you direct them to the actual content instead?
- Is your site a mirror of another site, or does it provide valuable and unique content?
- Is your site an affiliate site that is actually set up to sell products through various affiliate programs?
- Is your text legible and easy to read, or are you trying to use a yellow font on a lime-green background, for example? Your site could get rejected if the text is difficult to read, or if the point size is too small or even too large.
- Is there more to your site than one page? If not, create additional pages before submitting your site to the directories.
- Did you use your important keyword phrases in your title and description on the submission form? Directories don't look at your actual tags, so what you put on the submission form is crucial. Use your important keywords!

- With directories, you sometimes can submit only the main page of your site, so choose your subcategory wisely. If you're working with the ODP, you can submit your site in a couple of categories, but get your page listed in one area first, and then submit it to another area.

In Appendix C and on the CD-ROM, we also provide a checklist that you can print and use to analyze your Web site in terms of the directories.

**TIP** For an article that provides 10 suggestions for getting your site listed in the ODP as well as 10 things to avoid, visit **http://www.onlinewebtraining.com/information/odp.html**

## Conclusion

When considering the overall design of your individual pages and your Web site as a whole, be sure to remember the power of the search engines and directories. Although you tend to design your pages with your users in mind, which is as it should be, you can't forget the search engines. Without them, you may not get the traffic your site deserves.

So create simple, easy-to-use pages. Your users and the search engines will appreciate it! Give the engines links to other pages and help them find those pages. Keep each page focused on one particular topic, and try to keep each domain geared toward one general topic.

Remembering these simple guidelines will put you firmly on the road to success with your Web site!

# ANALYZING TECHNOLOGY THAT CAN BE DETRIMENTAL TO SEARCH ENGINE RANKINGS

**In This Chapter**

In previous chapters, we mention various problem areas that will put you immediately at a disadvantage when dealing with the search engines. Remember that your goal is to "even the playing field," then to give yourself an edge over the competition.

One of the most problematic strategies when working with the engines is frames, which we'll cover later in this chapter. We'll also cover JavaScript, another problematic strategy, which can easily push your important keyword-containing text farther down on the page, thus decreasing your keyword's prominence. Keep in mind that *anything* that pushes your keywords toward the bottom of the page can hurt your page's relevancy.

Flash, although certainly impressive, can be a killer to search engine rankings, as can dynamic HTML. Even tables and image maps can present problems, all of which we cover in this chapter.

While we certainly cover the problem areas, we also cover workarounds for those problems, which includes the use of cloaking software. Keep in mind that you can also use your technology-jammed pages as interior pages of your site, and not worry about trying to get them into the engines' indexes.

## Avoiding Frames

If you want to use one strategy that could get you in trouble with your visitors, their browsers, and the search engines, pick frames.

Yes, Internet-savvy folks know how to get out of someone else's frames. But are all your visitors Internet savvy?

How confident are you that virtually none of your visitors will be accessing your page using older browsers?

How important is it for your site to be found in the search engines?

Most search engines can't read the content of frames. They can only read the content of the `<NOFRAMES>` tag. Not only that, but frames increase the file size, which can decrease your overall keyword weight.

Frames definitely have some disadvantages!

Although frames do have a couple of advantages, their disadvantages far outweigh the good. In fact, it would be to *your* advantage to keep these two facts in mind:

- Only very large, complex Web sites need to use frames.
- Very few top 10 Web sites use frames.

If your site uses frames, what is your solution?

Get rid of the frames! You can probably accomplish the same look by using tables, and tables definitely don't present the problems that frames do.

If getting rid of the frames isn't an option, you'll need to consider some workarounds.

First off, be sure to use the <NOFRAMES> tag on your frameset page. The tag goes immediately after the first frameset tag, because you want the keyword-rich text to appear as close to the top of the page as possible. Do not place it above the first frameset tag, because it will be incompatible with some browsers.

If you use frames, remember to include a home link at the bottom of each of your pages so that your viewers will be able to navigate your site. By clicking on the home link, the viewers are taken back into the frames and all is well.

Also, use the TARGET="_TOP" command to link to your home page, which prevents a page from appearing inside another framed page; failure to do so will cause viewers who click on "home" to view a new set of frames within the main content frame:

```
<a href="index.html" TARGET="_TOP">Home</a>
```

Within the <NOFRAMES> tag, create a mini Web site and use your keyword phrase in it. Be sure to add links to other areas of your site to give the spiders something to index. Use META tags that accurately describe your page.

Next, for those keyword phrases that are important to your business, create non-framed pages that are optimized for those keywords. These will be additional doorways into your site, and you'll use the doorway page strategies that we cover in Chapter 18, "Basic Optimization Strategies."

**FIGURE 21.1**

The main page of a framed site.

Figure 21.1 shows an example of the main page of a framed site for one of our students (**http://www.maremmatoscana.com**), although it actually doesn't look like the traditional use of frames.

The page also is using Flash and a "Get URL" command inside the animation, instead of a redirect tag. For more information about this strategy, see "Making Flash Pages More Searchable," later in this chapter.

Listing 21.1 shows the source code.

### Listing 21.1
### Source code for a Web page using frames.

```
<HTML>
<HEAD>
<TITLE>MaremmaToscana.com : food and wine of Tuscany-Italy</TITLE>
<META name="keywords" CONTENT="<br> italian wine,extra virgin olive
oil, food of italy,truffles,italy,leather
handicraft,maremma,tuscany,on line shop,buy,on line">
<META name="description" content="Italian wine, extra virgin olive
oil, grappa,truffles and leather handicraft of Maremma Tuscany for on
line purchase">
<META http-equiv="keywords" name="keywords" CONTENT="italian wine">
<META http-equiv="Content-Type" content="text/html; charset=iso-8859-
1">
```

```
</HEAD>
<FRAMESET rows="10%,*,10%" framespacing="0" border="0"
frameborder="NO" bordercolor="#000000" cols="*">

  <FRAME src="sopra.htm" name="su" scrolling="NO">

  <FRAMESET cols="20%,*,20%" framespacing="0" border="1"
frameborder="YES" bordercolor="#000000">

    <FRAME src="destra.htm" name="destra" scrolling="NO"
frameborder="NO" marginwidth="0" marginheight="0"
bordercolor="#222222">

      <FRAME src="main.html" name="main" scrolling="NO"
frameborder="NO">

      <FRAME src="sinistra.htm" name="sinistra" scrolling="NO"
frameborder="NO" marginwidth="0" marginheight="0"
bordercolor="#222222">

  </FRAMESET>

  <FRAME src="sotto.htm" name="giu" scrolling="NO">

</FRAMESET>

<NOFRAMES>

<BODY bgcolor="#FFFFFF">

<META name="keywords" CONTENT="<br> italian wine, on line shop,extra
virgin olive oil, truffles, italy, leather handicraft, maremma
tuscany, ITALIAN WINE ">

<META name="description" content="Italian wine,extra virgin olive
oil,grappa,truffles and leather handicraft of Maremma Tuscany for on
line purchase">

<META http-equiv="keywords" name="keywords" CONTENT="italian wine">

<H2> <Italian wine from Maremma Tuscany : exclusive wines,
extravirgin olive oil, grappa, stock saddles, leather handicraft from
Italy for on line order> </H2>

<P> <Genuine products from Maremma, a wild area in the south of
Tuscany. Red and white wines and cold pressed, unfiltered, low
acidity extravirgin olive oil></P>

<P><Order on line truffles and leather handicraft from an ancient
land></P>

<A HREF="avp/italian_wine_av.htm"><IMG SRC="gifcheat.gif" BORDER="0"
alt="italian wine"></A>

<A HREF="avp/truffles_av.htm"><IMG SRC="gifcheat.gif" BORDER="0"
alt="truffles"></A>

<A HREF="avp/olive_oil_av.htm"><IMG SRC="gifcheat.gif" BORDER="0"
alt="olive oil"></A>

</BODY>

</NOFRAMES>

</HTML>
```

First, notice that the site uses title, META description, and META keyword tags. It also uses an http-equiv=keywords tag, which works with many of the engines. The http-equiv=content tag can be deleted.

Next, notice the content of the <NOFRAMES> tag, which we've highlighted in yellow. The designer chose to give the site every edge over the competition that he could by using other META description and keyword tags. He also used a headline tag. Note that he included links to other pages in the site as well, which are actually doorway pages optimized for particular engines. In other words, through this <NOFRAMES> tag, he's effectively given the engines something to index, and he's given them a key into the rest of the site.

**TIP**  Search Engine Watch has an excellent tutorial on using frames at **http://searchenginewatch. com/webmasters/frames.html**.

Another workaround for frames, as for several of the strategies presented here, is to use cloaking, which we cover later in this chapter in the "Cloaking as a Solution to Problematic Technologies" section.

---

### Additional Notes about Frames

Stephen Mahaney of Planet Ocean, a well-respected guru in the search engine industry, cautions those who use frames to test their pages on a WebTV browser, particularly if their customer base consists of a large portion of WebTV users. Because WebTV tries to combine frames, it sometimes can mess up the page. According to Mahaney, WebTV is the largest single browser demographic that currently doesn't support frames well.

Mahaney's *Unfair Advantages* e-book also cautions about shopping carts and frames:

Also keep in mind that shopping cart pages on a secure server that are wrapped in frames from a non-secure server won't show the "closed-lock" icon on the browser window. You need to break out of the frame when leading people to the secure pages or they will understandably think the page is non-secure—even though it is. This may cost some sales because that secure lock icon is looked for by a lot of consumers.

To subscribe to Mahaney's newsletter, *Planet Ocean's Search Engine News,* visit **http:// www.searchenginehelp.com/moreinfo**.

## Minimizing JavaScript Code

In a nutshell, JavaScript can push your keyword-containing text farther down on the page, thereby reducing its prominence and relevancy. Some JavaScript is relatively short and shouldn't present problems. Other JavaScript is quite lengthy and can be detrimental to search engine rankings.

 **TIP**   When viewing the source code of a page that contains JavaScript, if *you* have to scroll through several pages of script, so do the engines, and the rankings of the page will probably suffer.

What are some workarounds? When possible, place the JavaScript toward the bottom of the page, so that the important body text comes first. Or create content-rich information or doorway pages that do not use JavaScript and bring in traffic that way.

Another option is to move the JavaScript to a separate external .js file, and then reference that file in the ⟨HEAD⟩ section of your page.

By moving the majority of the Java off your page into a totally separate file, you'll reduce the amount of code on your Web pages, which can lead to better search engine rankings. This method will also allow you to reuse the code on other pages without duplicating it over and over again. As a result, you'll be minimizing your work if you need to make changes to the JavaScript at a later date.

To accomplish this, move any JavaScript code that you would normally place in the ⟨HEAD⟩ section of your Web page into a separate .js file. This file should contain only your JavaScript code with no other HTML codes. You can reference it like this:

```
<Script language="JavaScript" src="namethisfile.js">

</Script>
```

Then, when the browser loads the page, it will follow the link to get to the JavaScript code. An important consideration is that some servers may not recognize the .js file type, so experiment on your server to see if it works for you.

 **FIND IT ONLINE**   In Figure 21.2, you'll see the main page of a Web site that uses JavaScript. To view this page online, visit **http://www.gbitech.com/**.

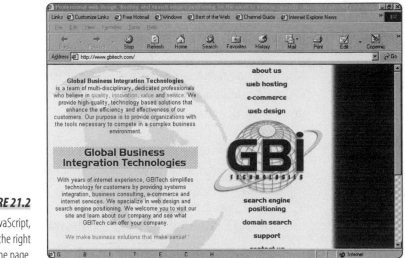

*FIGURE 21.2*

The main page of a site that uses JavaScript, and an example of navigation on the right side of the page.

This is the site of one of our students, and Listing 21.2 shows the source code of the <HEAD> section before she removed the JavaScript and placed it in a separate file. For brevity's sake, we've removed seven pages of JavaScript, but this will still give you a very good idea of what she was up against in the beginning.

### Listing 21.2
### A partial listing of JavaScript in a Web page header.

```
<HTML>
<HEAD>
<TITLE>Professional web design, hosting and search engine positioning
for the small to medium size businesses</TITLE>
<META Name="Description" Content="With years of internet experience,
we specialize in web design and search engine positioning.  Let
GBITech provide you with sensible business solutions.">
<META Name="Keywords" Content="professional web design,search engine
positioning,website promotion,quality,rankings,increased hits,web
hosting">
<META Name="Distribution" Content="Global">
<META Name="Rating" Content="General">
<META Name="Robots" Content="All">
<Script Language="JavaScript">
<!-- hide this script from non-javascript-enabled browsers
if (document.images) {
```

```
aboutf_f1 = new Image(247,29); aboutf_f1.src = "gfx/aboutf.gif";
aboutf_f2 = new Image(247,29); aboutf_f2.src = "gfx/aboutf_f2.gif";
aboutf_f3 = new Image(247,29); aboutf_f3.src = "gfx/aboutf_f3.gif";
hostingf_f1 = new Image(247,30); hostingf_f1.src = "gfx/
hostingf.gif";
hostingf_f2 = new Image(247,30); hostingf_f2.src = "gfx/
hostingf_f2.gif";
hostingf_f3 = new Image(247,30); hostingf_f3.src = "gfx/
hostingf_f3.gif";
ecommercef_f1 = new Image(247,30); ecommercef_f1.src = "gfx/
ecommercef.gif";
ecommercef_f2 = new Image(247,30); ecommercef_f2.src = "gfx/
ecommercef_f2.gif";
ecommercef_f3 = new Image(247,30); ecommercef_f3.src = "gfx/
ecommercef_f3.gif";
designf_f1 = new Image(247,31); designf_f1.src = "gfx/designf.gif";
designf_f2 = new Image(247,31); designf_f2.src = "gfx/
designf_f2.gif";
designf_f3 = new Image(247,31); designf_f3.src = "gfx/
designf_f3.gif";
front2a_r06_c2_f1 = new Image(326,49); front2a_r06_c2_f1.src = "gfx/
front2a_r06_c2.gif";
front2a_r06_c2_f3 = new Image(326,49); front2a_r06_c2_f3.src = "gfx/
front2a_r06_c2_f3.gif";
front2a_r06_c2_f4 = new Image(326,49); front2a_r06_c2_f4.src = "gfx/
front2a_r06_c2_f4.gif";
front2a_r06_c2_f5 = new Image(326,49); front2a_r06_c2_f5.src = "gfx/
front2a_r06_c2_f5.gif";
front2a_r06_c2_f6 = new Image(326,49); front2a_r06_c2_f6.src = "gfx/
front2a_r06_c2_f6.gif";
front2a_r06_c2_f7 = new Image(326,49); front2a_r06_c2_f7.src = "gfx/
front2a_r06_c2_f7.gif";
front2a_r06_c2_f8 = new Image(326,49); front2a_r06_c2_f8.src = "gfx/
front2a_r06_c2_f8.gif";
front2a_r06_c2_f9 = new Image(326,49); front2a_r06_c2_f9.src = "gfx/
front2a_r06_c2_f9.gif";
front2a_r06_c2_f10 = new Image(326,49); front2a_r06_c2_f10.src =
"gfx/front2a_r06_c2_f10.gif";
searchf_f1 = new Image(247,42); searchf_f1.src = "gfx/searchf.gif";
searchf_f2 = new Image(247,42); searchf_f2.src = "gfx/
searchf_f2.gif";
searchf_f3 = new Image(247,42); searchf_f3.src = "gfx/
searchf_f3.gif";
****Deleted 7 pages of JavaScript from here****
</HEAD>
```

Now let's look at the source code after she removed the JavaScript and placed it in separate .js files:

```
<HTML>
<HEAD>
<TITLE>Professional web design, hosting and search engine positioning
for the small to medium size businesses</TITLE>
<META Name="Description" Content="With years of internet experience,
we specialize in web design and search engine positioning.  Let
GBITech provide you with sensible business solutions.">
<META Name="Keywords" Content="professional web design,search engine
positioning,website promotion,quality,rankings,increased hits,web
hosting">
<Script Language="JavaScript" src="docimage.js"></Script>
<Script Language="JavaScript" src="scroll.js"></Script>
<Script Language="JavaScript" src="bannersetup.js"></Script>
</HEAD>
```

What a difference! Moving the JavaScript to a separate file certainly brought the page's keyword-containing body text toward the top of the page.

**NOTE** Another advantage of using external .js files is that some browsers will cache the file on the client's computer, thus saving download time on other pages that use the same file.

## Making Flash Pages More Searchable

Although certainly impressive, Flash can create search engine ranking problems. At this time, none of the major search engines index Flash content, so any content within Flash files is invisible to them.

So if you have a page that contains only Flash content, the search engines will see a blank page, which won't do your site much good in the rankings.

Not only that, but often sites that use Flash also use a redirect tag of some sort to go to the main content of the site. Redirect tags are frowned upon by most of the engines, although certain redirects are better than others.

**FIND IT ONLINE** Let's look at an example of a site that uses Flash. Although it's impossible to view the full scope of the technology in a book, you can visit the page online at **http://www.se-optimizer.com** to see how it really works.

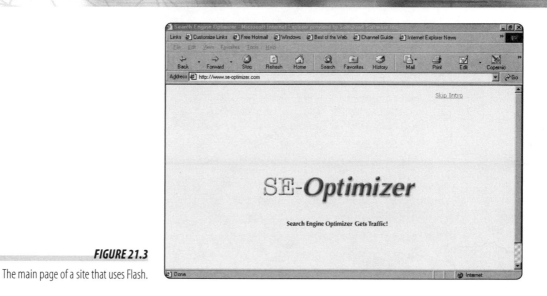

**FIGURE 21.3**

The main page of a site that uses Flash.

Figure 21.3 shows the main page of the Search Engine Optimizer site, complete with the way the screen looks when the Flash is finished, right before we're redirected to another page. Listing 21.3 lists the source code.

### Listing 21.3
### Source code for a site that uses Flash.

```
<HTML>
<HEAD>
<TITLE>Search Engine Optimizer</TITLE>
<META name="keywords" content="search engine optimizer, search engine
rankings, web positioning tools">
<META name="description" content="Search Engine Optimizer software
will analyze your Web pages and suggest changes that will boost your
search engine rankings!">
</HEAD>
<BODY bgcolor="white">
<CENTER>
<TABLE border="0" cellpadding="0" cellspacing="0" width="550">
<TR>
<TD>
<DIV align="right">
<!-- search-engine.html-->
```

```
<!-- SE-Optimizer-->
<!--Search Engine Optimizer Gets Traffic!-->
<A HREF="search-engine.html"><font face="Verdana,Arial,Helvetica"
size="2" color="gray">Skip Intro</FONT></A></DIV>
<P><object classid="clsid:D27CDB6E-AE6D-11cf-96B8-444553540000"
codebase="http://active.macromedia.com/flash2/cabs/
swflash.cab#version=4,0,0,0" id="SEO_intro" width="550" height="400">
<PARAM name="movie" value="images/SEO_intro.swf">
<PARAM name="quality" value="high">
<PARAM name="bgcolor" value="#FFFFFF">
<PARAM name="play" value="true">
<PARAM name="loop" value="false">
<PARAM type="type" value="application/x-shockwave-flash" name="">
<PARAM type="pluginspage" value="http://www.macromedia.com/shockwave/
download/index.cgi?P1_Prod_Version=ShockwaveFlash" name="">
<EMBED src="images/SEO_intro.swf" quality="high" bgcolor="#FFFFFF"
width="550" height="400" play="true" loop="false" type="application/
x-shockwave-flash" pluginspage="http://www.macromedia.com/shockwave/
download/index.cgi?P1_Prod_Version=ShockwaveFlash">
</OBJECT></TD>
</TR>
</TABLE>
</CENTER>
</BODY>
</HTML>
```

Look over the source code again. Is there anything for the engines to index? Other than the title and META tags, no. Not only that, but if the page had not redirected to another page, and if additional content had been added after the Flash, the body text would have been pushed toward the bottom of the page, which would still have presented ranking problems.

Although this is certainly an impressive page that is advertising an excellent piece of software, because of the technology used, the site had to create a workaround in order to achieve top rankings.

So what are some workarounds for the Flash?

- Add a <NOFRAMES> tag with content-rich information in the tag.
- Create effective doorway pages that don't use Flash, and direct traffic to the site in this manner.
- Use cloaking software, and keep the impressive main page of the site as it is.

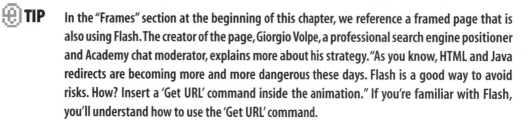

**TIP** In the "Frames" section at the beginning of this chapter, we reference a framed page that is also using Flash. The creator of the page, Giorgio Volpe, a professional search engine positioner and Academy chat moderator, explains more about his strategy. "As you know, HTML and Java redirects are becoming more and more dangerous these days. Flash is a good way to avoid risks. How? Insert a 'Get URL' command inside the animation." If you're familiar with Flash, you'll understand how to use the 'Get URL' command.

## Checking Tables for Keywords

How could we possibly include tables in a list of strategies that could be detrimental to search engine rankings?

Simple. If you're not using your keywords in your table columns, and if your navigational column is on the left-hand side of the page, your important keyword-containing body text has been pushed toward the bottom of the page. Also keep in mind that tables break apart when engines read them.

The solution is easy. Use keywords in your tables! In other words, if you use tables for precise text or image placement, be sure to use keyword in those tables as well. You can also experiment with moving the navigation column to the right-hand side of the page. Although we generally think of navigation bars as being on the left-hand side, that's certainly not set in stone.

Going back to our JavaScript example, now let's look at the page in terms of the tables by examining Figure 21.2. The navigation on this page is on the right-hand side of the page, and it certainly is effective.

## Linking Beyond Image Maps

You'll encounter a couple of problems if you use image maps. First, if the image map is large, it will push your keyword-containing text to the bottom of the page. We've harped on that enough, and you get the picture.

Second, the engines can't follow links in an image map, so be sure to use HTML links elsewhere on your page for the engines to spider.

**FIND IT ONLINE** Figure 21.4 presents an example of an image map as found at the Concierge.com Web site. You can view the site online at **http://www. concierge.com/cgi-bin/maps.cgi?link=intro**.

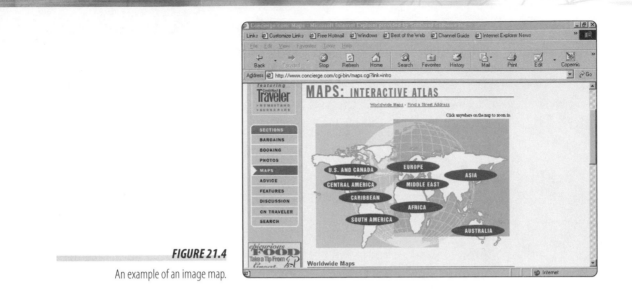

**FIGURE 21.4**

An example of an image map.

In this example, visitors can click on any of the regions on the map, and they'll be taken to another page.

## Working with Dynamically-Created HTML

Dynamically-created HTML is anything that's created on-the-fly, such as database-delivered content. It is also any HTML content, whether database-delivered, PHP, JSP, ASP, or CGI, that is created only after the request for the page is made to the server. Already, you can see the potential problems looming before you. First off, if the content is created on-the-fly depending on user interactivity, there's nothing for the engines to index.

Also, if the dynamic URLs have symbols in them, the engines generally won't index them. The symbols act as stop signs, and the engines quit indexing when they spot the symbol.

What kind of symbols are we talking about? In particular, the question mark (?), but other symbols include and (&), percent (%), plus (+), and the dollar sign ($).

Not only are symbols a problem, but many search engines avoid indexing URLs that include a reference to the CGI bin directory, because they could fall into the trap of the database feeding the engine an infinite number of URLs.

So with dynamic pages, we have a couple of problematic situations. If the URLs contain a symbol or a reference to the CGI bin directory, we probably won't be able to get the pages indexed at all. But if they don't, we should be able to get the pages indexed, but because there's no content for the engines to index, we'll have ranking difficulties.

If you have dynamically generated pages that are generated without special parameters in the URL and without giving any indication that the server is generating them on-the-fly, you should be able to get the pages indexed. But without content, the pages probably will still have ranking problems, unless the site has a good solid link and/or click-through popularity.

To tell whether a page is able to be indexed, try deleting everything from the question mark (?) on. If the page loads correctly, you should be able to get it indexed. If it doesn't, you'll need a workaround.

Also, you should avoid using symbols in your URLs if at all possible. Some programs, such as Apache and Cold Fusion, allow you to translate symbol-containing URLs with engine-friendly URLs, so that's an option, too.

As with many of the techniques presented here, content-rich static pages can serve as workarounds for dynamic content that can't be indexed.

Cloaking is another workaround for database-delivered content.

**TIP**   An Academy student has achieved much success with his database-delivered site, Cruise Discounts Online. One of his pages, **http://www.cruisediscountsonline.com/ Royal-Caribbean-cruise-line/index.asp**, was created completely by using data from an Access database table, and at the time of this writing, ranked #4 in Google for searches of the keyword phrase, "Royal Caribbean cruise line."

**FIND IT ONLINE**   He uses the same page as the mainframe at **http://www.cruisediscountsonline.com/ CruiseRoyalCaribbean.html**, which has ranked high at NBCi in the past. Be sure to take note of his effective `<NOFRAMES>` tag. As Ed King, owner of the site says, "Who said that frame pages cannot be used successfully?"

Then again, Ed has spent a lot of time learning search engine optimization strategies and working on his site. Everything on his site points to that one overall theme: cruises.

## Developing Strategies for Other Problem Areas

Besides the strategies already mentioned, keep in mind these additional potential problem areas:

- **Pages that are slow to load or access.** After submitting your page, if it takes longer than 60 seconds for the engines to access it, your page may not get indexed at all. This applies to AltaVista, Excite, and probably other engines as well. Also, some of the engines, such as Excite, don't seem to like slow-loading pages, either.

- **Drop-down menus.** If you use drop-down menus on your pages, be sure to include actual HTML links to your interior pages as well. If you rely on your drop-down menus to direct the spiders to other pages on your site, you may be very disappointed when the pages aren't indexed. Also make sure that your drop-down menus aren't pushing your important body text toward the bottom of the page.

- META **refresh tags.** Do your best to stay away from META refresh tags. Regretfully, the tag has gotten a bad name, and most of the engines take one look at a page that's using a META refresh and consider the page to be spam. Use a Java redirect instead.

- **Graphics before text.** Because the engines can't see your graphics, begin your pages with text, if at all possible. Don't rely on ALT tags, because not all the engines recognize them.

- **Irrelevant** META **tags.** Some HTML editors stick in irrelevant META tags like a generator or author tag. Don't confuse the engines with tags that aren't necessary. Remove them and clean up your HTML.

## Cloaking as a Solution to Problematic Technologies

Cloaking, also known as *dynamic page substitution* or *Food Script,* has gotten a bad name in some circles, so let's set the record straight.

First off, what is *cloaking?* Cloaking is when scripts are created and placed on a Web site's server that can detect the IP addresses of search engines' spiders. When the script detects a search engine spider, it serves up a different page than what a visitors to the site see.

With cloaking, you actually create engine-specific pages and optimize them. The script will recognize when HotBot's spider is visiting, for example, and it will serve up the special HotBot-specific page. When AltaVista's spider visits, it will serve up AltaVista's page. Yet when visitors click through to the site, they see a totally different page.

Cloaked pages are stripped to the bone. In other words, they're plain and simple HTML documents that don't use any of the strategies that could possibly be detrimental to top rankings. Cloaked pages don't use frames, JavaScript, tables, Flash, or anything else.

With cloaking, you're giving the engines what they want to see: simple pages. And you're giving your visitors impressive pages that are sure to make them trust your company and ultimately buy your products or services.

## When Is Cloaking Needed?

Let's say that you're working with a Web site that is using dynamic content. You know the problems you're going to have in getting the page ranked in the top 10. Not only that, your keyword phrase is competitive, and you need every edge over the competition that you can get.

Cloaking gives you that edge. It evens the playing field by eliminating all of the strategies that could possibly present ranking problems, so you're dealing with a Plain Jane page that's sure to appeal to the search engines.

Or let's say that you're in an extremely competitive business such as online casinos. About the only way you can compete is to use cloaking, because most of your competitors do.

You also may choose to use cloaking if your site is composed of frames.

Another reason for using cloaking is if you're presented with your company's Web site and told to optimize it for the engines, yet you're not allowed to make any changes to the page. It's rather difficult to optimize a page effectively if you can't work with it.

Not only that, but after positioners have spent hours and hours working on a Web site and struggling with rankings, they don't want a competitor to come along and steal their valuable code. Cloaking protects the code.

Because more and more professional search engine positioners are using cloaking these days, does this mean that you should cloak every one of your pages?

Definitely not. If your circumstances warrant cloaking, go for it. If you're having ranking problems, it's certainly something to consider. If you're not, there's no reason to use cloaking.

For one thing, cloaking costs a little bit more than pocket change. Most cloaking software costs in the neighborhood of $1,000. So cloaking isn't for the faint hearted. It's for those with ranking difficulties who are willing to go the extra mile to get top rankings.

How do the search engines feel about cloaking? Their main goal is to provide relevant content to their users. They want to make sure that pages get indexed under keywords that are relevant to the site's page. As long as your cloaked pages reflect the content of the actual pages, you don't use any spamming techniques, and you're on the up-and-up, you should have no problems with cloaking.

Will cloaking have an adverse effect on link or click-through popularity? This question comes up frequently when cloaking is discussed, so we went to John Heard, one of the leading authorities on cloaking, for the answer.

> Cloaking systems cannot affect link popularity or link relevancy. To a search engine's robot, cloaking doesn't "exist" because it is not visible to it. As far as the spider knows, it's seeing the same pages as anyone else visiting the site. In our promotion efforts, cloaking systems are a benefit, both to the spiders and to the web site owners, because it allows you to deep link from the home page to important pages within the site, perhaps links that you wouldn't normally put on the home page for humans, but that you do want spidered and indexed. That is crucial to those pages' link popularity, because if a site's home page doesn't even link to the page, it is not viewed as that important to the spider and either won't be indexed or it might not be kept in the index. Incoming link popularity from other sites is not affected by the target site, but you can affect outgoing link popularity "from" your site with cloaking. One example is, say that you want to put links up to

other sites, *but* you don't want to pass on the link popularity from your site. With cloaking, you can show humans the links, but hide them from the spiders if necessary.

Heard is well known and respected in the search engine industry for his IP Delivery cloaking software, as well as being the main researcher for Planet Ocean.

## Important Cloaking Considerations

When considering cloaking, keep in mind that it's actually not the cloaking software that is so important. It's the updates to that software. In other words, you need to go with a very reputable company that you can trust to provide updates every time the engines' spiders change their IP addresses. If you don't get constant updates, the software will do you no good.

For an excellent cloaking software program, consider IP Delivery (**http:// www.ip-delivery.com/foodscript/**). John Heard backs IP Delivery, so you know you're in good hands with this software.

Another top-notch cloaking software program is Traffic Titan. Learn more at **http://position-it.com/traffictitan/**.

**TIP**    For an article about cloaking and its pros and cons, visit **http://www.onlinewebtraining.com/ information/cloaking.html**.

For an online tutorial on using cloaking, visit **http://www.rookiesnstars.com/position/**.

Fantomaster publishes an excellent newsletter pertaining to cloaking, and they also sell cloaking software at a fraction of the price of most of the other software on the market. The following URL deserves a good, long look: **http://www.fantomaster.com/fasmbase0.html**.

Another important consideration when using cloaking is that Google caches pages and makes those pages viewable in the search results. See Chapter 24 on how to keep Google from caching your cloaked pages.

However, in recent months, Google has publicly stated that they consider any pages that use cloaking to be spam, and they're removing the pages from their index. Therefore, with the Google engine, we highly recommend not using cloaking, at least for the time being.

## Conclusion

When working with your Web site or designing new sites, keep in mind that certain strategies will present ranking problems. Are you willing to do what it takes to work around those problems? Will you be able to achieve the rankings you want, which translates to traffic to your site if you use those strategies?

Simply recognize that these potential problems exist, and then make educated decisions on the best way to handle them.

# STUDYING YOUR COMPETITION

**In This Chapter**

Resubmitting Competing Pages

Analyzing Competitors' Pages

Why Their Pages Are Beating Yours

No doubt about it—one of the best ways to learn how to boost your site's rankings is to study competing pages and learn why their sites are ranking higher than yours. In fact, submitting your competitors' pages to the engines can let you know that the top-ranking sites have earned the privilege of that top ranking, and you'll be able to study the sites that are truly on top.

In this chapter, you'll learn how to analyze your competition. You'll also learn why sites are ranking higher than yours when there appears to be no visible reason for it.

You can have search engine positioning strategies firmly fixed in your mind, but if you don't go to the engines to see who's really on top, you're spinning your wheels. Why is their page #1, when yours is #39 and holding? What are they doing that you can try?

Keep in mind that things change rapidly in this industry. What works today might not work tomorrow. If you study your competition and see what's working now, you'll be in a much better position to achieve top rankings for your own pages.

So visit an engine and run a search for your important keyword phrase. Visit each of those pages and study them closely.

By doing so, sometimes you'll hit gold and be able to apply the principles to your site. Other times, you'll have no idea why the site has achieved such good rankings, and you'll want to understand why.

In any event, by studying competing pages under your keyword phrase, you'll be in a much better position to understand what that particular engine likes to see at that point in time.

## Resubmitting Competing Pages

After you've searched for your keyword phrase at the engine but before you've studied those top 10 sites, resubmit their URLs to the engine.

*What? You're telling me to submit competing sites to the engine? Isn't that illegal or something?*

Not at all. It's a well-used strategy, and here's why.

When you study competing sites, you'll want to make sure that the pages you're analyzing have truly earned their top rankings.

*But they're in the top 10 rankings in the engine. How could they have not earned that ranking?*

There are numerous reasons why a page could be in the rankings yet not have actually earned that ranking. In Chapter 21, "Analyzing Technology That Can Be Detrimental to Search Engine Rankings," we study cloaking. With cloaking, the engines see a different page than what users see. So the page you're viewing actually did not "earn" the top ranking.

A similar strategy, although one that you won't want to try, is to swap out codes or tags once a top ranking is achieved. If a Web master is using this technique, you certainly wouldn't want to study the source code of the page, because it's not the source code that actually achieved the top rankings.

Other Web masters might swap out whole pages after a top ranking is achieved, so that the page you're viewing in no way resembles the page that was given the top ranking.

Later in this chapter, we cover other reasons why a page has achieved a top ranking when there appears to be no reason why. For now, let's look at the benefits of resubmitting competing pages:

- If any of the pages produce a 404 File Not Found message, you'll be removing them from the index, which will give your pages a chance to make it into the top rankings.
- If the pages or code was swapped out, the rankings on those pages will plummet, which could give your pages a push up the search engine rankings ladder.
- If the pages were given a top ranking under a different ranking algorithm, submitting them will cause the spider to reindex the page and give the page its true ranking based on today's algorithm.

*But that sounds rather underhanded—to submit the pages in hopes that their rankings will fall.*

Keep in mind that when the engine performs its next spider run, every one of those pages will plummet in the rankings anyway. You're simply speeding up the process for the purpose of analyzing the pages.

After all, you don't want to spend your precious time analyzing a page that won't be in the top 10 after the next spider run.

### How to Report Spammers to the Engines

If you've discovered a spammer among the search results for your particular keyword phrase(s), consider reporting the spammer to the search engine. After all, the engines are as keen on providing relevant content as you are, and they don't want to see spamming going on in their index.

| | |
|---|---|
| AltaVista | **http://doc.altavista.com/help/contact/search.html** |
| Excite | **http://www.excite.com/feedback/** |
| GO/InfoSeek* | **http://comments.go.com/comments.html/** |
| HotBot | **http://www.lycos.com/feedback/** |
| Lycos | **http://www.lycos.com/feedback/** |
| Northern Light | **http://www.northernlight.com/docs/gen_help_prob.html** |
| Yahoo! | **http://add.yahoo.com/fast/help/us/ysearch/cgi_feedback** |

*The GO search engine may be shut down by the time this book is published. See Chapter 17 for more information.

So resubmit the pages, and then wait for them to be reindexed. When they are, search for your keyword phrase again. Who is on top now? Is it the same 10 sites? In all likelihood, it won't be, and the strategy could even have given your site a boost in the rankings.

Then study those sites. Those are the sites that have truly earned a top 10 listing. Those are the sites that could provide valuable tips for the improvement of your own site's rankings. Learn from those on top, and see if their strategies can help you with your own site.

*Will I get into trouble for submitting someone else's pages to the engine?*

Not at all. In fact, many people submit pages that they feel are deserving of being in that engine's index. They have no connection to the site itself, but they'd like to see the pages in the index. After all, the engines want their indexes to include the best sites in various categories, and submitting those sites isn't a problem.

So find out which sites are beating yours in the competition, and resubmit those pages to the engine. Learn from their success, and try to apply some of their strategies to your own site. You may even find that your site moves up in the rankings as an added bonus.

## Analyzing Competitors' Pages

When analyzing competing pages, what should you look for? Be sure to study the page as it appears on the Web as well as the source code. We suggest to our students that they print out copies of the source code, which might make it easier to compare the pages.

Of course, you can also run the pages through a Web page analysis program like Search Engine Optimizer or Keyword Density Analyzer. See Chapter 18, "Basic Optimization Strategies," for the URLs for each of those programs.

When studying your competition, notice these things:

- Is the page using a title tag? Is the keyword phrase in that tag? Where in the tag is the phrase used? Is it used more than once? How long is the tag?

- Is the page using a META description tag? Does the keyword phrase appear in the tag, and if so, where? How many times is it used? How long is the tag?

- Is the page using a META keyword tag? Does the keyword phrase appear in the tag? Where? How many times is it used? Does the tag contain variations of the keyword phrase? Synonyms? How long is the tag?

- Where in the body text does the keyword phrase first appear? How often is it used? Does it appear toward the end of the page as well?

- What other keyword-containing tags are used? ALT tags? Headline tags? Style tags? Comment tags? Images?

- Is the keyword phrase used in the URL? In the domain name? In a subdirectory?

- What is the overall keyword weight, and what is the keyword weight of the visible body text?

- How many words are in the body of the page?

- Does the page use the keyword phrase in link text? How many related outgoing links are listed on the page?

- What is the site's link popularity? You can visit **http://www.linkpopularity.com** to find out.

- Is the page using frames? JavaScript? Dynamic content? Is the page using any of the techniques we discussed in Chapter 21, "Analyzing Technology That Can Be Detrimental to Search Engine Rankings"? Is your page? How do they compare?

- Is the entire site devoted to one central theme? Is your site?

- Is the page the index page of the site, or is it an interior or a doorway page?

- Is the page using spamming techniques in any way? If so, be sure to report the page to that particular engine. Almost all of the engines ask you to report spammers, so do it!

- Does the page provide relevant and related content in the form of body text, links, or other tactics, such as polls, contests, giveaways, etc.?

## Why Their Pages Are Beating Yours

When analyzing your competitors' pages and comparing them to yours, you'll more than likely be quite puzzled as to why a competitor's page is ranking higher than yours. There will appear to be no reason for it, but it's there.

---

### Don't Copy Competing Pages or Codes!

When we suggest that you study your competition, we are *not* suggesting that you copy their pages or codes.

Instead, we're suggesting that you analyze their codes to see what they might be doing right, and then transfer those strategies to your own site.

Don't copy their title tag—create your own. Don't copy their description tag—make yours better.

Model your page after your competition in terms of keyword use and length of page, but make sure that the content is yours alone.

It's quite easy to get into trouble for copyright infringement on the Web, so don't let it happen to you.

**TIP**

**FIND IT ONLINE** A quick and easy way to analyze competing pages, or even your own pages, is by visiting Mouse Click Application at **http://www.mouseclickapplication.com**. After downloading a very short file, you can then analyze any page that you visit by right clicking your mouse on the page itself, then choosing which tool you want to use.

Very handy tool—and it's *free*!

Let's look at a list of reasons, which you'll be able to refer back to when this happens to you:

- **Irrelevant search results.** It's a fact of life. Search results aren't always relevant. In fact, we searched on Lycos for the keyword phrase "buttered popcorn." Then we captured a screen shot to help explain various aspects of Lycos's search results, and we used this information in Chapter 24, "Engine-Specific Strategies." None of the results that show on that page are related in any manner to "buttered popcorn," but those are actual search results. So admit that it can happen and accept it, then move on.

- **Out-of-date pages.** If you're viewing a page that was spidered and indexed a year ago, you're probably viewing what the engine considered to be relevant at that time, which will be considerably different than what is relevant now. If you haven't resubmitted the page for indexing, you could actually be viewing an out-of-date page.

- **Cloaking.** If the page you're viewing has been cloaked, you're obviously not looking at the page that actually achieved the top search engine ranking, and resubmitting the page won't help. How can you tell whether a page has been cloaked? Compare the page size, title, and description from the page itself to the search results. If there's a difference, you can suspect that the page is cloaked. See Chapter 24 for information on how Google caches pages and makes those pages available in the search results.

- **Swapping Web pages or code.** If you're viewing a page where the page itself or its code has been swapped out after achieving a top ranking, you're not looking at the page that actually achieved the top rankings. Incidentally, the problem with using this tactic is that you never know when the engines' spiders will reindex the site. When the spider reindexes the site, your rankings will plummet.

- **New ranking algorithm.** Algorithms change so frequently, and what works today may not work tomorrow or next week.

- **Page popularity.** If the page has a good solid link popularity, it could be ranked significantly higher due to that one fact alone. Or if the page is visited often, the click-through popularity engines will give it a boost in ranking.

- **Search engine bugs or problems.** Let's face it: The search engines have problems too!

- **Reviewed by a human.** Many of the engines use human editors to review Web pages, and possibly your competitors achieved top rankings because they received a good review.

- **Listed in the engine's directory.** With a few of the engines, if your site is listed in their directory, your site automatically gets a boost in ranking.

- **Content-rich themed page.** If your competitors' pages are content rich and based on one particular theme or focus, they may get a boost in relevancy. Remember the importance of themes, and make sure that your Web site is focused on one main topic only.

**TIP**    Once your page achieves a top ranking, you may not want your competitors to submit your page for reindexing. If the algorithm has changed since your page was ranked, you may lose your top ranking. To prevent this from happening, use a META "noindex" tag, which will prevent the engines from reindexing the page. Of course, this only works for the engines that recognize the tag.

```
<META name="robots" content="noindex">
```

## Conclusion

When trying to achieve top rankings for your site, be sure to check out your competitors to see what they're doing. Analyze their pages and their tags, and compare them to yours. Decide if there's anything you can change that might help your rankings.

If you can't figure out why their pages rank higher than yours, remember that search results aren't always relevant, and don't waste your time worrying about it. Simply build a better page!

# PURCHASING KEYWORDS AT THE PAY ENGINES

**In This Chapter**

GoTo

Exploring Other Pay-per-Click Engines

Purchasing Internet Keywords through RealNames

Purchasing keywords at a search engine operates on a relatively simple principle: Whoever is willing to pay the most goes to the top of the rankings. You simply bid on your keyword phrase, depending on how much you are willing to pay per click-through. Then, whenever anyone clicks on the site through the pay engine, you're charged that amount.

You'll certainly find differing opinions about purchasing keywords at the pay engines. Some people spend thousands of dollars on keywords every month, but the return on their investment makes it worth every dollar.

Other people seem to toss their money away when they try to purchase keywords. It appears to be a waste of time and money, according to their experiences.

Are there helpful strategies that you can use when dealing with the pay engines? How can you get the most out of your marketing dollar when purchasing keywords?

This chapter covers the most important pay search engines, such as GoTo, and offers valuable suggestions that should help you achieve the most success if you decide to go this route.

You'll also learn about RealNames, or Internet Keywords, and how to gain traffic through this pay service.

**TIP** PayPerClickSearchEngines.com (**http://www.payperclicksearchengines.com/**) is an excellent resource for learning more about the pay engines.

## GoTo

**FIND IT ONLINE** GoTo, at **http://www.goto.com**, is by far the most popular pay engine, and its popularity continues to rise. With more than 100 million searches performed per month and more than 10 million click-throughs, they're definitely a powerful force on the Internet. In fact, GoTo is responsible for 2.9 percent of all searches as of December 1, 2000, according to Web Snapshot (**http://websnapshot.mycomputer.com/searchengines.html**). This effectively makes GoTo the #7 search engine in terms of popularity. Not bad.

GoTo is actually ahead of giants such as Lycos, HotBot, and Northern Light, which makes its importance even more clear.

So how much do keywords typically cost? There's nothing typical about purchasing keywords! Some keywords can be purchased for a penny or two, whereas others might go for $6 per click-through. In competitive areas such as online gambling, you can expect to pay major bucks to get on top.

Not only that, but a competitor can come along at any time and outbid you, so those bid amounts can constantly change.

One of the complaints that is often heard about GoTo is the fact that keywords are costing more and more. Where today you might pay $1.50 for a keyword, you may pay $3.20 for that keyword six months from now. As GoTo continues to build traffic, however, your site is apt to be seen by more people, so the return on your investment may be considerably higher.

Figure 23.1 shows a search performed at GoTo at the time of this writing for the keyword phrase "life insurance."

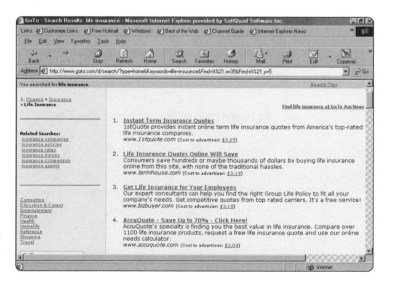

**FIGURE 23.1**

A search performed at GoTo for "life insurance."

Notice that the #1 site bid $3.25 per click-through to be in that esteemed spot; #4 paid $3.04. Although you can't see it on this screen, if you were to perform this search online, you would see that following the paid results, the non-paid results from Inktomi appear.

Here's an interesting consideration. Look at the titles and descriptions of each site in Figure 23.1. The #4 title of "AccuQuote - Save up to 70% - Click Here!" is certainly captivating. We'd all like to save 70 percent on life insurance.

Actually, #4 has a better description as well. Will the #1 site get more click-throughs than the #4? Possibly, but with a dynamite title and description, can you see how you can make up for the rankings?

Why is GoTo so popular with searchers? It could be its simple and easy-to-maneuver format. Instead of being a busy portal offering everything from horoscopes to stock quotes, GoTo's offerings are slim. It concentrates on giving you what you've come there for in the first place: a search engine.

Plus, searchers find that GoTo's results are more relevant than those from the other major engines. GoTo has a strict relevancy policy, and it monitors that policy closely. In other words, if you have a site that's devoted to office supplies, you can't purchase the keyword phrase of "online gambling" just to boost traffic to your site.

What if you and four other Web site owners bid the same amount for the same keyword phrase? Whoever places the bid first gets on top, followed by the others, in order of when they placed the bid.

## Advantages to Using GoTo

Besides GoTo's popularity and the relevancy of its results, there are many other advantages to purchasing keywords through GoTo:

- GoTo offers 40 search results per page, versus the traditional 10 of most engines. Therefore, your site can be #35 and still be on page 1 of the results.
- You pay only when someone clicks on your site, rather than on *page impressions*, which refers to the number of times someone has the opportunity to see your ad or listing.

- You have control over where you appear in the search results. Want to be #1? Have the money to do it? Go for it!

- When algorithms change, your site remains on top!

- You can instantly get a #1, or a #10, or whatever ranking, instead of spending weeks trying to get a top ranking in the traditional engines.

- You don't have to worry about optimizing your pages. You fork out the money, and voilá! You're on top!

- You can target your audience based on the keywords you choose. You don't have to create a series of doorway pages for various keywords. Just purchase those keywords and you're ready for traffic.

- If you're not getting enough traffic, you can modify your keywords at any time.

**FIND IT ONLINE**

- You can take advantage of GoTo's $99 Express Service at **http://www.goto.com/d/about/advertisers** and receive a personal consultation to help you come up with a list of 20 keywords.

- GoTo offers payment plans to help you manage your account.

- Because GoTo results are also seen in META search engines such as DogPile, you may find that your traffic increases significantly through the META search engines.

- GoTo now provides the top three search results at AOL Search and the top two search results at Netscape, which will certainly create more traffic for your GoTo keywords. As mentioned in Chapter 17, GoTo also provides its top three results to Lycos, HotBot, and AltaVista.

- The cost per click-through generally is less than the cost per lead in other forms of advertising.

**TIP**   Keyword Bid Optimizer (**http://www.paidsearchenginetools.com/**) is a subscription-based tool that will help you keep track of your keyword purchases through GoTo.

## Guidelines for Purchasing Keywords through GoTo

Before you jump into purchasing keywords, be sure to choose the most effective keywords that will bring you the most traffic. By far, those who make the most money from traffic at GoTo are those who take their time in choosing keywords and those who purchase more than one keyword.

**FIND IT ONLINE** As we mention in Chapter 18, "Basic Optimization Strategies," GoTo has a Search Term Suggestion Tool that will be valuable to you as you consider your keywords. Visit the tool at **http://inventory.go2.com/inventory/Search_Suggestion.jhtml**. In the future, this link may only work for keyword subscribers.

Or visit WordTracker and register for a free trial of its services at **http://www.wordtracker.com**.

Before visiting the online form at **http://www.goto.com/d/about/advertisers**, you'll want to keep these guidelines in mind:

- You must bid at least $.01 for each keyword, and increases to the bid amount must be in increments of $.01.

- Perform a search for your keywords and see what the keywords are going for. Where do you want to be in the rankings? How much are the sites paying per click-through? That's what you need to bid.

- According to GoTo's research, the #1 site gets clicked on three times more than the #5 site. But you can even those odds by creating effective titles and descriptions.

- Bid on 10 to 20 keywords at a time. As mentioned earlier in this section, those who purchase a large number of keywords have more success with this engine. An Academy student spends $10,000 a month on keywords at GoTo for his online casino, but it's well worth it for the traffic the engine sends his way.

- You must deposit $25 in order to bid on a keyword.

- Your keywords must be relevant to your site, and your title and description must relate to the keyword phrase. GoTo is watching this area closely, because it obviously wants its search results to continue to be relevant.

- Your title may contain up to 40 characters, and your description may be up to 190 characters, including spaces.

- You can purchase as many keywords as you want, but each keyword can link to one URL only.

- Choose targeted keywords. Don't choose general keywords, because the traffic won't convert to sales, and you may be throwing your money down the garbage disposal. Purchase keywords for your actual goods or services. If you sell "term life insurance" only, you don't want to purchase a general keyword like "insurance." Fine-tune!

- GoTo has a pluralization system, so if you purchase "motor homes," you'll also be found under "motor home."

- Some experts recommend bidding on a keyword phrase that is on the first page but that's below the fold, so that searchers have to scroll down to find your site. You may get less traffic, but the traffic will be more focused and possibly convert better to sales.

 **TIP**   For an in-depth article about GoTo, visit **http://www.onlinewebtraining.com/information/ goto.html**.

## Exploring Other Pay-per-Click Engines

With the popularity and success of GoTo, other pay-per-click engines have been created to try to tap into that market. As mentioned earlier, PayPerClickSearchEngines.com offers an impressive listing of the various pay-per-click engines, so be sure to check it out.

In the early days of any pay-per-click engine, you'll be able to purchase keywords for very little money. Of course, the traffic to the engine won't be ideal, either. Then as the engine gains in popularity and traffic, you can expect to pay more and more for your keywords, which is what has happened at GoTo.

Let's look at a couple of other popular pay-per-click engines.

### FindWhat

FindWhat (**http://www.findwhat.com**) has been in existence for more than a year now, and its traffic has continued to increase. According to Craig A. Pisaris-Henderson, president of FindWhat.com, the engine has 6,000 advertisers advertising more than 32,000 Web sites bidding on more than 4.2 million keywords and keyword phrases.

Like GoTo, FindWhat has an automated bidding system by which advertisers can bid for top placement for any keyword or keyword phrase. The system allows advertisers to choose their placement within FindWhat's results, and advertisers pay the bid amount whenever customers click through to the advertiser's site.

When purchasing keywords through FindWhat, look back over the guidelines for submitting to GoTo, because those suggestions will benefit you in FindWhat as well.

**FIND IT ONLINE**

Then visit **https://secure.findwhat.com/signup/signup.asp** and complete the online form.

## Kanoodle

**FIND IT ONLINE**

Kanoodle (**http://www.kanoodle.com**) is another pay-per-placement search engine that's rising in popularity. Keywords purchased at Kanoodle—and FindWhat, for that matter—are less expensive than keywords purchased at GoTo, so this might be the time to check out its system.

To purchase keywords through Kanoodle, look over the guidelines for submitting to GoTo, and then visit **https://safe.kanoodle.com/client_services/listings/**.

Kanoodle also offers an Express Service, which provides a consultant who will help you choose the most effective keywords for your Web site.

An interesting feature of Kanoodle is that the top three bids on any search term will receive free banner impressions within that search term results page. So being in the top three gives you an added bonus at Kanoodle.

## URLs for Other Pay-per-Click Engines

The URLs for the other two pay-per-click engines follow. Rocketlinks gets its supplemental (non-paid) results from its own engine, and 7Search uses supplemental results from Google.

**FIND IT ONLINE**

- Bay9—**http://www.bay9.com**
- 7Search—**http://7search.com/**

## Purchasing Internet Keywords through RealNames

RealNames' claim to fame is its impressive listing of partners, including AltaVista, MSN Search, LookSmart, Google, Inktomi, and many more.

But what exactly is RealNames?

RealNames, also known as *Internet Keywords,* is an alternative addressing system for the Web. As you know, many (most?) URLs are a convoluted mess and are extremely difficult to remember. Plus, they may or may not reflect the company that owns them.

With RealNames, people can type in the names they recognize from TV ads, newspaper articles, etc., and they'll be able to go straight to that Web site.

RealNames is seeking to make it easier for users to find companies, or even individuals, on the Web. Its goal is to improve navigation through this addressing system, similar to the way the White Pages of a phone book works.

The next goal of RealNames is to offer the equivalent of the Yellow Pages, where people can search according to keywords pertinent to the business they're looking for. However, one of the things you, as a business paying to be in its listing, must decide is the type of search matching best suited to your keywords—partial or complete.

RealNames has approximately one million Internet Keywords in its database, and it claims to cover more than 70 percent of the Web through its partners.

### Understanding How Partial or Complete Matches Affect Results

Because RealNames covers more than 70 percent of the Web, does this mean that if you purchase an Internet Keyword, you'll have a presence in each of those partners?

Not exactly, and here's why.

Some of RealNames' partners support *partial matches,* whereas others don't. With partial matches, if users type in a keyword that appears in the middle of the Internet Keyword, your site will show up in the search results.

Let's say that your company's name is Crystal Clear Water USA, and you purchase the Internet Keyword of "spring water." Someone visits one of the partners that support partial matching and performs a search for "water." Because "water" appears in your Internet Keyword, your site will appear in the search rankings.

But let's say that you purchase the Internet Keyword of "Crystal Clear Water USA." If someone searches for "spring water" at one of the partners that do **not** support partial matching, your site wouldn't appear. Instead, the person would have to search for "Crystal Clear Water USA" for your site to appear in the results.

These partners support *complete matches*, which means they will not pull sites that have keywords in their title.

Currently, the partners that support partial matches are AltaVista, iWon, About.com, and the META engines—such as Dogpile and Metacrawler.

With the rest of RealNames' partners, users will have to type in the Internet Keyword exactly as it was purchased in order for your site to appear in the rankings.

With the differences between partial and complete matching in the back of your mind, you need to decide how you want your site to be found and in what engines.

If you don't have a strong presence in AltaVista, you may want to purchase Internet Keywords that are loaded with keywords, because that engine supports partial matching.

If you want to build brand loyalty, purchase Internet Keywords for those brands. If you have a new company with little name or brand recognition, it might be to your benefit to purchase an Internet Keyword that reflects your domain name.

It's certainly always a good idea to purchase Internet Keywords for your company name as well.

## Planning for the Costs of Internet Keywords

You can purchase an Internet Keyword for $100 a year, which is certainly easy on the advertising budget. When you reach 1,000 resolutions, or click-throughs, RealNames will contact you to set up a different Internet Keyword solution, such as 20,000 resolutions for $3,000.

Is it worth $100 a year? If you spend some time considering your company's needs and choosing an appropriate and effective Internet Keyword, it can easily be worth $100 a year.

## Viewing Internet Keywords in Action

Figure 23.2 shows a search performed at one of RealNames' partners, AltaVista, for the keyword phrase of "online courses."

Notice this statement toward the top of the page:

```
online courses - Click here for a list of Internet Keywords related
to online courses
```

Because this statement appears at the top of the page before the actual AltaVista search results, can you see how this could help you in the rankings with AltaVista?

Clicking on the link brings you to Internet Keyword search results, as Figure 23.3 shows.

Figure 23.3 shows the Internet Keyword search results for the search term of "online courses." Notice how AltaVista resolves the search by using partial matching.

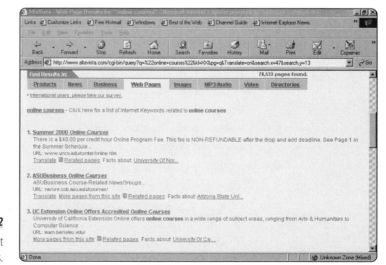

**FIGURE 23.2**

A search at AltaVista showing Internet Keyword results.

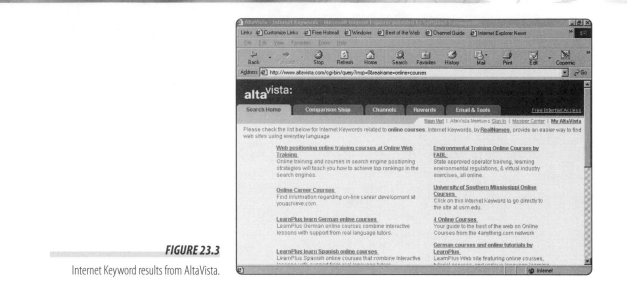

**FIGURE 23.3**

Internet Keyword results from AltaVista.

What determines which sites get on top of the rankings? RealNames' algorithm is based on three things: locale, relevance, and usage. Click-through popularity has a strong influence on which sites appear first in the rankings.

## Submission Tips for RealNames

**FIND IT ONLINE**

To purchase an Internet Keyword through RealNames, visit **http://customer.realnames.com/Virtual.asp?page=Eng_Subscribe_GetYourKeywords**.

If you keep these submission tips in mind, you'll have more success with your Internet Keyword:

- Spend some time determining how you want to be found and in which engines. If you want a strong presence in AltaVista, for example, be sure to add keywords to your Internet Keyword choice.

- You can't purchase a generic keyword like "dogs." Instead, you'll have to add keywords to the front or back of the keyword to make it more specialized. For example, you could register "Stan's Miniature Pinscher Dogs," and when someone searches for "dogs" through any of the partners who use partial matching, your site will be in the search results.

- Keep your title at around 80 characters and your description around 128 characters. Make sure that your title and description are captivating!

- You can send people to your home page through your Internet Keyword link, or to another page on your site.

- After your submission is reviewed, you'll be notified as to whether it was accepted or rejected. If it's rejected, you'll know why, and you can make some changes and resubmit.

- If you want to make changes to your account, you can call customer service. The changes will need to go through the review process before being implemented.

## How RealNames Is Marketing Internet Keywords

Does the average person know what "RealNames" or "Internet Keywords" are?

Probably not. RealNames is working hard at changing that, however.

For example, RealNames has adopted a logo that will be used through all its partner sites when presenting Internet Keyword results. This logo is a red circle with a blue arrow in it (see the search results in Figure 23.4).

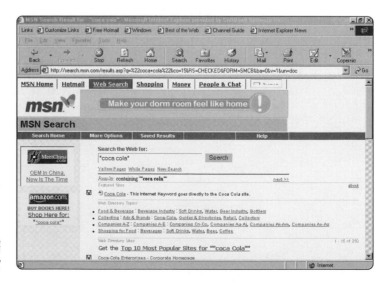

**FIGURE 23.4**

Search results at MSN for "coca cola."

Toward the top of the search results, look for this statement:

```
Coca Cola - This Internet Keyword goes directly to the Coca Cola site.
```

Before the sentence begins, you'll see the RealNames logo. This logo is one of RealNames' strategies for increasing public awareness about Internet Keywords.

Another way of increasing public awareness is through a draft proposal to institute an industry standard for Internet Keywords, which is to be considered by the *International Engineering Task Force* (IETF) this year.

Of course, the company also uses traditional advertising to increase public awareness. Another way RealNames is being pulled into the limelight is through its impressive listing of clients, which includes Panasonic, Coca Cola, and Hewlett-Packard.

**TIP** For a detailed article about RealNames, visit **http://www.onlinewebtraining.com/ information/realnames.html**.

## Conclusion

If you're having ranking problems with the major engines, and your back pocket is full enough, you may want to try the pay-per-click engines. You'll certainly save yourself some time by not having to optimize pages and then wait weeks for the results. You can simply pick and choose your rankings and where you want to appear based on how much money you're willing to spend.

Another alternative to using pay engines is to purchase an Internet Keyword through RealNames, which certainly can benefit your site through RealNames' impressive listing of partners.

C H A P T E R   2 4

# ENGINE-SPECIFIC STRATEGIES

**In This Chapter**

AltaVista

Excite

FAST/All the Web

Google

HotBot

GO/InfoSeek

Lycos

Northern Light

When working with your Web pages, you'll want to consider creating engine-specific pages, which will certainly do better in the targeted engines. As you learned in previous chapters, it's almost impossible to have one single page that will do well across the engines because each engine uses a different ranking algorithm.

To help you learn and understand how each engine operates and what makes that engine different from the others, we outline some of the engines' major characteristics in this chapter.

So study this information carefully, and then create engine-specific pages optimized for one or two keyword phrases only. Then watch your rankings and traffic soar!

As stated in Chapter 17 and other related chapters, Disney announced its intentions to shut down GO.com at the end of February 2001. So, at the time of the writing of this book, we aren't sure what's going to happen to the search engine and the GO directory. It may be sold, or it may be shut down altogether.

We are keeping the information on GO in the book, in the hopes that the engine will be kept alive and sold to another company. In this manner, you'll still have some excellent background information about GO and ways to work with the engine.

## AltaVista

**FIND IT ONLINE**

http://www.altavista.com

Submission URL: **http://www.altavista.com/cgi-bin/query?pg=addurl**

As mentioned in Chapter 17, "The Importance of Search Engines to the Success of Your Online Business," AltaVista pulls results from several other sources and provides those results to you on its search results page.

Understanding how the engine works with the other directories that feed into it will help save you time and energy. Plus, if you are unable to get a top ranking in the engine itself, you'll know that you can still have a solid presence in AltaVista by being visible in some of the directories and services that provide results to the engine.

Let's begin by performing a search at AltaVista, which will give you an idea of how the results from other sources appear. In Figure 24.1, we searched for the keyword phrase "utility software."

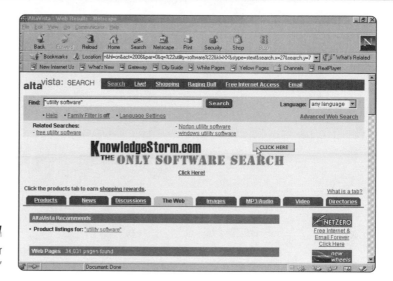

**FIGURE 24.1**

Search results at AltaVista for "utility software."

 **TIP** Notice the section below the Find box where you can perform another search. This "Related Searches" section gives you ideas for other keywords that might be effective for your Web pages, so when that section appears in the search results, pay attention to it!

In Figure 24.1 in the "AltaVista Recommends" section, you'll see a link to "Product listings for utility software." Clicking on that link will take you into AltaVista's shopping results. Below that, you'll see the number of Web pages the engine found in this search: 34,031.

In Figure 24.2, we've scrolled down on the page to see additional results.

Before the actual search results in Figure 24.2, you'll notice this statement:

> **utility software** - Click here for a list of Internet Keywords related to **utility software**

Those results come from RealNames, an alternative naming system for the Web. Internet Keywords results from RealNames should now always appear before the regular search results, according to AltaVista's new contract with RealNames. You can find more information about RealNames and other pay engines in Chapter 23, "Purchasing Keywords at the Pay Engines."

In this example, following the Internet Keyword results, you'll see numbered results from AltaVista's main index, which are created when its spider, Scooter, crawls the Web and indexes pages.

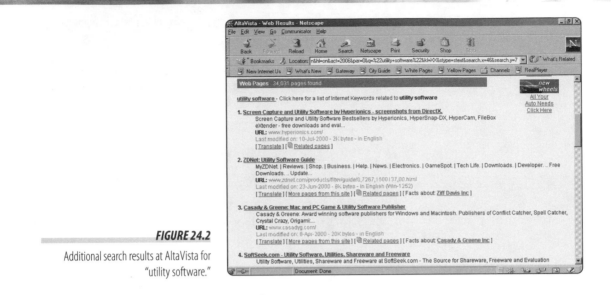

**FIGURE 24.2**

Additional search results at AltaVista for "utility software."

Figure 24.3 shows the bottom of the first page of search results for "utility software."

In Figure 24.3, "Have you ever tried these resources?" offers results from sources such as EXP.com (Find an Expert), WorldPages.com, and LookSmart.

Next, you'll see this section "Browse web sites selected by editors for 'utility software'."

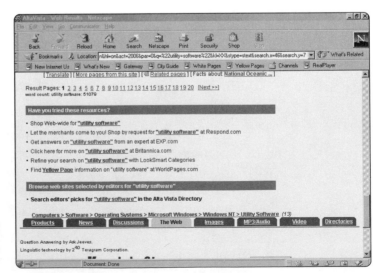

**FIGURE 24.3**

The bottom of the first page of AltaVista results for "utility software."

This information comes from AltaVista's directory, which takes results from the LookSmart directory.

By studying this information, you can see where you can have a presence in AltaVista, even if your Web pages aren't actually listed in the AltaVista index.

## Strategies for Working with AltaVista

When creating pages for AltaVista, keep these strategies in mind:

- Submit one to five pages a day to AltaVista, but no more.
- You can submit all important pages of your site to the engine, but the engine may only accept the main URL through its submission process. Therefore, be sure to place links to your other important pages on the main page of your site so that AltaVista's spider can crawl the links and find your other pages.
- Expect it to take 8 to 12 days for your pages to get in the index. As with all engines, however, it may take considerably longer.
- Most top-ranking pages with AltaVista don't use <META> tags, so try not using <META> tags on your AltaVista pages. If you do use <META> tags, don't use your important keyword phrase in those tags. Use synonyms of the phrase instead.
- Use your keywords in the following areas with AltaVista:

  <TITLE> tag

  Headline tags

  ALT attributes

  Domain names

  Link text

  Http-equiv tags

  URL

  Names of images

  Style tags
- The limit on <TITLE> tags is 78 characters, including spaces.
- The limit on description tags is 150 characters, including spaces.
- Try longer pages with AltaVista, even around 500 words.

- Link popularity is a major issue with AltaVista, so work hard at getting other Web sites to link back to your site. "Related" sites are the key to building good strong link popularity.

- AltaVista seems to prefer sites that have been in its index for a while.

- If you let AltaVista spider your links and find the pages itself, you may gain a boost in relevancy for those pages.

- Concentrate your keywords near the top of the page.

- Searches are generally *case sensitive* with AltaVista, which means that searches performed in all capital letters, all lowercase letters, or capitalized first letters will produce different search results. So be sure to use all variations of your keywords in your tags and text with this engine.

What can't AltaVista index? Visit this URL to find out:

***Find It*** **ONLINE**  **http://doc.altavista.com/adv_search/ast_haw_wellindexed.shtml**

**TIP**  If there's one search engine that takes a hard core approach to stopping spam, it's AltaVista. So, be very careful to make sure your pages are on the up-and-up when dealing with this engine. Read over the spam warnings, listed in the following section, carefully. Make sure that your link pages and site maps contain text, and get rid of all duplicate pages.

## AltaVista and Spamming

***Find It*** **ONLINE**  AltaVista considers the techniques mentioned in this section to be spamming. Following Figure 24.4 outlining those techniques, we explain what we believe AltaVista means by these spamming techniques. You can find this screen shot at **http://www.altavista.com/cgi-bin/query?pg=addurl**.

### AltaVista's Spamming Policy

Following is an explanation of Alta Vista's spamming policy:

- **Pages with text that is not easily read, either because it is too small or is obscured by the background of the page.**

   Like most engines, AltaVista doesn't like "hidden text." By this, we mean hiding text by using the same color font on the same

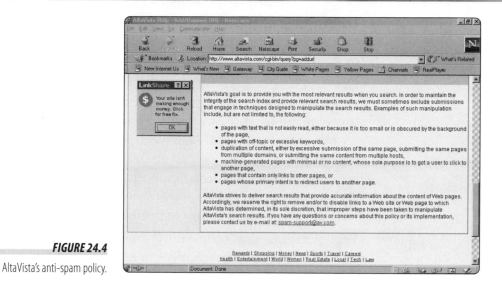

**FIGURE 24.4**

AltaVista's anti-spam policy.

color background. Visitors to the site won't see the hidden text unless they highlight the page. But the search engines will see and index it.

Also, like most engines, AltaVista doesn't like tiny text in a point size lower than the standard of 3. Have you ever seen a Web page where below the body text, you have to scroll down past a large blank area, only to find keywords written over and over again at the very bottom of the page? Most viewers will never see that tiny text because they won't scroll down that far on the page. But again, the engines will see it.

- **Pages with off-topic or excessive keywords.**

  One thing you never want to do with any engine is to use your keywords over and over and over again in the tags or body text. Most of the engines have spam guards in place that will detect this abuse, and your site won't get in the index anyway, or the engine may ban your site altogether.

  Also, you don't ever want to use keywords in your tags that aren't relevant to that particular Web page. In other words, if you have a Web page about "lowfat cooking," you won't want to use an off-topic word in your tags, such as "sex"; just to try to get more traffic to your site. Your tags *must* reflect the content of your page. Plus, just using an off-topic word doesn't mean you'll get a top ranking for that word.

- **Duplication of content, either by excessive submission of the same page, submitting the same pages from multiple domains, or submitting the same content from multiple hosts.**

  Don't create dozens of identical or almost identical pages and expect to get top rankings. Some software programs allow you to create hundreds of *doorway pages,* which are pages that are highly optimized for one keyword phrase only and generally for one engine only. These software programs then go through and substitute your keywords for another keyword; the text remains the same, with only the keywords swapped out. Using this technique can only get you in trouble with AltaVista.

  With AltaVista, don't constantly submit your pages over and over again. When you make changes to the page, resubmit it. But if no or very few changes have been made, don't resubmit. Better yet, let AltaVista find the changed pages on its next spider run.

  AltaVista also doesn't like you to submit pages from *mirror sites,* which are identical Web sites created under different domains. Some large companies will have mirror sites, possibly one on the West coast, one on the East coast, and one in the UK, in order to divide the traffic to those sites and prevent an overload to their servers. But if you submit identical pages from each of those domains, you run the risk of getting every one of those domains kicked out of AltaVista's index.

- **Machine-generated pages with minimal or no content, whose sole purpose is to get a user to click to another page.**

  In the past, Web masters often created dozens of doorway pages containing little or no content, sometimes even containing just the keyword phrase in the middle of the page. They would get these pages ranked high in the engines and then direct traffic from those pages to the real "meat" of their Web site.

  These pages are no longer effective in the engines for several reasons. First, almost all of the engines consider the content of your Web pages to be critical when determining *relevancy,* which is how well a Web page provides the information a user is looking for, as measured by that particular engine's algorithm. The higher the relevancy of your page, the higher your rankings in the engines. So Web pages with no content won't do well in search engine results these days.

Instead of bringing in visitors through these "splash pages," where the sole purpose of the page is to get a user to click to another page, bring your visitors in to the real content of your site.

In this manner, you can't lose—with the engines or your Web site visitors.

- **Pages that contain only links to other pages.**

  This guideline is one of the most confusing of AltaVista's anti-spamming guidelines. Exactly what they mean by "links to other pages," no one knows. We've tried to interview the engine to get more information, but like everyone else who has tried, we've run up against brick walls.

  Therefore, we can only offer our opinion of what the engine means by this rule.

  AltaVista doesn't like to see pages of links that are there strictly to direct the spider to other pages in your Web site. This is a very common practice because you certainly want to place links to all important pages of your site in front of the engines at all times.

  Also, site maps are simply pages of links, so does AltaVista consider site maps to be spamming? We don't think so.

  So to keep out of trouble with AltaVista, put a paragraph or two of text at the top of your pages of links. Use your important keyword phrase in that text. If possible, add a paragraph or two of text in other places on the page.

  Rather than submit site maps to the engine, put a link to the site map on the main page of your site, which you will certainly want to do anyway, and let the engine find and spider the link itself.

  Make sure that your site map follows the same format as the rest of your site, so that it's obvious that the page is legitimate and used as a navigational tool for your visitors.

- **Pages whose primary intent is to redirect users to another page.**

  With AltaVista, don't use <META> *refresh tags*, no matter how slow they are. <META> refresh tags are used to redirect traffic to another page.

  Have you ever clicked on a link and then noticed that the URL where you ended up is different than the URL you actually clicked on? The site is often using a redirect tag to direct you to another site.

Regretfully, there are some legitimate reasons for using redirect tags. But with AltaVista, you're better off not using them at all, or if you feel that you have to use a redirect tag, use a Java redirect instead.

You can find more information on spamming and redirect tags in Chapter 22, "Studying Your Competition."

### What Could Happen if You Spam AltaVista?

With AltaVista in particular, spamming can get you kicked out of the index with little hope of returning. If you spam AltaVista, the following may happen:

- Your page may not be allowed in the index.
- Your entire domain may be kicked out of the index.
- Other domains that can be connected to you may be kicked out of the index, too.

It's difficult to get back in the good graces of a search engine if the engine has kicked you out for spamming. It takes many e-mail messages and phone calls and many anxious moments.

It's just not worth it.

**Don't spam. It's as simple as that.**

## Excite

http://www.excite.com

Submission URL: **http://www.excite.com/info/add_url**

In comparison to AltaVista, Excite's search results are relatively simple and to the point. Where AltaVista pulls in results from several other sources, Excite pulls in results from one, LookSmart, and that's only if you request the information.

Figure 24.5 shows a search conducted at Excite for "swimming pool supplies." Notice the list of "Top 10 Web Site Results," which are pulled from Excite's index.

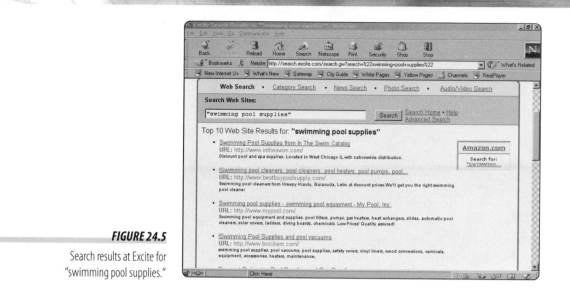

**FIGURE 24.5**

Search results at Excite for "swimming pool supplies."

To access Excite's directory, which pulls results from LookSmart, you click on the "Category Search" link at the top of the search results page.

At the time of this writing, Excite was beta testing the use of Internet Keywords as provided by RealNames, so those results will be seen in the search results, too.

## Strategies for Working with Excite

When creating pages for Excite, keep these strategies in mind:

- Expect it to take one to three weeks for submitted pages to get in the index.
- Submit no more than 25 pages per day.
- Excite often won't accept interior or doorway pages through the submission process. Be sure to add links on your main page to all important pages of your site, and give the engine other pages to index.
- Excite doesn't consider <META> tags when determining relevancy.
- Although it doesn't consider the <META> description tag when determining relevancy, the engine still uses the content of the description tag in the search results.

- The <TITLE> length limit is 70 characters, including spaces.
- The description length limit is 395 characters, including spaces.
- Link popularity is very important with this engine, so be sure to work hard toward getting other related sites to link back to your site.
- Excite asks you to specify the category you want to be listed in when you submit your site, so spend some time considering the most appropriate category for your site.
- Submit your site to LookSmart in order to be in the Excite directory.
- Use keywords in the following tags with Excite:

  <TITLE> tags

  Headline tags

  URL

  Style tags

  Near the top of each paragraph

  Domain names
- Use synonyms of your keywords.
- Try using your keywords in bold.
- Link from all instances of your keywords to other pages on your site.

**FIND IT ONLINE** For more information on getting listed in Excite, visit **http://www.excite.com/info/getting_listed/**.

**NOTE** With Excite, make sure that you submit the main page of your site before submitting any interior pages. If you don't, you may find that the interior pages won't make it into the index until you submit the main page.

Excite places much more relevancy on main pages over interior or doorway pages.

## Excite and Spamming

Excite considers the following strategies to be spamming:

- Repeated series of words
- Abnormal word densities
- Hidden text

## FAST/All the Web

*Find It*
**ONLINE**

http://www.alltheweb.com/

Submission URL: **http://www.alltheweb.com/add_url.php3**

With FAST now powering the main results at Lycos, its importance has soared. At the time of this writing, though, the search results between Lycos and FAST were still different, which is why the engines have been included separately. Little is known about FAST in comparison with the other major search engines.

When working with FAST, keep these guidelines in mind:

- It takes between 20 to 40 days for submissions to make it into the index. In other words, FAST isn't fast!
- FAST indexes the content of <TITLE> tags up to around 1,100 characters, including spaces.
- FAST doesn't index the content of <META> tags.
- The engine uses the first 250 characters at the top of your page as the description of your site in the search results.
- FAST indexes the content of <noframes> tags.

**TIP**    FAST doesn't use the contents of a META description tag as the description of your site in the search results. Therefore, it's imperative that you make sure that the first text on your page is appropriate to be a description of your site in those all-important results. Check this carefully!

## Google

*Find It*
**ONLINE**

http://www.google.com

Submission URL: **http://www.google.com/addurl**

If there's one thing you need to remember about Google, it's the way the engine uses links. The engine indexes many URLs without actually visiting the pages, which accounts for a half million of the Web pages in Google's index. So some of your pages may be in the Google index, but the engine may not have actually visited those pages.

Therefore, when working with Google, put links to other pages on your site in several areas to help the engine find those links and index them.

Because of the importance Google places on links, your page may not make it into the index if it has no other pages linking back to it. When performing a search at Google, you're presented with the top 10 results. In Figure 24.6, look at the bottom of the results for a link to "Try Our Web Directory." This takes you into the Google directory, where sites from the Open Directory Project are ranked according to Google's link analysis system.

In Figure 24.6, notice the "Cached" link to the right of each URL in the search results. When Google indexes a page, it saves a picture of that page in its cache. Clicking on the link will show you a copy of the page that the engine saw when it last indexed the page, which may or may not be like the page that's currently in the index.

Therefore, if you're using cloaking strategies, be sure to insert the following `<META>` tag in the `<head>` section of your Google page, which should prevent the engine from saving a picture of the page.

```
<META NAME="ROBOTS" CONTENT="NOARCHIVE">
```

We discuss cloaking strategies in Chapter 21.

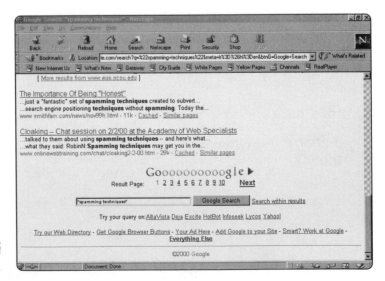

**FIGURE 24.6**

Search results at Google.

## Strategies for Working with Google

When creating pages for Google, keep these strategies in mind:

- Google indexes pages within one to two months.
- Submit around 10 pages a day to Google.
- <META> tags are not considered when determining relevancy.
- The <TITLE> length limit in the search results for Google is 83 characters, including spaces.
- The description length limit is 144 characters, including spaces.
- The description found in the search results is taken from the most relevant portions of the page, so make sure the first text on your page is appropriate for a description of the page and uses your important keyword phrase.
- Link popularity is very important with Google.
- On your main page, include links to all important pages on your site.
- Use keywords in the following tags with Google:

  <TITLE> tag

  ALT attributes

  Headline tags

  No frames tags

  Link text

  Drop-down form boxes

- Use large point sizes with Google, and place keyword phrases in bold.
- Both ingoing and outgoing related links are important with Google.

**TIP** What should you remember about Google? It's simple: link, link, and link! Be sure to use linking strategies between your related pages and important related sites in your industry. Link to those important sites, and ask them to link back to you. Because of the way Google follows links, if you put the links in front of the engine, you'll rapidly find that you have a multitude of pages listed in the Google index.

## Google and Spamming

As mentioned earlier, if your page has no links pointing to it whatsoever, Google considers the page to be spam. So before submitting a page to Google, make sure that it has links pointing to it.

Also, like many of the major engines, Google considers <META> refresh tags to be spamming. Use Java redirects instead. Or, better yet, don't use redirect tags at all.

Google has publicly announced that it considers cloaking to be spam as well as the use of hidden text. Google also doesn't like to see hidden links on a page as well as sites that participate in link exchange programs for the sole purpose of artificially boosting a site's link popularity. In recent months, many sites have found themselves booted out of Google for using any of the previously mentioned strategies, so be very careful.

## HotBot

http://www.hotbot.com

Submission URL: **http://hotbot.lycos.com/addurl.asp**

Pay Submission URL: **http://www.positiontech.com/index2.htm**

Unlike the other major engines, HotBot is quite willing to let you know who is powering its search results.

This is good to know because, recently, searches made within minutes of each other have pulled up entirely different results from different sources in HotBot.

In Figure 24.7 for the keyword phrase "New Orleans real estate," notice the following words across the top of the page:

PEOPLE WHO DID THIS SEARCH ALSO SEARCHED FOR

As with AltaVista, HotBot is actually helping you come up with additional keyword phrases that might be relevant to your site, so pay close attention to this area of the search results when working on your own pages.

Below this area, notice these words:

FROM THE LYCOS NETWORK

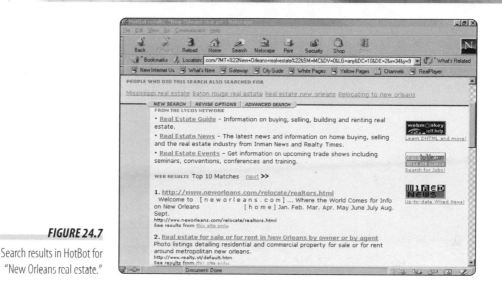

**FIGURE 24.7**

Search results in HotBot for "New Orleans real estate."

Because Lycos owns HotBot, you'll find links back and forth between the two engines, which may help you if you have a strong presence in either of the engines.

Below "WEB RESULTS Top 10 Matches," you'll find the top 10 sites pulled from Direct Hit. How do we know they're from Direct Hit? Because at the bottom of the search results page, you'll see a graphic with these words:

Powered by Direct Hit

Clicking to the next page, you'll see another 10 results, but these results are pulled from the Inktomi search engine, as evidenced by the graphic at the bottom of the page shown in Figure 24.8. In fact, the Inktomi engine powers HotBot.

Right above the HomeScape.com banner, notice the "SECOND OPINION." Again, the engine is giving you the option of searching in Lycos.

**TIP**

**FIND IT ONLINE**

If you want a good, strong presence in the Inktomi engine (which powers HotBot and provides search results to most of the pay engines, AOL Search, NBCi, and more), consider using Inktomi's pay submission service. Benefits include being added to the index within 48 hours and respidering every 48 hours. In fact, at the time of the writing of this book, sites who used Inktomi's free submission service were getting penalized in the rankings. In the future, you'll likely find that the free add URL service at Inktomi will be discontinued. For more information, visit **http://www.positiontech.com/index2.htm**.

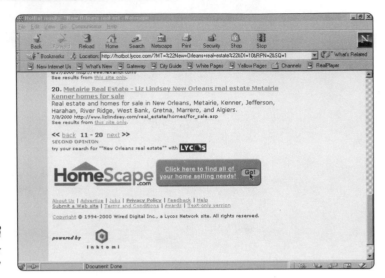

**FIGURE 24.8**

Additional search results at HotBot for
"New Orleans real estate."

## Strategies for Working with HotBot

When creating pages for HotBot, keep these strategies in mind:

- HotBot generally indexes pages within a couple of weeks after submission.
- The daily submission limit is 50 pages.
- HotBot considers <META> tags when determining relevancy.
- HotBot also uses the <META> description tag as the description of the page in the search results.
- The <TITLE> length limit is 115 characters, including spaces.
- The description length limit is 249 characters, including spaces.
- Site popularity is important, because Direct Hit provides the top 10 search results for HotBot.
- Use keywords in the following tags with HotBot:

    <TITLE> tags

    Headline tags

    Early in the body of the page

    <META> author tag

    URL

    Domain names

<META> tags

Link text

Style tags

## HotBot and Spamming

With HotBot, your pages are penalized in the rankings if you use any of these techniques:

- Keyword stuffing
- Invisible text, such as using ‹ › around text that are not tags
- Tiny text
- Submission of identical pages
- Irrelevant keywords
- Same color font on same color background

## GO/InfoSeek

http://www.go.com/

Submission URL: **http://addurl.go.com/dynamic/landNotLogged**

We may sound like a broken record here, but Disney has announced its intentions to shut down GO.com at the end of February 2001. This means that the search engine and GO directory will either be shut down for good or sold to another company. We're keeping the engine's information here, in case the engine is sold. However, we haven't included a screen shot of GO, since the look of the engine will totally change if it's sold.

You can learn more about Disney closing GO.com in Chapter 17.

Several factors can greatly influence your rankings in GO, including having your site listed in the GO Guides, which is GO's directory, and having a high link popularity. As with most of the major engines these days, it's crucial for you to spend some time building links to and from other Web sites in your related area.

Having your site listed in the GO Guides can help your rankings in the main GO index as well.

### Becoming a GO Guide Editor

Like the Open Directory Project, editors for the GO Guides are volunteers. Once you reach a certain level, you're able to accept submissions into the directory, and you're also able to make sure that your own sites are listed. In fact, being a GO Guide editor is the surest way to make certain that your site is listed in the GO directory because the actual submission process isn't successful many times.

Also, being an editor allows you to submit your site to more than one category, which can influence your site's rankings in those categories.

To learn more about being a GO Guide editor, visit **http://guides.go.com/**.

With the possibility of the GO Directory being shut down, many of the GO Guides have moved to Wherewithall Search. For more information, visit **http://www.wherewithal.com/**.

## Strategies for Working with GO

When creating pages for GO, keep these strategies in mind. However, remember that if another company purchases the engine, the engine's algorithm could totally change.

- If you pay to submit to GO, your site will be added to the index within 48 hours. If you use the free submission service, it may take 10 weeks for your site to get added, and there's no guarantee that it will.
- With GO, you can submit only the main page of your site through its submission process. So be sure to add links to all your other pages on the main page of your site, so the engine can spider and find those other pages.
- The daily submission limit is 25 pages per day.
- The <TITLE> length limit is 70 to 75 characters, including spaces.
- The description length limit is 150 characters, including spaces.
- GO considers the content of <META> tags when determining relevancy.
- GO uses the <META> description tag as the site's description in the search results.
- Link popularity is very important with GO/InfoSeek.

- GO's AddURL form is down on the weekends and on holidays. During that time, submit your sites by e-mail.
- Adult sites must be submitted by e-mail.
- Use keywords in the following tags with GO/InfoSeek:

  <TITLE> tags

  Early in the page

  Headline tags

  Link text

  Style tags

  URL

  Names of images

  Domain names

- Use keyword phrases in bold in the body of your page.
- Use synonyms of your keyword phrase.
- GO likes longer pages, around 1,000 words.
- Don't target more than one page for the same keyword phrase.
- Use commas to separate keywords in the <META> keyword tag.
- Some top-ranking sites don't use the <META> keyword tag, so consider eliminating it if you need a boost in relevancy.
- Be sure to include a visible privacy policy if running banner ads with the GO Network.

**TIP** GO clearly states to NOT submit any URL more than once. So, submit your main page to GO, either through their paid submission service or their free add URL page, and then don't submit it again.

## GO/InfoSeek and Spamming

To avoid getting into trouble with GO for spamming, avoid these techniques:

- Overuse or repetition of keywords
- Use of keywords that don't relate to the content of the site
- Use of a <META> refresh tag
- Use of the same color font on the same color background

- Duplication of pages with different URLs
- Use of different pages that bridge or link to the same URL

## Lycos

http://www.lycos.com

Submission URL: **http://www.lycos.com/addasite.html**

As with many of the major engines, Lycos pulls results from several different sources: FAST, the Open Directory Project, and Direct Hit. The main search results are pulled from FAST, though at the time of this writing, searches performed at each engine are still different.

In a search for "buttered popcorn" in Lycos, as shown in Figure 24.10, four Web sites are listed below the heading of "Popular." These sites were pulled from Direct Hit based on user popularity.

After the first four sites, the regular search results for Lycos follow, which are called "Web Sites." These sites are pulled from the ODP, FAST, and Lycos's own crawler-based index.

Because FAST is now powering the main search results in Lycos and because of Direct Hit's and the ODP's importance with this engine, be sure to submit your pages to those directories.

**FIGURE 24.10**

Search results at Lycos for "buttered popcorn."

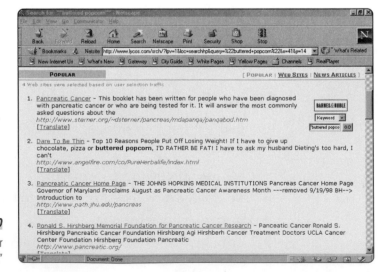

## Strategies for Working with Lycos

When creating pages for Lycos, keep these strategies in mind:

- Sites submitted to Lycos generally get accepted into the index within four to six weeks.

- There are no submission limits with this engine, but always use caution when submitting a large number of pages to any engine. Spread the submissions out over several days, instead of submitting hundreds one right after the other.

- Lycos doesn't consider <META> tags when determining relevancy.

- Lycos picks the first text on the page and uses it as the description of your site in the search results. Therefore, make sure that the first text on your page appropriately describes your site.

- The <TITLE> length limit is 60 characters, including spaces.

- The description length limit is 255 characters, including spaces.

- Site popularity is important with this engine, as evidenced by the Direct Hit results, which are shown in the "Popular" heading in the search results.

- Use keywords in the following tags with Lycos:

     <TITLE> tags

     Text in <noframes> tags

     Body text

     Headline tags

     Domain name

     Near the top of each paragraph

     URL

     Directory name

- Use synonyms of your keywords.

- Run your site through an HTML validator because poor HTML code could cause your site not to get indexed at all.

- The average of number of words per page is 300, but shorter pages do well in the engine, too.

**TIP**  Patience is a virtue when working with Lycos, since it can take literally months for a page to make it into the Lycos index. With Lycos, don't ever "throw away" or remove Web pages from the index. Instead, create new pages. You never know when old pages will once again gravitate to the top of the listings. In fact, this is a good strategy to use with all of the engines.

## Lycos and Spamming

Lycos considers these elements to be spamming:

- Keywords repeated over and over again
- Duplicate pages
- Hidden or invisible text
- Double word occurrences
- Tiny text

## Northern Light

*Find It*
**ONLINE**

http://www.northernlight.com

Submission URL: **http://www.northernlight.com/docs/regurl_help.html**

When visiting Northern Light's main page, you'll quickly see why researchers keep coming back to this engine time and time again. Not only can you perform a simple search, but you can also perform a business search, news search, search for stock quotes, and more. You can even select a source, such as through the "Special Collections" section, the *Wall Street Journal* or even city and regional newspapers.

Another popular feature of Northern Light is its blue Custom Search Folders, which group results below topic areas. For example, a search for "John Kennedy" produced Custom Search Folders on topics such as "White House," "Bay of Pigs Invasion," "Warfare," and more, as you can see in Figure 24.11.

Clicking on any of the Custom Search Folders at the left of the screen produces results based on the topic of that folder.

Because some of the folders are actually company-related folders, how can you get your own Custom Search Folder in Northern Light?

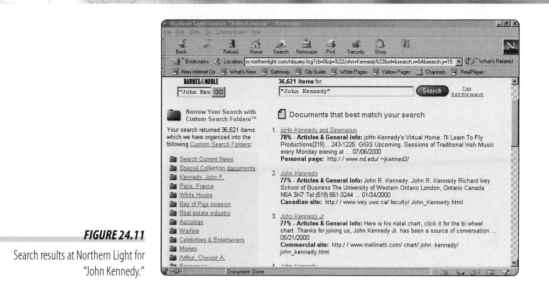

***FIGURE 24.11***

Search results at Northern Light for "John Kennedy."

You can't. Custom Search Folders are created dynamically according to the unique results for each search. According to the engine, it doesn't exercise any editorial control over which folders appear for certain searches or which sites appear within a given folder.

**TIP** **Though Northern Light doesn't have the popularity with Web surfers that many of the other major engines enjoy, it is still a very popular engine with researchers. Long pages do well with this engine, so give the engine what it wants to see: content!**

## Strategies for Working with Northern Light

When creating pages for Northern Light, keep these strategies in mind:

- Northern Light indexes pages within two to four weeks after submission.
- There are no daily submission limits, but use good judgment when submitting several pages to this or any engine.
- Northern Light doesn't consider <META> tags when determining relevancy, and it doesn't use the <META> description tag as the description of the page in the search results.
- The <TITLE> length limit is 80 characters, including spaces.

- The description length limit is 150 to 200 characters, including spaces.
- Use keywords in the following tags with Northern Light:

  <TITLE> tags

  Headline tags

  Beginning of the body text

  Link text

- Use synonyms of your keyword phrase.
- Site popularity is important with this engine.

### Northern Light and Spamming

With Northern Light, don't use the same color font on the same color background. Other than that, as with all engines, don't stuff the body text or tags with keywords, don't overdo the use of doorway pages, don't use lightning-fast <META> refresh tags, and so forth.

## Conclusion

Because the major search engines are so important to the success of any Web site, take time to study the engines' likes and dislikes and create pages accordingly designed to boost traffic to your site.

And be sure to stay away from all spamming techniques. Getting into trouble with the search engines over spamming can be disastrous to a Web site.

For further information on the status of the GO search engine and directory, visit the authors' related Web site at **http://www.kerri-leigh.com/wsar**.

# STRATEGIES FOR WORKING WITH DIRECTORIES

**In This Chapter**

General Guidelines for Working with Directories

Yahoo!

Open Directory Project (ODP)

NBCi

LookSmart

Although you were briefly introduced to the important directories in Chapter 17, "The Importance of Search Engines to the Success of Your Online Business," you didn't learn any tips and strategies for working with those directories.

For example, what do human editors like to see on a Web site? What would make them reject a submission?

If your Web site doesn't make it into the index, what can you do? What if you need to make a change to your listing?

In this chapter, we dig deeper into each of these directories so you can learn effective strategies for working with them and apply those strategies to your own site.

## General Guidelines for Working with Directories

You can apply many of the strategies for working with directories across the board to all directories.

But the main thing to remember when working with directories is that directory submissions go before a human editor, so it's crucial that your pages are top-notch without any glaring problems or errors.

When working with directories, keep these important facts in mind:

- The tags on your page make no difference to directories.
- <META> tags have no effect, either.
- How you complete the submission form determines your placement in directories.
- Editors visiting your page will determine whether to accept it into the index.
- Most directories have alphabetical listings, so if your site falls in the early part of the alphabet, it can make a huge difference in your rankings.
- In most cases, you can only submit the main page of your site to directories, instead of individual interior or doorway pages.

- You submit your site through the category path that best suits your site, instead of through a central Add URL page.
- Editors can and will make changes to your title, description, and category.

## Tips for Getting Accepted into Directories

When submitting to directories, keep these important tips in mind:

- Spend time looking through the directory to find the subcategory that's just right for your site. Search for your competitors' pages. What categories are your competitors listed in? Don't try to submit to upper level categories. Instead, drill down to find the most appropriate subcategory for your site.
- Create a businesslike and professional-sounding title and description for the submission form. Be honest and sincere, and don't sound like a snake oil salesman.
- Fill in the submission form completely. Enter the complete URL, and double-check it carefully. Make sure you aren't misspelling anything. Be sure to use your important keyword phrase in the title and/or description of your site on the submission form.
- If you place a "last updated on <date>" notice on your site, make sure that you update the site on a regular basis.
- Put a copyright notice on your site.
- If you have a physical address, consider putting that on your Web site. Some directories, like Yahoo!, require a physical address. Plus, it's a way for your customers to get in touch with you.
- Make it easy on the editor to accept your site into the index. Follow the directory's guidelines explicitly, create effective titles and descriptions, choose the most appropriate subcategory, and be polite!
- Make sure your site is top-notch. Do all of your graphics load? Do all of the links work? Is the page readable, or does the background make it almost impossible to read the words? Is the background color offensive? Is the point size too small or too large?

## Top 10 No-No's when Working with Directories

If you want your Web site to be successfully listed in directories, make sure that you stay clear of these tactics:

- Don't list your title and description on the submission form in ALL CAPS, which is considered yelling on the Internet and is extremely annoying.

- Don't use keywords over and over again in the title or description that you enter on the submission form. For example, don't use the following as the description of your site:

   Fresh vegetables, corn, green tomatoes, Irish potatoes, broccoli, asparagus

- Instead, create a title that's sure to gain the approval of the editor, like this:

   Fresh garden vegetables delivered straight from the garden to your front door!

- Don't *demand* anything of an editor. Don't try to tell the editors how to do their job. Don't express anger if it takes several weeks for your site to be considered. Your site's future depends on the approval of these overworked, underpaid editors. It's just as easy for them to reject your submission, so be extremely nice.

- Don't submit to upper level categories, such as "Health." Instead, find the most appropriate subcategory for your site, such as this:

   `Health/Diseases and Conditions/Diabetes/Research/Insulin Therapy`

- Don't submit your site until it's ready for traffic. Don't submit a site with a huge "Under Construction" sign on the first page and nothing else. Don't submit a site with broken links or missing graphics. Many editors will reject sites that consist of one page only. Check your grammar and punctuation carefully. Submit a top-notch site!

- Don't submit your site to every category you can think of. Editors can see all of your submissions to the index. If you overdo your submissions, the editors will know this, and you may be labeled a spammer.

- Don't submit your site every single day until it is accepted into the index. Submit your site, wait two weeks, and submit it again.

- Be careful when using technology such as Flash or Shockwave. Many editors reject submissions that require them to download an add on before being able to view the page. Also, editors reject submissions that cause their browsers to crash, so test your site out on several different machines and browsers.

- Don't purchase several domains and set up mirror sites using the same pages as on the original domain. Using this tactic can get you labeled a spammer in record time, and you won't be able to get any of your sites into the index.

- Don't use Yellow Page tactics to try to get higher in the alphabetical listing. For example, don't put AAA in front of the name of your Web site on the submission form in order to try to get on top of the rankings for your keyword phrase. If your Web site is legitimately named something like AAASoftware Deluxe, however, you can certainly use that as the name of your site on the submission form.

- If you are in the process of setting up a new online business, consider naming the business with a letter that's early in the alphabet. Because directories list sites in alphabetical order in most cases, this could put you at the top of the rankings. Be sure to use that name when you register the domain, and use the name throughout the Web site itself.

**TIP** Regretfully, URLs frequently change in this industry. So, if you're looking for the submission URL for any of the search engines or directories, look for the Submit a Site link, which is generally toward the bottom of the engine's or directory's main page. With some of the directories, however, you'll actually submit through the categories in which you want your site to appear, so there isn't a central submission URL.

## Yahoo!

**FIND IT ONLINE**

http://www.yahoo.com

By far, Yahoo! is the most important search facility on the Internet and packs a mean punch when determining the success of your site.

When you perform a search at Yahoo!, search results appear in this order:

- Yahoo! categories
- Yahoo! Web sites
- Web pages from Google

Why is this order important? Because when you search for your own site, you'll want to know if the site is in Yahoo!'s database or the supplemental index supplied by Google. You want to be in both for maximum coverage, but your main concern is to get in Yahoo!'s database.

When searching inside a category at Yahoo!, you may also be presented with a Most Popular Sites section, which is judged according to click-through popularity. Then, you'll see new and reviewed sites followed by the sites in the Yahoo! directory.

Let's look at an example. Figure 25.1 shows a keyword search of "insulin resistance." Notice the "Yahoo! Category Matches" at the top of the page. Below the category matches, you see four "Yahoo! Site Matches," which come from Yahoo!'s index of Web sites. At the bottom of the page, you see "Go To Web Page Matches," which comes from Google.

You can see how having a presence in Google will certainly help you in Yahoo! Ideally, however, you want to be in both indexes.

**FIGURE 25.1**

Search results at Yahoo! for "insulin resistance".

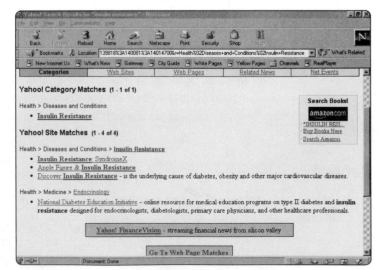

## Strategies for Working with Yahoo!

In addition to the general strategies for working with directories listed at the beginning of this chapter, keep these tips in mind:

- Use this submission strategy when working with Yahoo!:

  1. Submit your site.
  2. Wait two weeks, and if your site isn't accepted into the index, submit it again.
  3. Wait two more weeks, and if your site still isn't accepted, send an e-mail to Yahoo! (See "Yahoo! Contact Information," later in this chapter.)
  4. Look at your site carefully and make any changes that you think may be preventing your site from getting indexed. Consider submitting to a different category with less submissions.
  5. Wait two more weeks, and if your site isn't accepted, send another e-mail.
  6. Wait two more weeks, and if you've heard nothing, call Yahoo!'s toll-free number. (See "Yahoo! Contact Information," later in this chapter.)
  7. Wait two weeks, and if you haven't heard anything, call Yahoo!'s toll-free number again.

  *FIND IT*
  **ONLINE**

  Continue this strategy until you get accepted or until Yahoo! explains to you why your site isn't being accepted into the index. Throughout this process, look closely at your site and follow the guidelines listed in this chapter and on Yahoo!'s Web site at **http://docs.yahoo.com/info/suggest/**.

- It generally takes two to eight weeks for sites to make it into Yahoo!'s index. If the site is being submitted in a particularly busy subcategory, it may take longer.

- Your title length should be approximately 40 characters long, including spaces, and your description length should be 200 characters. Use your keyword phrase in your description.

- Begin your description with a capital letter and follow with lowercase letters, except when using proper nouns. In other words, don't use a description like this:

  Delicious Fresh Fruit Baskets In A Variety of Sizes and Prices

A Yahoo! editor would have to remove those capital letters, which means an extra step for the editor. Will this prevent your site from getting indexed? Possibly, and it will more than likely cause a delay in indexing.

- Don't use submitting software with Yahoo!. Submit your site manually.

- Yahoo!'s submission form allows you to send a short comment, so take advantage of this by entering a short statement about your site, if appropriate.

- If your site is commercial, you must submit it to the "Business and Economy" category.

- You can suggest two subcategories for your site. Often, Yahoo! will accept your site into a category appropriate for the content of your site and also into a regional area.

- Search for your competition and see where they're listed in Yahoo!. Also, see which categories appear first. If your site fits in the first category, choose that one. After all, most searchers start at the top and choose the first category. Ideally, that's where you want to be.

- If your site contains information about a particular event where indexing time is of the essence, be sure to indicate this on the submission form.

- For $199, you can submit your site through Business Express, which means that Yahoo! will look at your site and consider it for acceptance into the index within seven days. Using the express service doesn't guarantee entry into Yahoo!'s index. You'll have some recourse if the site isn't accepted into the index, however, and you can go back and make some changes and resubmit the site. Although using the service doesn't guarantee acceptance, we've seen instances where seemingly unindexable sites have made it into the index in this manner, so it's certainly worth a good long look.

**FIND IT ONLINE**

For more information about Business Express, visit **http://www.yahoo.com/info/suggest/busexpress.html**.

- Use your important keyword phrase in the description you enter on the submission form. You'll have to use your company's name as the title, but you might be able to tack on keywords at the end of the company name and get it to go through. For example, if the actual name of the company is Allied Company, you might use the following:

Allied Company's Steel Pipes

- Never use any marketing hype when submitting to Yahoo!.
- Don't use brand names in your titles or descriptions.

 **TIP** If you have a business-related site, you must go through the Business Express and pay $199 for your site to be added to the Yahoo! index. However, the benefits are many when using Business Express, since most of the sites submitted do get into the index. For more information, visit **http://help.yahoo.com/help/bizex/**.

## Yahoo! Contact Information

If your site doesn't get into Yahoo! after your first submission, which it probably won't, follow the submission guidelines in "Strategies for Working with Yahoo!" in the preceding section.

 **FIND IT ONLINE** Yahoo! offers an e-mail address for those who are having submission problems. The address is **url-support@yahoo-inc.com**.

In your e-mail, mention the URL of your Web site and any pertinent information about the site. The e-mail should be short and to the point. Don't go on and on expanding on the virtues of your site. The editors want information quickly and easily. Give it to them and get out!

After submitting the site by e-mail, if your site still doesn't make it into the index, try calling 408-731-3333 in the U.S. and Canada or 001-408-731-3333 from outside the U.S. and Canada.

When you call, leave your name, URL, phone number, e-mail address, and the date you submitted your site on the answering machine.

## Submitting Changes to Your Yahoo! Listing

 **FIND IT ONLINE** If you want to change your Yahoo! listing, you need to complete a change form located at **http://add.yahoo.com/fast/change**.

Yahoo! doesn't like to make changes, however, so if you can't prove to them that the change is necessary for the benefit of Yahoo! users, they won't make it.

What kind of changes would benefit Yahoo! users? If you've moved your Web site to a different domain, for example, the change is necessary so that Yahoo! users will be able to find your site. Or, if you've changed the focus of your site and it's no longer listed in the appropriate category, that would be considered a needed change.

However, submitting a change to get your important keyword phrase listed in the title or description probably won't be considered a needed change and it won't go through.

If you have a legitimate reason for submitting a change form, however, you can certainly try to get other things associated with your listing changed at the same time. Just don't be surprised or disappointed if the extra changes don't go through. In all likelihood, they won't.

When submitting a change form to Yahoo!, keep Yahoo!'s guidelines in mind, as shown in Figure 25.2.

In fact, these guidelines are excellent tips for submitting to Yahoo! in general.

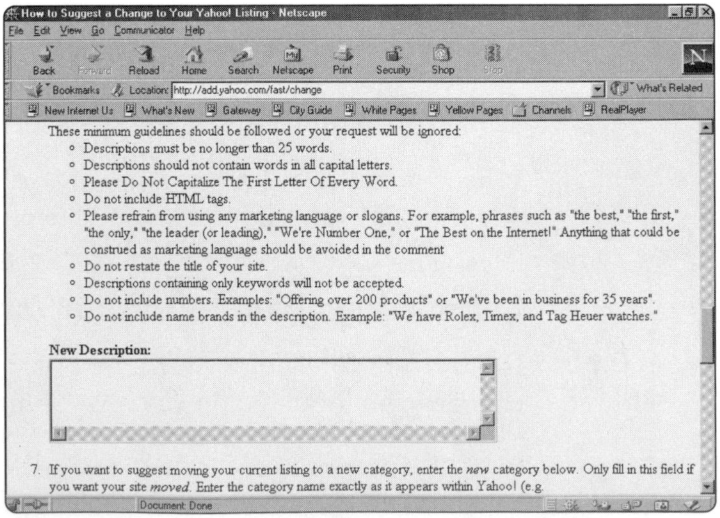

**FIGURE 25.2**

Yahoo!'s guidelines for submitting a change form.

If your change form doesn't go through the first time, go through a process similar to the one outlined in "Strategies for Working with Yahoo!," earlier in this chapter. In other words, submit the change form; wait two weeks; submit the change form again. Wait two weeks, and send Yahoo! an e-mail. When sending an e-mail to get a listing changed, give Yahoo! this information in the e-mail:

- URL
- Title of the site
- Description of the site
- Complete subcategory path
- Reason you want the change to go through
- Dates you submitted the change forms

Wait two weeks, and send Yahoo! another e-mail, always outlining the steps you've taken to get the change form to go through. If the form still doesn't go through, call Yahoo!'s toll-free number as mentioned in the preceding section, "Yahoo! Contact Information."

Above all, be *nice* when writing to Yahoo!. They don't owe you a thing, and they don't have to make changes to your listing. So prove to them that the change will benefit Yahoo! users, and you may be lucky enough to see the change go through.

## Open Directory Project (ODP)

The ODP is a human-edited directory that consists of thousands of volunteer editors. Because volunteer editors largely run the ODP, it's come up against some fairly intense criticism. Some editors won't let competitors into their own categories, for example, which is certainly against the ODP guidelines.

 **NOTE**   **http://dmoz.org**

 *Find It*
**ONLINE**   The history behind "dmoz" began with the start of the directory, then named Gnuhoo. When Netscape purchased the directory, it became known as Newhoo. "Mozilla" is the original inside name for the Netscape Navigator browser, and it's also the name of the lizard you see on Open Directory Project Web pages. So, "dmoz" actually stands for the "directory of Mozilla." Because the ODP is free to anyone to use, it became known as the organization that handles Open Source, which is how the Open Directory Project name came into being.

Also, the ODP has never offered a helpful set of editor guidelines. Often, editors are accepted into the fold only to be told to "edit," but not told much else. To give the directory credit, it has certainly come a long way in providing better guidance and more guidelines for new editors, but it still has a long way to go.

Criticism aside, no one can doubt the power behind this group of volunteers. The ODP provides directory results to many of the major engines, such as AOL Search, Netscape Search, HotBot, and Lycos. That's a tough act to follow, and no one is even trying.

The directory did take a major blow in July 2000, however, when AltaVista chose LookSmart to power its directory, when in the past, it had been a combined effort between LookSmart and the ODP. Why did AltaVista make the change? Simple—LookSmart paid it to do so. After all, why should AltaVista use free directory listings from the ODP when it can get paid to use LookSmart's?

Figure 25.3 shows a list of directories found in the ODP. Each of ODP's partners lists the results differently, however, and runs the results through its own algorithms. So results at AOL won't be the same as results from Netscape, for example.

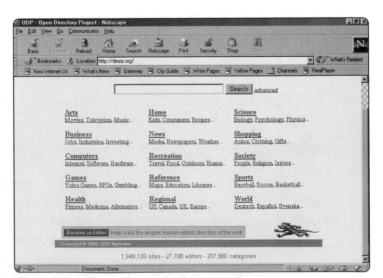

**FIGURE 25.3**

The main page of the Open Directory Project (ODP).

In Figure 25.3, notice the number of sites listed in the directory at the time of this writing (almost two million), and notice the number of editors (almost 28,000).

## Strategies for Working with the ODP

For guidelines on submitting to the ODP, be sure to review the "General Guidelines for Working with Directories," earlier in this chapter. Also, in addition to the following tips, review the guidelines for Yahoo!:

- As opposed to Yahoo!, which only allows you to submit the main URL of your site, you can submit your site to a couple of subcategories at the ODP. Make sure that your site belongs in both subcategories, however, and don't submit to more than two. Many editors at the ODP won't let a site into more than one subcategory, so choose your initial subcategory wisely.

- Be sure to use your important keyword phrase in the title and description on the submission form.

- Also, editors at the ODP write detailed messages to each other on the submission forms for each site. So don't ever submit to numerous subcategories at the ODP, mirror sites, affiliate sites, and so on. You'll find yourself labeled a spammer, and you'll find that every door going in to the ODP is locked to you.

- If you participate in several affiliate programs, which is certainly a very lucrative business these days, don't try to submit the URLs to the ODP. The ODP doesn't like affiliate sites or links, and that will get your submission rejected faster than you can hit the Submit button.

- Another difference between Yahoo! and the ODP is that you can actually write to your editor at the ODP. The editors' nicknames are listed at the bottom of the search results. So if you're having problems getting into the ODP or if you'd like to change your title or description, write to your editor.

- Again, don't write a lengthy e-mail that is sure to aggravate busy editors. Instead, write a short e-mail that lists your URL, the title of your site, the description, and the complete category path. Don't make the editor guess at the category. Give explicit information, and you'll have a much better chance at getting in the index.

- Remember to be nice and professional. Don't tell editors that you submitted to their subcategories months ago, so you wonder if they are even doing any work. Believe us, with an e-mail like that, the only work editors will be doing on your site is writing nasty notes to other editors and rejecting your submission.
- Keep on the good side of the editors. They can be extremely valuable to your Web site.

## Signing Up To Be an ODP Editor

If you have some time on your hands, consider signing up to be an ODP editor. Pick a subcategory without much traffic and one that doesn't have an editor. Complete the form at ODP's site by choosing the "Become an Editor" link on the main page. You may have to submit a request several times to get in, but it will certainly give you valuable insight into the workings of a directory.

What kind of information is required when you submit a request to become an editor? You need to state a reason for wanting to become an editor, and you need to tell the ODP which subcategory you'd like to edit. Before submitting the request, spend time at the directory and find a subcategory that no one else is editing. Don't choose a seemingly busy subcategory. Choose a quiet category that will allow you to prove to the ODP that you can be an effective editor. Then find a couple of links appropriate for that subcategory because you'll be asked to provide those links when you submit the request to become an editor.

**TIP** Why would you want to be an editor at the ODP? Simple. Being an editor gives you an "insider's view" into the workings of a major directory. You'll understand which submissions work and which don't, and you'll know how to improve your own directory submissions. Being on the "other side" will help you understand what editors go through when editing sites, and you'll be sure never to make mistakes again!

Can being an ODP editor help your own site? If you're the editor of the subcategory where your site is listed, you'll have the capability to make changes to your site as needed. Also, you'll be able to read what other editors have written about your site and submissions, which can help you make decisions on submitting to additional categories.

Some editors will mark their own site as "cool," which means that the site will appear at the top of the listings followed by a little palm tree graphic. It is not recommended that you do this with your own site, however. If your site is of the caliber to be considered "cool," let another editor make that decision so it won't look as if you're trying to manipulate the rankings.

## NBCi

**http://www.nbci.com**

**FIND IT
ONLINE**

Submission URL: **http://www.nbci.com/LMOID/resource/
0,566,home-1078,00.html?st.sn.ft.0.surl**

Previously known as Snap, NBCi is a vital directory with many interesting features. When performing a search at NBCi, search results come from three sources, in this order:

1. Main NBCi Directory
2. LiveDirectory
3. Inktomi Index

Let's take this a step further. When you first submit to NBCi, you're actually submitting to the LiveDirectory. Submissions generally make it into the index within hours, which certainly is a plus at a time when most major engines take weeks or even months to index pages.

To make it into the main NBCi directory, which is your ultimate goal, your site must have a high click-through popularity. So with NBCi, site popularity (or click-through popularity) is important, as opposed to link popularity, which is such an issue with engines like AltaVista and Excite.

The more popular your site becomes in terms of the number of visitors who click through to your site from NBCi, the higher up in the index your site will go. Once your site reaches a certain level, it's automatically placed in front of a human editor who will decide whether your site will be accepted into the main NBCi directory. This is certainly something to strive for because those results appear first in the search results.

Figure 25.4 shows "Related Searches," which we mention in previous chapters as being good spots for considering additional keyword phrases for your site.

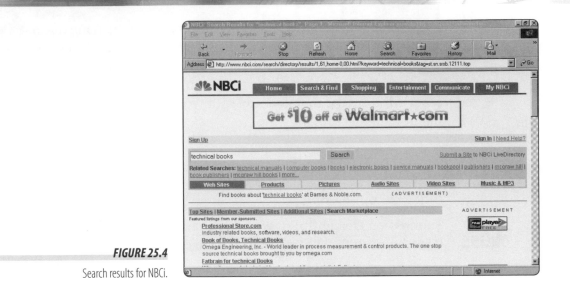

**FIGURE 25.4**

Search results for NBCi.

Also, notice that the first results on the page are paid results from sponsors of NBCi. Then, notice the categories of "Top Sites," "Member-Submitted Sites," and "Additional Sites" along the bottom of the figure. "Top Sites" are those that are reviewed by editors and are in the main NBCi directory. Following those sites are the LiveDirectory results (Member-Submitted Sites), followed by results from Inktomi (Additional Sites).

## Strategies for Working with NBCi

When working with NBCi, the general guidelines listed at the beginning of this chapter will be very helpful to you. Keep these specific strategies in mind as well:

- The limit for your title at NBCi is 128 characters, including spaces. The limit for your description is 255 characters.
- You can't submit to a second category at NBCi, although editors may place your site in an additional category.
- When submitting changes to an existing listing, search for the site in NBCi. Find the site in the search results, and click Update found on the last line of the site's description.

- Use your important keywords in the title and description on the submission form. Also, use your keywords in style tags and in the URL itself with NBCi.

- Web sites submitted to NBCi should consist of more than one page. The main page of the site is preferred over interior pages.

- If you place a physical address on your site, your site may have to be listed in the regional areas of NBCi, so keep this in mind if you don't want to be in the regional listings.

**TIP** A very unique element about NBCi is how fast the directory indexes new submissions. In fact, you can often submit your site to NBCi and then receive an acceptance e-mail within an hour or two. Remember that the way to progress up to the main NBCi directory is through click-throughs. So, once you submit to NBCi, make sure that you click on your site in the search results, and prove to the directory that your site deserves to be promoted.

## Submitting to NBCi

Whereas some of the major directories, such as Yahoo! and LookSmart, have adopted pay submission programs, NBCi is still determined to remain free, at least at the present time.

However, as many of the engines and directories take a shift toward pay submissions, you can expect some of the others to follow suit. After all, what are the engines and directories in business for, if not to make money?

## LookSmart

**FIND IT ONLINE** http://www.looksmart.com

In July 2000, AltaVista announced its plans to use LookSmart as the sole power behind the AltaVista directory. Prior to that time, the ODP and LookSmart provided results, so this move effectively cut off ODP results from AltaVista.

Also in recent months, LookSmart announced a partnership with Gale Group to provide business and premium magazine and periodical content for free to those who use the LookSmart directory.

With big-name magazines such as *Scientific American* and *Rolling Stone* included, you can see how this service can rapidly build traffic to the LookSmart directory.

As you can see in Figure 25.5, LookSmart not only provides directory results through its category listing, but it also provides global and city directories. In fact, LookSmart's international directories are quite popular on a regional basis, with the French market eagerly awaiting the release of the French version of the directory.

## Strategies for Working with LookSmart

As with the other directories, be sure to read "General Guidelines for Working with Directories," earlier in this chapter. Also, keep these specific guidelines in mind:

- On LookSmart's submission form, there's a place for you to indicate which keywords you consider to be important to your site. Put some thought into this area and add your relevant keywords.

- Limit your title to 35 characters, including spaces, and your description to 145 characters, or 20 words. Use your important keyword phrase in your title and/or description.

- To have your site considered for more than one subcategory, duplicate this process.

- Submitting your site to LookSmart won't guarantee that it will be accepted into the index.

- The placement of your site in the index is determined by editors, so the only way to make your site appear more prominently is to improve its content, design, or usefulness.

- You can't request that your site be listed in a "Best of the Web" category. Editors determine this designation.

- Sites that contain only a few pages, as well as pornographic sites, are excluded from the directory.

- Sites that are rich in content and relevant to the work, leisure, and home lives of busy people stand a better chance at getting accepted.

- To update your LookSmart listing, visit **http://www.looksmart.com/h/info/confirm.html**.

## Submitting to LookSmart

At the time of this writing, LookSmart offers two submission choices. With Express Submit, site owners pay a few hundred dollars to insure that their site appears in the index within 48 hours. Basic Submit is half the price, but site owners will find themselves waiting for eight weeks for their listing to appear. Non-profit organizations can still submit their sites for free.

**TIP** Is it worth the expense to submit your site to LookSmart? Most experts say yes. After all, with LookSmart providing the main directory results to AltaVista and Excite, even if your site isn't listed in the main index for either of those engines, you'll have a presence in LookSmart. Plus, if your site is new, having it appear in the index within 48 hours is a definite plus.

## Conclusion

Directories are a totally different ballgame than search engines, and different strategies need to be employed to achieve success.

Hundreds of directories are spread across the Internet, but the ones listed here are certainly the most important. If there are directories associated with your particular industry or field, however, be sure to consider those and submit your site.

Use the general guidelines listed in this chapter, and your submission will stand an excellent chance at getting accepted into these all-important directories.

# PART VI

# HOW SECURE IS YOUR WEB SITE?

# ANALYZING SECURITY RISKS

**In This Chapter**

Understanding the Types of Attacks

Examining Your Internal Vulnerabilities

Employing a Thorough Security Policy

Warding Off Creepy Crackers

Every week, we hear or read about yet another cracker attack (cleverly phrased as a *hacker attack* by those who don't know better) or some other breach of security. Whether the problem is the stereotypical teenage evil-doer in front of his computer in a dark room or the unthinking employee who tosses a printout of personal information and passwords with the evening trash, security breaches are too common and easily avoided. At the very least, you should strive to make your site as unappealing to crackers as possible. In this chapter, you will examine the ways your site might be vulnerable and look at how you can reduce your risks.

**NOTE** A hacker is an intelligent or skilled programmer who has learned how to manipulate a system. Hacker has been a positive term for several years, but many now use the term to imply malicious intent. Throughout this chapter, we will use the term hacker as it was originally intended. In those instances when we bring up malicious or criminal behavior, we will use the term cracker.

### Grasping the Importance of Security

How do you create a perfectly secure computer? There's only one way: Lock it in a room requiring biometrics for entry, then unplug it.

In other words, there is no such thing as a completely secure computer.

It's a frightening truth, but if you are aware of the risks involved with storing information in a computer system, you can greatly reduce the chance that you will be a victim of a successful cracker attack. If you are an e-merchant, you must be aware of other types of attack that can leave your customers and their private information vulnerable.

An e-business's first priority is the customer, and most customers' concerns boil down to one thing: privacy. Personal information can include everything from names to phone numbers to credit card numbers. To protect your customers' privacy, you should do everything in your power to secure that information.

Imagine that a cracker breaks your system and sucks it dry of credit card numbers, bank account information, and home phone numbers. Yikes! This is a Very Bad Thing. To avoid such a situation, you might be tempted to make your site impervious to attack. Banish the thought now. Again, there is no such thing as a completely secure system, and to believe that you have achieved such a thing will only leave you open to attack. Instead, make your site as secure as you possibly can, implement constant improvements to security, and produce a site that is as unpalatable to crackers as possible.

## Understanding the Types of Attacks

How can your server be compromised? Several methods of attack exist, but if you group them together, you'll find they fall into one of very few categories: unauthorized access, intercepted or false information, denial of service, and malicious code.

### Unauthorized Access

Unauthorized access is exactly what it appears to be: Someone who shouldn't have been playing with your hard drive has done so. How does this happen? You'd be surprised at how easy it is for crackers to gain access to systems where they don't belong. The most preventable but most common method of access revolves around passwords. How are passwords compromised? We discuss this more in Chapter 28, "Prevention, Detection, and Recovery," but suffice it to say that if your name is Joe Bob and your password is JoeBob, your account is more likely to fall under attack. Likewise, if your password is a dictionary word, you're in trouble.

Unauthorized access is also where the issue of back doors comes in. Remember that by default, some operating systems are shipped with those back doors wide open, and if the system Administrator is too busy making eyes at the cute new Web developer to close those doors, that system will be vulnerable to attack.

**NOTE**   A back door refers to an inconspicuous means of gaining access to a system or manipulating a system.

Last year, the FBI and the U.S. Senate's Web pages were replaced by pages that crackers created and uploaded to their Web servers. These are examples of unauthorized access.

### Intercepted and False Information

The next type of attack revolves around information that has been tampered with. If you're dialing into your Internet service provider on a phone line, you're vulnerable to attack, because twisted-pair wire (telephone wire) is easy to tap. Don't call out the FBI, though. It's unlikely that anyone is sitting outside your house, trying to find out all the details of your personal and financial life.

An example of this type of attack would be your neighborhood cracker pitching a tent outside your home, tapping into your phone line, and intercepting your online banking transactions. He then could change information in that transaction (if he knows the proper format of the message and the message has not been encrypted) so that the money ends up in his own account in the Bahamas.

## Denial of Service

Denial of service usually occurs due to malicious code or the exploitation of a security hole in a server, but it boils down to a huge disruption for all the decent, hardworking system Administrators out there.

Denial of service is a deceptively dangerous type of attack. Several methods are used for this particular attack flavor, but the most common and effective method is a distributed attack. With a distributed attack, several crackers or programs lay dormant around the Internet. At a specific time, the crackers or programs flood a single server, inundating it with requests for a response or with data until it slows to a crawl or even crashes. Either way, the server is unable to deal with the genuine requests its users are trying to make.

Other types of attacks that lead to denial of service can be surprisingly simple. For example, the command `ping`, which is used to determine whether a server is available, can be used to overwhelm a buffer, causing the system to crash.

A SYN Flood attack effectively does the same thing, except that it uses the TCP/IP protocol to accomplish this feat. With TCP/IP, a request is performed in two stages. First, the cracker pretends to use a different server and sends a request for a connection to the victim server. Then the victim server must send an acknowledgement to the requesting server before the connection can be made.

Because the originating server did not actually request a connection, acknowledgements are ignored until the victim server times out the request. In other words, the server finally breaks the connection and then can accept a new request. During this period, while the victim continues to send acknowledgements to the falsified server, it uses up processing time and memory. Crackers can automate this attack so that the victim server is flooded, and again, no other requests for connection to that server can be made. In effect, the server is down for the count and unavailable.

Of course, platform-specific methods of attack exist as well. You should be aware of the existence of these methods and make sure that you have the latest version of your Web server or its patches, so that you will be less vulnerable to these attacks.

## Malicious Code

Finally, we have malicious code. Malicious code breaks down into three general categories: viruses, worms, and Trojan horses.

**TIP**   Remember that malicious code is any code created to cause damage to a system, whether by tricking users into revealing information, propagating endless processes, or destroying data and spreading to other systems.

### Viruses

Undoubtedly, you've heard of viruses—from Happy99.exe to the Melissa macro virus and even the LoveLetter virus in all its variations. In essence, a computer virus shares two characteristics with a physical virus. First, it replicates, and then it destroys. Viruses are dangerous for two reasons. First, they destroy or corrupt valuable information, possibly sending some of the more sensitive data to the virus writer for that person's own diabolical use. Second, viruses hide in transmissions to other systems, whether through e-mail, a network connection, or even a floppy disk passed around the office, and they replicate on these other systems.

## Worms

In 1988, a young college student at Cornell University created an infamous Internet worm that wreaked havoc on the university system tied to the Internet. The worm was a program that replicated itself (like a virus) but did not destroy information. Instead, it spawned processes as it replicated. The worm spread throughout the network, tying up servers all over the U.S. Since then, we don't see worms as frequently as we see viruses, but they still exist. And they perform the same function: They replicate and spread to cause denial of service.

## Trojan Horses

The last type of malicious code is a Trojan horse. Recall the story of the original Trojan horse, that massive wooden structure the Greeks used to infiltrate and destroy Troy. The modern-day Trojan horse is the same idea.

A Trojan horse destroys information, much like a virus, but in this case, the malicious code is actually hidden within what the victim believes is a perfectly safe program. For instance, you download the latest release of Bloody Star Battle Warrior Civilization Simulation, not realizing that, as you kill off the Mighty Zorlonz, the malicious code is hard at work in the background, destroying information on your computer. Or worse yet, your Trojan horse is sending sensitive information stored on your computer to someone else.

## Other Malicious Code

In addition to Trojan horses, viruses, and worms, other malicious code exists that falls into similar categories. We discuss these categories due to the popularity of this malicious code in the cracker world and to keep you aware of the dangers that exist for your site.

A *logic bomb* is a type of virus. Like a virus, it implants itself in your computer and makes itself the running program. It allows the program you were running originally to continue, so that you never notice that something is wrong. But unlike a virus, a logic bomb waits. A regular virus hatches its plot immediately and begins to erase information, send itself out via mass e-mails, or shut down your computer.

A logic bomb waits until something happens—a trigger—inside the computer. The trigger could be you clicking on something onscreen, pressing a certain key, or even performing a specific string of actions (clicks, keystrokes, etc.). As soon as you hit the trigger, the logic bomb engages and begins to destroy information.

Viruses have evolved over the last several years. Originally, viruses were just executable code. Then anti-virus software learned to detect these viruses by watching for certain actions. So virus writers began to write viruses with varying instructions that performed the same action. For example, the commands MOV and MOVX might do the same thing, but they look different when they're in machine code, so virus writers would swap between the two commands to confuse the anti-virus software.

Then viruses were encrypted. To counteract this method, anti-virus software identified viruses by noting the unique signatures of the encryption algorithms that virus writers use. Now the new danger is *polymorphic viruses.* Polymorphic viruses actually *change* each time they are decrypted and run so that the next victim's version will be different from the previous victim's. Some anti-virus software can detect polymorphic viruses, but the stakes are rising, and detection has become more difficult.

**TIP** What can you do to avoid the pitfalls of malicious code? First, be aware of what is out there. Read articles about the latest viruses, and keep up-to-date on the progress being made to counteract new attacks. Second, upgrade your anti-virus software. Make sure systems connected to your server have the latest updates. Third, pray that nothing hits your site. And finally, make certain your security policy (which we discuss later in this chapter in "Employing a Thorough Security Policy") accounts for the aftermath of such an attack. The "Warding Off Creepy Crackers" section of this chapter lists some ways to arm yourself. And, as we discuss in Chapter 28, recovery methods after an attack are just as important as prevention methods, if not more so.

## A ("Cracked") Mirror World

Consider a mirror world attack to be a hybrid, the offspring of hijacking and a Trojan horse, where *hijacking* means a user is whisked off to another site without having requested to download that site. Suppose that Susie Surfer heads to cheapomusic.com to buy the latest Nine Inch Nails release. The site comes up with no problem, though perhaps the URL suddenly looks longer than usual, with CGI variables strung throughout. As Susie fantasizes about Trent Reznor, she adds the CD to her shopping cart, then checks out. She gives her credit card number, password, etc., then logs out and waits impatiently for the CD to arrive. It never does. What *does* arrive is her credit card statement with charges around the world and at cheapomusic.com amounting to more than her mall-job salary. What happened?

Crackers hijacked Susie to their mirror world site, which looked and acted just like cheapomusic.com's site. When she gave them her login, password, and credit card number, they captured that information, sold her credit card number to other criminals, and even accessed her account at cheapomusic.com to charge their own musical appetites to her card. How can you avoid causing such distress to your customers? Consider using a digital certificate so customers can verify the identity of the site. We discuss digital certificates in Chapter 27.

## Packet Sniffing

Packet sniffing is the same idea as wiretapping. Information on the Internet is split into packets, which are sent individually. When crackers employ sniffing, they can actually read exactly what is being sent, in plain text. To be able to do this, a network card must be run in promiscuous mode, so that it is allowed to see traffic passing through the server. Thankfully, this method is becoming more difficult now that such modes are more restricted, but it is still very possible for crackers to read your e-mail, password (in plain text!), credit card numbers, files, and any other data you make available by sending it to other servers.

To ensure that any packet-sniffed information cannot be read (at least not easily), encrypt your messages, your data, etc., before they leave your machine. Likewise, if your customers must send information to you, be sure that the information is encrypted before it is transmitted. And, of course, check that your network cards are not vulnerable to sniffers.

## Password Cracking

How do crackers get to your password? It's easier than you may think. How can you prevent them from finding out your password? It's even easier. Two tips are guaranteed to make your password almost impossible to break—if the encryption on your password is strong enough, that is. First, change your password regularly. Second, choose a password that has nothing to do with your personal or professional life, and make sure it cannot be found in a dictionary.

**TIP**  If you change your password often, it does become more difficult to remember. However, if what you're accessing with that password is important (and if it's password protected, it's probably of some small importance at least), you should make the effort. If you forget your password, it's always possible to contact the system Administrator and have a new temporary password created for you, which you should change immediately. Some online groups will even e-mail your password to you, reveal your password with the proper answers to given cues (your dog's name, your refrigerator brand, the city where you were born, etc.), or issue you a new and temporary password. Changing your password often will ensure that, if crackers do learn what it is, you can change it to lock them out before you even realize they are using your account.

Likewise, if you require or allow your customers to log in to your site, be sure to give them the same courtesy. Encourage frequent password changes, and make it easy for them to do so. Make sure they can easily gain access to their account again if they forget their password, but also make sure that the e-mail you send the new password to is the same you have on file for that user, or make sure your users can answer key questions to verify their identity before mailing a new password to them.

As for using a nondictionary password, there's a very easy explanation. Some encryption algorithms, such as those used on Unix systems, are one-way. That means whatever you've encrypted can't be decrypted. On Unix systems, however, the password file is sometimes stored publicly, which means any Joe Schmoe can read it. This isn't necessarily a bad thing, because all Joe will see is gobbledygook— your password encrypted. He can't look at your password and tell what that password is, and he can't use the encrypted form of the password to gain access to your account, so this is no big deal. Unless your password is in the dictionary. Suppose that you use the word "security" as your password. In the password file, it may look like "zl54oP1h." Crackers can run your password against a dictionary encrypted with the same algorithm that encrypted your password. That means when the comparing program runs your encrypted password against the encrypted word "security" in the encrypted dictionary, it will inform crackers of the match. Then they have your password.

To counteract this possibility, use alphanumeric passwords, and even include other characters such as an exclamation point or an asterisk. You can even create a phrase like "computersr2cool." And again, encourage your users to use nondictionary-style passwords. Be sure to check their choices for a good length, numbers, or nonalphanumeric characters.

## Spoofing

Crackers can impersonate someone on another machine by performing IP spoofing. Remember that IP stands for *Internet protocol* and is used to refer to an IP address. An IP address is the address of the network card on a computer or server. So by spoofing an IP, crackers make another server believe that they are located at a different server than they really are. The SYN Flood and Ping o' Death are examples of IP spoofing.

Spoofing can trick a server into believing that crackers are coming from a trusted address, and the server will allow the crackers access without requiring a password. If the crackers gain privileged access from this spoofing, they can tamper with information on the server or create other problems. Obviously, to counteract this problem, a server should require authentication (logins and passwords) from everyone, whether or not the server can assume that the origin of the user is trusted.

## Examining Your Internal Vulnerabilities

One of the first steps you can take to discourage crackers is to examine your site for possible areas of vulnerability. When you understand how attacks work, you can look at your system for weaknesses that translate into an invitation for prying eyes. Start with examining the many aspects of your software: custom scripts by in-house developers, commercial applications, your operating system, and your server software. Even if your site is strong, it is only as secure as the training and awareness of the people operating it.

## Avoiding Bug Exploitation

Security breaches may not originate with a malicious attack. Indeed, some of the worst security issues occur due to lack of preparedness rather than crackers on the prowl.

Any software developer will tell you that it's impossible to write bug-free code. Indeed, it's very difficult to determine how new code or other programs will interact with well-established and well-tested code. For example, have you ever installed new software, and all of a sudden, your computer crashes every time you restart it or the program? Even though some software goes through rigorous testing, it's very difficult to determine how it will interact because different computers have different components and different software running on them.

The Web is no different. It runs on software that allows communication between several machines, and that software is prone to bugs. What can happen if you have an undiscovered bug running rampant on your own system? To start, your system could crash, causing your boss to fire you. Very bad. The bug could cause a corruption of data, loss of data, or loss of connectivity. Customers would riot in the streets, and again, you'd find yourself scouring the newspaper for job openings.

Although bugs can cause problems on their own, they also can be exploited and used for an attack. With the knowledge that bugs are bound to exist in any software (and an operating system is software), crackers use those bugs to gain unauthorized access to computers running those particular operating systems. Crackers communicate newfound bugs to one another, and they try to use those bugs to tap into systems they otherwise would not be able to access. Once they are in those systems, they can access, change, or destroy information.

To counteract bug-induced problems, make sure that you download new patches for software as they become available. If you use software that has a bug that you know about, you can write to the software

### Bug Background

Dr. Grace Hopper, a rear admiral in the U.S. Navy, first used the term "bug" to describe a computing error. The computer she was using, the Mark I, was not working properly for some reason. After investigating, a co-worker found the source of the problem: a dead moth inside the computer.

Hopper noted the malfunction in the logbook and even taped the moth to the page. The logbook is on display at the Naval Surface Weapons Center. Today, any problem or mistake in coding that results in a computing error is called a "bug."

company and ask whether it has created a patch for this problem (if it even knows about the problem), or you can build your own patch.

## Safeguarding Your Site's Operating System

As we mentioned, your site's operating system is vulnerable to attack because it is a piece of software. We most often hear about Windows-related attacks in the news, probably because the Windows operating system is so prevalent. However, attacks are just as easy to commit against other operating systems. It's a matter of crackers caring enough to delve into the operating system to find its weaknesses, and then actually implementing an attack. Use these sites to read about the weaknesses of your operating system:

*FIND IT*
**ONLINE**

- If you use Microsoft Windows NT, be sure to read its security information at **http://www.microsoft.com/ntserver/security/ techdetails/default.asp**. In addition, Microsoft provides an area in its TechNet section dealing with available security tools and checklists: **http://www.microsoft.com/technet/security/tools.asp**.

- If you use a Unix server, a plethora of excellent information is available. Australia's *Computer Emergency Response Team* (CERT) offers a security checklist at **ftp://ftp.auscert.org.au/pub/auscert/ papers/unix_security_checklist**.

- If you use a Macintosh or other system to host your Web server, be sure to watch the software company's Web site for security updates and announcements. In addition, you can use the list of resources we include in this chapter to watch for general announcements regarding security in general.

## Keeping Your Site's Web Server Secure

Just like your server's operating system, the Web server itself is software and is therefore vulnerable to attack. And as you should with your operating system, check the vendor's Web site often for security updates and checklists. Here are the three most common Web servers used today:

*FIND IT*
**ONLINE**

- If you use Microsoft IIS, download Microsoft's security checklist at **http://www.microsoft.com/security/products/iis/CheckList.asp**.

- Netscape's Enterprise Server security information is located at **http://netcaster.netscape.com/products/security/resources/notes.html**. Unfortunately, this information is combined with all of Netscape's products. To find the main product page for Enterprise, see **http://home.netscape.com/enterprise/v3.6/index.html**.

- The Apache Web server page is located at **http://www.apache.org**, and you can search for bugs of every type (security included) at **http://bugs.apache.org**.

## Avoiding Social Engineering and Human Error

Don't be fooled into believing that your most secure assets are your employees. When cracker Kevin Mitnick appeared in March 2000 before members of Congress to discuss security issues, he declared that social engineering was an extremely viable way of gaining the information he needed to crack a site.

What is social engineering? It's getting the information you want from human beings by pretending to be someone you're not, cajoling employees, or intimidating them. You can take several precautions to avoid becoming a victim of social engineering.

First, document your company's policy on giving out sensitive information by phone or e-mail. Make sure everyone is aware that not all sweet-talking callers are truly who they say they are. If employees are aware of what is considered sensitive information, they will be less likely to give away something they shouldn't.

Then train your employees. Show them situations that could be misinterpreted as perfectly benign requests for sensitive information. Let them know the risks involved, and let them see what could happen as the result of just a small information leak.

## Protecting Data at Risk

When crackers compromise your system, what data is at risk? To put it bluntly, everything is at risk. You could lose your entire system, the programs on it, and any data you store on the server. That data could be yours, or it could be your customers'. Either way, the loss is bad, and the only way to avoid mayhem and a bevy of lawyers at your door is to protect that data. As you decide how to handle the information you store, you should consider the possibilities of loss and what to do to counteract potential loss.

To begin, analyze the type of information you store on your server:

- Do you store customer information on the same system as the Web server? (By *system,* we are referring to your internal network, if you have one.) If so, what precautions do you use to protect the information from crackers?

- Is your information segregated among partitions on your server?

- What roadblocks have you erected between your data and the outside world? For example, do you use a firewall of some sort?

- Do you store information that could potentially create a huge loss, such as credit card numbers? If so, do you store this information in plain-text files, or do you encrypt it?

- Have you disabled dangerous commands such as `rm -rf /*` to users who don't need permission to implement these types of commands?

- Do you limit access to your information? How?

## Employing a Thorough Security Policy

A security policy is vital to your company, both in regard to the relationship with your customers and to your own means of recovery and future prevention. With so many concerns for the protection of your customers' privacy, you must make an effort to address as many potential security holes as possible. You also must plan for recovery from any problems or attacks that may affect your site.

Although we go into more detail in the next few chapters about further considerations as you analyze your security policy, you will begin to consider your policy in this section. We begin in Chapter 9, "Analyzing Your Engineering Process," to discuss documentation. Your security policy is one piece of that documentation, but it can be just as important, if not more so, as any other piece of documentation you draft for your site design project.

**CAUTION**   There is one caveat with the security policy. You should definitely share with your customers the protections you use and the level of security you offer, but your security policy must not become public information in its entirety. Why?

Imagine that you record everything related to the security of your site and server in your security policy. Then you post the entire document to the Web for public consumption. You may impress thousands with the number of considerations you've incorporated into your security design, but you've also just invited crackers world wide to have first dibs at bringing your site to its knees.

Your security policy contains information that people outside of your group need not know. For example, you don't want crackers to know exactly how you will counter a cracking attempt. You also don't want them to find out what type of encryption you use or where you keep the encrypted files.

Again, your security policy is vital, but keep it from sight so that crackers are not tempted to use it against you.

You need to keep several consideration in mind as you draft your policy. We discuss some of these items in this section.

## Predicting Possible Attacks

First, decide what types of attacks could make your site susceptible:

- Suppose that your site is connected to the Web, so a denial-of-service attack is a possibility, as is the defacement of your page. What else could happen?
- What types of attack make your server susceptible? Your entire system?
- Who has access to the system? What, if any, type of access is granted to users?
- What back doors have you sealed?
- How is your information segregated?

## Taking Steps for Prevention

Next, consider methods of prevention. Again, we cover the issues out-lined here in more detail in the next few chapters, but you should begin to consider the inclusion of this information in your security policy:

- Do you use the best encryption available?
- What security protocols do you use through your Web site? What protocols do you use for your server?
- Do you use a firewall? If so, what kind?
- Do you employ user authentication? What kind?
- Do you back up your information? How? Where do the backups reside?
- Do you use physical security measures to prevent the physical stealing of hardware, information, etc. or to avoid loss due to natural disasters, power outages, etc.?
- Do you use an intrusion detection system? What type? How often is it monitored, or does it use automatic notification when it detects an intruder?
- Have you disabled dangerous commands and tools, such as `rm` or `setuid`?
- Have you partitioned your data as part of a plan to set hurdles for crackers who want to damage a great deal of your information?

## Planning Recovery

When an attack or problem occurs, how will you recover?

- How long will it take to recover damaged or lost data? Must it be shipped physically from another location, or is it available electronically?
- While the affected partition(s) is down, how will you keep your services running? To avoid the side-effect here of a denial of service, do you have the system capacity to run your company as if it were business as usual?
- What process do you have in place during recovery to get the system running normally again?

- What process do you have in place to keep future attacks or problems from recurring?
- What process do you have in place to identify the culprit who caused the system to go down?
- How much information regarding the attack or problem will you release to the public?

Using your answers to the questions posed here, you can certainly extract more information to include in your security policy. But there is one more consideration to be made at this point: How much of this information should be made public? Remember to consider the legal aspects of what you publicize, as well as what information will harm your business. Also remember not to disclose details about your recovery, prevention, and detection methods, because crackers can and will use those clues about your system in their next attack.

## Warding Off Creepy Crackers

It's easier than you'd think to get rid of crackers before they do any damage. In fact, you can start off with just a few guidelines that can keep you relatively safe from attack. We discuss protection in depth in the next few chapters, but this section will get you started.

First, don't tempt the Fates. Don't place huge ads on your pages declaring that all transactions are 110 percent secure, 400 percent guaranteed. If you do this, you're asking for trouble. Instead, boast about your SSL if you must. Just don't entice crackers to prove you wrong about your perfect security.

Second, keep up-to-date with security issues and concerns. Know what attacks your system is most likely to suffer. Know how to counteract those attacks to the best of your ability. If crackers try to break your system and instead find that you've done a nice job of keeping them out, they're more likely to leave you alone and hunt for an easier target.

Finally, don't be afraid to err on the side of security. Yes, there's a delicate balance between ease of use and tight security, but there is also a happy medium in there. Don't make your users type in eight passwords to gain access to a Telnet session with your server, but also don't leave the key in the front door with a sign in the yard that says, "Hey, I'm not home."

## Monitoring Cracker and Security Sites for Information You Need

When fighting crackers, you must think like them. If security is a huge issue for you and your development team (as it should be), you should read everything you can find on the security issues that affect or could affect you—including any issues related to the Web, the software you use, and the software your customers use. All these issues relate to your own system, because anything that affects the systems around you will affect your own.

The following list of sites will help you remain on top of security issues. Make a habit of visiting these sites regularly, not just when you have a problem on your hands.

### Cracking/Hacking Sites

These sites are run by hackers and perhaps a cracker or two. They provide a wealth of information you can use to learn about the latest goings-on in the world of cracking.

*Find It*
**ONLINE**

- L0pht Heavy Industries, perhaps the most popular/infamous hacker site—**http://www.l0pht.com/**
- Attrition.org, another popular hacker site with a huge catalog of security information—**http://www.attrition.org/**
- @stake, formerly Hacker News Network, covers the latest security news and fosters an "open source" mentality to disseminate security information—**http://www.atstake.com/**

### Security Sites

The following sites are run by security professionals, activists, and government communities.

*Find It*
**ONLINE**

- SecurityFocus, a security-related community for discussion and news—**http://www.securityfocus.com/**
- InfoWar, the InfoSec and InfoWar portal—**http://www.infowar.com/**
- Computer Emergency Response Team (CERT), responsible for researching security issues and providing recovery services—**http://www.cert.org/**

- NetworkIce.com, a company that deals in security software and maintains a discussion area for security issues—**http://www.networkice.com/**. The discussion area is located at **http://advice.networkice.com/Advice/default.htm**.

- Securiteam.com, an information area for security news, reviews, and issues—**http://www.securiteam.com**.

- @stake, a security company that provides security-related news—**http://www.atstake.com/**

## Arming Yourself with Preventive Technology

The following two sites provide information about software tools that can help you analyze security risks at your Web site and with your server. Remember that you can help secure your site by thinking like crackers, so using their tools will help you find your own vulnerabilities. However, be careful that you don't generate your own Internet worm or destroy all the files on your server. Read the documentation (if the tool comes with any) before using the tool. Have a feel for what should happen if the cracking attempt is successful.

**FIND IT ONLINE**

- Computer Incident Advisory Capability keeps a list of tools for security analysis and improvement at **http://ciac.llnl.gov/ciac/ SecurityTools.html**.

- The National Institute of Standards in Technology offers a list of tools for analysis at **http://cs-www.ncsl.nist.gov/tools/tools.htm**.

## Conclusion

Security is a major concern with anyone operating on the Web. Even if you have protected yourself with a firewall, encryption, and user authentication, crackers of every level of experience—from script kiddies to seasoned pros—can attack your site or exploit a weakness in your system unless you make efforts to plug all holes.

Fortunately, the Web also offers copious tools, checklists, and articles to keep you abreast of the latest in security issues. If you make the effort to stay in the loop, you will find yourself more protected than most companies.

# MINIMIZING RISKS TO DATA INTEGRITY AND CONFIDENTIALITY

**In This Chapter**

Understanding Stored Data Risks

Transmitted Data Risks

Protecting Data

Safeguarding Against Site Integrity Risks

Analyzing Your Data Security

Using Software to Secure Your Data

In this chapter, you'll look at the risks related to data integrity and confidentiality, and you'll learn how to protect important information from unauthorized access.

In Chapter 26, "Analyzing Security Risks," you examined security risks in general. Now you'll look at risks to your data specifically.

The scope of this book and the volatile nature of computer security preclude an in-depth list and analysis of the variety of issues related to this topic. However, we include a list of recommended reading in Appendix A, as well as a list of online resources in Chapter 26.

## Understanding Stored Data Risks

When you store data, it is susceptible to unauthorized access, destruction, or alteration. Unfortunately, the Internet increases these risks dramatically: Given the right time and resources, anyone could break into any system connected in any way by using the interconnectedness of the Internet.

Suppose that Evil Eric takes advantage of a hole in a CGI script and gains access to your password file. He runs a dictionary program against the file and finds out that one of your silly content editors used the word *scrumptious* as his password. Eric logs in as your content editor and proceeds to work his way behind your firewall, logging in once again as your editor, gaining access to files you thought were protected.

This would be a Very Bad Thing.

What if a virus makes its way via e-mail into your company's Inboxes, sending information to the virus writer, then deleting all files with .doc, .txt, .wp, and .html extensions?

Knowing that any file connected to a Web server or to the Internet is vulnerable, you should be aware of certain types of information when considering security issues:

- Personal or sensitive information relating to customers, such as contact information, credit card numbers, personal preferences, etc.
- Passwords

- Files not meant for public consumption (*hidden files*)
- Files accessible from the system hosting the Web server, such as proprietary company information stored within reach of the Web server

Although we consider possible dangers related to security in Chapter 26, let's look more closely at data-related risks.

## Unauthorized Access

When crackers connect to your server, they first need to gain access to the files within. They may do this by cracking passwords, using back doors to gain superuser status, abusing loopholes through server commands, applying social engineering, etc. Regardless of the method used, once they have gained access, your data is at risk. In this section, *unauthorized access* refers to the act of viewing sensitive, private, or proprietary information.

Consider proprietary company information accessible through your Web server. Is this information protected behind a firewall? Is it on a separate server? Is it further password protected? How many additional layers of security have you used to protect the information within?

Consider sensitive customer information. Are credit card numbers stored within? If so, are they encrypted? Does your database require a password to view certain information? Can any Joe Schmo off the Web streets gain access to customer contact information?

Consider passwords in /etc/passwd. Is this file viewable to outsiders? Can crackers manipulate executables in your CGI directory to have that file e-mailed to them? Certainly you'd like to think that users would follow instructions and choose hard-to-guess passwords or non-dictionary words, but can you be sure crackers won't correlate an encrypted password with the correct plain text?

When you analyze your server to gauge the level of risk for unauthorized access, consider the type of information you have stored on your server or that is accessible via your server, and take into account the level of security you need to enact in order to protect that data. Include this information in your security policy.

## Destruction of Data

The destruction of data can cause much wailing and gnashing of teeth. If recovery from backups (if you bothered to make backups) fails, what can you do? Basically, you're stuck back at square one, forced to rebuild your system from scratch.

Crackers don't necessarily have to have direct access to data to destroy it. Using malicious code such as viruses or Trojan horses, they can delete or corrupt files. These programs can reach into your system with a simple e-mail attachment.

With the proper access and a single `rm -rf /*` command, crackers can delete everything on your server. If CGI executables are not properly secured, crackers can feed extra commands into the shell, destroying data. As you write your security policy, consider the risks associated with data destruction, and be aware of the methods crackers can use to delete files.

## Alteration of Data

When data is altered, it can become unusable or incorrect. Either way, if you don't have backups of the correct data, you may be in trouble. In any case, unauthorized alteration of data presents a large problem that you must consider and address in your security policy.

### Unusable Data

What do we mean by unusable? If Kyle the Code Kiddie decides one day to mess with some files on your system, he could run a program that would insert or flip random bits in that file. Later, when you try to open that file in a text editor, you'll see fun bits of gobbledygook.

*Unusable data* refers to data that has been altered so that you can no longer access it for its intended purpose. The file containing the data still exists, but the information within it is gone.

### Incorrect Data

What do we mean by incorrect? Assume that Christie Cracker has just changed database information so that the price of your 13-inch

Super-Deluxe Widget now stands at $.01—a savings of 99.95 percent. Not bad for a 13-inch widget. Unfortunately, that's quite a bit of money you lose each time someone orders a widget for that price.

In this case, the data is still usable. Programs or scripts that access the information still can perform calculations and incorporate that data into Web pages that access the price for this widget. However, the data is incorrect. Your company is forced to change the amount before too much damage occurs.

### Detecting Altered Data

How can you tell when data has been altered? Usually, your best bet is to use log files and programs that inform you each time the content of a file has changed.

You might also consider an *intrusion detection system* (IDS) to inform you of the potential for data integrity risks before they occur. An IDS alerts the system administrator when it detects suspicious activity. The IDS considers any activity suspicious if it falls outside the parameters of typical activity on the server it inspects. We discuss intrusion detection more in Chapter 28, "Prevention, Detection, and Recovery."

Consider the dangers of altered data when writing your security policy, and include risks and methods of detection.

## Transmitted Data Risks

When data is in transit between servers, it's at great risk of being compromised. As data bounces through phone lines and between routers, wiretaps and packet sniffers may intercept the information, alter it, spoof it, etc. Paranoid? Perhaps. But where sensitive information is concerned, paranoia is better than compromised data.

In this section, you'll look at some of the risks associated with data in transit.

**NOTE**    A good system administrator is a paranoid system administrator. Consider everything that could go wrong, and secure your system against each possible attack.

## Interception

As packets of data move through routers toward their destination, sniffers can intercept the packets and save a copy for malicious use. This information may be sensitive for privacy reasons, or it may contain data that crackers can abuse (such as credit card numbers or an order to sell 250 shares of stock in YeOldWidgetShoppe.com). Whatever the case, you should make efforts to ensure that any data in transit is secured against unauthorized viewing.

**TIP**  To avoid the interception of login information when users attempt to access your server remotely, require secure shell sessions with tools such as SSH or OpenSSH, and disable telnet, rlogin, etc.

In your security policy, remember to analyze the risks associated with intercepted data. How likely is interception, how can you prevent it, and what damage could interception cause?

## Web Spoofing

Some Web servers may be used as proxies without your knowledge or intent. When this occurs, the user accesses a site that may seem perfectly legitimate. However, the cracker's site is passing along altered information or capturing the user's input or available data, and the user may well have no idea that this is happening.

Usually, users can determine that a Web site is being spoofed because the spoofing site's URL prepends the target site, as in this example:

```
http://evilsite.com:80/http://where_I_wanted_to_be.com/
```

In addition, users can see, in the status bar of the browser, that any links from the page have the evil site's URL prepended to the target URL. This is a sure sign that the target Web site has been spoofed.

**CAUTION**  If users try to surf behind a firewall or use a proxy such as Anonymizer.com, they may see another site prepended to the target site—but the prepended site is not actually spoofing.

The bad news is that simple JavaScript can overwrite the contents of the URL.

You can help protect your visitors from Web spoofing by encouraging them to view your site's certificate during secured sessions. Using the certificate authenticated in SSL, users can determine whether the site they have accessed really belongs to your company and not a malicious cracker waiting to steal their credit card information.

## Protecting Data

When you're aware of the dangers involved with the data you store on your servers, you have a better chance of protecting that data against malicious attack. Although no protection is guaranteed to be 100 percent secure, you can at least know that you have done all you can to discourage crackers from attacking your valuable data.

### Back Up Your Data!

As any freshman computer science major knows, the only way to preserve your sanity is to back up everything. What should you back up? Any data you can't replace. The only exception should be software that you can reinstall from copies you keep offsite or in a fireproof safe.

For the ultimate in security, back up files offsite. This ensures physical security as well as the capability to replace lost data. So if your site is hit by a series of earthquakes, fires, and floods, you can rest assured that your data will survive, even if you don't.

If you can't afford or don't need physical security, at least back up your data to tapes or to a system that sits behind a heavily armored firewall or that is configured to receive data and not to send anything.

### Use Encryption

*Encryption* is the process of converting a readable file into gobbledygook. How does this work? Remember back to grammar school days, when you would write in secret code to your friend two rows away? Recall that you used a key, where a = t and g = c...that was a basic method of encryption. In short, you take *plain text*, which anyone can read, and transform it using a key into *ciphertext*, which looks like nonsense to anyone who doesn't know better. To decrypt the message, recipients must have both the key used to encrypt the message

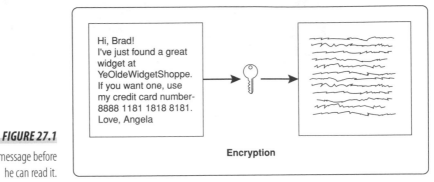

**Encryption**

**FIGURE 27.1**

Brad must decrypt Angela's message before
he can read it.

and the algorithm used to encrypt it. If they have the key but not the algorithm, their key is useless. Figure 27.1 shows how an encrypted message appears to the recipient before it is decrypted.

Encryption can solve a variety of issues related to the security of data, either in storage or in transit. When storing data such as credit card numbers or contact information, seriously consider storing it only if it's encrypted. If sensitive information is stored in plain text on your server, you risk unauthorized access and possibly malicious action against the person whose information was just compromised.

You also may consider encryption of information transmitted from one server to another. Using PGP (Pretty Good Privacy) or other public-key encryption methods, you can not only protect data from unauthorized viewing, but because messages are also encrypted with the sender's private key, the recipient knows that the message came from the sender.

## Digital Signatures

Digital signatures ensure authentication of the sender. In other words, digital signatures do not necessarily require encryption, but they place a "stamp" on a message that only the sender can generate and that cannot be altered. One example is the use of a sender's private key to encrypt a message. When the recipient receives this privately encrypted message, she can decrypt it using the sender's public key to confirm that the message actually came from the purported sender.

## *Public Key Encryption*

Public key encryption involves two sets of keys: Angela's and Brad's public and private keys. Public keys are encryption keys available to the general public. Angela posts her public key on her Web site for Brad to access, and Brad sends his public key via attachment in an e-mail to Angela. Private keys are kept secret. Only Angela has access to her private key. Only Brad has access to his private key.

Figure 27.2 shows the path of a message encrypted using public key encryption.

When Angela decides to send an encrypted message to Brad, she takes her plain-text message (which anyone can read) and encrypts it both with Brad's public key, which he sent to her in an e-mail, and her own private key, which only she can access. Then she sends her message to Brad.

When Brad receives Angela's encrypted message, he decrypts it using Angela's public key from her Web site. Then he decrypts it yet again using his private key. When the message reveals itself, he knows two things:

- Because Angela's public key decrypted the message properly, her private key encrypted the message. This means the message definitely came from Angela.
- Because his private key was able to decrypt the message properly, he knows Angela encrypted it with his public key, so the message was intended for him, and nobody else was able to read it.

Therefore, public key encryption guarantees two things. One: Nobody but the person for whom the message was intended can read the message. Two: The identity of the sender is verified when the message is decrypted using the sender's public key.

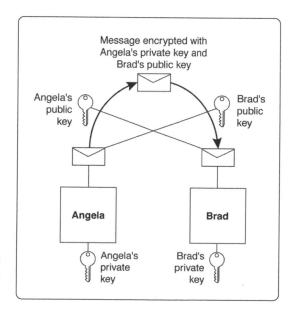

**FIGURE 27.2**

The path of a public-key encrypted message from Angela to Brad.

What happens if a cracker intercepts the message, alters the information, and resends it? First, the cracker would have to decrypt the message using the public key, in which case, he will be unable to re-encrypt and send the altered message because he does not have access to the private key.

If the cracker saves a copy of the message and resends it later, a problem could arise. For example, if the message was an order to sell 250 shares of stock, and the cracker resends the message a day later, a total of 500 shares of stock might be sold. The sender and receiver can avoid problems by using time stamps to verify that the message is authentic and has not been "replayed" by a cracker.

## Secure Sockets Layer (SSL)

*Secure Sockets Layer* (SSL) is a protocol that adds an additional layer of security to data transmissions via the Web. It is a layer beneath the HTTP protocol that allows authentication of both client and server, as well as provides encryption for all communication between the authenticated parties.

How do you use SSL? If your Web server is already SSL-enabled, you need only alter the URL you use…slightly. For example, if you have a Web page at

```
http://www.kerri-leigh.com/cgi-bin/pay_me_money.pl?amount=lots
```

and you want to have all information sent from this page be secure, you need only add a wee little s, as you can see here:

```
https://www.kerri-leigh.com/cgi-bin/pay_me_money.pl?amount=lots
```

SSL is extremely popular as a tool used for secure ordering and passing sensitive information from browser to server.

 **TIP** Remember to register for a site certificate from a source such as VeriSign (**http://www.verisign.com**).

## Forced Password Integrity

If you enforce a few rules related to passwords on your company's server(s), you can avoid quite a few security issues:

- When a user enters a new password, check that it contains numbers as well as letters to ensure that the password can't be found in a dictionary.

- Encourage users not to incorporate personal information—such as names, birth dates, or other identifiers—into their passwords. Passwords should not be obvious.

- Enforce regular password changes.

- Encourage users not to write down their passwords.

- Inform users that they are never to share their passwords with anyone under any circumstances, even with IT personnel.

- Lock out users after a certain number of unsuccessful login attempts. Users must verify their identity before IT can unlock their account and allow them access to the system.

- Use a series of questions related to personal information that allows users to verify their identity. Let users determine these questions and answers when creating their accounts.

# Safeguarding Against Site Integrity Risks

Because the entire point of having a Web server is so that the general Web population can access it, Web sites are very vulnerable to attack. In 1999, several government sites came under attack, as did a slew of commercial sites. In some cases, your options for staving off an attack are fairly limited, but there are a few steps you can take.

Before you look at how to maintain site integrity, consider the possible types of attack you may have to contend with.

## Vandalism and Defacing

Imagine opening your Web site one morning, coffee cup in one hand, bagel in the other. But instead of seeing your Web site, you see a satire of your site, with not-so-subtle jibes at your company and a few tirades about capitalism in general.

Not a Good Thing.

Your site has been vandalized. How did this happen? Crackers created a new HTML file—or set of HTML files—and then cracked your system and uploaded the new files over the original ones. The result is the equivalent of Web graffiti.

As long as you have your original pages backed up (preferably offsite, because the vandals may well have destroyed data while uploading these new and not-so-improved pages), replacing the vandalized pages is easy. However, you must still track down how the crackers entered your system and plug those holes.

## Denial of Service

Denial-of-service attacks can be implemented in a variety of ways, but the end result is always the same—customers who want to access the victim site are unable to. *Denial-of-service* (DoS) attacks involve flooding a server with traffic that it is unable to handle.

Most often, the attack occurs by tricking a server into requesting a response from another server, but the other server won't respond because it never communicated with the victim server in the first place. The victim server waits until it times out for the response that never comes. If enough of these faked requests occur, the server's response rate to legitimate requests slows to a crawl.

If these faked requests originate from a large array of systems, the attack is known as a *distributed denial of service* (DDoS). DDoS attacks are more lethal because of the amount of traffic they generate to the victim servers. Many times, the systems that host the DoS traffic-generating programs don't even belong to the crackers, and system administrators may be completely unaware that their system is being used for a DDoS attack.

DoS attacks have become a very popular way for crackers to target and hurt businesses. And unfortunately, the security hole that allows DoS attacks to occur rests with the protocols used in these requests. As long as any system exists that can host these attacks, and as long as crackers find this type of attack effective against their enemies, DoS attacks will occur. However, you can find patches to limit the effectiveness of these attacks by using load shedding.

## Hijacking

*Find It*
**ONLINE**

With a wee bit of social engineering or a touch of conniving, crackers can change your DNS information so that anyone typing in **http://www.yeoldewidgetfactory.com** will end up at the cracker's site instead of yours. This is known as *hijacking*. A site that is hijacked can lead to relatively minor situations, such as defacing. However, the site can also be used to fool your customers into revealing credit card numbers or other sensitive information.

The problem rests at InterNIC and must be resolved at that level. Unfortunately, security will increase, making life more difficult for those who must change information InterNIC has stored for any particular domain. In exchange for lost convenience, however, your site will be better protected from crackers who would hijack it.

## Analyzing Your Data Security

Now that you've looked at a few of the dangers related to the security of stored and transmitted data, you can use the following list to determine how secure your site's data is:

- Do you store sensitive or proprietary information on a server connected to any network?

- Do you encrypt sensitive or proprietary information?

- Do you authenticate users attempting to gain access to sensitive data?

- Do you use protections such as anti-virus software and e-mail attachment policies to protect against malicious code?

- Do you use password aging?

- Do you check new passwords to make sure they follow your company's password guidelines? Remember that these guidelines should be enacted for both company employees and customers.

- Do you make regular backups of your data?

- Do you use an intrusion detection system?

- Do you allow for remote login access? Do you require secure login shells?

- Do you disable certain tools for remote users?

- Do you restrict directory access for remote users?
- Do you restrict directory access for employees, depending on their job types and access needs?
- Do you use a firewall?
- Do you have a site certificate?
- Do you use digital certificates?
- Do you use SSL?
- Does your security policy address risks as well as policies and procedures related to data?

## Using Software to Secure Your Data

This section includes software tools and solutions related to securing data.

For data recovery software and tips, visit these sites:

- CBL Data Recovery—**http://www.cbltech.com/**
- Enhanced Software Technologies—**http://www.bru.com**
- NetMass—**http://www.systemrestore.com/**

Check out these sites for General Security Solutions:

- CyberSafe—**http://www.cybersafe.com/**
- Check Point—**http://www.checkpoint.com/**

You can also download OpenSSH, , free at **http://www.openssh.com/**. This program allows users to remotely and securely access your server.

## Conclusion

Data is the commodity at most risk online, and although the list of dangers related to stored or transmitted data is seemingly endless, you can take steps to protect yourself from lost data or misused information. The most important steps you can take include enacting tight password rules, backing up data regularly, using encryption, and researching risks daily.

# PREVENTION, DETECTION, AND RECOVERY

**In This Chapter**

Anticipating Physical Security Needs

Employing Prevention Methods

Detecting an Intruder

Responding to an Attack

Attending Seminars and Conferences

In previous chapters, you explored the dangers related to security and data integrity. In this chapter, you will look at the methods of prevention, detection, and recovery as they relate to e-commerce Web servers.

Prevention, detection, and recovery are integral to the overall security of a system. If your company does not make efforts to protect its system from danger, to detect possible dangers to the system, and to use an established process to recover from attacks or security issues, your system will remain extremely susceptible to attack.

## Anticipating Physical Security Needs

Tectonic plates can be a nasty element of nature. Especially when they move, rippling the Earth's crust, causing buildings to shake, fall down, and destroy all your computer systems.

Especially when you neglected to back up your systems offsite. Oops.

When analyzing the security of data and systems, people rarely stop to consider Mother Nature in all her forms. Whether it's dust, fire, flood, lightning, alligators gone mad, or leaky pipes that soak the lab, if you fail to back up your system and keep the backup copies offsite, you're asking for trouble.

Mother Nature isn't your only nemesis, though. Disgruntled employees, thieves, and bumbling fools also conspire against you. If anyone has access to the physical components of your system, they can wreak havoc on your life…and your stock value.

Stop to analyze your physical security, and consider the following:

- Is your system backed up? Are the backups offsite, in fireproof, earthquake-proof, waterproof safes?
- Should you keep physical components of your system behind locked doors? Who should have access?
- Do you need to use biometrics, such as retinal scans, fingerprinting, or voice recognition, to ensure the physical safety of your system?
- Should you use ID cards or badges to ensure the physical safety of your system?

- Do you need to use psychological testing to ensure that none of your employees will take out their frustrations on your system by taking it out with a high-powered rifle?

**NOTE** Biometrics is not just good sci-fi fare anymore. In 2000, Siemens, the electronics company, announced a new method of user authentication—a fingerprinting mouse. Passwords will become obsolete, thanks to the physical security provided by biometric devices such as these.

## Employing Prevention Methods

As you saw in the previous two chapters, Web Administrators must deal with a slew of security issues. As an Administrator, your best bet is to stay on top of the latest security news and to know about any new security holes, viruses, or attacks related to the software you use. We cover some general prevention techniques in this chapter.

### Keeping Up-to-Date with Research

Read, read, read, read, read. We can't stress this enough. Security holes are found weekly, if not daily, and are posted to a variety of sources. If you research the software you use, as well as the particular hardware setup you use, you'll find an amazing number of problems and their solutions. If you're aware that there's a problem before someone exploits a weakness on your system, you can prevent a great deal of lost time and money. You also can review warnings and methods of attack to be prepared in case of an assault; know how to detect one and how to recover from it.

We highly encourage you to take advantage of the following resources and the news they disseminate:

*FIND IT ONLINE*

- Computer Incident Advisory Capability—**http://ciac.llnl.gov/**
- Forum of Incident Response and Security Teams—**http://www.first.org/**
- TruSecure's ICSA Labs—**http://www.icsalabs.com/**
- Computer Security Resource Center—**http://csrc.ncsl.nist.gov/**
- InfoSec and InfoWar—**http://www.infowar.com/**

- System Administration, Networking, and Security Institute—**http://www.sans.org/**
- AntiOnline.com—**http://www.antionline.com/**
- XForce—**http://xforce.iss.net/**
- CERT (formerly Computer Emergency Response Team)—**http://www.cert.org/**
- Computer Security Institute—**http://www.gocsi.com/**

## Implementing Version Control

In Chapter 9, "Analyzing Your Engineering Process," we discuss the importance of version control as an element of configuration management and sound engineering process. Now consider the security aspects of version control. Imagine that your summer intern just finished commenting all of the undocumented scripts that reside on your server. He checks them into version control...then suddenly howls and screams fill the halls.

The comments weren't commented after all.

Now you have a problem. The world is trying to access your pages, but the scripts that generate those pages aren't working. You're losing money by the bucketload, and it's all because of an intern functioning on two pots of coffee and a power nap who forgot that Perl comments and C++ comments are different birds.

Except that there *is* no problem, because you've implemented version control. All you need to do is undo the last check-in, and your scripts are restored. You then send the intern back to school to learn how to comment code.

Companies often have version control software sitting around the office, ready to be used. But some engineers and coders resist using the software. After all, it adds an extra layer of work to an already genius bit of code. Who needs version control, anyway?

We all do. Use it. It not only contributes to solid engineering practices, it also keeps you out of trouble when the world turns upside down and your recently updated scripts and Web pages no longer work properly.

## Setting up Virus Protection

As you learned in Chapter 26, "Analyzing Security Risks," viruses and other malicious code can create massive problems with your system, your data, and your sanity. Anti-virus software can keep you out of trouble. Remember to update your software and to check all incoming files for infection before allowing them to execute anywhere near your Web server.

 **NOTE**   Remember not to allow e-mail to be within reach of your Web server, or restrict the scope of users' e-mail to their private directories on the server. Also establish a protocol to ensure that nobody will upload a virus file to the Web server, where it can be executed.

The following list of anti-virus software can help protect your server from the perils of viruses:

*Find It*
**ONLINE**

- Symantec's Norton Anti-Virus—**http://www.symantec.com/product/**
- Network Associates' McAfee—**http://www.mcafeeb2b.com/**
- Command Software Systems' Command Anti-Virus—**http://www.commandcom.com/products/product_info.html**
- Computer Associates' InnoculateIT— **http://www.cai.com/products/inoculateit.htm**

## Separating Your Data

If your data resides in different physical locations (whether it's a series of servers or even just hard drives), you are better able to protect it from attack. Consider the following situations:

- Malicious code is attempting to format the current partition, but it can't reach into another partition because there is no direct path between the two.
- A denial-of-service attack has managed to wipe out one hard drive in your system. Luckily, the other drives can share the added load until the drive is free from attack.
- You use a separate server to test the software you're about to use online. The new software has an insidious bug that alters every file within reach. It doesn't affect the server containing your entire Web site because it cannot reach it.

### Polymorphic Viruses

A new strain of viruses has been making its way into mainstream Virusville. These new viruses are called *polymorphic* because of their ability to change the code that anti-virus software uses to identify them.

Viruses have evolved over the years, as this list shows:

- *Simple* viruses are those that are easily detected. They always display a "signature" by which anti-virus software can detect them.
- *Variable* viruses are more difficult to detect, because they actually use variable commands to cause the same result. For example, if machine code such as 4F82 2102 has the same result as two lines of machine code (4E20 2200 39FA 2102), then the virus simply swaps between these two commands. If there are several instances of this variable code and two or more options for variance, the detection can become quite complicated.
- *Encrypted* viruses are also more difficult to detect because their encrypted files don't allow detection software to determine the code (and, therefore, the virus "signature"). Anti-virus software can detect suspicious files, however, by using the "signature" of commonly used encryption algorithms.
  - *Polymorphic* viruses change each time they replicate by mutating the telltale decryption code.

Symantec has created anti-virus software that fools the polymorphic virus into executing its malicious code within a virtual machine. The software watches for signs that a virus has begun executing its nasty payload, and then it warns users that the suspicious file does indeed carry a virus.

---

- You use an array of servers to host different portions of your site. Users can't tell the difference—it's a smooth transition between the servers. When one server goes belly up one morning, only a small portion of your site is unavailable while you replace that server.

## Safeguarding Scripts and Multimedia

In Chapter 29, "Avoiding the Dangers of Interactive Web Sites," you'll look at ways to protect your site and your visitors from multimedia and scripting-related attacks. Remember that visitors can protect themselves against the perils of multimedia by turning off those options in their browsers, however. Keep this in mind, and if you use any multimedia or scripting (such as ActiveX or JavaScript), try to use a backup means of communicating your site's content for those who won't be able to see it.

Also, you might consider limiting the amount of scripting and multimedia your site uses if you're concerned about the security issues associated with them. If you're willing to take the chance that users may not be able to view your bells and whistles or content, check out Chapter 29 for ways to protect yourself against malicious users of your scripts.

## Requiring User Authentication

How can you easily and effectively authenticate users on your Web site? If you use a Unix-based system, it's a piece of cake using .htaccess files.

What are .htaccess files? In each directory of your secret Web site area, you should include an .htaccess file that restricts access to any files or subdirectories within that directory, according to a password file you create. You don't need to repeat the .htaccess file in subdirectories, but if you want further restrictions in certain subdirectories, you will have to create separate .htaccess files within those subdirectories, with separate password files for each.

### Step 1: Create an .htaccess File

To create an .htaccess file, first go to the directory you want to protect. In this example, we'll use the directory /home/httpd/html/secret-widget-society/ (a.k.a. secret-widget-society/). In the example below, [yows]# is the Ye Olde Widget Factory server prompt.

```
[yows]# cd /home/httpd/html/secret-widget-society/
```

Now, using your favorite text editor, open a file named .htaccess for editing.

```
[yows]# vi .htaccess
```

Create your file according to the restrictions you want to use for this directory. In this case, we'll hide our passwords and logins in the file auth-secret-widget-society located in the directory /home/widgets/.

```
AuthType Basic
AuthName 'The Secret Widget Society'
AuthUserFile /home/widgets/auth-secret-widget-society
```

```
<Limit GET POST>
require valid-user
</Limit>
```

In this example, we'll allow anyone who's listed in the auth-secret-widget-society file to have access to our secret-widget-society/ directory. However, we can also limit access according to domain name, hostname, IP address, group, or username. For example, the following .htaccess file will limit access to those accessing your site from the yeoldewidgetshoppe.com domain:

```
AuthType Basic
AuthName 'The Ye Olde Widget Shoppe Secret Widget Society'
AuthUserFile /home/widgets/auth-yowf-secret-widget-society
<Limit GET POST>
order deny, allow
deny from all
allow from .yeoldewidgetshoppe.com
require valid-user
</Limit>
```

## Step 2: Create a Password File

Now we'll create our password file using the htpasswd command. We'll start by creating a login account for user minnieme.

```
[yows]# htpasswd -c /home/widgets/auth-secret-widget-society
minnieme
Adding password for minnieme
New password: ilovedrevil
Re-type new password: ilovedrevil
[yows]#
```

## Step 3: Add to Your Password File

To add more users to the list of valid users in your htpasswd file, type the following at your server prompt:

```
[yows]# htpasswd /home/widgets/auth-secret-widget-society bloomer
Adding password for bloomer
New password: noclap4tink
```

```
Re-type new password: noclap4tink
[yows]#
```

Notice that the only difference is the lack of the -c option, which orders that a new file be created. If you decide to redo this auth-secret-widget-society file, you need only create a new login and password using the -c option.

### Step 4: Test the Access Restrictions

If you view the password file /home/widgets/auth-secret-widget-society, you'll find that the passwords are encrypted. The same security dangers exist for these passwords that exist for those in /etc/passwd. If you use or create a program that allows users to add a new login or change their password for access to your secret widget society directory, test for password integrity.

Now open your Web browser and test the access restrictions by typing the following URL:

```
http://www.yeoldewidgetshoppe.com/secret-widget-society/
```

A window should open that requests a username and password. Figure 28.1 shows such a window. Try using the minnieme username with the ilovedrevil password. If the window disappears and the Secret Widget Society page reveals itself, you have seen success.

Try again, using an incorrect username and/or password, and make sure that access is denied. Figure 28.2 shows the error you would receive.

**FIGURE 28.1**

The user authentication window for htaccess files.

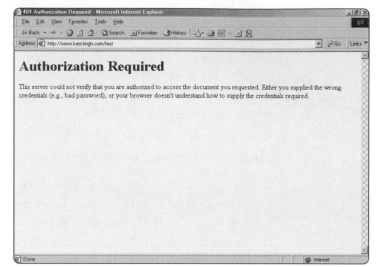

*FIGURE 28.2*

Authentication failed.

## Detecting an Intruder

An *Intrusion Detection System* (IDS) will alert you when it detects suspicious behavior on your system—behavior that indicates that a stranger is in your system, perhaps even with superuser privileges. An IDS might be located on a single machine, or it might protect an entire network. It might look for strange activity, altered files, or activity that had been previously tagged as threatening by the software vendor or the system administration.

An IDS should be able to do the following:

- It should detect behavior that is defined outside of the norm. This could mean that a user is performing abnormal actions, or it could mean that abnormal results are occurring because of a user action.

- It might also be aware of common attack types and styles, so that it can detect a possible attack in the making, no matter how normal or benign the current system activity may seem.

- Although IDSs are, by nature, heavy resource consumers, your IDS should be able to perform its duties without draining the entire system.

- If the system shuts down, the IDS should be able to recover without user intervention.

- Because some cracker attacks are focused on IDSs, your IDS should be able to withstand an attack.
- You should be able to configure the IDS to work with your own unique system. This also means it should respond well to system upgrades.

Here is a list of IDS software you can use on your system:

- Network ICE—**http://www.networkice.com/html/ products.html**
- Cisco Intrusion Detection System—**http://www.cisco.com/warp/ public/cc/pd/sqsw/sqidsz/**
- RealSecure—**http://www.iss.net/securing_e-business/ security_products/intrusion_detection/index.php**
- Kane Security Monitor—**http://www.intrusion.com/Products/ monitor.shtml**

## Responding to an Attack

When an attack occurs, you must be on your toes, cleaning up the mess the attacker made, getting your system back online, finding out how the attack occurred, and patching the holes the attacker used to infiltrate your system.

This section discusses the elements of recovery from attack: how to do it, and how to prepare for it.

### Understanding the Importance of Backups

We've already discussed why backups are important as a method of recovery. Besides, that much is obvious—if you don't have a backup, you can't restore any files you lose during an attack.

By backing up your system, you prevent crackers from doing permanent damage to your system. Some cracking attacks are meant solely to cause a disruption of service to your customers. If a mean, nasty cracker deletes all your files on your site, you can rest assured that service is disrupted for only as long as it takes you to reload the files to your Web server. The attack would be successful if your backup plans require more than a few hours to implement.

Your security policy should clearly outline how to restore the system via backups after an attack. Even if your backups are offsite, you should have the capability to restore functionality to your server within hours—at the very most—of the attack so that business as usual only experiences a minor hiccup.

Once again, we must stress the importance of using offsite backups unless you have the time, money, and resources to properly protect your system and data onsite.

## Plugging the Holes

Naturally, after an attack occurs, you'll want to make sure it doesn't happen again. Your first inclination may be to shut down everything related to the problem, but this is hardly useful. By doing so, you deny either your customers or your employees access to something they once used often. You make their lives more difficult...and that isn't productive.

Instead of turning off functionality, do some research. There may be a way to take away a small bit of convenience in order to maintain current functionality with higher security. What steps can you take to find the information you need? Then when you find the culprit(s), you should try to help others who might face the same risks.

### Looking for Answers

After you experience an attack, try these suggestions to find your vulnerabilities:

1. Look at your software documentation, including any alerts posted at the software company's Web site. The creator of the software may have a download or a set of instructions you can use to patch the hole.

2. If you are unable to find any information at the software company's site, contact the company. You may be one of the first to fall victim to this particular weakness, and the company will want to know about it.

3. Look at security sites to find others who have encountered the same problem or who found the potential hole before it was exploited. Experiment with their recommended fix to see whether your site is still vulnerable.

4. If all else fails, come up with your own patch, publicize the problem, and wait to see if the software company comes up with a solid fix.

### Where to Publish Your Findings

If your company policy allows you to disclose details of attacks, you might consider giving back to the community by posting your own security hole—now patched, of course—online so that others are aware of the new bug in whatever software or of the new attack style. Naturally, you won't want to publish anything if the bug is already public knowledge and your company failed to patch the hole before a cracker took advantage of it.

**TIP** If the bug that allowed an attack can be traced to a weakness in software, remember to contact the company that created the software. Give it the opportunity to take action before you tell the world about the weakness. It may be able to create a fix for the problem that works better than any patch you or others might have used, and the company will have an opportunity to contact its customers about the problem.

## Responding Quickly

When attackers already have hit your system for the sole purpose of destroying data, why give them the pleasure of knowing they also caused a denial of service to occur? The only way to address an attack is quickly. If you have set procedures in place to deal with the aftermath of an attack, your customers may hardy recognize that anything bad happened.

Again, keep in mind that a side-effect of many attacks is denial of service. If your response is swift and sure, you'll avoid the problems associated with this side-effect.

## Reporting the Attack to Officials

After an attack occurs, your company's policy may be to sweep it under the rug and continue to pretend impenetrability to both customers and the general public. Many companies choose not to publicize an attack and do not pursue the prosecution of crackers because they don't want to lose trust from their customers or the public.

However, keep in mind that pretending that the problem never happened means three things:

- The crackers are still on the loose, possibly richer, knowing they got away with it and telling all their friends about how they managed the attack.
- That same attack may be used against another company.
- If crackers know you won't prosecute, they may try to return to the scene of the crime and attack again.

When a cracking attempt occurs, you can take steps to inform officials of the attempt. When a successful attack is launched against your site, you have ample opportunity to turn over documentation of the attack to officials and the possibility of seeing the cracker prosecuted.

You can contact the following people:

- First, let the software vendor know of the vulnerability the cracker exploited. Give the vendor an opportunity to create a patch before the news becomes public.
- Also consider contacting vendors of security software you may be using. If a cracker circumvented their security measures, they'll want to know.
- Then contact the system administrators for other affected servers. Can you trace the origins of the attack, for example, at least back one server? Did the cracker use your site to attack another?
- Many local law enforcement agencies have become more aware of the dangers related to computer security and will actively investigate security incidents. Contact your local police department in case of such an incident. Also look into state and international law enforcement if you have reason to believe that either or both should be involved.

- Contact your local FBI field office (you can find yours at **http://www.fbi.gov**).

You can also find more information about reporting computer crimes from the following sources:

- Critical Infrastructure Assurance Office—**http://www.ciao.gov/**
- National White Collar Crime Center—**http://www.nw3c.org/home.htm**
- National Infrastructure Protection Center—**http://www.nipc.gov/**
- Computer Crime and Intellectual Property Section of the Criminal Division of the United States Department of Justice—**http://www.cybercrime.gov/**

## Attending Seminars and Conferences

The following list of seminars and conferences can help you become better educated and remain knowledgeable about security issues:

- MISTI—MIS Training Institute—**http://www.misti.com/**
- InfoSec—**http://www.misti.com/conference_show.asp?id=OS01**
- National Information Systems Security Conference—**http://csrc.ncsl.nist.gov/nissc/**
- Computer Security Conference—**http://www.gocsi.com/**
- SANS—**http://www.sans.org/**

## Conclusion

You should prepare for an attack, even when you don't expect one. In this chapter, you learned how to prepare for an attack by setting out procedures in your security policy, employing methods of prevention, using intrusion detection systems, carrying out recovery procedures, and reporting any attacks to the proper people.

C H A P T E R    2 9

# AVOIDING THE DANGERS OF INTERACTIVE WEB SITES

**In This Chapter**

Analyzing Scripts and CGI for Risks

Safeguarding Databases

Practicing General Good Sense

A Web site without some form of interactivity is, invariably, a site on its way to the Web graveyard. Yet each day, more users turn off their browsers' capabilities to display interactive features at Web sites. Why? Because of security issues. In this chapter, we discuss the dangers of interactive features provided by plug-ins, ActiveX, Java and JavaScript, CGI scripts, and databases.

## Analyzing Scripts and CGI for Risks

Scripting languages are great for adding a bit of excitement to your Web pages. JavaScript can issue pop-up windows to draw users' attention to some element of the page. Perl and PHP can be used to interact with the database, create on-the-fly pages according to the identity of the user or even the date, and help you track page use. These languages can be very handy tools.

They can also be the cause of some potentially serious security problems, however. Let's look at each of these three tools—JavaScript, Perl, and PHP—to consider the problems you might encounter by including them on your site and how to overcome those potential problems.

### Limiting Interactivity

Interactive Web sites have become customary fare for Web surfers. Unfortunately, many tools used to create interactive Web sites are rife with security issues. Such tools include Netscape plug-ins (which are probably the most secure of any tool used today), Java, and ActiveX. Each of these has its own means of dealing with security issues. Users trust these tools less each day, however, as news anchors increasingly tell tales of horror related to the abuse of these tools.

**NOTE** When you build your site, keep in mind that many users will have turned off their Java and ActiveX capabilities. They'll refuse to download a plug-in. They'll even disable JavaScript. Remember to give these users the option of viewing your site without missing content and without risking the security of their systems and data.

## JavaScript

JavaScript is great for manipulating the browser window itself, as well as including interactive features inside the window. You can use JavaScript to validate a form, for example, forcing users to fill it out completely before activating the Submit button. You can also use this language to force your own set of messages into browsers' status bars, located in the lower left corner of the window.

Unfortunately, these great features of JavaScript also make it the tool of choice when crackers decide to use Web spoofing—a.k.a. a *mirror world* attack—on your site. With this tool, crackers can fool users into coming to their site, and those users believe they are actually on yours. Meanwhile, the crackers are capturing your users' login and password information, credit card numbers, and anything else they choose to request from the unknowing users.

What can you do about this? Not much. Users can turn off JavaScript capabilities on their browsers, disallowing any of this spoofing activity to occur. But if your site uses JavaScript in any way, they might have it turned on. Most users enact low security settings on their browsers.

You can watch for links on the Web that seem to go to your site but actually don't. Also, stay in touch with customers. Remember that active attacks of this flavor will be propagated via e-mail that uses HTML to create links to the mirror world site. Be aware when suspicious e-mail goes out to your customers. Include your own employees on customer mailing lists to ensure that only your own e-mails go to the customer group.

Along the same vein, protect your e-mail lists like you do credit card numbers. Encrypt them if necessary, but at the very least, don't sell them to the world. It's bad customer service to spread your customer e-mail list to anyone willing to pay (and there are plenty willing to pay for a valid list of e-mail addresses). But you also may endanger your customers if a less-than-honorable group gets your list and approaches your customers pretending to be your company.

## Perl and CGI

CGI, or *Common Gateway Interface,* is a powerful tool for interacting with the server during a user's session at your site. CGI can be implemented using Perl, shell scripts, and executables written in languages such as C/C++.

**CAUTION** Never, ever, ever use shell scripts for CGI. Anything you can do in a shell script (such as ksh, tcsh, sh, bash, etc.), you can do in Perl. Shell scripts are very insecure and open the door to security issues that could affect the operation of your server, as well as the integrity of the data it holds.

Although C/C++ is faster than Perl because it is compiled rather than interpreted, it's not as secure. Be sure to investigate the potential security issues of C/C++ if you choose to use that language.

No matter which language you use, the following tips will help you create solid programs with security in mind:

- Plot out your program, no matter how small, using flowcharts or other means to check the logic you intend to use. If your program encounters logical errors during execution, you may open your system to attack.

- Watch for side-effects caused by your program's manipulation of data. If a side-effect could potentially cause a fatal error, your program may open the system to attack.

- Check HTML input fields for bad data. In Perl, you can strip out dangerous characters or isolate input that matches a particular format. In a field where users must enter their e-mail address, for example, you might match alphanumeric characters, periods, and the @ symbol, or you may choose to eliminate white space, semicolons (;), ampersands (&), etc.

- Limit the size of input text fields using the MAX parameter.

- Remember that crackers may try to save your form to their hard drive, alter parameters and input information (such as options in a select field), and submit directly from their hard drive. Filter requests that don't come from your own server, and check that any hard-coded values from a form are valid.

- Validate parameters before you pass them to the shell. If you're programming in Perl, you can use the `-T` (taint) flag (`#!/usr/bin/perl -T`) for automatic checking of possibly tainted variables before they go to the system. This function also taints any variables "touched" by the automatically tainted user-supplied values. You can untaint a variable by using character-matching and regular expressions. The taint flag also requires that you define the `PATH` environmental variable if you plan to use system calls within your program.

- Don't put any dangerous executables in your cgi-bin directory, and limit the scope of any scripts that reside in that directory. Use the /tmp directory for any temporary or lock files you use, for example.

- Use absolute pathnames for everything.

- Set permissions on your CGI scripts to ensure that they are not world writable.

- Check exit values of system calls to ensure that a fatal error has not occurred or will not occur.

- If your program dies, make sure it exits gracefully.

- Anticipate crackers. Go through your program and find ways to crack your own system.

- Keep access log files, if your server does not, that let you know how the program executes each time. Did it fail? Where? Why? What time? What was going on in the system at the time of failure?

- Know which methods of system access are secure and which are not for the programming language you use.

- If you must use SUID (setuid) or GUID (getuid), isolate the code that accesses the system in SUID/GUID mode. Make sure that the access is minimal in this mode and that the code that runs in this mode does not interact directly with the rest of the code in your program.

- Watch for potential denial-of-service issues with your scripts. Can your program deadlock over resources? Can it enter an infinite loop at some point? Set your server to time out any process that runs beyond a reasonable amount of time to ensure that these denial-of-service issues never come up.

- Test your system. Then test it again. Then test it with others. Then in the spirit of good engineering process, bring your changes or implementations before a board of review to ensure that your programs run efficiently, effectively, and securely. Then test your system again.

## PHP

PHP, a hypertext preprocessor that allows you to create dynamic Web pages, has its own set of security issues of which you should be aware. Any amount of dynamic page design has its inherent problems, because you use user input (whether direct or not) to influence what happens on a page. Just as with CGI, you must be careful to watch for potential security holes in your code.

To start, be sure to implement the level of security your server requires during installation. Read the documentation included with your version of PHP to be sure you are aware of the holes you can close before anyone has the opportunity to exploit them. You can also run your scripts in "safe mode," which is similar to the taint mode you can use for Perl—in both cases, the interpreter/parser will disable certain potentially harmful actions.

---

### Secure Perl System Access

If your CGI program accesses the shell to perform some task, know your options and choose the level of security that best fits your needs.

Obviously, if your program is very restricted and accessible to a very small number of trusted people, you need not be quite as concerned about the level of security of each system call method.

Consider the following code snippets:

```
$user_input = $query->param('user_input');
'/usr/bin/go $user_input';              #very dangerous!
system '/usr/bin/go $user_input';       #still dangerous!
system '/usr/bin/go', $user_input;      #much better!
$user_input =~ m/[a-zA-Z0-9\._@]*/;
system '/usr/bin/go', $user_input;        #much, much better!
```

In general, you should exercise the same judgment with PHP that you would with any other method of dynamic design or interactivity:

- **Trust no one.** Believe that there's a user out to cheat or break your system. If you design your code as if you were a paranoid freak, you'll probably save yourself some grief.

- **Check everything.** Input, return values, signals, etc. should receive equal attention in your scripts. Don't allow anything to pass you by when it could cause fatal errors for users or even your system.

- **Use every precaution.** Don't think that one small hole will never be found—it will! Avoid the financial loss and the huge stress by plugging every hole you can find, and then cement that solution with stronger adhesive.

- **Trust no one.** Everyone is out to get you.

If you keep these thoughts in mind, you may actually come through unscathed.

## Safeguarding Databases

Almost every commercial site online now uses at least one database to supply information to the pages, to track users at the site, and to deal with every facet of making a sale to customers. The type and amount of information stored in databases makes for quite a tempting source of illegal activity for crackers.

Because every database package has its own set of security problems and implementations, we'll forgo a discussion of the individual software and look instead at what you can do in general to secure information you keep in your database.

## Segregating Data

You might consider the value of using more than one database to store information. Your customer database might be separate from your product database, for example. Naturally, if you have a large system, separate databases might be ideal to begin with. Smaller operations may need only one database to store all information, however, from tracking affiliates to the product price list.

When you segregate data, use a different set of usernames and passwords for accessing each. We don't mean that customers will need several usernames and passwords to access their accounts—we mean, for example, the username and password required by your system's database interface to connect to the database. If crackers manage to compromise one database, they may not necessarily have the tools to automatically grab information from another database—they'll have to start from scratch to determine the new passwords.

## Encrypting Sensitive Information

Encryption of sensitive information may seem like common sense, but some companies have refused to recognize the importance of this necessary procedure. In 1999, a cracker managed to obtain a list of credit card numbers from a *plain-text listing on an e-commerce server.* Not only were the numbers in readable form, but they were stored in a flat text file, providing no additional security to the sensitive data.

Clearly, this is unacceptable.

When you record sensitive information, such as credit card numbers, personal identification information, passwords, etc., encrypt it. Every roadblock you place in the crackers' way is one more deterrent to them compromising your system. Check your database software documentation to find out how to encrypt sensitive data fields in your database tables.

## Setting Privileges

The account that accesses your database from the Web site should *not* have the same access privileges as the account your marketing department has. Your marketers might need access to add product descriptions to the product table, for example. They might need to deactivate or delete a product that your company no longer sells to the Web public. Do you want to leave a potential hole in your database that allows your customers to do the same if they're wily enough? Certainly not.

Likewise, do you want your engineers to have access to your customer database? Do you want them to be able to read personal and sensitive information about anyone who's registered at your site? Probably not, unless some element of their job requires them to have this type of access.

Remember one of the tenets of good security—that of least privilege. Give users the least amount of privilege they can have and still be able to do what they need to do on your Web site. In most cases, a read-only privilege will do just fine. Where their personal information is concerned, however, you'll want them to be able to add, modify, and delete at will in order to retain control over their own information.

## Practicing General Good Sense

What can you do, in general, to ensure that your site is as secure as you can make it?

- Check all return values during the execution of scripts or programs.

- Limit the size of input to avoid the overflow of your buffer.

- Give users the opportunity and capability to quickly and easily report any problems they encounter. Follow up on those problems and address them immediately.

- Document all code thoroughly, both with comments and with external and easy-to-read user documentation to ensure that new developers or managers can pick up where the last developer left off.

- Use version control of your code to ensure that your scripts can return to the last known stable state if the new version does not work out.

- Check all input, and weed out anything that isn't expected of that input or that could potentially cause problems. If you ask for an e-mail address, for example, be sure to check it against a regular expression that looks for a series of alphanumeric characters, possibly including dashes or periods, followed by an "at" (@) sign and another series of alphanumerics, plus dots and dashes. This way, you automatically weed out semicolons, slashes, and other evil characters.

- Isolate directories for particular purposes so that PHP files will be parsed only if they're in your /php directory, CGI files will be executed only if they're located in your /cgi-bin directory, etc.
- Don't put any shell commands or executable programs in your cgi-bin directory.
- Use safe mode or taint mode for all your files.
- Trust no one.

## Conclusion

Although security issues abound where interactivity is concerned on Web sites, you can improve the safety of your site for your users and yourself by following a few easy procedures. Whether you offer visitors an alternative to plug-ins, ActiveX, and Java; or you use sound programming and engineering principles in designing and executing CGI code, you help both yourself and your customers by being more security-minded. Your customers will thank you for it, and your boss may decide not to fire you.

# PART VII

# TRACKING TRAFFIC TO BENEFIT YOUR SITE

# USING REFERRER AND SESSION LOGS

**In This Chapter**

Tapping the Power of Referrer Logs

Using Session Logs to Track Activity

Suggested Software

Often, a company will spend an enormous amount of time improving its site in an effort to build traffic. The company's Web master will analyze the site's design, optimize pages for the search engines, develop an impressive security system, and so forth.

Then that Web master will totally drop the ball when it comes to analyzing the site's valuable traffic.

If you don't take time to analyze your traffic, you won't have the full picture of your Web site, and you won't be in a position to make changes based on proven experiences and patterns.

Analyzing referrer log files is one of the final steps in Web site analysis—part of the "bottom line." It's the measuring tool for determining the success of your analysis efforts.

In this chapter, you'll learn what referrer logs are and why they're so important. Then you'll discover exactly what you need to be looking for in your referrer logs. You'll also look at using log files to find dead links on your site and using session logs to track clickstream sales.

## Tapping the Power of Referrer Logs

When someone visits your site, server software counts and tracks, or *logs*, that visit. The software also keeps a record of it for a certain period of time. Some of that saved information is called a *referrer log*.

Referrer logs can help you analyze the traffic to your site, and you can use that information to strengthen your online business.

Although each referrer log offers slightly different information, let's look at some of the more common information you can get from a referrer log file:

- Which engines have sent you traffic
- What keywords were used to find your site
- Which pages were accessed the most or the least
- Which spiders have visited your site
- The user profile by region
- Average length of time someone remains on your site
- Average number of user sessions or page views per day

- Top entry and exit pages
- Top-referring sites
- Summary of activity by day
- Server errors
- Bandwidth, which is the measure (in kilobytes of data transferred) of the traffic on the site
- Type of technology used by your visitors.

But isn't simply glancing at your traffic log files enough? Why do you have to analyze them? This section shows you how to get the most from the information that referrer logs have to offer.

 **TIP**    For an article comparing packet sniffing to log file analysis, visit **http://www.webtrends.com/ solution/whitepapers/packet.htm**.

## Understanding the Importance of Referrer Logs

Using referrer logs, you'll learn which engines are sending you the most traffic. You then can boost your optimization strategies for those engines by creating additional pages for other relevant keyword phrases. This could increase your traffic even more.

Or, if you know that you're not getting any traffic at all from a particular engine, you'll be able to consider strategies for findability in that engine.

Through your referrer logs, you may discover that you're being found through keyword phrases that you haven't even considered before. If that's the case, you certainly don't want to change those pages and lose the traffic. Or, if you're being found under a keyword phrase in one engine, wouldn't it be worth creating pages for the other engines for that same keyword phrase to see if you can bring in some additional traffic?

You can also find out through which pages you're losing visitors. Why are you losing visitors? What changes can you make to keep them from leaving?

By the same token, with referrer logs, you can learn through which pages you are gaining the most traffic. What strategies are you using on those pages that you can transfer to other pages?

Simply put, a referrer log can give you an enormous amount of information and serve as a road map for future changes to your site.

## Viewing Your Referrer Logs

Ask your ISP to provide referrer logs in extended log format. Then you'll probably want to use a software program to help you read and analyze the data.

Referrer log information in raw data form isn't exactly easy reading. Here's an example:

```
208.148.200.54 - - [1/May/2001:21:03:36 -0800] "GET /index.html HTTP/
1.0" 200 4356 "http://www.altavista.com/cgi- bin/query?
pg=aq&text=yes&d0=1%2fmay %1f01&q=relationship+marketing%2a
+AND+relationship marketing%2a&stq=30" "Mozilla/2.0 (compatible; MSIE
5.0; SK; Windows 98)"
```

It's a mouthful, isn't it?

However, through the above entry, you can learn the following:

- The IP address of your visitor—`208.148.200.54`
- The date and time of the visit—`[1/May/2001:21:03:36 -0800]`
- The first file requested—`"GET /index.htm HTTP/1.0"`
- The fact that the request was completed—`200`
- The number of bytes that were transferred—`4356`
- Where your visitor came from and the keywords used to find your site—`"http://www.altavista.com/cgi-bin/query? pg=aq&text=yes&d0=1%2fmay %1f01&q=relationship+marketing%2a +AND+relationship marketing%2a&stq=30"`
- Browser and operating system of the visitor—`"Mozilla/2.0 (compatible; MSIE 5.0; SK; Windows 98)"`

Although the raw data provides valuable information to you, you can easily see that it requires some effort to analyze it yourself.

Figure 30.1 shows an example of some data from a referrer log program. The data shows the top-referring search engines for this sample Web site.

You can see how much easier it is to study referrer log information when analyzed by a software program. Later in this chapter, we

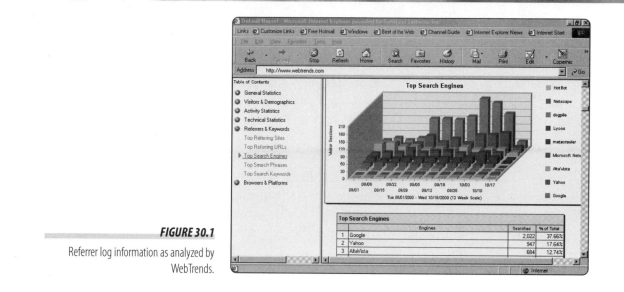

**FIGURE 30.1**

Referrer log information as analyzed by WebTrends.

discuss some free and pay software programs that will analyze your referrer logs for you.

## Analyzing Referrer Logs

When analyzing your referrer log information, what should you look for?

- **Number of page views per day.** Page views (or page impressions) refer to how many "hits" your site has had to HTML pages only. A hit is an action on a Web page, such as when a user views a Web page.

- **Number of user sessions per day.** A *user session* refers to the activity of one visitor to a Web site.

- **How long users are staying on your pages.** How long did users stay at your Web site? Are they finding what they're looking for, or are they getting frustrated and leaving? If visitors are immediately clicking out of your site, maybe it's time to set up an onsite search engine. After all, once you get visitors to your site, you want to make sure they find what they're looking for. We discuss onsite search engines in Chapter 31, "Tracking with Log Files from Onsite Search Engines."

**TIP**

*FIND IT*
**ONLINE**

Ginette Degner, Professional Search Engine Optimizer and owner of Search Engine Services (**http://www.searchengineservices.com**), explains that the length of time users spend on the site tells her whether they're actually reading the pages or clicking in only to leave immediately. This lets her know if she's conveying the purpose of the site adequately. Perhaps her pages are listed under the wrong keyword phrases, and visitors aren't finding what they're looking for and immediately leave.

- **Most-requested and least-requested pages.** Which page is getting the most visits? Look closely at the content and simply produce more of the same throughout your site. Which page is getting the least visits? This information can tell you which areas of the site might need to be expanded or dropped altogether.

- **Top entry pages.** How are people first coming into your site? Which pages are bringing you the most traffic? What about some of your other pages? What can you do to make them top entry pages, too?

- **Top exit pages.** Where are you losing visitors from your site? What offsite links are your visitors clicking on the most? Do you need to revamp the page in order to retain your visitors? Or do you need to get rid of the page altogether?

- **Single-access pages.** Which pages are being viewed by themselves, where visitors aren't even clicking to go to another page? Look at these pages to see what you can provide on the page to keep up the interest of your visitors.

---

### Using Top Exit Pages Information to Strengthen Your Site

Ginette Degner offers this example of using the top exit pages information in the referrer log file to strengthen a client's site.

*A client insisted upon having a second intro page that played their radio commercial, so you clicked on the index page to enter and were stuck in a second media-enhanced page. We could see half of our traffic leaving right there and going no further into the site, which was a really big clue that it was a turn off to the surfing public.*

*A lesson to corporate sites—a Web site is the wrong place to be vain. Serve up your product or service immediately or pay the price with an impatient dotCom'r.*

- **Errors, such as 404 pages.** If your visitors encounter too many error messages when visiting your Web site, the professional image of your site will fall, and you may lose your visitors along with the sales.

- **Most active countries.** If you want a corner of the international market, study this data carefully. How many user sessions are being generated for each country that's important to your business? Are you creating highly targeted information pages for your international keywords?

- **Top-referring sites and URLs.** Are the top-referring sites members of your affiliate network? How many of your affiliates are sending you traffic? If you're not getting much traffic through affiliate links, you need to look closely at your affiliate program and do some revamping.

- **Top-referring search engines.** Which search engines are sending you the most traffic? Create additional pages for those engines and try to boost your traffic. Do you have some top-ranking pages in certain search engines, but you're not seeing coinciding traffic through those engines? If so, you may need to rethink your keyword strategy, because those impressive #1s won't do you any good if traffic doesn't follow.

- **Keywords that searchers are using to find your site.** If you're being found under a particular keyword in one engine but not another, boost efforts in the other search engine and try to bring in more traffic. Also, study this section closely for any holes in your keyword-thinking strategies. Are you being found by keywords that you didn't know you were being found under? Can you create additional pages optimized for those keywords for some of the other engines?

- **Browsers used by your visitors.** Check periodically to make sure that the technology offered at your Web site can be used by the majority of your visitors. In other words, if many of your visitors are accessing the Web using older browsers, you will want to be careful about using technology that will prevent them from fully using your Web site.

- **Visiting spiders.** Which search engine spiders have visited your site recently? When did they spider your site, and how many pages? After submitting your pages to the engines, be sure to monitor this section closely for spider activity. How long did it take for the spiders to hit your pages after submission, and how long did it take for the pages to make it into the indexes? Watch for patterns.

Also remember to compare a site's traffic from month to month to see how your overall promotion efforts are working.

**TIP**    For an excellent article on referrer log programs, visit the Web Developer's Virtual Library at **http://www.wdvl.com/Internet/Management.**

## Using Your Log Files to Find Dead Links

One of the first sections you should review in your referrer log file is your listing of 404 pages. When most visitors find a 404 file, they rarely go back to the root domain to try to find the information. They simply leave.

Plus, 404s signify one thing: unprofessionalism.

Not only that, but some search engines that run across numerous 404s in one domain are beginning to eliminate the entire domain from their index.

So look at your listing of 404s and fix the errors. By doing so, you'll be improving your traffic and your reputation.

Figure 30.2 shows the portion of a referrer log that deals in 404 files.

Eliminate the 404s and problem areas, and you'll have a much more efficient and professional site.

## A Step-by-Step Approach to Analyzing Referrer Logs

Use this step-by-step guide to analyze your own referrer logs. Remember that, depending on the program you use, you may have slightly different entries than what we mention here. This will give you a good guideline to follow, though.

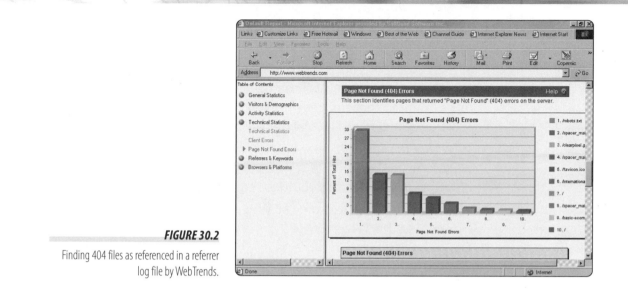

**FIGURE 30.2**

Finding 404 files as referenced in a referrer log file by WebTrends.

Also remember that we include checklists in Appendix C and on the CD-ROM. You can print these checklists and use them while you're doing your own analysis.

- **How many page views is your site getting per day?** Keep track of your page views and compare them from week to week, then month to month. Remember that *page views* (or *page impressions*) refer to how many hits your site has had to HTML pages only. Remember that a hit is an action on a Web page, such as when a user views a Web page.

- **How many user sessions is your site getting per day?** Keep track of your user sessions and compare them from week to week, then month to month. Remember that a *user session* refers to the activity of one visitor to a Web site.

- **How long are users staying on your pages?** The average U.S. user spends 49 seconds viewing a page. What is your average? If it's less than 30 seconds, your visitors aren't staying long enough to buy anything. Are visitors not finding what they're looking for immediately and then leaving? Have you considered setting up an onsite search engine?

- **Which pages of your site are requested the most?** Can you use similar strategies on other pages to boost traffic to those pages?

- **Which pages of your site are requested the least?** Do you need to expand the content of those pages? Do you need to clarify the links going to those pages or link to them more often? Are there any pages you need to consider dropping altogether?

- **What are the top entry pages for your site?** In other words, how are people first coming into your site? What about some of your other pages? What can you do to make them top entry pages, too?

- **What are your top exit pages?** Where are you losing visitors from your site? What offsite links are your visitors clicking on? Do you need to revamp the pages in order to retain your visitors, or do you need to consider changing your navigation or even getting rid of some of the pages altogether?

- **Which pages are being viewed by themselves, where visitors aren't even clicking to go to another page?** What can you provide on the page to keep up your visitors' interest?

- **Do you have any 404 files on your site?** Check the log files for 404 error messages and clean up your site.

- **Are visitors from other countries visiting your site?** If you're trying to work in the international market, check your log files for the most active countries. How many user sessions are being generated for each country that's important to your business? How you can beef up efforts to improve those numbers? Have you created highly targeted information pages for your international keywords?

- **Which sites are sending you the most business?** What sites should be sending you business but aren't? In other words, are you getting business from your affiliate network, if you have an affiliate program in place?

- **What are your top-referring search engines?** Consider creating additional pages for those engines, and try to boost your traffic. If you have some top-ranking pages in certain search engines, but you're not seeing coinciding traffic through those engines, rethink your keyword strategy.

- **Which keywords are searchers using to find your site?** If you're being found under a particular keyword in one engine but not another, boost efforts in the other search engine and try to bring in more traffic. Are you being found under keywords that you didn't know you were being found under? Can you create additional pages optimized for those keywords for some of the other engines?

- **How many of your visitors are using older browsers?** Are you using any technology that will prevent them from fully using your Web site?

- **Which search engine spiders have visited your site recently?** When did they spider your site, and how many pages? Keep track of how long it took for the spiders to hit your pages after submission, and how long it took for the pages to make it into the indexes.

## Using Session Logs to Track Activity

As we discuss in previous chapters, session logs are vital to tracking the effectiveness of your site design and marketing campaigns. Session logs are only slightly different from referrer logs. Instead of parsing log files recorded by the server for each file request, you can actually determine page view information rather than those determined solely by *hits*, which may include image and multimedia files.

In this section, we discuss what session logs are and how you can generate them.

## Defining Session Logs

To begin, let's define the concept of a session log. Earlier in this chapter, we define referrer logs as text files that record hits to your site, giving you valuable information about how users came to your site. Well, now that those users have happened upon your beautiful pages, how are you to determine where they go from there? And just as important, how do you differentiate among different visitors at your site?

In short, a session log is a record of a single user's journey through your site. Unlike with referrer logs, session logs actually record a user's entire *visit* to your site. From here, you can see what the user is doing.

To determine the effectiveness of your site's layout, it helps to be able to track each visitor to your site. Do visitors click through several related pages before leaving? Or do they go directly to the information they wanted, spend some time on that page, then leave? Do they seem to hunt around for your product catalog before finally getting to that page, spending approximately six minutes there, and ordering something, or do they give up after hitting a few areas of your site?

What can session logs tell you about your site?

- How users found the page they just hit
- How long users spent on a particular page
- How many pages users hit before leaving
- What page/area users hit when they decided to leave
- Total time of each visit
- If they return later
- The browser and operating system each user has
- What errors users encounter

Obviously, when looking at this list, it's easy to see the importance of maintaining a session log. However, we must remind you that moderation is key. If you're not careful, you can compromise the privacy of your visitors, and then you'll lose credibility and business.

**TIP** Remember to include information about the data your session logs collect in your privacy policy. Let users know what you're collecting, who will see this information, what they can do to correct or delete the information you've collected, and how you intend to use the data.

## Setting up Session Logs

You have a few choices when deciding how to record visits to your site.

- **Server side includes.** Using SSI, you can pass certain environmental variables to a script to record a user's view of a page.

- **Cookies.** We discuss these in Chapter 8, "Getting to Know Your Customer."

- **Database-driven pages.** With the help of CGI and a database, you can record valuable information about a user's visit in your database, where the data can easily be mined.

- **Parsing server logs.** Although not quite as useful as a full-fledged session log, you can sometimes grab information from servers that have configured their logs to gather enough information for your needs. Simply have your system Administrator configure the server to capture as much information as you need, then write a script or program to find distinct users and patterns within the log files.

- **Web bugs.** Web bugs are unnoticeable scripts that, when called in an HTML <IMG> tag, perform the tracking in secret, returning a clear GIF or other inconspicuous image file. Unfortunately, because many companies have used Web bugs covertly to track users, they have a bad reputation.

- **Non-covert <IMG> tracking.** You can use a Web bug-style method to track users without causing wailing and gnashing of teeth. Simply call on a CGI script through the use of an <IMG> tag, and instead of returning a clear GIF, return an image file that lets users know you've tracked their movement to that page.

You have numerous choices for gathering session log information, but how do you implement the process?

If you use Perl to write your HTML, then within your page-generating script, add the code in Listing 30.1 as a subroutine or a snippet of your whole script.

### Listing 30.1
### Using Perl to implement session logs

```
$hostname = $ENV{'HTTP_HOST'};      #The following environmental
variables tell
$browser = $ENV{'HTTP_USER_AGENT'};      #everything you could wish to
know...almost.
$requesting_ip = $ENV{'REMOTE_ADDR'};
$username = $ENV{'REMOTE_IDENT'};
```

```
$date = $ENV{'DATE_LOCAL'};
open (LOGFILE, ">/my/logfile/path/file");      #Print the Information
you've gathered to a log file…
print LOGFILE
"$date\t$hostname\t$requesting_ip\t$browser\t$username\n";
close LOGFILE;
```

To use an image file, such as a Web bug or a non-covert image, simply include code such as Listing 30.1, as well as the additional return of an image file, shown in Listing 30.2.

### Listing 30.2
### Using an image file to track activity

```
use CGI;
$page = new CGI;
$img = "/home/httpd/html/imgs/myimg.gif";     #Define the image file,
open it, and print it
open (IMG, "$img");         #to the Web page
$img_size = -s $img;
read IMG, $return, $img_size;
print $page->header(-type=>'image/gif'), $return;
close IMG;
```

Remember, if you use script-generated pages, you can also create a unique ID for users for a specific session, and then pass that ID from page to page. Consider this example:

```
use CGI;
$page = new CGI;
$ID = $page->param('ID');
…
print qq[<a href="/goto/new/page/page.cgi?incoherent=yes&ID=$ID">Want
a new job?</a><br>];
```

## Suggested Software

Referrer log software ranges from free to rather costly, depending on the quantity and quality of information it supplies.

Some host servers provide referrer log analysis programs for their members, so check with your host server to see what log analysis

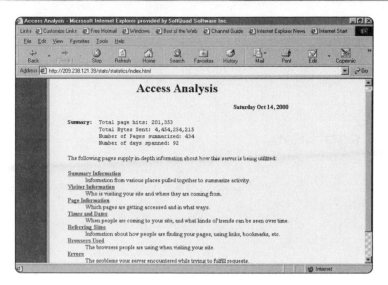

**FIGURE 30.3**

An analysis by MKStats listing links to various categories.

programs are available to you.. In Figure 30.3, you'll see the analysis information that's provided by MKStats for Verio members.

Remember, you can use server logs and the software listed below to generate lists of sessions. You need only parse the resulting files to determine individuals among the page hits.

These programs are available for free:

- Analog—**http://www.statslab.cam.ac.uk/~sret1/analog**
- Webalizer—**http://www.mrunix.net/webalizer**
- eXTReMe Tracking—**http://www.extreme-dm.com/tracking/ ?home**
- Northern Web's Keyword Sniffer (free Perl script)—**http:// www.northernwebs.com/set/kw_install.html**
- bitlog—**http://www.yassou.net/devel/**

The following programs are available for a fee:

- WebTrends—**http://www.webtrends.com**
- FlashStats—**http://maximized.com/products/flashstats**
- Funnel Web—**http://www.activeconcepts.com/prod.html**

**NOTE**

**FIND IT ONLINE** WebTrends also offers a Web-based version of their popular log analysis software. You simply insert a small code onto your pages, and the fee-based service, called WebTrends Live, analyzes your traffic for you. For more information, visit **http://www.webtrendslive.com/ ordertracking_info.htm**.

## Conclusion

You've spent an enormous amount of time and energy analyzing your Web pages in terms of design, search engine placement, Web security, and more. Now that you've seen that hard work pay off in terms of traffic, don't let your efforts go to waste by stopping there.

Take the time to analyze your log files. Find out where you're getting traffic and where you're losing it. Make adjustments accordingly, and watch your site become even more of a raging success.

# TRACKING WITH LOG FILES FROM ONSITE SEARCH ENGINES

**In This Chapter**

Why Do You Need an Onsite Search Engine?

Setting Up an Onsite Search Engine

Translating Log Information into a Better Site

Finding a Site Search Engine

Your site is generating a lot of traffic, thanks to your analysis efforts. You've spent considerable time and energy getting to this point, and you have a right to be proud of your accomplishments.

You're using an impressive and comprehensive referrer log program, and you're analyzing your traffic and applying that knowledge to further strengthen your Web site.

So why would you need an onsite search engine? Your customers are finding you, and you have all the analysis features you need. Why complicate things by adding something else?

This chapter explains the benefits of using an onsite search engine, how simple it is to set one up, and how its vast features can complement your referrer log program.

Learn why it's so important for business sites to offer an onsite search engine, and discover some free and pay programs that can greatly enrich your site.

## Why Do You Need an Onsite Search Engine?

The benefits of an onsite search engine can be divided into two distinct categories:

- Helping potential customers find what they're looking for once they reach your site
- Using log files to track what those customers are looking for

As we covered in Chapter 2, "Analyzing Your Site's Structure for Maximum Accessibility," visitors to your site are generally search dominant or link dominant, with 50 percent being search dominant. Simply put, give your potential customers what they want to see when they visit a site looking for information: a site search engine.

### Helping Customers Find What They're Looking for on Your Site

All your search engine positioning strategies and additional online marketing efforts are in vain if people can't find what they're looking for once they reach your site.

How many times have you conducted a search at a search engine, then visited one of those top 10 sites, only to find absolutely no reference to the topic you're searching for? How much time do you spend digging through the site for the topic? Do you perform a cursory glance at the main page, then go back to the search engine for another try?

Do you want to lose traffic in that manner?

A much smarter option is to provide an onsite search engine and help your visitors find exactly what they're looking for. Even if you've done some rearranging of your site since the spider's last visit, your potential customers can still find what they need quickly and easily.

As stated in Chapter 2, if your site contains more than 200 pages, you need an onsite search engine. Smaller sites will benefit greatly from one as well. Intranets or extranets can also use a site search engine to help organize large amounts of unstructured text.

With services like SearchButton.com, anyone can set up an onsite search engine within minutes, even without server access. Or you can install search engine software on your own server.

**FIND IT ONLINE**   Let's look at an example of a real search performed at the Academy of Web Specialists site (**http://www.academywebspecialists.com**). In Figure 31.1, you'll see a search for "ecommerce training."

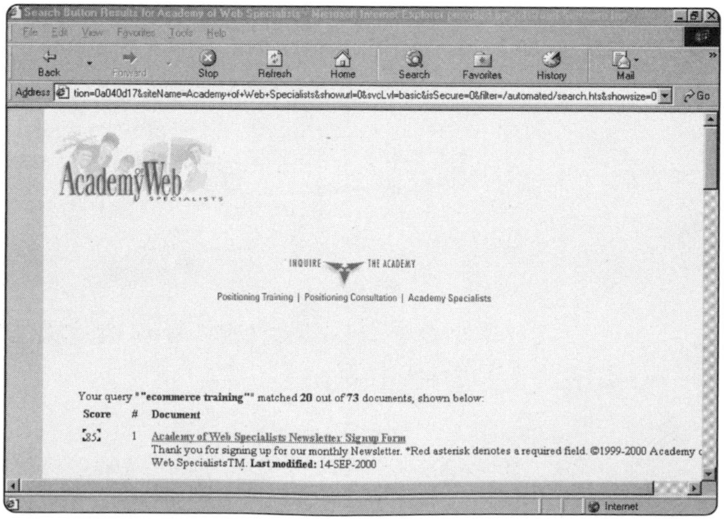

**FIGURE 31.1**

A search for "ecommerce training" at the Academy of Web Specialists.

Let's take a look at the valuable information that an onsite search engine can provide to a Web owner.

## Using Log Files to Track What Those Customers Are Looking For

Besides giving your potential customers easy access to your content through an onsite search engine, you can learn valuable information through the log files of the engine—things you can't find out through referrer logs.

**NOTE** Keep in mind, however, that not all site search engines provide logs, so be sure to find out whether the one you're interested in does, if this aspect is important to you.

**FIND IT ONLINE** Figure 31.2 shows a sample screen shot of the most popular searches performed by an onsite search engine, SearchButton (**http://www. searchbutton.com**).

As you can see, Figure 31.2 lets you know what people are searching for once they get to your site. It also lets you know how many results the onsite search engine found for that search.

In Figure 31.3, you'll see a search performed at TechTV, one of InfoSpace's clients. Notice that the search results are returned in a

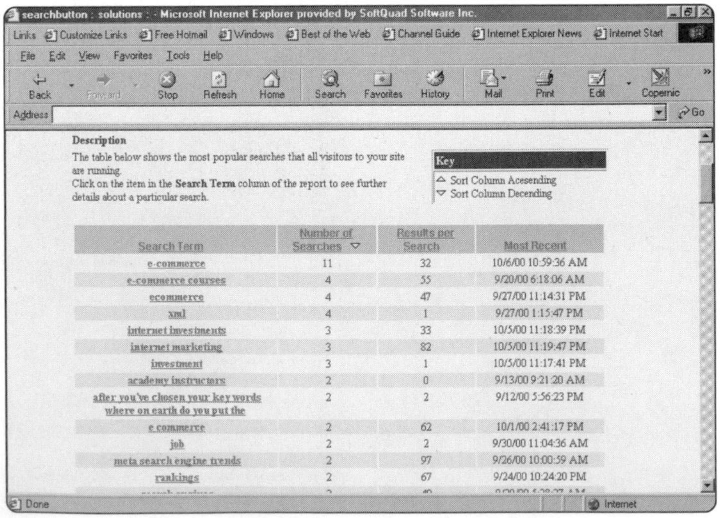

**FIGURE 31.2**

Most popular searches performed at a sample site.

> ## An Added Consideration: Onsite and Offsite Searches in a Branded Environment
>
> Some services, such as InfoSpace, provide both onsite and offsite search capabilities for their clients, all within a branded environment.
>
> In previous chapters, we discuss the importance of branding or name recognition on the Internet. And, because nine out of ten people on the Internet use the Web to search, search capabilities are crucial to the success of a site.
>
> Steve Stratz with InfoSpace explains,
>
> > Search provides a site's users with a necessary tool that will make their experience a pleasant one, and this is where our search offerings are different than our competitors, as we'll provide search (Web and site search) in a site's branded environment. The same is true for other offerings, including yellow and white pages, maps, classifieds, horoscopes, etc. The key here is these services are brand agnostic and improve the user experience.

branded environment: TechTV's. Also, notice that the results actually came from Dogpile, a META search engine owned by InfoSpace.

Notice that the search is branded using TechTV's format, rather than the results appearing to have come from InfoSpace.

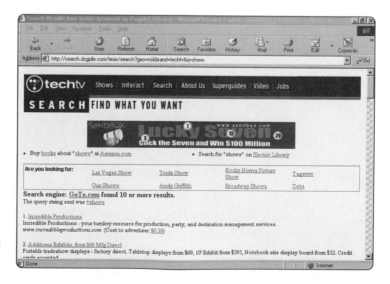

**FIGURE 31.3**

A search performed at TechTV.

## Setting Up an Onsite Engine

If you use a service such as SearchButton.com or Atomz, you simply subscribe to their service, and their spider visits your site and indexes all of the text. With these services, you have no hardware or software to install.

After the spidering is complete, you add a few lines of HTML and a search form, which you can cut and paste from the service's site, and that's it. Your site is now searchable.

Obviously, if you install your own software, you'll have numerous issues to consider. Because there are so many versions of search engine software that operate on different platforms, it's impossible to outline those issues here.

Our main objective is to let you know that there are some very simple solutions to the need for a site search engine—solutions that don't need to cost you three fortunes to set up.

 **TIP** When creating pages on your site, be sure to use title, META tags, and headline tags to make it easy for the site search engine to learn what's relevant on that page.

 **FIND IT ONLINE** SearchButton offers a list of "Hints on Making Your Site More Search Friendly" (see Figure 31.4). View the tips online at **http://www.searchbutton.com/resources/tips.html**.

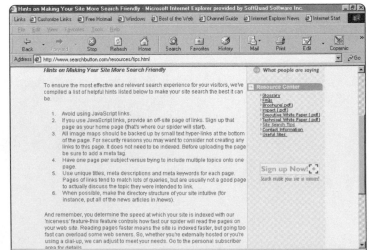

*FIGURE 31.4*

Hints on Making Your Site More Search Friendly, by SearchButton.com.

These tips will help you make your site more searchable for the benefit of your users.

## Translating Log Information into a Better Site

Again, depending on which site engine you choose, you'll have different log files or no log files at all. We'll look at some features included in the more popular site search engines these days and the facts they offer, which you can use to improve your site.

You can use the information you glean from a site search engine with the information from a referrer log program to learn more about the traffic to your site and to make adjustments and changes as needed. Some of the features deserve a more in-depth look, so we'll cover them more thoroughly in this section.

Use this list to test the features of your onsite engine and check the information each provides:

- **Most popular searches.** Which keywords are people searching for when they get to your site? Are you providing enough information about that particular topic? Do you need to create subpages and expand in any way?

- **Most frequent visitors.** Which visitors performed the most frequent searches on your Web site over a certain time period? This report shows the address of the computer visitors were using when searching. Clicking on the address of the computer brings up the search terms each visitor was searching for, the date, and how many pages were found.

- **Searches that produce no results.** This important feature is covered more in-depth later in this chapter. Make sure your onsite engine includes this feature.

- **Summary of searches performed at your site.** With this report, you're able to view the raw search data for your site.

- **Monthly report when errors are found, such as 404s, bad HTML, etc.** Besides learning about 404 error messages, you'll also learn whether any of your pages contain bad HTML. Then you can make changes to your pages so that your visitors won't be presented with an unprofessional Web site.

- **Search activity reports.** Some onsite search engines provide a detailed search activity report, which compiles all search activity on your site into one handy report.

- **Click-through reports.** Where are your visitors going once they get to your site? How often is your server down?

- **Server performance reports.** These reports simply outline how your server is performing.

- **Creating a site map and automatically updating it.** This capability is available with FreeFind; see details on this later in this chapter.

- **Generating a "What's New" page and automatically updating it.** This capability is available with FreeFind; you'll find more information following this list.

- **Content monitoring.** FreeFind allows your visitors to keep a watch on certain pages of your site by notifying them when the content has changed. This is certainly an important traffic builder, because anyone who registers for the service is asking to be invited back to your site again and again.

- **Offsite search capabilities.** InfoSpace provides offsite search capabilities, which means that you can actually be on another site that offers a link back to the original site and then search the original site from that location.

- **E-mail sent to visitors when results of a determined search have changed.** You can use NetMind Search-It's unique tracking system to send out e-mail to visitors when results of a determined search have changed. This valuable feature allows you to "invite" visitors back to your site when you begin offering what they were looking for in the first place. What a valuable marketing tool!

Again, these features won't be available on all of the site search engines. If you have multiple sites, some site engines may search through all of your sites.

## Looking at Searches That Produce No Results

Knowing about searches that produce no results is probably one of the most valuable pieces of information from a site search engine's log files. Think about it. You'll be able to learn what people are searching for that you lack in your pages.

Look over this area carefully. Can you create pages for any of those keywords that produced no results?

If your site actually doesn't provide the information or goods and services, can you refer visitors to another domain to learn more?

For example, if your visitors are searching for "mechanical engineering supplies," but you don't offer those items, do you partner with a company that does? Direct your visitors there!

Figure 31.5 shows a screen shot of a SearchButton report on searches that produced no results.

In this example, four searches were performed for the term "e-commerce." The owners of this site would be smart to create a page that is optimized for that keyword phrase and give visitors what they want to see.

## Creating and Updating a Site Map

FreeFind will automatically generate a site map. When your site changes, it will create a revised map. Considering how helpful site

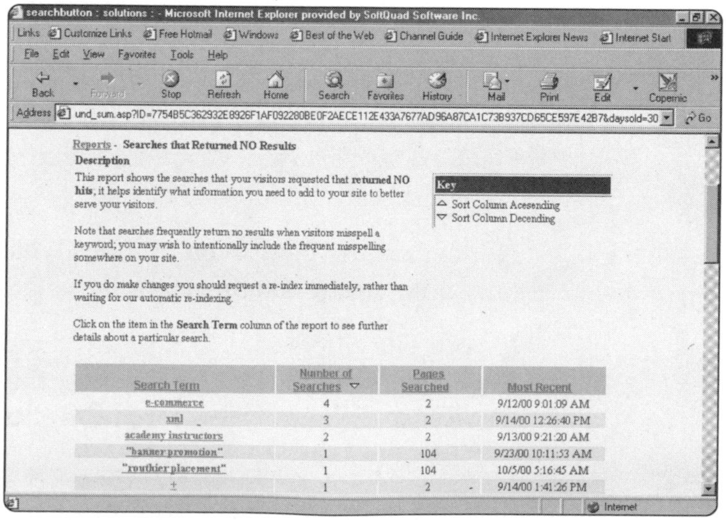

**FIGURE 31.5**

Searches that produced no results.

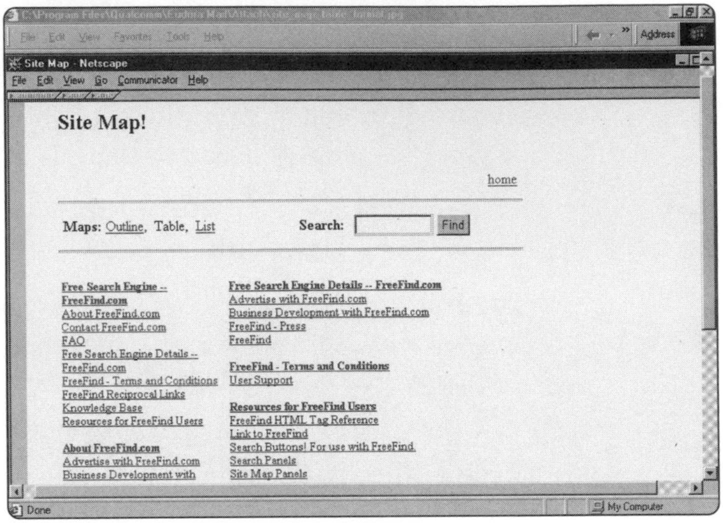

**FIGURE 31.6**

A site map in table format.

maps are to the navigation of your site and to the search engines, this is an extremely valuable feature.

Figure 31.6 shows a site map created by FreeFind, which provides the site map in two formats: outline or table.

## Generating and Updating a What's New Page

FreeFind generates a What's New page for your site. Not only could this could save you an enormous amount of time, but it also could be very beneficial to your visitors by informing them of pages featuring new products, updates to existing product pages, and more.

Figure 31.7 shows a What's New page created automatically by FreeFind.

Notice that the page even outlines what has changed on the site, totally automating the process for you.

If your site offers manuals of any kind, such as software manuals, tutorials, operating guidelines, etc., the What's New page would be invaluable to your visitors for finding out where you've made changes to those manuals.

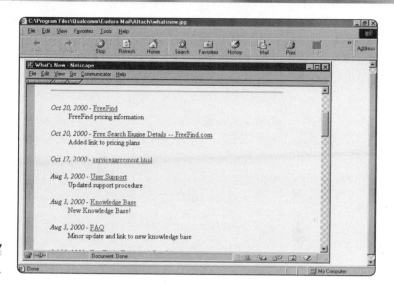

**FIGURE 31.7**

An automatic What's New page.

## Finding a Site Search Engine

Site search engines can be anything from free, simple Web-based search engines to massive programs that cost thousands of dollars. Much depends on how large your site is as well as the size of your pocket book, plus how much time you want to spend setting it up.

Before you choose a site search engine, be sure to see what type of logging capabilities the engine has. If a site search engine doesn't offer valuable logging capabilities, you may want to consider a different engine.

Let's look at some pros and cons of various onsite search engines, starting with SearchButton, FreeFind, ht://Dig, and InfoSpace, and then concluding with a list of other engines you might want to consider.

### SearchButton

**FIND IT ONLINE**

If you want to set up a search engine for your site within minutes with no hardware or software installations, SearchButton (**http://www.searchbutton.com**) is the way to go. Their search engine provides an impressive listing of log files, and the service is customizable.

SearchButton's Customer Support area is second to none, so if you experience any problems, they'll have you back in business in no time.

## FreeFind

Like SearchButton, FreeFind (**http://www.freefind.com**) can be set up within minutes and is located on its server. But unlike SearchButton, FreeFind is free! The initial indexing limit of this free engine is 32MB of HTML or 2,000 pages, but most sites qualify for free expansion upon request.

The features of this program are quite impressive, including automated site maps, automated What's New pages, content monitoring, and logging reports. On the downside, the logging reports FreeFind provides aren't as extensive as those provided by SearchButton, so you'd have to weigh the pros and cons and make a decision as to your unique needs.

What reports does FreeFind generate? The program generates daily site search activity reports, common queries, and most recent queries.

Another helpful feature of FreeFind is that visitors can search on the site itself or perform Web searches. You can schedule the reindexing of your site at any time or at regularly scheduled intervals.

## ht://Dig

ht://Dig (**http://www.htdig.org**) is a free CGI script that works well with large or small sites or even groups of sites. On the downside, the software is difficult to set up. It takes someone with a knowledge of the software running on your server and the configuration of the server to install it.

Once ht://Dig is installed, however, it's impressive and powerful and gives very relevant results.

Another downside is that the program doesn't offer log files, other than a log detailing how the installation went.

ht://Dig comes with installation instructions, and the Web site offers FAQs, a mailing list, and configuration and installation information.

You won't have a Customer Support department to fall back on if you encounter difficulties, however.

## InfoSpace

InfoSpace (**http://www.infospace.com/about/corporate/cobrand.htm**) provides portal packages created around your own unique branding. Services include Yellow Pages, search capabilities, stock quotes, maps, a calendar, an address book, instant messaging, and even Web-based e-mail.

## Other Suggestions

- SiteSearch (**http://www.gd-ind.com/sitesearch/**)—A freeware CGI script that is a good solution for small sites only. It doesn't index the site, so using it on a site containing more than a few hundred pages is impractical because of the time it would take to perform the search.

- site Search (**http://www.agl.uh.edu/~saljxk/site_Search/**)—A search engine written in Perl. This program is shareware, and if you use it for commercial purposes, you'll need to register and pay a nominal fee.

- Excite (**http://www.excite.com/navigate/**)—Excite for Web Servers 1.1 is a free and unsupported software that works on all platforms and helps visitors navigate through your local content. EWS uses Perl, which comes with the product.

- Atomz (**http://search.atomz.com/**)—Atomz.com Search adds a powerful search engine to your site with no hardware or software to install. The service is free for small sites with less than 500 pages. The Results page is customizable with no banner ads. Its Prime Search plan is a pay plan geared toward larger Web sites.

- PicoSearch (**http://www.picosearch.com/**)—PicoSearch is a free, hosted search engine for your site that can be installed in minutes. Basic service is free for sites up to 1,500 pages. The service offers multisite and partitioned searches, and Boolean searches as well.

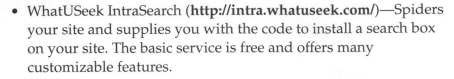

- WhatUSeek IntraSearch (**http://intra.whatuseek.com/**)—Spiders your site and supplies you with the code to install a search box on your site. The basic service is free and offers many customizable features.

- NetMind Search-It (**http://www.netmind.com/html/ wmsearchit.html**)—A free search engine with a unique Web page tracking service that will inform your users by e-mail when the results of a determined search have changed. Search-It is powered by ht://Dig and NetMind.

- Inktomi Search Software (**http://software.infoseek.com/**)— Previously known as Ultraseek Server offered by InfoSeek, Inktomi Search Software is a search engine for Unix-based systems. You can download a trial version and use it for 30 days.

- AltaVista's Hosted Search Services (**http:// solutions.altavista.com/products/hss-overview.html**)— AltaVista provides several different search packages, from a small custom site index to the use of AltaVista's massive Web index.

## Conclusion

Once you get visitors to your site, are you making it easy for them to find what they're looking for? Or are your visitors getting frustrated and leaving, taking their business with them?

The solution is simple. Set up an onsite search engine and point your visitors in the right direction. Not only will you be helping your customers, you'll also have access to valuable log files that can help you provide even better information for your visitors.

# TRACKING ONLINE SALES TO DETERMINE THE EFFECTIVENESS OF MARKETING CAMPAIGNS

**In This Chapter**

Tracking Hits and Sales through Online Advertising Methods

Tracking Software or Services

Strangely, online businesses often don't track their hits, much less their sales, from advertising method to closing of the sale. This is almost unheard of in brick-and-mortar businesses, but the online arena hasn't yet come up to par.

An entire book could be written about tracking sales, and several probably have. In this chapter, we offer some basic suggestions for tracking hits and sales through various online advertising models, and we suggest some software programs to simplify your task.

If you don't track your online hits and sales, how will you know whether the amount it costs you per response or sale is worth the expense?

You won't.

In other words, if you send out a press release, how much did it cost you per sale to send out that release? Is the cost justified based on the response and subsequent sales?

Not only is the cost per sale important, but the amount of people who respond to that ad is important. If your response was great but your sales were poor, you may have fallen down in your sales approach, even though your advertising campaign itself was a success.

If you don't know how much it actually costs you per response or sale, you won't know whether it's worth your while to advertise by that method again or whether it might be more beneficial and cost effective to choose a different method with a better response and less expense.

Tracking sales gives you concrete information about the per-person cost of each form of advertising. It enables you to make educated decisions about future advertising methods based on what actually brought you the most business for the least cost.

Tracking your sales lets you know exactly how effective each advertising campaign really was.

## Tracking Hits and Sales through Online Advertising Methods

Whether you participate in banner exchanges, send out press releases, purchase print ads, or advertise by direct e-mail, you'll want to be able to track your sales to determine the effectiveness of the campaign.

> ### *Creating Customized Splash Pages to Track Sales*
>
> One means of tracking sales is by creating customized splash or entry pages.
>
> Susan O'Neil, president of @Web Site Publicity, Inc. (**http://www.websitepublicity.com**), a Web marketing company specializing in search engine optimization and co-author of *Maximize Web Site Traffic*, explains a very simple method of tracking sales:
>
> > *The Internet provides easy, efficient opportunities to track an organization's marketing efforts. For example, each time I issue a press release, I include the company's URL, and I code the URL differently each time by creating a customized "splash" page to receive any traffic generated by that particular release. So, my first press release would present my URL as **www.websitepublicity.com/pr1**. My second release would be **www.websitepublicity.com/pr2**, etc.*
> >
> > *I do the same thing with each banner ad, each print ad, every newsletter sponsorship and direct mail piece, so I can gauge what language and what formats elicit the best results as measured in web traffic.*
> >
> > *There's no excuse for not tracking results—otherwise you're shooting in the dark. Besides, when it's time again to bring your promotional budget upstairs for approval, won't you be more effective when you can say: X% of your Web traffic was produced by search engine optimization, X% by banner ads, X% by the public relations campaign, etc.? Use your knowledge of past results to fuel future endeavors.*

Chapter 30, "Using Referrer and Session Logs," gives you information on tracking clickstream sales. Also, for more information on getting to know your customers by tracking demographics, see Chapter 8, "Getting to Know Your Customer."

Now let's look at some forms of online advertising for tips on how to track responses and sales through those advertising means.

## Affiliate Programs

Tracking affiliate sales through affiliate software programs is easy, simply due to impressive software programs such as My Affiliate Program.

Affiliate software programs make it simple for you to track sales by assigning a tracking URL to each affiliate. These affiliate numbers can be used on print order forms, banner ads, links, signature lines, and even beside phone numbers as extensions—all are ways to keep track of who recommended the person to your site.

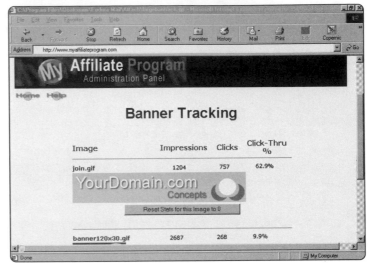

**FIND IT
ONLINE**

Figure 32.1 shows a Banner Tracking Report from My Affiliate Program (**http://www.myaffiliateprogram.com**).

Notice how easy it is to see the click-through percentage for each of your banner campaigns.

With My Affiliate Program, you can also view the current statistics of your affiliate program. Figure 32.2 shows a Current Stats report sorted by affiliate IDs.

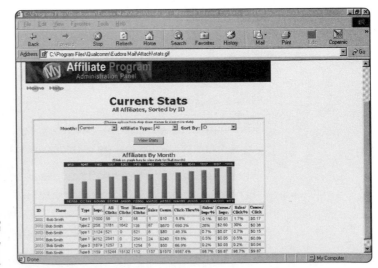

Notice the comprehensive information at your fingertips through these stats.

## Informal Affiliate Programs

*FIND IT*
**ONLINE**

Informal and very small affiliate programs may create separate splash pages for each of their affiliates, with a redirect that takes traffic into the actual site. Then by looking at log files, the affiliate owner can determine where those sales originated. If you want to track your affiliate sales yourself, for example, you can assign separate pages to each affiliate, such as **http://www.myproduct.com/atc.html**.

In this example, the affiliate is given a special page (atc.html), and all traffic routed through that page is credited to that particular affiliate. Although this method is impossible to keep up with on a large scale, it certainly offers the advantage of building a good solid link popularity with related links.

An even more informal means would be to simply include a "How did you learn about our business?" question in your online sales form. Needless to say, this isn't a very effective or efficient means of tracking sales.

## Using Your Affiliate Software Program to Track Other Sales

If you use your own affiliate software program, such as My Affiliate Program, you can use the program to track sales through other forms of advertising, such as press releases, e-mail marketing, online ads, and more.

As you know, most affiliate tracking numbers are rather long and convoluted, and you probably wouldn't want to use them in your advertising campaigns.

Jeff Doak, head of Software Development for My Affiliate Program, explains how to use a short URL and direct traffic through your affiliate program for tracking purposes:

> *Yes, there is a fairly easy way to use a short URL; you simply create a "redirect" page that redirects to your normal affiliate link. So if your normal affiliate link was:*
>
> http://www.theaffiliateprogram.com/cgi-bin/a/b.cgi/3151
>
> *you could create a page called "go.htm" at your domain:*

http://www.acws.com/go.htm

*and that page would include a meta refresh tag. Then in your email ads or whatever, you use the shorter URL to advertise.*

You'll create a new affiliate number just for that campaign, and all sales through that number will be accounted for, giving you a clear picture of the hits conversion to sales for that campaign.

If you don't have your own affiliate software but use a revenue-sharing network such as Commission Junction, be sure to change the percentage of the affiliate sales to 0 percent so that you won't be charged a percentage for those sales.

### Are Using Robots.Txt Files Necessary?

As we discuss in the search engine chapters of this book, having mirror pages is considered spamming by the major engines. So if you create duplicate entry or splash pages for hit-tracking purposes, should you use a robots.txt file to keep the engines out of those pages?

That's certainly a possibility and should be considered, especially if you've fallen out of the rankings for an engine and think there's a possibility of this being a problem. However, Ginette Degner, director of Marketing with Harris Publishing, doesn't go to the trouble:

*With the slashing of personnel at search engines, I do not think there will be enough human power to devote to hanging me out to dry because I have lots of test marketing pages. They are not linked to the true index page and I am not trying to trick anyone. I am only concerned with running my day-to-day marketing efforts, and the search engines are but a part of it.*

*We will also try to tailor the page to the banner ad we have out. For example, if the banner was meant to draw a specific demographic/ theme, we would change the copy on the page to appeal toward that specific group.*

For more information on multiplying the reach of your online business through an affiliate program, see Chapter 6, "Multiplying the Reach of Your Web Site through Affiliate Programs."

## Banner Ads and Exchanges

As we suggested earlier, an excellent way to track traffic from banner ads is by creating duplicate splash or index pages. This will allow you to keep up with which banner ads are bringing you traffic and which aren't, and which you need to forget about in the future.

Using this type of tracking method, you can determine which banners are effective, and even if banners placed in certain places on the page actually bring more traffic than banners placed in other areas.

Degner uses two ways to track banners and their effectiveness. She uses a rotating banner script that shows clicks and exposures broken down into percentages. Then when she buys banner ads, she sends visitors to a special page so she can track the effectiveness of the banner and make sure she's not being cheated if she's paying per click-through. Degner also uses banners or buttons in the lower right-hand corner of a Web page, because this is where the mouse pointer always ends up.

---

### *Banner Tips*

Ginette Degner offers this helpful advice when using banner ads:

*You must remember that people don't go to sites to click on banners. I try to create two types of banners.*

*1. The kind that just makes you click.*

*2. The kind that prequalifies you as my customer.*

*Here's an example of #1:*

*http://www.harrisdigitalpublishing.com/bannerfarm/investor.html*

*The Money Poll Banner is what I use just to get clicks. It does not prequalify anyone, but you are driven to click…just to see what you get! I use this type of banner when buying a cost-per-impression campaign.*

*Here's an example of #2:*

*http://www.harrisdigitalpublishing.com/bannerfarm/images/turbodrop1.gif*

*This is an example of using a banner to prequalify the click-through. We also try to create a banner that does not look like a banner at all. People are more comfortable clicking on what they see as more links in a site.*

## Search Engines and Pay Engines

In Part V, "Creating Engine-Friendly Web Sites," we discuss purchasing keywords through the pay engines. Be sure to monitor your referrer logs closely to keep track of the success of your marketing campaign.

Keep in mind, however, that Dogpile and other META search engines also use GoTo results. So if your figures don't match those of GoTo's, look at your log files for referral traffic from Dogpile, which is where the discrepancies may lie.

Also remember that the top three results at AOL are now from GoTo, and the top two results are from Netscape. That certainly could contribute to discrepancies as well.

---

### *Add a Tracking URL for Your GoTo Account*

GoTo partners with hundreds of Web sites, all of which can send traffic to your site if you purchase keywords from GoTo. A representative from GoTo explains:

*While searches from these sites return GoTo's results, your server logs will not always reflect GoTo's URL. In fact, your logs will sometimes show our partner's URL, not ours. If you would like to track the amount of traffic you receive from GoTo, we recommend that you change the URL you have listed with us to a tracking URL.*

To do this, go to GoTo's DirecTraffic Center (**https://secure.goto.com/s/dtc/center**). To change a URL such as **http://www.mysite.com/** to a tracking URL, add ?source=goto to the end. The URL will look like this: **http://www.mysite.com/?source=goto**.

If the URL already has a question mark in it, you will have to add &source=goto to the end. For example, if your URL is **http://www.mysite.com/search.cgi?q=lightbulb**, you'll change it to **http://www.mysite.com/search.cgi?q=lightbulb&source=goto**.

If the URL has a pound sign (#), the ?source=goto will need to be inserted before the # sign. For example, if your URL is **http://www.mysite.com/#bulldog**, you'll change it to **http://www.mysite.com/?source=goto#bulldog**.

GoTo's rep adds,

*Once you've converted the URL in your listings to a tracking URL, you should be able to look for source=goto in your access logs. If your Web server behaves normally, it should appear once for every click-through on one of your GoTo search results.*

---

**TIP**   If you convert your URL to a tracking URL with GoTo, take time to monitor the new tracking URL to make sure it's working properly. Also, don't put the modified URL on your site or distribute it.

Also, keep in mind that if you modify the URL, the modified listing will appear as a new entry in the search results. This means that if you've bid on a term that other advertisers have bid the same amount for, your listing with the modified URL will appear as the last listing for that item.

The pay engines as well as RealNames have an account area for you to monitor your keyword purchases, so visit those areas and keep track of your visitors.

**FIND IT ONLINE**   If you purchase a lot of keywords through GoTo, the *Keyword Bid Optimizer* (KBO) can help you keep track of the bids and optimize your keyword strategies. Visit **http://www.paidsearchenginetools.com/** to learn more.

## E-commerce Packages

Many e-commerce packages offer tracking capabilities, such as Marketer's Choice. Marketer's Choice offers a fully integrated shopping cart system featuring a tool called Ad Tracker (**http://www.1shoppingcart.com/**). Company representative John Lee explains how Ad Tracker works:

> *Ad Tracker will let you know which of your ads are working, not working, visit-only-with-no-sales, sales, and so on. So using the Ad Tracker, business owners can perform a customized "surgical operation" on their different ad campaigns to maximize the return.*

Simply put, Ad Tracker will track the click-through rate of every ad you create. When you place an ad, you direct the traffic to Ad Tracker first. Ad Tracker records the click and then sends the traffic to your site. This system eliminates the need to create special pages for each ad campaign, and you can visit its site to check the number of hits your ad has received.

Marketer's Choice also offers a Coupon Tracking System that will help you monitor special sales.

## Signature Lines

Don't forget the power of signature lines when considering an online marketing campaign. Use signature lines and have all your employees do the same. Include your company name, URL, possibly a brief statement about the company, phone number, etc.

You can even use a special URL in your signature line to direct traffic through a splash page or a special affiliate URL to track any traffic and subsequent sales that might come from displaying your signature line.

## Press Releases, Phone Tracking, Opt-in E-mail Marketing, and More

When someone contacts your company, whether through e-mail, mail, or the phone, try to track the advertising method used to find your business. The means of tracking the traffic can be anything from a simple print spreadsheet that you can use when you ask new customers how they heard of your business to sophisticated software programs, which we discuss in the next section.

Although it's not feasible to ask every single person who calls or sends you an e-mail where they heard of your business, be sure to do what you can to track the traffic generated from special advertising campaigns by using the strategies mentioned in this chapter.

When possible, run all advertising campaigns through your affiliate software, which will not only tell you the response of each campaign but the resulting sales as well. You'll then have a clear picture of the per-response and per-sale cost of each advertising campaign, and you can determine what's working and what isn't for future ad campaigns.

## Exit Surveys

How much business are you losing to potential customers who abandon your shopping cart? According to BizRate.com, two thirds of e-commerce shoppers abandon their shopping cart after they've selected an item for purchase.

BizRate.com offers a Non-Buyer Exit Survey that will capture feedback from departing visitors at different exit points on your site.

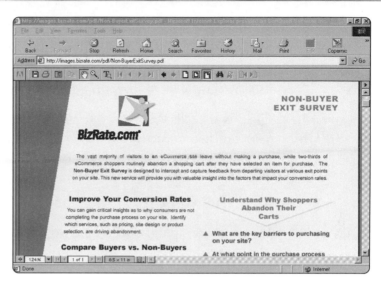

**FIGURE 32.3**

BizRate's Non-Buyer Exit Survey.

Through this survey, you can learn how to improve your conversion-to-sales rate, compare buyers to non-buyers, identify which promotions are successful, and identify which tools motivate visitors to buy.

In Figure 32.3, you'll see a screen shot listing more information on BizRate's Non-Buyer Exit Survey.

***Find It*
ONLINE**

For more information about BizRate.com, visit **http://merchant.bizrate. com/oa/research_consulting/custom_research.xpml**.

## Tracking Time

If you're in a service-oriented business, be sure to track the time your employees spend on various projects.

***Find It*
ONLINE**

Gil Vidals, owner of a successful search engine optimization firm called PositionGeek.com (**http://www.positiongeek.com**), tracks the time each of his optimizers spend on their clients' sites.

Vidals explains,

> *It's important to track the time invested by the SEO in each project, so they can calculate the total return on investment. Keeping track of the time can be done on pencil and paper or via time tracking software.*

*It's important to make sure you are profitable. If you find out that your real rate ends up being $15 per hour, then you have to either make your process more efficient or else charge more. (Actually both would be best.)*

"SEO" stands for Search Engine Optimizer in the above quote.

**FIND IT ONLINE** Clockware sells Web-based time-tracking software called Tock, which you can use to capture time for project cost accounting. Visit **http://www.clockware.com/** to learn more.

## Test the Market

If your ad campaigns aren't paying off for you, rather than scrap them altogether, try making a few simple changes.

Change the headline of the campaign. Revise the "call for action." Cut down the length. Reduce the price. Offer free shipping. Write a more effective ad copy.

Try changing things one step at a time. Track the results. Determine which is the most effective, and take it to the next step.

# Tracking Software or Services

If you use your affiliate software program and run ad campaigns through it, you'll have ready-made tracking software already in place, with very little additional effort.

Besides the programs already mentioned in this chapter, you might consider some other tracking software programs.

### Swiss Army App

**FIND IT ONLINE** The Enterprise Version of Swiss Army App at **http://www.swissarmyapp.com** is an impressive one-stop software program for analyzing your Web site. Features include submitting your site to the engines and FFA (Free For All) sites, checking your link popularity, checking your engine rankings, searching for broken links, analyzing keyword density, and much more.

The program also offers tracking features, such as a Campaign Analyzer that will track the effectiveness of your marketing campaigns

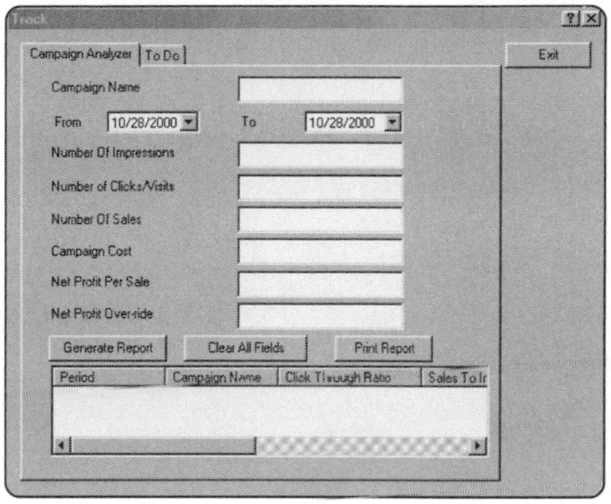

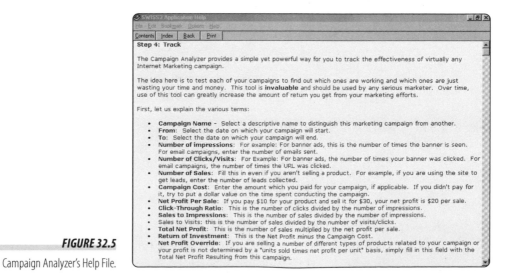

**FIGURE 32.4**

Swiss Army App's Campaign Analyzer.

over time. It automates your marketing testing process by tracking your click ratio, sell ratio, *return on investment* (ROI), and more. And, it allows you to test each of your campaigns to find out which ones are working and which aren't.

Figure 32.4 shows the program's Campaign Analyzer and the type of information that is available through the program, such as Number of Impressions, Number of Sales, Campaign Cost, and more.

Figure 32.5 explains the comprehensive information you can glean from the program.

**FIGURE 32.5**

Campaign Analyzer's Help File.

**FIND IT ONLINE** For more information about Swiss Army App for Web masters (Enterprise Edition), visit **http://www.robinsnest.com/swissarmy.html**.

## CommerceTrends Analysis

**FIND IT ONLINE** WebTrends (**http://www.webtrends.com/products/commerce/default.htm**) offers a software package that will summarize the traffic brought to your site as a result of your marketing campaigns, including the cost of the campaign, the forecasted revenue, and the return on your investment. The analysis includes a visitor conversion ratio of qualified leads to total visits for each marketing campaign.

Figure 32.6 shows a Marketing Campaigns Summary.

The summary is divided up between marketing campaigns, and you're able to see the total revenue, cost, ROI, and percent ROI per campaign.

**FIND IT ONLINE** WebTrends offers several software programs that produce numerous and valuable reports for your site. For sample reports, visit **http://www.webtrends.com/reports/reports.asp?reports=position**.

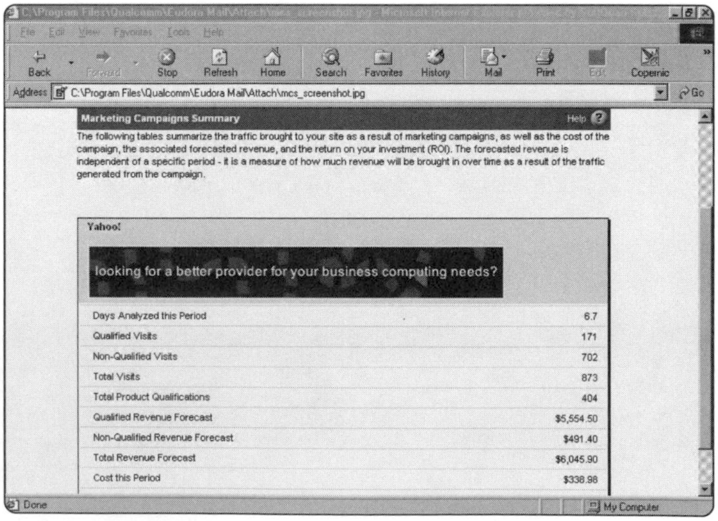

**FIGURE 32.6**

A Marketing Campaigns Summary by CommerceTrends Analysis Software.

### eContact

eContact is a sophisticated software program that tracks customer inquiries from start to finish, whether through e-mail, phone, on the Web, or other electronic customer interactions.

The software, available at **http://www.quintus.com**, gives companies the capability to manage, control, track, and report on customer relationships across any mix of electronic channels and the capability to deliver consistent, personalized service across electronic channels.

### LEADtrack

LEADtrack Software (**http://www.leadtrack.com/**) tracks sales from all sources, such as space ads, public relations, trade shows, and so forth. Web-related sales can be indirectly tracked after the purchase if you can identify the source of the lead.

## Conclusion

To determine the effectiveness of any advertising campaign, you must have a system in place to track the hits and sales of that campaign. By carefully tracking the hits and sales of each campaign, you'll be able to decide which advertising campaigns are working for you.

# PART VIII

# APPENDIXES

# RECOMMENDED READING LIST

## Programming and Scripting Languages

Castagnetto, Jesus, et al. *Professional PHP Programming.* Wrox. February 2000.

Christenberry, Johnie, et al. *CGI Fast and Easy Web Development.* Prima Tech. August 2000.

Christiansen, Tom, et al. *Perl Cookbook.* O'Reilly and Associates. August 1998.

Holzner, Steven. *Perl Black Book.* CoriolisOpen Press. 1999.

Lemay, Laura and Denise Tyler. *Teach Yourself Web Publishing With HTML 4 in 21 Days.* Sams Publishing. February 2000.

Thomasson, Michael. *ASP 3 Fast & Easy Web Development.* Prima Tech. July 2000.

Wall, Larry. *Programming Perl,* Third Edition. O'Reilly and Associates. July 2000.

## Databases

Date, C.J. *An Introduction to Database Systems.* Addison-Wesley. October 1999.

Descartes, Alligator and Tim Bunce. *Programming the Perl DBI.* O'Reilly and Associates. February 2000.

King, Tim, et al. *MySQL and mSQL.* O'Reilly and Associates. 1999.

## Security

Brenton, Chris. *Mastering Network Security.* Sybex. 1999.

Garfinkel, Simson and Gene Spafford. *Practical Unix and Internet Security,* Second Edition. O'Reilly and Associates. April 1996.

Garfinkel, Simson and Gene Spafford. *Web Security and Commerce.* O'Reilly and Associates. June 1997.

Pfleeger, Charles. *Security in Computing,* Second Edition. Prentice Hall. 1997.

Stoll, Clifford. *The Cuckoo's Egg: Tracking a Spy Through the Maze of Computer Espionage.* Pocket Books. 1995.

## Networks and Servers

Laurie, Ben and Peter Laurie. *Apache: The Definitive Guide.* O'Reilly and Associates. February 1999.

Minasi, Mark. *Mastering Windows NT Server 4.* Sybex. February 2000.

## Miscellaneous

Nielsen, Jakob. *Designing Web Usability: The Practice of Simplicity.* New Riders Publishing. December 1999.

Nobles, Robin and Susan O'Neil. *Streetwise Maximize Web Site Traffic.* Adams. 2000.

# RECOMMENDED WEB SITES

## Affiliate Software and Information

- Affili Source—**http://www.affilisource.com/**
- Affiliate Directories
  **http://www.2-Tier.com/**
  **http://www.Associate-It.com/**
  **http://www.CashPile.com/**
  **http://www.ClicksLink.com/**
  **http://www.WebAffiliatePrograms.com/**
- Affiliate Program Links
  **http://www.affiliate-programs.org/**
  **http://www.affiliatetips.com/**
  **http://www.associateprograms.com/search/newsletter.shtml**
- Affiliate Seminars and Conference—**http://seminars.internet.com/**
- AffiliateMatch—**http://www.AffiliateMatch.com/**
- Banner Exchange Programs
  **http://store.bcentral.com/le/**
  **http://www.bannerswap.com/**
  **http://www.bannerexchange.mycomputer.com/**
  **http://www.exchange-it.com/**
  **http://www.free-banners.com/**
  **http://www.webmasterexchange.com/** (only for sites dedicated to Web design issues)
- Be Free—**http://www.befree.com**
- ClickTrade—**http://www.clicktrade.com**
- Commission Junction—**http://www.cj.com**
- eCommerceBase.com—**http://www.ecommercebase.com/subcats.php3?id=23**
- Internet Affiliate Marketing Summit (AffiliateForce)—**http://affiliateforce.com/**
- LinkShare—**http://www.linkshare.com**
- My Affiliate Program—**http://www.myaffiliateprogram.com**
- OnlineBusiness.com—**http://onlinebusiness.com/news_affiliate_marketing.html**

- PlugInGo—**http://www.plugingo.com**
- Pro-Track—**http://www.affiliatesoftware.net**
- ReveNews—**http://www.revenews.com/**
- WebMarketing World—**http://www.thunderlizard.com/ wmw.html**
- Webmaster-Programs—**http://webmaster-programs.com/Ezine/ Subscribe.htm**

## Browsers

- HotJava—**http://java.sun.com/products/hotjava**
- Konquerer—**http://www.konqueror.org/**
- Lynx—**http://www.lynx.browser.org**
- Microsoft Internet Explorer—**http://www.microsoft.com/ windows/ie**
- Netscape Navigator—**http://www.netscape.com/download/**
- Opera—**http://www.opera.com**
- Web TV—**http://developer.webtv.net/design/tools/viewer/**

## Communities

- Allaire Forums—**http://www.forumspot.org/**
- Boards2Go—**http://www.boards2go.com/**
- "Building Electronic Communities" (article)—**http:// www.totalnetval.com/7-steps.htm**
- "Community Building and Moderator Guidelines" (article)— **http://www.well.com/confteam/hosting.html**
- Conferencing Software for the Web—**http://thinkofit.com/ webconf/**
- Entervision's Live Broadcasting over the Web— **http://www.magicweb.com/technology.htm**
- eShare's Expressions—**http://www.eshare.com/products/ internet/expressions/index.html**
- Evoke Communications—**http://excite.webconference.work.com/ excite/index.shtml**

- Excite's Forum Guidelines—**http://www.excite.com/ communities/resources/standards/boards/**
- Forum One—**http://www.forumone.com/capital/index.htm**
- Freebiescenter Directory—**http://www.freebiescenter.com/ webmaster/cgi.html**
- iChat Rooms—**http://www.ichat.com/community/rooms**
- Intel's Video Conferencing—**http://www.intel.com/proshare/ conferencing/**
- Invitation Services—**http://www.cnet.com/internet/0-1497812-7-1883617.html**
- LearnSpace by Lotus—**http://www.lotus.com/home.nsf/ welcome/learnspace**
- LibWeb—**http://libweb.sourceforge.net/**
- Lycos Calendar by AnyDay—**http://anyday.lycos.com/**
- Meeting Tools—**http://www.zdnet.com/downloads**
- Microsoft NetMeeting—**http://www.microsoft.com/windows/ NetMeeting**
- Mimio's WebEx—**http://www.mimio.com/meetings/index.html**
- Online Community Report—**http://onlinecommunityreport.com/**
- Online Community Toolkit—**http://www.fullcirc.com/ community/communitymanual.htm**
- Salon Table Talk—**http://tabletalk.salon1999.com/webx**
- Sametime by Lotus—**http://www.lotus.com/home.nsf/welcome/ sametime**
- Seven Golden Rules for Building Community— **http://software.oreilly.com/news.cfm?ID_News=189**
- Sharewire—**http://www.sharewire.com/**
- Sun's Java Chat Rooms—**http://developer.java.sun.com/ developer/community/**
- vLab Classroom—**http://www.mentortech.com/vlab/class.shtml**
- Wanvas Online Whiteboard Editor—**http://www.zdnet.com/ downloads**

- Web Crossing—**http://www.webcrossing.com/40/**
- WebBoard by O'Reilly—**http://webboard.oreilly.com/**
- WWWBoard—**http://www.worldwidemart.com/scripts/ wwwboard.shtml**
- Yahoo!'s Community Guidelines—**http://docs.yahoo.com/info/ guidelines/community.html**
- Yahoo!'s Termination Policy—**http://docs.yahoo.com/info/terms/**

## Databases

- Microsoft SQL Server—**http://www.microsoft.com/Sql/**
- MySQL—**http://www.mysql.com**
- Oracle—**http://www.oracle.com/**
- PostgreSQL—**http://www.postgresql.org/**
- Sybase—**http://www.sybase.com/**

## Data-Mining Tools and Information

- Accrue Software, Inc.—**http://www.accrue.com/**
- The Association for Computing Machinery Special Interest Group: Knowledge Discovery and Data Mining (SIGKDD)— **http://www.acm.org/sigs/sigkdd/**
- AZMY—**http://www.azmy.com/**
- Blue Data Miners, Inc.—**http://www.bluedatainc.com/**
- Coremetrics—**http://www.coremetrics.com/**
- Data Distilleries—**http://www.ddi.nl/**
- Data Miner Software Kit—**http://www.data-miner.com/**
- Data Miners—**http://www.data-miners.com/**
- Information Discover, Inc.—**http://www.datamining.com/**
- Intellix—**http://www.intellix.com/**
- KDnuggets—**http://www.kdnuggets.com/**
- MyComputer.com's SuperStats—**http://v2.superstats.com/**
- Web Side Story—**http://www.websidestory.com/**

## Examples

- Academy of Web Specialists— **http://www.academywebspecialists.com**
- Amazon—**http://www.amazon.com**
- Amazon's Friends and Favorites area—**http://www.amazon.com/ exec/obidos/subst/community/community-home.html**
- Barnes & Noble—**http://www.bn.com**
- Cold Water Creek—**http://www.coldwatercreek.com**
- Concierge.com—**http://www.concierge.com/cgi-bin/ maps.cgi?link=intro**
- Cruise Discounts Online—**http://www.cruisediscountsonline.com/ Royal-Caribbean-cruise-line/index.asp**
- eBay Auction's "About Us" section—**http://pages.ebay.com/ community/aboutebay/index.html**
- Eudora's Technical Support—**http://www.eudora.com/ techsupport/**
- GameBlitz.com—**http://www.gameblitz.com**
- Global Business Integration Technologies— **http://www.gbitech.com/**
- Harris Publishing—**http://www.harrisdigitalpublishing.com/ freeprograms/index.html**
- Jelly Belly Online—**http://www.jellybelly.com**
- Maremmatoscana—**http://www.maremmatoscana.com**
- National Writers Union—**http://www.nwu.org**
- Online Web Training—**http://www.onlinewebtraining.com**
- Prima Publishing—**http://www.primapublishing.com**
- Prima's Site Map—**http://www.primapublishing.com/map.asp**
- PrimeGuide—**http://quiver.myprimetime.com**
- Sandals4Less—**http://www.sandals4less.com/**
- Search Engine Optimizer—**http://www.se-optimizer.com**
- Sport Fishing Magazine—**http://www.sportfishingmag.com/**
- Weather Channel—**http://www.weather.com/**

- Web Promotion Outsourced—**http://www.webpromotionoutsourced.com**
- Wired.com—**http://www.wired.com**

## Free Services

- 100FreeScreensavers.com—**http://www.100freescreensavers.com/customize.html**
- About.com's Freebies—**http://freebies.about.com/shopping/freebies/**
- Dominator—**http://www.e-gineer.com/e-gineer/domainator/index.phtml**
- javElink—**http://www.javelink.com/**
- Mouse Click Application—**http://www.mouseclickapplication.com**
- Netwhistle—**http://www.netwhistle.com**
- Reverse IP Lookup—**http://eamnesia.com/hostinfo/ipinfo.jhtml**
- Search Engine Simulator—**http://www.delorie.com/web/ses.cgi**
- Shields Up—**http://grc.com/**

## HTML Editors

- Allaire HomeSite—**http://www.allaire.com/homesite/**
- Arachnophilia—**http://www.arachnoid.com/arachnophilia**
- Macromedia DreamWeaver—**http://www.macromedia.com/software/dreamweaver**
- Microsoft FrontPage—**http://www.microsoft.com/frontpage**

## Keywords and How to Use Them

- Basic to Basics: META Tags—**http://www.webdeveloper.com/html/html_metatags.html**
- "Choosing the Right Keywords" (article)—**http://www.onlinewebtraining.com/information/keywords.html**
- How to Use HTML META Tags—**http://www.searchenginewatch.com/meta.htm**

- KeywordCount.com—**http://www.keywordcount.com/**
- META Tag Lawsuits—**http://searchenginewatch.com/resources/ metasuits.html**
- Roget's Thesaurus—**http://www.thesaurus.com/**
- Search Engine Tutorial for Web Designers— **http://www.northernwebs.com/set/index.html**
- Search Term Suggestion Tool at GoTo—**http://inventory.go2.com/ inventory/Search_Suggestion.jhtml**
- What can META do for You?—**http://www.hotwired.com/ webmonkey/html/96/51/index2a.html**
- What People Search For—**http://searchenginewatch.internet.com/ facts/searches.html**
- "Where to Place Your Keywords" (article)— **http://www.onlinewebtraining.com/information/ whereputkeywords.html**
- WordTracker—**http://www.wordtracker.com**

## Log Analysis

- Analog—**http://www.statslab.cam.ac.uk/~sret1/analog/**
- bitlog—**http://www.yassou.net/devel/**
- eXTReMe Tracking—**http://www.extreme-dm.com/tracking/ ?home**
- FlashStats—**http://maximized.com/products/flashstats/**
- Funnel Web—**http://www.activeconcepts.com/prod.html**
- Northern Web's Keyword Sniffer—**http://www.northernwebs.com/ set/kw_install.html**
- "Packet Sniffing Vs. Log File Analysis" (article)— **http://www.webtrends.com/solution/whitepapers/packet.htm**
- Referrer Log Article—**http://www.wdvl.com/Internet/ Management**
- Webalizer—**http://www.mrunix.net/webalizer/**
- WebTrends—**http://www.webtrends.com**
- WebTrends Live—**http://www.webtrendslive.com/ ordertracking_info.htm**

## Payment Plans

### Charging to Phone Bills or ISPs

- eCharge Phone—**http://www.echarge.com**
- iPIN—**http://www.ipin.com**
- Trivnet's WISP—**http://www.trivnet.com**

### Check Payments

- CheckFree—**http://www.checkfree.com**
- PayByCheck.com—**http://www.paybycheck.com**
- Yahoo! Bill Pay—**http://billpay.yahoo.com**

### Money Transfer Programs

- Achex, Inc.—**http://www.achex.com**
- Cybermoola—**http://www.cybermoola.com**
- PayMe.com—**http://www.payme.com**
- PayPal—**http://www.paypal.com**
- Yahoo! Pay Direct—**http://paydirect.yahoo.com**

## Privacy and Security

- @stake—**http://www.atstake.com/**
- Anonymizer.com—**http://www.anonymizer.com**
- Apache Web Server bugs search—**http://bugs.apache.org**
- Attrition.org—**http://www.attrition.org/**
- Better Business Bureau's Online Division—**http://bbbonline.com**
- Computer Emergency Response Team (CERT) (Unix server)—**ftp://ftp.auscert.org.au/pub/auscert/papers/unix_security_checklist**
- Computer Incident Advisory Capability—**http://ciac.llnl.gov/ciac/SecurityTools.html**
- "E-Privacy's Foggy Bottom" at Wired.com (article)—**http://www.wired.com/news/business/0,1367,38041,00.html**

- FTC's "Privacy Online: Fair Information Practices In the Electronic Marketplace"—**http://www.ftc.gov/os/2000/05/testimonyprivacy.htm**
- Hacker News Network—**http://www.hackernews.com/**
- Idzap—**http://www.IDzap.com**
- InfoWar—**http://www.infowar.com/**
- Internet Fraud Complaint Center—**http://www.ifccfbi.gov**
- JunkBusters Corporation—**http://www.junkbusters.com**
- L0pht Heavy Industries (infamous hacker site)—**http://www.l0pht.com/**
- Microsoft Windows NT security information—**http://www.microsoft.com/ntserver/security/techdetails/default.asp**
- Microsoft's IIS security checklist—**http://www.microsoft.com/security/products/iis/CheckList.asp**
- National Institute of Standards in Technology—**http://cs-www.ncsl.nist.gov/tools/tools.htm**
- Netscape's Enterprise Server product page—**http://home.netscape.com/enterprise/v3.6/index.html**
- Netscape's Enterprise Server security information—**http://netcaster.netscape.com/products/security/resources/notes.html**
- NetworkIce.com's discussion area—**http://advice.networkice.com/Advice/default.htm**
- OpenSSH—**http://www.openssh.com/**
- PrivacyChoices—**http://www.privacychoices.org/resource.htm**
- Privacy.net
  **http://privacy.net/anonymizer/**
  **http://www.privacy.net**
- Privada—**http://www.privada.com**
- PrivaSeek—**http://privaseek.com**
- Security Focus—**http://www.securityfocus.com/**
- Somebody's Proxy Server—**http://www.somebody.net**
- TrustE—**http://www.truste.com**
- VeriSign—**http://www.verisign.com**
- Zero-Knowledge—**http://www.zeroknowledge.com**

## Promote Your Site

- Anaconda Products—**http://anacondapartners.com/ap_products.shtml**
- Autobots—**http://autobots.net/**
- BizLinks for Entrepreneurs—**http://youonline.net/free_sub.htm**
- Business Course in Permission E-Mail Marketing—**http://www.email-solutions.com/moreinfo**
- CataList—**http://www.listserv.net/lists/listref.html**
- CNET's Download.com—**http://download.cnet.com**
- Content Provider Network—**http://www.pocketcd.com/content.asp**
- Coupons.com—**http://www.coupons.com**
- CyberFiber NewsGroups Directory and Search—**http://www.cyberfiber.com/index.html**
- Directory of Publicly Accessible Mailing Lists—**http://paml.net/**
- eBook Directory—**http://www.ebookdirectory.com/**
- eBooks Portal—**http://ebooks.searchking.com/**
- Email Mailing Lists—**http://www.cuenet.com/ml.html**
- Experts.com—**http://www.experts.com/**
- Ezine News Wire—**http://www.ezinenewswire.com**
- Free fax services

  **http://www.fax-away.com/free/**

  **http://www.freefax.com.pk/**

  **http://www.tpc.int/sendfax.html**

  **http://www.efax.com/**
- Huge Index of Mailing Lists—**http://www.geocities.com/Eureka/6146/index.html**
- InfoJump—**http://www.infojump.com**
- iSyndicate—**http://www.isyndicate.com/services/**
- The List of Lists—**http://catalog.com/vivian/interest-group-search.html**
- ListQuest—**http://www.listquest.com/**
- Liszt—**http://www.liszt.com/**

- Low Bandwidth—**http://www.disobey.com/low/**
- Mailback.com—**http://www.databack.com/mailback.htm**
- Maintaining a newsletter or e-zine
  **http://www.listbot.com/**
  **http://www.topica.com/**
- Mind-It—**http://www.netmind.com/html/wmmindit.html**
- Net-Announce—**http://www.erspros.com/cgi-bin/neta/na-webart.pl**
- Netsites—**http://www.egroups.com/group/netsites**
- New-List—**http://listserv.classroom.com/archives/new-list.html**
- Poll Control Center—**http://www.misterpoll.com/pollwiz.wga**
- Promo Loop—**http://www.promoloop.com**
- Save.com—**http://www.save.com**
- Setting up a mailing list—**http://www.useit.com/alertbox/20000820.html**
- Setting up a newsletter or e-zine—**http://www.academywebspecialists.com/information/ezines.html**
- Tile.Net—**http://tile.net/lists/addlist.html**
- The Ultimate Guide to Creating and Marketing eBooks—**http://www.ultimateguidetoebooks.com**
- Whizdiary—**http://www.whizdiary.com/**
- Yahoo!'s Net Events—**http://www.broadcast.com/**
- Yahoo!'s search for an expert—**http://search.yahoo.com/search?p=experts**

## Scripting and Programming Languages

- Java
  **http://java.sun.com/**
  **http://javaboutique.internet.com/**
- JavaScript
  **http://www.javascript.com/**
  **http://javascriptweenie.com/**

- JScript—**http://msdn.microsoft.com/scripting/jscript/default.htm**
- Perl

    **http://www.perl.com**

    **http://www.perl.org**

    **http://www.cpan.org**
- PHP—**http://www.php.net/**
- VBScript—**http://msdn.microsoft.com/scripting/vbscript/default.htm**
- Visual Basic/ActiveX

    **http://www.vbhow.to/**

    **http://browserwatch.internet.com/activex.html**

## Scripts

- CGI Forum—**http://www.cgiforum.com/**
- CGI Forum's poll script—**http://www.cgiforum.com/directcgi/search.cgi?query=polls**

## Search Engines and Directories

### Directories

- LookSmart

    **http://looksmart.com**

    **http://www.looksmart.com/h/info/confirm.html**
    (to update listing)
- NBCi/Snap

    **http://www.nbci.com**

    **http://home.nbci.com/LMOID/resource/0,566,-1077,00.html?st.sn.ld.0.1077**

- Open Directory Project (ODP)

  **http://dmoz.org**

  **http://directory.netscape.com/Computers/Internet/WWW/ Searching_the_Web/Directories/Open_Directory_Project/ Sites_Using_ODP_Data**

- Yahoo!

  **http://www.yahoo.com**

  **http://www.yahoo.com/info/suggest/busexpress.html** (Business Express)

  **http://add.yahoo.com/fast/change** (change form)

  **url-support@yahoo-inc.com** (submission problems)

## Helpful URLs Related to Search Engines

- @Web Site Publicity Inc.—**http://www.websitepublicity.com**
- Academy of Web Specialists Online Search Engine Training— **http://www.onlinewebtraining.com**
- "Cloaking: Beauty or Beast?" (article)—**http:// www.onlinewebtraining.com/information/cloaking.html**
- Cloaking Tutorial by Bill Gentry—**http://www.rookiesnstars.com/ position/**
- Creating Effective Doorway Pages— **http://www.onlinewebtraining.com/information/ doorway_strategies.html**
- "Doorway Pages at Search Engine Watch" (article)—**http:// searchenginewatch.internet.com/webmasters/bridge.html**
- Global Web Positioning—**http://www.globalwebpositioning.com**
- PositionGeek.com—**http://www.positiongeek.com**
- Problems Using Trademarked Terms—**http:// searchenginewatch.internet.com/sereport/9805-metatags.html**
- Robots.txt File (tutorial on how to create)—**http://country- art.com/class/robotstxt.htm**

- Search Engine Advice—**http://www.searchengineadvice.com**
- Search Engine Related Articles—
  **http://www.onlinewebtraining.com/information/
  search_engine_articles.html**
- Search Engine Services—**http://www.searchengineservices.com**
- Search Engine Showdown—
  **http://www.searchengineshowdown.com/**
- Search Engine Watch—**http://www.searchenginewatch.com**
- "Ten Suggestions for Getting Your Site Listed in the ODP"
  (article)—**http://www.onlinewebtraining.com/information/
  odp.html**
- Theme-Related Articles by Michael Campbell—**http://www.1-
  internet-marketing.com/vault/**
- Tutorial on Using Frames at Search Engine Watch—
  **http://searchenginewatch.com/webmasters/frames.html**
- WebSearch at About.com—**http://websearch.about.com/
  internet/websearch/**

## Newsletters about Search Engines

- Academy of Web Specialists' Newsletter—
  **http://www.academywebspecialists.com/newsletter.html**
- Fantomaster's Cloaking Newsletter—**http://
  www.fantomaster.com/fasmbase0.html**
- Internet Day (not only about search engines)—
  **http://internetday.com/**
- Market Position Newsletter—**http://www.webposition.com/
  newsletter.htm**
- Planet Ocean's Search Engine News (monthly newsletter and
  *Unfair Advantages* book)—**http://www.searchenginehelp.com/**
- Search Engine Watch (offers free and pay newsletters)—
  **http://www.searchenginewatch.com**
- *The Vault* and Search Engine Reports—**http://www.1-internet-
  marketing.com/vault.htm**

## Onsite Search Engines

- AltaVista's Hosted Search Services—
  **http://solutions.altavista.com/products/hss-overview.html**
- Atomz Search—**http://search.atomz.com/**
- Excite for Web Servers 1.1—**http://www.excite.com/navigate/**
- FreeFind—**http://www.freefind.com**
- "Hints on Making Your Site More Engine Friendly" (article)—
  **http://www.searchbutton.com/resources/tips.html**
- HtDig—**http://www.htdig.org/**
- InfoSpace—**http://www.infospace.com/about/corporate/
  cobrand.htm**
- Inktomi Search Software—**http://software.infoseek.com/**
- NetMind Search-It—**http://www.netmind.com/html/
  wmsearchit.html**
- PicoSearch—**http://www.picosearch.com/**
- SearchButton.com—**http://www.searchbutton.com**
- site Search—**http://www.agl.uh.edu/~saljxk/site_Search/**
- SiteSearch—**http://www.gd-ind.com/sitesearch/**
- WhatUSeek IntraSearch—**http://intra.whatuseek.com/**

## Pay Engines and Information

- 7Search—**http://7search.com/**
- Article about GoTo—**http://www.onlinewebtraining.com/
  information/goto.html**
- bay9—**http://www.bay9.com**
- FindWhat—**http://www.findwhat.com**
- GoTo—**http://www.goto.com**
- GoTo's DirecTraffic Center—**https://secure.goto.com/s/dtc/
  center**
- Kanoodle—**http://www.kanoodle.com**
- Keyword Bid Optimizer—**http://www.paidsearchenginetools.com/**
- PayPerClickSearchEngines.com—
  **http://www.payperclicksearchengines.com/**

- RealNames—**http://web.realnames.com**
- RealNames article—**http://www.onlinewebtraining.com/ information/realnames.html**

## Report Search Engine Spammers

- AltaVista—Send an e-mail to **spam-support@av.com**
- Excite—**http://www.excite.com/feedback/**
- GO/InfoSeek—Send an e-mail to **comments@GO.com**
- HotBot—Send an e-mail to **feedback@hotbot.com**
- Lycos—Send an e-mail to **webmaster@lycos.com**
- Northern Light—**http://www.northernlight.com/docs/ gen_help_prob.html**
- Yahoo!—Send an e-mail to **url-support@yahoo-inc.com**

## Search Engine and Submission URLs

- AltaVista

  **http://www.altavista.com**

  **http://www.altavista.com/cgi-bin/query?pg=addurl**

  **http://doc.altavista.com/adv_search/ ast_haw_wellindexed.shtml**
- Excite

  **http://www.excite.com**

  **http://www.excite.com/info/add_url**
- Fast/All the Web

  **http://www.alltheweb.com/**

  **http://www.alltheweb.com/add_url.php3**
- GO/InfoSeek (GO may be shut down by the time this book is published.)

  **http://www.infoseek.com/**

  **http://www.go.com/ AddUrl?pg=SubmitUrl.html&svx=CTOC_Add_url**

- Google

  **http://www.google.com**

  **http://www.google.com/addurl**
- HotBot

  **http://www.hotbot.com**

  **http://hotbot.lycos.com/addurl.asp**
- Lycos

  **http://www.lycos.com**

  **http://www.lycos.com/addasite.html**
- Northern Light

  **http://www.northernlight.com**

  **http://www.northernlight.com/docs/regurl_help.html**

## Search Engine Software Programs

- Hi-Verify and Microsoft FrontPage—**http://www.hisoftware.com/ hiverify.htm**
- IP-Delivery—**http://www.ip-delivery.com/foodscript/**
- Keyword Density Analyzer (GRKda)— **http://www.grsoftware.net/search_engines/software/grkda/ grkda.html**
- Search Engine Optimizer (SEO)—**http://www.se-optimizer.com/**
- Site Promoter—**http://www.sitepromoter.com**
- Swiss Army App—**http://www.swissarmyapp.com**
- TopDog—**http://www.topdog2000.com**
- Traffic Titan—**http://position-it.com/traffictitan/**
- WebPosition Gold—**http://www.webpositiongold.com**
- Website Promoter—**http://www.cyberspacehq.com**

## Search-Related Services

- Consortium for Ethical Search Engine Optimization (CESEO)— **http://www.ceseo.org/**
- Cyrsh Technologies—**http://www.cyrsh.com**

- EZ Ranking Reports—**http://www.ezrankingreports.com**
- Link Popularity.com—**http://www.linkpopularity.com**
- Mouse Click Application—**http://www.linktriad.com/**
- PositionPro—**http://www.positionpro.com**
- Robots.txt Syntax Checker—**http://www.tardis.ed.ac.uk/~sxw/ robots/check/**
- Search Engine Simulator—**http://www.delorie.com/web/ses.cgi**
- SearchMechanics—**http://www.searchmechanics.com**
- Submit Director—**http://www.submitdirector.com**
- WordTracker—**http://www.wordtracker.com**

## Vertical Directories and Search Engines

- Community Search by SearchButton—**http://www.searchbutton.com/solutions/features/ CustomServices.html**
- Quiver—**http://www.quiver.com**
- SearchLogic—**http://www.1port.com/**
- Twirlix—**http://www.twirlix.com**
- Web Wombat—**http://webwombat.com**

## Shopping Carts

- @Retail—**http://www.atretail.com**
- Cart32—**http://www.cart32.com**
- CartIt—**http://www.cartit.com**
- Check It Out—**http://ssl.adgrafix.com**
- EasyCart—**http://www.easycart.com**
- Make-a-Store Order Page—**http://www.make-a-store.com**
- Marketer's Choice—**http://www.1shoppingcart.com/**
- SalesCart—**http://www.salescart.com**
- Shoptron—**http://www.shoptron.com**
- WebSiteTool—**http://www.websitetool.com**

## Software Programs

### Anti-Virus

- McAfee.com—**http://www.mcafee.com/**
- Norton (Symantec)—**http://www.norton.com/**

### Free Software Sites

- AnalogX—**http://www.analogx.com**
- Freshmeat—**http://www.freshmeat.net**

### Miscellaneous Software Programs

- Audio Web Pro—**http://www.audiowebpro.com**
- BizRate's Non-Buyer Exit Survey—**http://merchant.bizrate.com/oa/research_consulting/custom_research.xpml**
- Bulk E-Mail Software Superstore—**http://www.americaint.com/**
- Business Course in Permission E-Mail Marketing (includes software program)—**http://www.email-solutions.com/moreinfo**
- CGIVote—**http://www.analogx.com/contents/download/network/cgivote.htm**
- CommerceTrends Analysis—**http://www.webtrends.com/products/commerce/default.htm**
- eContact—**http://www.quintus.com**
- Favicon—**http://www.favicon.com/**
- LEADtrack—**http://www.leadtrack.com/**
- MailLoop—**http://www.mailloop.com**
- Master E-Book Generator—**http://www.willmaster.com/master/ebook/index.shtml**
- Master Recommend—**http://www.willmaster.com/master/recommend/index.shtml**
- Swiss Army App—**http://www.swissarmyapp.com**
- Tock—**http://www.clockware.com/**

- Updates time on your site
  **http://www.worldwidemart.com/scripts/textclock.shtml**
  **http://www.worldwidemart.com/scripts/C++/textclock.shtml**
  **http://www.zdnet.com/devhead/resources/scriptlibrary/javascript/time.html**
- World Trade Server by RegiSoft—**http://www.regisoft.com**

## Source Code Control Tools and Resources

- Continuus/WebSynergy—**http://www.continuus.com**
- CVS (Concurrent Versions Systems)—**http://www.cvshome.org**
- Microsoft Visual SourceSafe—**http://msdn.microsoft.com/ssafe/**
- MKS Web Integrity—**http://www.mks.com/products/wi/**
- Rational ClearCase—**http://www.rational.com/products/clearcase/index.jsp**
- Software Engineering Institute—**http://www.sei.cmu.edu**
- WebCrisis.com: Inability to Maintain—**http://www.mks.com/press/coverage/wi/crisis.htm**

## Statistics

- ActivMedia Research—**http://www.activmediaresearch.com**
- MediaMetrix—**http://mediametrix.com/landing.jsp**
- Nua Internet Surveys—**http://www.nua.org/surveys**
- Search Engine Watch's Referral Traffic Chart—**http://searchenginewatch.com/reports/statmarket.html**
- Search Engine Watch's Size of Engines Chart—**http://searchenginewatch.com/reports/sizes.html**
- Useit.com—**http://www.useit.com**
- Web Snapshot—**http://websnapshot.mycomputer.com/searchengines.html**

## Web Servers

- Apache Web Server—**http://www.apache.org**
- Microsoft Internet Information Server—**http://www.microsoft.com/ntserver/web/exec/feature/Datasheet.asp?RLD=71**
- Netscape's Web Server—**http://home.netscape.com/enterprise/v3.6/index.html**

# CHECKLISTS

## *Page Design Checklist*

| Check | Answer | Notes |
|---|---|---|
| Have you tested your pages individually for usability? | _____ | _____ |
| Have you tested your pages individually on different browsers? | _____ | _____ |
| Have you tested your pages on different systems? | _____ | _____ |
| Have you checked that color schemes are easy on the eye? | _____ | _____ |
| Have you used a familiar user interface? | _____ | _____ |
| Do you open links in new browser windows? | _____ | _____ |
| Have you included biographical information about the people behind the site? | _____ | _____ |
| Do you provide archived content? | _____ | _____ |
| Have you checked for linkrot? | _____ | _____ |
| Have you checked that all relocated pages within your site have been addressed in links? | _____ | _____ |
| Have you created a custom 404 error page that keeps users on your site? | _____ | _____ |
| Do you sacrifice content for bells and whistles? | _____ | _____ |
| Have you checked for fast download time on each page? | _____ | _____ |
| Are your page titles relevant and concise? | _____ | _____ |
| Have you considered the amount of vertical scroll on each page? | _____ | _____ |
| Have you eliminated horizontal scroll on all pages? | _____ | _____ |
| Have you eliminated splash screens? | _____ | _____ |
| Are your pages easily bookmarked? | _____ | _____ |
| Do you warn users of links to non-HTML files? | _____ | _____ |
| Do you include contact information on each page? | _____ | _____ |
| In forms, can users easily tab between input fields? | _____ | _____ |
| Are graphics quickly downloaded? | _____ | _____ |
| Have you checked to be sure that graphics do not break up the flow of the page? | _____ | _____ |
| Have you eliminated annoying background sound? | _____ | _____ |
| Have you eliminated annoying animated graphics or text? | _____ | _____ |
| Are links integrated with text? | _____ | _____ |
| Is page design consistent? | _____ | _____ |
| Do pages have copious amounts of white space? | _____ | _____ |

## Page Design Checklist (continued)

| Check | Answer | Notes |
|-------|--------|-------|
| Does the page design cause the user to look at the entire page? | _____ | _____ |
| Have you eliminated crowded pages with content concentration in a single area? | _____ | _____ |
| Are fonts readable? | _____ | _____ |
| Have you included a copyright notice on each page? Is this necessary for your site? | _____ | _____ |
| Do you use interactivity well? | _____ | _____ |

## Site Design Checklist

| Check | Answer | Notes |
|-------|--------|-------|
| **Navigation:** | | |
| Are all major areas linked from the main page? | _____ | _____ |
| Does your navigation naturally progress from page to page? | _____ | _____ |
| Are all important areas of your site listed on your navigation bar? | _____ | _____ |
| Are you using an onsite search engine? | _____ | _____ |
| Do you have a site map? | _____ | _____ |
| Is it obvious what each major area of your site contains? | _____ | _____ |
| Do you provide navigation across the top and bottom of your pages? | _____ | _____ |
| Is there enough on your pages "before the fold" to explain what your site is about? | _____ | _____ |
| Are there any "dead ends" on your site? Check your site closely. | _____ | _____ |
| Do you have an "About Us" section that describes your company, products, and services? | _____ | _____ |
| Do you provide contact information on the main page and on all major sections of your site? | _____ | _____ |
| **Customer Support:** | | |
| Is it obvious where to go to obtain customer support or help? | _____ | _____ |
| Do you provide contact information for the various departments in your company, including e-mail addresses, phone numbers, etc.? | _____ | _____ |

## *Site Design Checklist (continued)*

| Check | Answer | Notes |
|---|---|---|
| Do you provide information on how to set up your products, if applicable? | _____ | _____ |
| Do you provide FAQs about your products or services? | _____ | _____ |
| Do you provide an online user manual? | _____ | _____ |
| Does your site contain warranty information? | _____ | _____ |
| Do you have a troubleshooting area? | _____ | _____ |
| Is your customer support area searchable? | _____ | _____ |

**Database-Driven Sites:**

| Check | Answer | Notes |
|---|---|---|
| Does your database track hits? | _____ | _____ |
| Does your database automatically change the content of the page depending on the time, date, or other factors? | _____ | _____ |
| Does your database provide automatic fill-in of online forms? | _____ | _____ |
| Are you using your database to retrieve e-mail addresses for future use? | _____ | _____ |

**Intranets and Extranets:**

| Check | Answer | Notes |
|---|---|---|
| Are your intranet and extranet different enough from your Internet to avoid confusion, yet still maintain a similarity to remind your users of where they are? | _____ | _____ |

## *Community Checklist*

| Check | Answer | Notes |
|---|---|---|
| **Getting Set Up (Which Community Features Are Important to Your Business?)** | | |
| Special interest groups? | _____ | _____ |
| If so, for what areas? | | _____ |
| Bulletin boards? | _____ | _____ |
| Chat capabilities, such as: | | |
| Chat software? | _____ | _____ |
| Chat rooms? | _____ | _____ |
| Video conferencing? | _____ | _____ |
| Live lecturing/courses? | _____ | _____ |
| Vertical search engine? | _____ | _____ |
| Vertical directory? | _____ | _____ |

## *Community Checklist (continued)*

| Check | Answer | Notes |
|---|---|---|
| Free e-mail? | _____ | _____ |
| Mailing list? | _____ | _____ |
| Group calendar? | _____ | _____ |
| White board? | _____ | _____ |
| File sharing? | _____ | _____ |
| Articles? | _____ | _____ |
| Questions and answers? | _____ | _____ |
| Free Web space? | _____ | _____ |
| Members database? | _____ | _____ |
| Group buying? | _____ | _____ |
| Invitation services? | _____ | _____ |
| Community search? | _____ | _____ |
| Industry-specific features? | _____ | _____ |
| Promoting your community (How are you advertising?) | _____ | _____ |
| Signature lines? | _____ | _____ |
| Company newsletter? | _____ | _____ |
| Company printed materials? | _____ | _____ |
| Your Web sites? | _____ | _____ |
| Search engines and directories? | _____ | _____ |
| Mailing list? | _____ | _____ |
| Yahoo! events? | _____ | _____ |
| Newsgroups? | _____ | _____ |
| Other Web sites? | _____ | _____ |
| Through existing members, offering special promotions? | _____ | _____ |
| Press releases? | _____ | _____ |
| Your intranet and extranet? | _____ | _____ |
| Recommend scripts? | _____ | _____ |
| Autoresponders? | _____ | _____ |
| Are you scheduling expert chat sessions and marketing them heavily? | _____ | _____ |

**Managing Your Community:**

| Check | Answer | Notes |
|---|---|---|
| Have you assigned existing members/leaders to leadership positions? | _____ | _____ |
| Have you offered perks to those members for participating? | _____ | _____ |

## Community Checklist (continued)

| Check | Answer | Notes |
|---|---|---|
| Have you developed community goals? | _____ | _____ |
| Have you developed a system for measuring those goals and the outcome? | _____ | _____ |
| Have you visited other online communities to get ideas to implement in yours? | _____ | _____ |
| Have you implemented community guidelines and posted them? | _____ | _____ |
| Have you developed and posted guidelines for removing members? | _____ | _____ |
| Have you posted guidelines on how you're protecting the privacy of your members? | _____ | _____ |
| Is your community working? | _____ | _____ |
| Are you meeting your goals for new members? | _____ | _____ |
| Is your traffic increasing in various community areas? | _____ | _____ |
| Is your link popularity increasing? | _____ | _____ |
| Are new interest groups, new bulletin boards, and new chat rooms being created faster than those that are fading out? | _____ | _____ |
| Are you getting referrals from current members? | _____ | _____ |
| Do you have good solid attendance in chat sessions? | _____ | _____ |
| Are you getting good ideas for future products? | _____ | _____ |
| Is the community proving beneficial to your Customer Support areas? | _____ | _____ |
| Are you getting positive feedback from members? Implement a means for members to give feedback! | _____ | _____ |
| Are your moderators participating and keeping discussions going? | _____ | _____ |
| Are you listening to feedback from members and implementing changes as needed? | _____ | _____ |
| Are you using the community to announce new products and services? | _____ | _____ |
| Are you constantly adding new content? | _____ | _____ |
| Is your user interface simple and easy to use? | _____ | _____ |
| Are you retrieving valuable e-mail addresses and saving them for future promotions? | _____ | _____ |

## Boosting Traffic Checklist

| Check | Answer | Notes |
|---|---|---|
| Are you using free software or service to get traffic to your site? | _____ | _____ |
| Are you giving away promotional items at your site? | _____ | _____ |
| Are you using discount coupons? | _____ | _____ |
| Have you checked into partnering with another company to provide promotional items? | _____ | _____ |
| Do you offer discounts and sales on a regular basis? | _____ | _____ |
| Do you visibly promote those sales on your site? | _____ | _____ |
| Do you provide free articles or information at your site? | _____ | _____ |
| Have you considered free shipping, even just during a promotional period? | _____ | _____ |
| Do you send out a newsletter or e-zine? | _____ | _____ |
| Do you offer expert columns on your site? | _____ | _____ |
| Do you provide frequently answered questions about your goods, services, or your industry in general? | _____ | _____ |
| Do you use autoresponders as a means of relaying more information? | _____ | _____ |
| Have you considered giving away a free e-book to get traffic to your site? | _____ | _____ |
| Is it appropriate to offer a free course or tutorial pertaining to your goods or services? | _____ | _____ |
| Are you allowing your valuable content to be used by other sites as a means of promoting your own site? | _____ | _____ |
| Are you using reminder services for your customers? | _____ | _____ |
| Is your content constantly updated and fresh? | _____ | _____ |
| Are you using polls to determine what your visitors want to see on your site? | _____ | _____ |
| Are you using interesting polls that will get your visitors to return to see the results? | _____ | _____ |
| Do you offer contests or sweepstakes? | _____ | _____ |
| Are you using a personal icon? | _____ | _____ |
| Do you provide free fax services? | _____ | _____ |
| Can visitors send articles on your site by fax to someone else? | _____ | _____ |
| Can visitors send your site's articles by e-mail to someone else? | _____ | _____ |
| Are you retrieving all e-mail addresses and storing them in a database for future promotions? | _____ | _____ |

## *Boosting Traffic Checklist (continued)*

| Check | Answer | Notes |
|---|---|---|
| Do you offer awards on your site? | _____ | _____ |
| Is your ad copy captivating and professional? | _____ | _____ |
| Have you considered providing a vertical engine or directory as a means of increasing traffic? | _____ | _____ |
| Are you making each user's visit a personal experience by using interactive features? | _____ | _____ |
| Are you using recommend scripts so visitors can recommend your site to others? | _____ | _____ |
| Are you using an online scheduler for appointments, if appropriate for your business? | _____ | _____ |
| Are you promoting your business through signature lines? | _____ | _____ |
|    Banner ads? | _____ | _____ |
|    Search engines and directories? | _____ | _____ |
|    Mailing lists? | _____ | _____ |
|    E-zines? | _____ | _____ |
|    Newsgroups? | _____ | _____ |
|    Press releases? | _____ | _____ |
|    Linking programs? | _____ | _____ |
|    Permission e-mail marketing campaigns? | _____ | _____ |
|    Affiliate programs? | _____ | _____ |
|    Writing expert articles for other publications, Web sites, newsletters, etc.? | _____ | _____ |
|    Newsletters? | _____ | _____ |
|    Offline means? | _____ | _____ |

## E-commerce Checklist

| Check | Answer | Notes |
|---|---|---|
| Does your site design allow users to maintain control of their browsing experience? | _____ | _____ |
| Is the site navigable? | _____ | _____ |
| Is page layout consistent and straightforward? | _____ | _____ |
| Is content concise? | _____ | _____ |
| Do you provide interactive and immediate customer service? | _____ | _____ |
| Do you address security concerns? | _____ | _____ |
| Do you address privacy concerns? | _____ | _____ |
| Are product images available? | _____ | _____ |
| Are they clear? | _____ | _____ |
| Do order buttons or "Add to Cart" buttons look like buttons or links? | _____ | _____ |
| Do you limit advertisements to pages that will not interrupt your users' shopping experience? | _____ | _____ |
| Can users easily scan pages for content? | _____ | _____ |
| Is all product information clearly visible and easy to find? | _____ | _____ |
| Do you provide a secure server for shopping? | _____ | _____ |
| Do you provide a product catalog? | _____ | _____ |
| Is your shopping cart easy to use? | _____ | _____ |
| Does your shopping cart allow for easy navigation to previous tasks? | _____ | _____ |
| Is your shopping cart secure? | _____ | _____ |
| Do you include shipping information with products? | _____ | _____ |
| Do users know when to expect the product to be shipped? | _____ | _____ |
| Do you accept a variety of payment options? | _____ | _____ |
| Do you use interactivity to build relationships with customers? | _____ | _____ |
| Do you personalize areas of the site for customers? | _____ | _____ |
| Do you maintain contact with customers via e-mail, newsletters, and announcements? | _____ | _____ |
| Do you provide a community for customers? | _____ | _____ |
| Do you provide an affiliate program to advertise your products and increase your customer network? | _____ | _____ |

## *Log Analysis Checklist*

*Instructions: Look at your log files and compare them from week to week.*

| Check | Week of: _____ | Week of: _____ |
|---|---|---|
| Page views per day? | _____ | _____ |
| User sessions per day? | _____ | _____ |
| How long are users staying at your site? | _____ | _____ |
| Most-requested pages? | _____ | _____ |
| | _____ | _____ |
| | _____ | _____ |
| | _____ | _____ |
| Least-requested pages? | _____ | _____ |
| | _____ | _____ |
| | _____ | _____ |
| | _____ | _____ |
| Top entry pages? | _____ | _____ |
| | _____ | _____ |
| | _____ | _____ |
| Top exit pages? | _____ | _____ |
| | _____ | _____ |
| | _____ | _____ |
| Single-access pages? | _____ | _____ |
| | _____ | _____ |
| | _____ | _____ |
| Errors/404s? | _____ | _____ |
| | _____ | _____ |
| | _____ | _____ |
| Most active countries? | _____ | _____ |
| | _____ | _____ |
| | _____ | _____ |
| | _____ | _____ |

## *Log Analysis Checklist (continued)*

| Check | Week of: _____ | Week of: _____ |
|---|---|---|
| Top-referring sites? | _____ | _____ |
| | _____ | _____ |
| | _____ | _____ |
| | _____ | _____ |
| Top-referring search engines? | _____ | _____ |
| | _____ | _____ |
| | _____ | _____ |
| | _____ | _____ |
| Keywords? | _____ | _____ |
| | _____ | _____ |
| | _____ | _____ |
| | _____ | _____ |
| Browsers used? | _____ | _____ |
| | _____ | _____ |
| | _____ | _____ |
| | _____ | _____ |
| Visiting spiders? | _____ | _____ |
| | _____ | _____ |
| | _____ | _____ |
| | _____ | _____ |

**Additional Questions:**

| | | |
|---|---|---|
| How are you recording session logs? | _____ | _____ |
| How many pages do your users hit before leaving? | _____ | _____ |
| Are your visitors returning later? | _____ | _____ |

## *Search Engine Checklist*

Name of Engine: _____

Name/URL of Page: _____

Keyword Phrase: _____

| Check | Answer | Notes |
|---|---|---|

**Keywords:**

| Check | Answer | Notes |
|---|---|---|
| Are you using a highly focused keyword phrase, rather than a keyword that's too general? | _____ | _____ |
| Are you optimizing the page for one to two keyword phrases only? | _____ | _____ |
| Are you using regional keywords, if appropriate? | _____ | _____ |
| Are you using the longest version of your keyword phrase? | _____ | _____ |
| Are you using specific product names and services as keywords? | _____ | _____ |

**Where to Place Keywords:**

| Check | Answer | Notes |
|---|---|---|
| Are you using your keyword phrase at the beginning of all tags, including the title, description, headline, etc.? | _____ | _____ |
| Are you using your keyword phrase at the beginning of your body text? | _____ | _____ |
| Are you using a title tag? | _____ | _____ |
| Are you using a description META tag if appropriate for this engine? | _____ | _____ |
| Are you making use of headline tags, possibly in a graduated format? | _____ | _____ |
| Are you using your keyword phrase to create effective link text? | _____ | _____ |
| Are you overusing your keyword phrase? | _____ | _____ |
| What is your keyword weight for the page? | _____ | _____ |
| Is your page close to the root domain? | | |
| Are you using your keyword phrase in ALT tags if this engine considers the contents of ALT tags? | _____ | _____ |
| Did you name the page after your keyword phrase? | _____ | _____ |
| If the page is in a subdirectory, did you name the subdirectory after the keyword phrase? | _____ | _____ |
| Did you change the names of your images to reflect the keyword phrase? | _____ | _____ |
| Are you using subdomains? | _____ | _____ |
| Is the domain named after your keyword phrase? | _____ | _____ |
| Are you using keywords in a <style> tag? | _____ | _____ |

---

### *Search Engine Checklist (continued)*

Name of Engine: _____

Name/URL of Page: _____

Keyword Phrase: _____

---

| Check | Answer | Notes |
|---|---|---|
| **Titles and Descriptions:** | | |
| Is your title tag captivating and designed to bring in traffic? | _____ | _____ |
| Is your keyword phrase used toward the beginning of the tags? | _____ | _____ |
| Are your tags written with a capital letter starting the tag, and followed by all lowercase letters, unless you're using proper nouns? | _____ | _____ |
| Are you using your company name in the title tag instead of a keyword phrase? Don't! | _____ | _____ |
| Is your title easy to read? | | |
| If this engine uses the content of description tags, is the description tag captivating and designed to attract business? | _____ | _____ |
| Is your description tag easy to read? | | |
| If this engine doesn't use a description META tag, is the first text on your page appropriate as a description of the page in the search engine results? | _____ | _____ |
| **Navigation/Linking:** | | |
| Are you linking to all important pages of your site from this page? | _____ | _____ |
| If you own additional domains, are you linking to those pages too, if they're related in content? | _____ | _____ |
| Are you linking to popular sites that are related in content to your site? | _____ | _____ |
| Are you using effective link text when linking both on and off your site? | _____ | _____ |
| Are you using a site map containing links to all important pages of your site? If so, have you added some content to the page as well? | _____ | _____ |
| Are you working toward building good solid related link popularity? | _____ | _____ |
| **Problems:** | | |
| Does the page begin with text rather than a graphic, if at all possible? | _____ | _____ |
| Are you using technology that could create ranking problems, such as frames, lengthy JavaScript, database-delivered content, etc.? | _____ | _____ |

## *Search Engine Checklist (continued)*

Name of Engine: _____

Name/URL of Page: _____

Keyword Phrase: _____

| Check | Answer | Notes |
|---|---|---|
| Does your HTML editor stick in any irrelevant tags that could be hurting your ranking? | _____ | _____ |
| If you're using tables, do you use your keyword phrase in the tables? | _____ | _____ |
| If you're using frames, have you created a mini Web site in a `<noframes>` tag and added valuable content in this manner? | _____ | _____ |
| If your site is database delivered, have you created static pages as well? | _____ | _____ |
| If you're using lengthy JavaScript, have you moved most of it to a separate .js file? | _____ | _____ |
| If you're using an image map, have you provided text links to interior pages as well? | _____ | _____ |

**Spam:**

| Check | Answer | Notes |
|---|---|---|
| Are you using a redirect tag? If you're using a `META` refresh tag, use a Java redirect instead. | _____ | _____ |
| Are you using keyword stuffing in tags or in the body text? | _____ | _____ |
| Are you using tiny text? | _____ | _____ |
| Are you using hidden text? | _____ | _____ |
| Is your keyword weight too high? | _____ | _____ |
| Are you using keywords that don't pertain to the content of the page? | _____ | _____ |
| Does the page contain links only? If so, add content! | _____ | _____ |
| Is this page a mirror of another page? | _____ | _____ |
| Do you have other pages optimized for the same keyword phrase? | _____ | _____ |

**Other:**

| Check | Answer | Notes |
|---|---|---|
| Is the page full of valuable content? If not, did you add content through a `<noframes>` tag? | _____ | _____ |
| How long is the page? The average word count for top-ranking pages across the board is 450 words. | _____ | _____ |
| Is your data segregated, so that the focus of each page is kept separate? | _____ | _____ |

## *Directory Checklist*

Name of Engine: _____

Name/URL of Page: _____

Keyword Phrase: _____

| Check | Answer | Notes |
|-------|--------|-------|
| Is your site ready for traffic? | _____ | _____ |
| Do all graphics load? | _____ | _____ |
| Do all links work? | _____ | _____ |
| Has your site been updated recently? | _____ | _____ |
| Is contact information provided on the main page? | _____ | _____ |
| Do you list a physical address on your page, if appropriate? | _____ | _____ |
| Is there more than one page of the site? | _____ | _____ |
| Does the site contain original content? | _____ | _____ |
| Do visitors have to download a plug-in before being able to effectively view the site? | _____ | _____ |
| Do you have a copyright notice on your page? | _____ | _____ |
| Is this a mirror site of another site? | _____ | _____ |
| Is this a site that is strictly set up for the purpose of selling affiliate programs? | _____ | _____ |
| Is the main page just a splash page, where visitors have to click to go to another page? | _____ | _____ |
| Is your text easy to read? | _____ | _____ |
| Is the font and background color pleasing and professional? | _____ | _____ |
| Is the site ready for the scrutiny of a human editor? | _____ | _____ |
| Did you choose the most effective category(s) for your site? | _____ | _____ |
| Did you create an effective title that uses your important keyword phrase, if possible? (Some directories will only let you use the name of the business as the title.) | _____ | _____ |
| Is your title length within the limits of the directory's guidelines? | _____ | _____ |
| Does your title contain more than just a series of keywords? | _____ | _____ |
| Is your title written in all caps? It shouldn't be! | _____ | _____ |
| Did you create an effective description that uses your important keyword phrase? | _____ | _____ |
| Is your description length within the limits of the directory's guidelines? | _____ | _____ |
| Does your description contain more than just a series of keywords? | _____ | _____ |

## *Directory Checklist (continued)*

Name of Engine: _____

Name/URL of Page: _____

Keyword Phrase: _____

| Check | Answer | Notes |
|-------|--------|-------|
| Is your description written in all caps? It shouldn't be! | _____ | _____ |
| Did you follow submission guidelines explicitly? | _____ | _____ |
| If this is the second or third time to submit to the directory, did you allow ample time for the editor to accept it into the index when previously submitted? | _____ | _____ |
| Did you use any marketing hype? | _____ | _____ |
| Did you use brand names in your title or description? As a general rule, don't! | _____ | _____ |
| Did you consider submitting through the express services, if available for this directory? | _____ | _____ |

## *Competitor's Checklist*

Your Page: _____

Your Ranking: _____

Your Link Popularity: _____

Competing Page: _____

Their Ranking: _____

Their Link Popularity: _____

Search Engine: _____

Keyword Phrase: _____

| Check | Your Site | Competing Site |
|-------|-----------|----------------|
| Uses a title tag? | _____ | _____ |
| Keyword placement in title? | _____ | _____ |
| Length of title? | _____ | _____ |
| Uses keyword more than once? | _____ | _____ |
| Uses a description tag? | _____ | _____ |
| Keyword placement in description? | _____ | _____ |
| Length of description? | _____ | _____ |
| Uses keyword more than once? | _____ | _____ |
| Uses a keyword tag? | _____ | _____ |

## Competitor's Checklist (continued)

Your Page: _____

Your Ranking: _____

Your Link Popularity: _____

Competing Page: _____

Their Ranking: _____

Their Link Popularity: _____

Search Engine: _____

Keyword Phrase: _____

| Check | Your Site | Competing Site |
|---|---|---|
| Keyword placement in keyword tag? | | |
| Length of keyword tag? | | |
| Uses keyword in other variations? What are they? | | |
| Uses synonyms? What are they? | | |
| Order of <HEAD> section? For example, is the title tag the first tag on the page? If not, what is? | | |
| Uses any irrelevant tags in the <HEAD> section? What are they? | | |
| Does text appear before an image? | | |
| Uses frames? | | |
| Uses JavaScript? | | |
| Moved Java to a separate .js file? | | |
| Uses tables? | | |
| Uses a large image map? | | |
| Uses flash? | | |
| Dynamically generated site? | | |
| Where in the body text does the keyword phrase first appear? | | |
| Length of page? | | |
| Keyword weight of body text? | | |
| Keyword weight of entire page? | | |
| Keyword weight of individual keywords in keyword phrase? | | |
| Where at the end of the body text does the keyword phrase appear? | | |

## *Competitor's Checklist (continued)*

Your Page: _____

Your Ranking: _____

Your Link Popularity: _____

Competing Page: _____

Their Ranking: _____

Their Link Popularity: _____

Search Engine: _____

Keyword Phrase: _____

| Check | Your Site | Competing Site |
|---|---|---|
| Uses keywords in: | | |
| ALT tags? | _____ | _____ |
| Style tags? | _____ | _____ |
| Two title tags? | _____ | _____ |
| Http-equiv tags? | _____ | _____ |
| Image names? | _____ | _____ |
| Domain name? | _____ | _____ |
| Subdirectory name? | _____ | _____ |
| Name of URL? | _____ | _____ |
| Headline tags? | _____ | _____ |
| Link text? | _____ | _____ |
| How many outgoing, related links appear on the page? | _____ | _____ |
| Does the page focus on one theme alone? | _____ | _____ |
| Does the entire site focus on a related theme as well? | _____ | _____ |
| Is this an index page? | _____ | _____ |
| An interior page? | _____ | _____ |
| A doorway page? | _____ | _____ |
| Is the page visibly linked to and from the main page of the site? | _____ | _____ |
| Is the page using any spamming techniques? If so, what are they? | _____ | _____ |
| Is it possible that the page is cloaked? | _____ | _____ |
| Is the site listed in the engine's directory? | _____ | _____ |
| Other comments and observations: | _____ | _____ |

## *Security Checklist*

| Check | Answer | Notes |
|-------|--------|-------|

**YOUR SECURITY POLICY**

Do you have several policies, or at least separate versions
of your policy, that target employees, IT, managers,
and customers? _____ _____

Does your document state its purpose? _____ _____

Does your document state the intended audience? _____ _____

Does your document state the resources it covers? _____ _____

Does your document state risks associated with
each resource? _____ _____

Does your document state rights of users/customers? _____ _____

Does your document state rights of those accessing
your system? _____ _____

Does your document state the responsibilities of the
target audience? _____ _____

Does your document define levels of security regarding
your system and information? _____ _____

Does your document define the process to be
implemented during system upgrades? _____ _____

Does your document define an upgrade/maintenance
schedule for your system? _____ _____

Does your document state physical security risks? _____ _____

Does your document state physical security methods? _____ _____

Does your document state prevention methods? _____ _____

Does your document state detection methods? _____ _____

Does your document state recovery methods? _____ _____

Does your document state access policies,
including password aging? _____ _____

**YOUR SYSTEM'S SECURITY**

**Prevention:**

When do you back up your system? _____ _____

What parts of your system do you back up? _____ _____

Do you use version control on all files on your system? _____ _____

Do you use virus protection? _____ _____

Do you partition your data? How? _____ _____

Do you limit the access that scripts and multimedia
have within your system? _____ _____

Do you require user authentication for all system access? _____ _____

### Security Checklist (continued)

| Check | Answer | Notes |
|---|---|---|
| **Detection:** | | |
| Do you have an intrusion detection system? | _____ | _____ |
| Have you defined a process for detection? | _____ | _____ |
| Do your system administrators train to learn new detection methods? | _____ | _____ |
| Do you regularly update your IDS software? | _____ | _____ |
| **Response:** | | |
| Do you have a defined process for security breach responses? | _____ | _____ |
| What types of attacks/breaches will you publicize? | _____ | _____ |
| What process will you use to publicize attacks? | _____ | _____ |
| Do you have a solid timeline for response? | _____ | _____ |

# INDEX